Fromm

AMON

POSTCARDS

FROM

CANCÚN, COZUMEL & THE YUCATÁN

Quiet beach towns dot the Yucatán Peninsula. See chapter 4. © Robert Landau Photography.

Cancún is a social place, both in the water and out. See chapter 3. © Markova/Mexico/ The Stock Market.

Frommer's® 2001

Cancún, Cozumel & the Yucatán

by David Baird and Lynne Bairstow

WITHDRAWN

IDG Books Worldwide, Inc.
An International Data Group Company
Foster City, CA • Chicago, IL • Indianapolis, IN • New York, NY

ABOUT THE AUTHORS

David Baird (chapters 1, 4, 5, 6, and Appendix A) is a writer, editor, and translator based in Austin, Texas. He spent part of his childhood in Morelia, Mexico, and later lived for 2 years among the Mazatec Indians in Oaxaca, while he was doing graduate fieldwork.

Lynne Bairstow (chapters 1, 2, 3, and 4) is a writer specializing in travel and the Internet, who has lived in Puerto Vallarta, Mexico, at least part time for the past 9 years. She now lives there year-round, and was assisted in her research for this book by Claudia Velo. In a previous professional life, Lynne was a vice president for Merrill Lynch in Chicago and New York.

They are also the authors of *Frommer's Mexico*.

IDG BOOKS WORLDWIDE, INC.

An International Data Group Company
919 E. Hillsdale Blvd.
Suite 400
Foster City, CA 94404

Find us online at **www.frommers.com**

ISBN 0-0286-3873-5
ISSN 1064-1416

Editor: Kelly Regan, Claudia Kirschhoch, Matthew Garcia
Production Editor: Jenaffer Brandt
Photo Editor: Richard Fox
Design by Michele Laseau
Staff Cartographers: John Decamillis, Roberta Stockwell, Elizabeth Puhl
Page Creation by IDG Books Indianapolis Production Department

Front cover photo: Cancún hotel zone overview
Back cover photo: Kukulkán Pyramid at Chichén-Itzá

SPECIAL SALES

For general information on IDG Books Worldwide's books in the U.S., please call our Consumer Customer Service department at 1-800-762-2974. For reseller information, including discounts, bulk sales, customized editions, and premium sales, please call our Reseller Customer Service department at 1-800-434-3422.

Manufactured in the United States of America

5   4   3   2

Contents

List of Maps

AN INVITATION TO THE READER

In researching this book, we discovered many wonderful places—resorts, inns, restaurants, shops, and more. We're sure you'll find others. Please tell us about them, so we can share the information with your fellow travelers in upcoming editions. If you were disappointed with a recommendation, we'd love to know that, too. Please write to:

Frommer's Cancún, Cozumel & the Yucatán 2001
IDG Books Worldwide, Inc.
909 Third Ave.
New York, NY 10022

AN ADDITIONAL NOTE

Please be advised that travel information is subject to change at any time—and this is especially true of prices. We therefore suggest that you write or call ahead for confirmation when making your travel plans. The authors, editors, and publisher cannot be held responsible for the experiences of readers while traveling. Your safety is important to us, however, so we encourage you to stay alert and be aware of your surroundings. Keep a close eye on cameras, purses, and wallets, all favorite targets of thieves and pickpockets.

A FEW WORDS ABOUT PRICES

The peso's value continues to fluctuate—at press time it was roughly 9 pesos to the dollar. Prices in this book (which are always given in U.S. dollars) have been converted to U.S. dollars at 9 pesos to the dollar. Most hotels in Mexico—with the exception of places that receive little foreign tourism—quote prices in U.S. dollars. Thus, currency fluctuations are unlikely to affect the prices charged by most hotels.

Mexico has a Value-Added Tax of 15% (Impuesto de Valor Agregado, or IVA, pronounced "ee-bah") on most everything, including restaurant meals, bus tickets, and souvenirs. (Exceptions are Cancún, Cozumel, and Los Cabos, where the IVA is 10%; as ports of entry, they receive a special 5% break on taxes.) Hotels charge the usual 15% IVA, plus a locally administered bed tax of 2% (in many but not all areas), for a total of 17%. In Cancún, Los Cabos, and Cozumel, hotels charge the 10% IVA plus 2% room tax. IVA will not necessarily be included in the prices quoted by hotels and restaurants. You may find that upper-end properties (three stars and above) quote prices without IVA included, while lesser-price hotels include IVA in their quotes. Always ask to see a printed price sheet, and always ask if the tax is included.

WHAT THE SYMBOLS MEAN

✪ Frommer's Favorites

Our favorite places and experiences—outstanding for quality, value, or both.

The following abbreviations are used for credit cards:

AE	American Express	EURO	Eurocard
CB	Carte Blanche	JCB	Japan Credit Bank
DC	Diners Club	MC	MasterCard
DISC	Discover	V	Visa
ER	enRoute		

FIND FROMMER'S ONLINE

www.frommers.com offers up-to-the-minute listings on almost 200 cities around the globe—including the latest bargains and candid, personal articles updated daily by Arthur Frommer himself. No other Web site offers such comprehensive and timely coverage of the world of travel.

The Best of Cancún, Cozumel & the Yucatán

The he Yucatán Peninsula welcomes more visitors than any other part of Mexico. Its tremendous variety draws every kind of traveler with an unequaled mix of sophisticated resorts, ancient Maya culture, exquisite beaches, and exhilarating adventures. Between the two of us, we've logged thousands of miles crisscrossing the peninsula, and these are our personal favorites: the best places to go, the best restaurants, the best hotels, and must-see, one-of-a-kind experiences.

1 The Best Beach Vacations

- **Cancún:** Essentially one long ribbon of white sand bordering aquamarine water, Cancún is Mexico's ultimate beach vacation. It's not only ideal for a beach vacation if you want tropical drinks brought to you while you lounge in the sand, but doubles as a great place for exploring Caribbean reefs, tranquil lagoons, and the surrounding jungle. The most tranquil waters and beaches on Cancún Island are those at the northern tip, facing the Bahía de Mujeres. See chapter 3.
- **Isla Mujeres:** If laid-back is what you're after, this idyllic island offers peaceful, small-town beach life at its best. Most accommodations are smaller, inexpensive inns—with a couple of unique, luxurious places tossed in. Bike around the island to explore rocky coves and sandy beaches, or focus your tanning efforts on the wide beachfront of Playa Norte. Here you'll find calm waters and *palapa* restaurants, where you can have fresh-caught fish for lunch. You're also close to great diving (in the Cave of the Sleeping Sharks), snorkeling just offshore, and Isla Contoy National Park, which features great bird life and its own dramatic, uninhabited beach. If all that tranquility gets to you, you're only a ferry ride away from the action in Cancún. See chapter 4.
- **Playa del Carmen:** This is one of our absolute favorite Mexican beach vacations. Stylish and hip, Playa del Carmen offers the incredibly beautiful beaches that this coast is known for, as well as an eclectic assortment of inns, B&Bs, and *cabañas*. Activity centers on the small but excellent selection of restaurants, clubs, sidewalk cafes, and funky shops that run the length of pedestrians-only avenida 5. You're also close to all the major attractions of the coast, including Tulum, *cenote* diving, and Cozumel Island (just 45 minutes by ferry). Enjoy it while it's a manageable size. See chapter 4.

Mexico

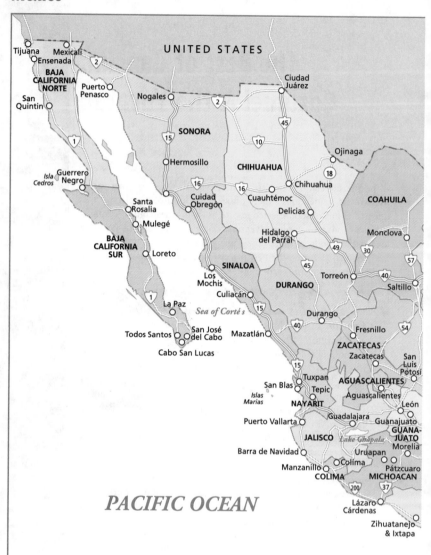

UNITED STATES

Tijuana
Mexicali
Ensenada
BAJA CALIFORNIA NORTE
Puerto Penasco
San Quintin
Nogales
Ciudad Juárez

2

SONORA

45

10

Hermosillo

CHIHUAHUA

Ojinaga

18

Isla Cedros
Guerrero Negro

16
16
Cuauhtémoc
Chihuahua

COAHUILA

Santa Rosalia
Cuidad Obregón
Delicias

Monclova

Mulegé

Hidalgo del Parral

BAJA CALIFORNIA SUR
Loreto

49
30
57

SINALOA

45

Torreón

40

Los Mochis

DURANGO

Saltillo

Culiacán

La Paz

Sea of Cortés

15

Durango

Todos Santos
San José del Cabo
Mazatlán

40

Fresnillo

54

Cabo San Lucas

ZACATECAS
Zacatecas

San Luis Potosí

15

Tuxpan

AGUASCALIENTES

San Blas
Tepic

Islas Marias

NAYARIT

Aguascalientes

León

Puerto Vallarta

Guadalajara
Guanajuato
GUANA-JUATO

JALISCO
Lake Chapala

Morelia

Barra de Navidad

Uruapan
Pátzcuaro

Manzanillo
Colima

COLIMA
MICHOACAN

200
37

PACIFIC OCEAN

Lázaro Cárdenas

Zihuatanejo & Ixtapa

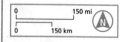

0   150 mi

0   150 km

N

UNITED STATES

Piedras Negras

Nuevo Laredo

85D

Monterrey   Matamoros

NUEVO
LEÓN   85

TAMAULIPAS

180

Ciudad Victoria

Ciudad Mante

Tampico

Gulf of Mexico

SAN LUIS
POTOSÍ

San Miguel
de Allende

Tuxpan

QUERÉTARO   Poza Rica

HIDALGO

Querétaro   180

Pachuca

Mexico City   Xalapa

Toluca   TLAXCALA

Cuernavaca   Tlaxcala   Veracruz

Puebla

MORELOS   PUEBLA   Orizaba

Taxco   95   Catemaco

Tehuacán   VERACRUZ

GUERRERO   1900   175   Coatzacoalcos

Chilpancingo   186

Acapulco   Oaxaca

200   OAXACA

Tuxtla   San Cristóbal
Gutiérrez   de las Casas

Salina   CHIAPAS
Cruz   Comitan

Puerto Escondido   Huatulco   *Gulf of*

Puerto   *Tehuantepec*   200
Ángel   Tapachula

Río Lagartos   *Isla
Mujeres*

Progreso   Valladolid

Celestún   180   Cancún

Mérida   *Cozumel*

YUCATÁN   Playa del
Carmen

Campeche   *Punta
Allen*

QUINTANA
ROO

CAMPECHE   Bacalar

261   *Majahual
Escárcega   Peninsula*

TABASCO   Chetumal

Villahermosa   186

Caribbean Sea

BELIZE

GUATEMALA

HONDURAS

EL
SALVADOR

*Bay of
Campeche*

3

- **Xcalak:** For many, the best beach vacation gets them far from "civilization." If living out fantasies of Robinson Crusoe is your ambition, the entire coastal area between Majahual and Xcalak is ideal for isolated beach getaways. Sportfishing and diving the Chinchorro reef (just offshore) are excellent ways to pass the days. Accommodations are rustic, but then, that's what you're looking for, right? Spirited adventurers can check out more details in chapter 4.

2 The Best Cultural Experiences

- **Streets and Park Entertainment** (Mérida): Few cities have so vibrant a street scene as Mérida. Throughout the week there are music and dance performances in plazas about the city—but on Sundays, Mérida really gets going. Streets are closed off, food stalls spring up everywhere, and you can enjoy a book fair, flea market, comedy acts, band concerts, and dance groups. At night, the main plaza is the place to be: People dance in the street in front of the town hall to mambos and rumbas. See chapter 5.
- **Exploring the Inland Yucatán Peninsula:** Travelers who venture only to the peninsula's resorts and cities will miss the tidy inland villages, where women wear colorful embroidered dresses and life seems to proceed as though the modern world (except for highways) didn't exist. Also not to be missed is the adventure of seeing newly uncovered ruins deep in jungle settings. See chapter 5.
- **San Cristóbal de las Casas:** The city of San Cristóbal is a living museum, with 16th-century colonial architecture and pre-Hispanic native influences. The highland Maya live in surrounding villages and arrive daily in town wearing colorful handmade clothing. The outlying villages are a window into another world, which gives visitors a glimpse of traditional Indian dress, religious customs, churches, and ceremonies. See chapter 6.
- **Regional Cuisine:** A trip to the Yucatán allows for a culinary tour of some of Mexico's finest foods. Don't miss specialties like *pollo* or *cochinita pibil* (chicken or pork in a savory *achiote* sauce); great seafood dishes; the many styles of *tamal* found throughout Chiapas and the Yucatán; and Caribbean-influenced Tabasco foods such as fried bananas, black beans, and yucca root.

3 The Best Archaeological Sites

- **Calakmul:** Of the many elegantly built Maya cities of the Rio Bec area in the lower Yucatan, Calakmul is the broadest in scope and design. It is also one of the hardest to get to—about 30 miles from the Guatemalan border and completely surrounded in jungle (actually, the Calakmul Biological Reserve). It is a walled city, with the tallest pyramid in the Yucatán—a city where the main inhabitants are the trees that populate the plazas. Go now, while it remains infrequently visited. See chapter 4.
- **Tulum:** Some dismiss Tulum as less important than other ruins in the Yucatán Peninsula, but this seaside Maya fortress is still inspiring. The sight of its crumbling stone walls is a stark contrast to the clear turquoise ocean just beyond. See chapter 4.
- **Uxmal:** No matter how many times you see Uxmal, the splendor of its stone carvings is awe-inspiring. A stone rattlesnake undulates across the facade of the Nunnery complex, and 103 masks of Chaac—the rain god—project from the Governor's Palace. See chapter 5.

- **Chichén-Itzá:** Stand beside the giant serpent head at the foot of El Castillo pyramid and marvel at the architects and astronomers who positioned the building so precisely that shadow and sunlight form a serpent's body slithering from peak to the earth at each equinox (March 21 and September 21). See chapter 5.
- **Palenque:** The ancient builders of these now-ruined structures carved histories in stone that scholars have only now been able to decipher. Imagine the magnificent ceremony in A.D. 683 when King Pacal was buried below ground in a secret pyramidal tomb—unspoiled until its discovery in 1952. See chapter 6.

4 The Best Active Vacations

- **Scuba Diving in Cozumel:** The reefs off the island of Cozumel are among the world's premier diving destinations, renowned for their deep walls covered with coral and sponges, teeming with life. Underwater caves and canyons also form part of this intricate reef system. Most hotels in Cozumel offer special dive packages, which make Cozumel's reefs accessible to everyone. Diving from Isla Mujeres is also quite spectacular, especially the Cave of the Sleeping Sharks. See chapter 4.
- **Cenote diving on the Yucatán mainland:** Dive into the clear depths of the Yucatán's *cenotes* (sinkholes or natural wells) for an interesting twist on underwater exploration. The Maya considered the *cenotes* sacred, and indeed, their vivid colors seem otherworldly. Most are located between Playa del Carmen and Tulum, and dive shops in these areas regularly run trips for experienced divers. See chapter 4.
- **An Excursion to Bonampak, Yaxchilán, and the Usumacinta River:** Bonampak and Yaxchilán—two remote, jungle-surrounded Maya sites along the Usumacinta River—can be reached by air (landing in a four-seater plane on a jungle airstrip), or by adding rafting and hiking to car travel. The experience could well be the highlight of any trip. See chapter 6.
- **Birding:** The Yucatán Peninsula, Tabasco, and Chiapas are an ornithological paradise, with hundreds of species awaiting the birder's gaze and list. One very special place is Isla Contoy, with over 70 species of birds, as well as a host of marine and animal life.

5 The Best Places to Get Away from It All

A handful of places in the Yucatán are perfect escapes—for a moment, a day, a week, or more of sublime tranquility. Some of these spots, while not posh, rate high on romance and ambiance.

- **Isla Mujeres:** If there's one island in Mexico that enables a respite from stress, it's Isla Mujeres. Though you'll find an ample selection of hotels and restaurants, they're as laid-back as are their patrons. Here, life moves along in pure *mañana* mode. Visitors mainly stretch out and doze beneath shady palms or languidly stroll about. And for many, the best part about this getaway is that it's comfortably close to Cancun's international airport, as well as shopping and dining, should you choose to reconnect. See chapter 4.
- **The Yucatán's Riviera Maya:** Away from the busy resort of Cancún, a string of quiet getaways, including Capitán Lafitte, Paamul, Xcalacoco, and a portion of Xpu-ha, offer tranquility on beautiful beaches at low prices. See chapter 4.

- **Tulum:** Near the Tulum ruins, about 20 beachside *palapa* inns offer some of the most peaceful getaways in the country. This stretch just might offer the best sandy beaches on the entire coast. Life here among the birds and coconut palms is decidedly unhurried. See chapter 4.
- **Rancho Encantado Cottage Resort** (Lago Bacalar; ☎ **800/505-MAYA** in the U.S.): The attractive *casitas* are the place to unwind at this resort, where hammocks stretch between trees. The hotel is on the shores of placid Lake Bacalar, south of Cancún near Chetumal, and there's nothing around for miles. But if you want adventure, you can head a kayak out on the lake, follow a birding trail, or take an excursion to Belize and the intriguing nearby Maya ruins on the Río Bec ruin route. See chapter 4.
- **Eco Paraíso Xixim** (Celestún; ☎ **991/6-2100**): In these crowded times, space is a luxury that's getting harder to come by. Space is precisely what makes this place so great: fifteen bungalows on 3 miles of beach bordering a coconut plantation. Throw in a good restaurant, a pool, and a couple of hammocks, and you have that rare combination of comfort and isolation. See chapter 5.

6 The Best Museums

- **Museo de la Isla de Cozumel** (Cozumel): More than something to do on a rainy day, this well-done museum is worth a visit any time. It unveils the island's past in an informative way not found anywhere else. There's a good bookstore on the first floor and a rooftop restaurant overlooking the Malecón and Caribbean. See chapter 4.
- **Museo de la Cultura Maya** (Chetumal): This new museum, one of the best in the country, features Maya archaeology, architecture, history, and mythology. It has interactive exhibits and a glass floor that allows visitors to walk above replicas of Maya sites. See chapter 4.
- **Museo Regional de Antropología** (Mérida): Housed in the Palacio Cantón, one of the most beautiful 19th-century mansions in the city, this museum showcases area archaeology and anthropological studies in handsome exhibits. See chapter 5.
- **Museo Regional de Antropología Carlos Pellicer Camara** (Villahermosa): This anthropology museum addresses Mexican history in the form of objects found at archaeological sites, with particular emphasis on the pre-Hispanic peoples of the Gulf Coast region. See chapter 6.
- **Parque Museo Olmeca de la Venta** (Villahermosa): The Olmec, considered Mexico's mother culture, are the subject of this park/museum, which features the magnificent stone remains that were removed from the La Venta site not far away. Stroll through a jungle setting where tropical birds alight, and savor these relics of the mysterious Olmec. See chapter 6.

7 The Best Shopping

Some tips on bargaining: Although haggling over prices in markets is expected and part of the fun, don't try to browbeat the vendor or bad-mouth the goods. Vendors won't bargain with people they consider disrespectful unless they are desperate to make a sale. Be insistent but friendly.

- **Resort wear in Cancún:** Resort clothing—especially if you can find a sale—can be a bargain here. And the selection may be wider than you have available at home. Most every mall on the island contains trendy boutiques specializing in locally designed and imported clothing. See chapter 3.

- **Duty Free in Cancún:** If you're looking for European perfume, fine watches, or other imported goods, you'll find the prices in Cancún's various duty-free shops hard to beat. Located in the major malls on the island and in downtown Cancún. See chapter 3.
- **Precious gemstones in Isla Mujeres:** Isla Mujeres, also a duty-free zone, offers an impressive selection of both precious stones and suburb craftsmen who can make jewelry designs to order. See chapter 4.
- **5th Avenue, Playa del Carmen:** Once Playa del Carmen was considered a shopping wasteland. All that has changed, and today, the pedestrian-only avenida 5 is lined with small boutiques selling batik clothing and fabric, Guatemalan textiles, Mexican dance masks, premium tequilas, Cuban cigars, and decorative pottery from Mexico's best pottery villages. See chapter 4.
- **Mérida:** It's *the* marketplace for the Yucatán, the best place to buy hammocks, *guayaberas,* Panama hats, and Yucatecan *huipils.* See chapter 5.
- **San Cristóbal de las Casas:** Deep in the heart of the Maya highlands, San Cristóbal has shops, open plazas, and markets that feature the distinctive waist-loomed wool and cotton textiles of the region, as well as leather shoes, handsomely crude pottery, and Guatemalan textiles. Highland Maya Indians sell direct to tourists from their armloads of textiles, dolls, and handmade miniature likenesses of Subcomandante Marcos—complete with ski masks. See chapter 6.

8 The Hottest Nightlife

While much of the Yucatán's nightlife expectedly is found in Cancún, that resort city isn't the only place to have a good time after dark. Along the Yucatán's Caribbean coast, nightlife is dominated by beachside dance floors with live bands, and extended "happy hours" in seaside bars. Cancún has the greatest variety and most sophisticated nightlife. Here are some favorite hot spots, from live music in hotel lobby bars to hip techno dance clubs.

- **Liquid, Coco Bongo, El Alebrije, Carlos 'n Charlie's, Ma'ax'O, and Dady'O:** These Cancún bars all offer good food, hot bands, and great dance floors. **Azucar Bar Caribeño** is a top spot for live Cuban and Caribbean rhythms in Cancún. See chapter 3.
- **The Lobby Lounge:** Located in Cancún's luxurious Ritz-Carlton Hotel, this is by far the most elegant evening spot on the island. The romantic live music, a selection of fine cigars, and over 120 premium tequilas (plus tastings) allow you to savor the spirit of Mexico. See chapter 3.
- **Forum by the Sea:** One place that has it all: The newest of the seaside entertainment centers in Cancún has a dazzling array of dance clubs, sports bars, fast food, and fine dining, with shops open late as well. You'll find plenty of familiar names here, including the Hard Rock Cafe and Rainforest Cafe. See chapter 3.

9 The Most Luxurious Hotels

Cancún, Cozumel, and the Yucatán Peninsula offer a long list of special places where the service is as polished as the quality of the establishment. Below are a few that should be on your short list of accommodations where you can indulge yourself.

- **Ritz-Carlton Cancún** (Cancún; ☎ **800/241-3333** in the U.S.): Thick carpets, sparkling glass and brass, and rich mahogany surround guests at this hotel, which clearly sets the standard for luxury in Cancún. The service is impeccable, leaving guests with an overall sense of pampered relaxation. See chapter 3.

- **Le Méridien** (Cancún; ☎ 800/543-4300 in the U.S.): It's the most intimate of the luxury hotels in Cancun, with a classy, yet understated sense of highly personalized service. Most notable is its 15,000-square-foot European Spa and Fitness Center, currently the largest in the state. See chapter 3.
- **Fiesta Americana Coral Beach** (Cancún; ☎ 800/343-7821 in the U.S.): Lavish use of imported marble and plenty of rich wood accents lead the way to luxurious rooms with views of the Bahía de Mujeres. The draws here are the sports facilities, a spa, its prime location across from the Convention Center, and one of the best beaches in the city. See chapter 3.
- **Puerto Isla Mujeres Resort & Yacht Club** (Isla Mujeres; ☎ 800/960-ISLA in the U.S.): Spacious individual villas face the Laguna Macax, where yachts glide up and anchor. Those who immerse themselves in the tranquillity and luxury of this 30-room enclave pass the word on to others, who dock for days or weeks on end. See chapter 4.
- **Presidente Inter-Continental Cozumel** (Cozumel; ☎ 800/327-0200 in the U.S.): Surrounded by shady palms, this hotel also has the best beach on the island, located right in front of Paraíso Reef. Favorite rooms are the deluxe beach-front rooms with spacious patios and direct access to the beach—you can even order romantic in-room dining on these patios, complete with a trio to serenade you. See chapter 4.

10 The Best Budget Inns

Some inns stand out for their combination of hospitality and simple-but-colorful surroundings. These are places guests return to again and again.

- **Suites El Patio** (Cancún City; ☎ 9/884-3500): This European-style inn welcomes many guests for repeat or long-term stays. Each room is unique, but all are tastefully decorated and surround a common, plant-filled corridor. Special packages combine Spanish lessons and accommodations. It's an oasis of cultured hospitality in one of Mexico's most commercial beach resorts. See chapter 3.
- **Hotel Safari Inn** (Cozumel; ☎ 987/2-0101): The comforts here are simple—a clean, basic room, a comfortable bed, good reading lights, powerful air-conditioning, and a great location. The inn is above the Aqua Safari dive shop (one of the top shops on the island) across from the dive shop's pier—you can book dives and a room at the same time. It's 3 blocks from the plaza and in the heart of the shopping district. What more do you need in Cozumel? See chapter 4.
- **Villa Catarina Rooms & Cabañas** (Playa del Carmen; ☎ 987/3-0970): These stylishly rustic rooms are nestled into a garden of tall palms, flowering trees, and singing birds. Just a block to the wide beach and tranquil Caribbean, it's also a short walk to the action of avenida 5. See chapter 4.
- **Hotel Dolores Alba** (Mérida; ☎ 99/28-5650): The new rooms at this hotel in Mérida offer all the comforts at a rate that other hotels in this category can't match. Add to this the new pool and large sunning area, and I call it a bargain. See chapter 5.

11 The Best Unique Inns

- **La Casa de los Sueños** (Isla Mujeres; ☎ 800/551-2558): Energizing colors and a tranquil ambiance will help put life back into perspective at this upscale B&B. The sculpted architecture frames pools that look out over Garrafon Reef to

Cancún across the bay. This nonsmoking property encourages healthful rejuvenation. See chapter 4.

- **Hotel Jungla Caribe** (Playa del Carmen; ☎ 987/3-0650): In a town filled with exceptional inns, this one's a standout. The eclectic decor combines neo-classical details with a decidedly tropical touch. The 26 rooms and suites surround a stylish courtyard restaurant and pool. You couldn't be better located—1 block from the beach, with an entrance on happening avenida 5. See chapter 4.
- **Cuzan Guest House** (Punta Allen Peninsula; ☎ 983/4-0358): Getting to the isolated lobster-fishing village of Punta Allen is half the adventure. Then you can retreat to one of the thatched-roof cottages, swing in a hammock, dine on lobster and stone crabs, and absolutely forget there's an outside world. There are no phones, televisions, or newspapers, and "town" is 35 miles away. Nature trips and flyfishing are readily arranged. See chapter 4.
- **Casa Mexilio Guest House** (Mérida; ☎ 800/538-6802 in the U.S.): Here, an imaginative arrangement of rooms around a courtyard features a pool surrounded by a riot of tropical vegetation. The rooms are divided among different levels for the sake of privacy, and connected by stairs and catwalks. Breakfast here provides an extra incentive for getting out of bed. See chapter 5.
- **Casa Na-Bolom** (San Cristóbal de las Casas; ☎ 967/8-1418): This unique house-museum is terrific for anthropology buffs. Built as a seminary in 1891, it was transformed into the headquarters of two anthropologists. The 12 guest rooms, named for surrounding villages, are decorated with local objects and textiles; all rooms have fireplaces and private baths, and breakfast is included. See chapter 6.
- **El Jacarandal** (San Cristóbal de las Casas; ☎ 967/8-1065): There are just four rooms here, and it isn't cheap, but a stay at this essentially private home—which includes all meals, drinks, and activities—is lodging as high-concept art. You can choose one of the horses from the stable and go on a morning ride, or take a guided trip to the Indian villages, the Huitepec cloud forest, and nearby Maya ruins. Meals are outstanding. See chapter 6.

12 The Best Restaurants

Best doesn't necessarily mean most luxurious. Although some of those listed below are fancy affairs, others are simple places to get fine, authentic Yucatecan cuisine.

- **Club Grill** (Cancún; ☎ 98/85-0808): The international cuisine served at this Ritz-Carlton restaurant is as excellent and elegant as the sumptuous setting. Soft, quiet, and utterly refined, dining here is a memorable experience. Also, there's a dance floor with oh-so-slow romantic music. See chapter 3.
- **La Dolce Vita** (Cancún; ☎ 98/84-1384): It's one of Cancún's longtime favorites, and remains untouched by newer arrivals. La Dolce Vita continues to draw diners with its blissfully flavorful dishes such as green tagliolini with lobster medallions, veal with morels, and fresh salmon with cream sauce, all served up alongside live jazz music. See chapter 3.
- **Zacil-Ha** (Isla Mujeres; ☎ 987/7-0279): With its sandy floor beneath thatched *palapas* and palms, it's hard to beat this relaxed and casual place for island atmosphere and well-prepared food. Along with its signature seafood and Caribbean cuisines, this restaurant continues to prove that vegetarian cuisine can be both artfully and tastefully prepared. It also offers special menus for those participating in yoga retreats on the island. See chapter 4.

- **Lobster House** (Cabaña del Pescador) (Cozumel; ☎ 987/2-4132): If you want an ideally seasoned, succulent lobster dinner, this is the place. If you want anything else, you're out of luck—lobster dinner, expertly prepared, is all that's served here. When you've achieved perfection, why bother with anything else? See chapter 4.

- **Prima** (Cozumel; ☎ 987/2-4242): The Italian food here is fresh, fresh, fresh—from the hydroponically grown vegetables to the pasta and garlic bread. And it's all prepared after you walk in, most of it by owner Albert Domínguez, who concocts an unforgettable shrimp fettuccine with pesto, crab ravioli with cream sauce, and crispy house salad in a chilled bowl. See chapter 4.

- **Media Luna** (Playa del Carmen; no phone): The inviting atmosphere of this sidewalk cafe on avenida 5 is enough to lure you in to dine. The expertly executed and innovative menu, together with great prices, makes it one of the top choices along the entire Caribbean coast. See chapter 4.

- **La Pigua** (Campeche; ☎ 981/1-3365): Campeche's regional food is seafood, and nowhere else will you find seafood like this. Mexican caviar, coconut-battered shrimp, and chiles stuffed with shark are just a few of the unique specialties. Thinking about La Pigua's pompano in a fine herb green sauce makes me want to start checking flight schedules. See chapter 5.

- **El Pórtico del Peregrino** (Mérida; ☎ 99/28-6163): There are few things so delightful as an evening spent dining at this elegant and unpretentious setting. The menu offers a varied assortment of national and international dishes with an underlying Mediterranean influence. Main courses are nourishing but not heavy, while the salads, soups, and vegetable dishes recommend themselves. See chapter 5.

- **Virrey de Mendoza** (Mérida; ☎ 99/25-3082): If you're in Mérida and feel like splurging for a night, this is the place. It specializes in highly refined versions of Mexico's most elaborate dishes. The Yucatecan specialties are superb—especially the seafood. The setting, lighting, and background music are first-rate. See chapter 5.

Planning Your Trip: 2
The Basics

A little advance planning can make the difference between a good trip and a great trip. When should you go? What's the best way to get there? How much should you plan on spending? What festivals or special events will be taking place during your visit? What safety or health precautions are advised? We'll answer these and other questions for you in this chapter. In addition to these basics, I highly recommend taking a little time to learn about the culture and traditions of Mexico. It can make the difference between simply "getting away" and truly adding understanding to your experience (see Appendix A).

THE REGION AT A GLANCE
Travelers to the peninsula will have an opportunity to see pre-Hispanic ruins—such as **Chichén-Itzá, Uxmal,** and **Tulum**—and the living descendants of the cultures who built them, as well as the ultimate in resort Mexico: **Cancún.** The peninsula is edged by the dull aquamarine Gulf of Mexico on the west and north, and the clear blue Caribbean Sea on the east. It covers almost 84,000 square miles, with nearly 1,000 miles of shoreline. Underground rivers and natural wells called *cenotes* are a peculiar feature of this region.

The interior of the peninsula is dotted with lovely rock-walled Maya villages and crumbling *henequén* haciendas. In contrast to the placid interior is the hubbub of the Caribbean Coast. From Cancún south to **Chetumal,** the jungle coastline is spotted with all kinds of development, from posh to budget, but it also hosts an enormous array of wildlife, including hundreds of species of birds. The Gulf Coast beaches, while good enough, don't compare to those on the Caribbean. National parks near **Celestún** and **Río Lagartos** on the Gulf Coast are home to amazing flocks of flamingos.

1 Visitor Information, Entry Requirements & Money

SOURCES OF INFORMATION
The **Mexico Hotline** (☎ 800/44-MEXICO) is an excellent source for general information; you can request brochures on the country and get answers to the most commonly asked questions.

More information (15,000 pages worth, they say) about Mexico is available on the Mexico Ministry of Tourism's Web site: **mexico-travel.com.**

The Yucatán Peninsula

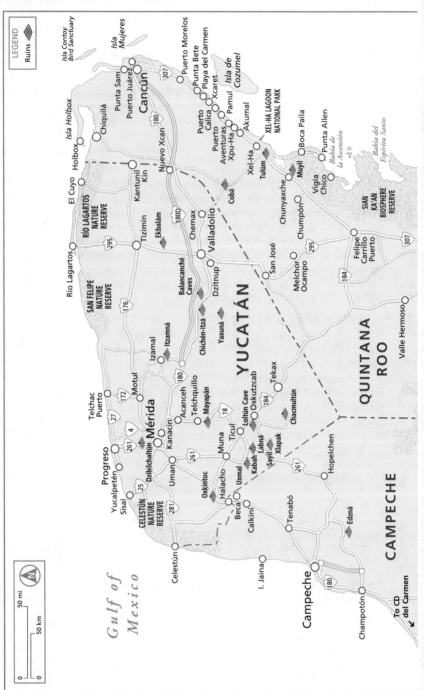

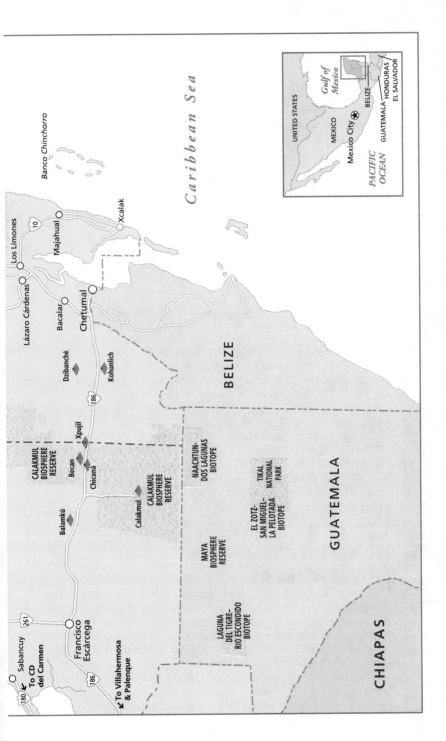

Banco Chinchorro

Caribbean Sea

Los Limones

Majahual

Xcalak

Lázaro Cárdenas

Bacalar

Chetumal

BELIZE

Dzibanché

Kohunlich

186

Xpujil

CALAKMUL
BIOSPHERE
RESERVE

Becan

Chicaná

CALAKMUL
BIOSPHERE
RESERVE

Balamkú

Calakmul

NAACHTUN–
DOS LAGUNAS
BIOTOPE

TIKAL
NATIONAL
PARK

EL ZOTZ–
SAN MIGUEL–
LA PELOTADA
BIOTOPE

GUATEMALA

MAYA
BIOSPHERE
RESERVE

261

Francisco
Escárcega

Sabancuy

To CD
del Carmen

186

To Villahermosa
& Palenque

180

LAGUNA
DEL TIGRE–
RIO ESCONDIDO
BIOTOPE

CHIAPAS

UNITED STATES

Gulf of
Mexico

BELIZE

MEXICO

GUATEMALA HONDURAS

EL SALVADOR

PACIFIC
OCEAN

Mexico City

13

The **U.S. State Department** (☎ **202/647-5225** for travel information and Overseas Citizens Services) offers a **Consular Information Sheet** on Mexico, with a compilation of safety, medical, driving, and general travel information gleaned from reports by official U.S. State Department offices in Mexico. You can also request the Consular Information Sheet by fax (☎ **202/647-3000**). The State Department is also on the Internet; check out **travel.state.gov/ mexico.html** for the Consular Information Sheet on Mexico; **travel.state. gov/travel_warnings.html** for other Consular Information sheets and travel warnings; and **travel.state.gov/tips_mexico.html** for the State Department's *Tips for Travelers to Mexico.*

The **Center for Disease Control Hotline** (☎ **800/311-3435, 404/639-3534**) is another source for medical information affecting travelers to Mexico and elsewhere. The center's Web site, **www.cdc.gov/**, provides lengthy information on health issues for specific countries. For travelers to Mexico and Central America, the number with recorded messages about specific health issues is ☎ **404/332-4555,** and the Web page is **www.cdc.gov/ travel/camerica.htm**. The U.S. State Department offers medical information for Americans traveling abroad at **travel.state.gov/medical.html**. This site provides general information and a list of air ambulance services.

MEXICAN GOVERNMENT TOURIST OFFICES   With the exception of the United States and Canada, Mexico's foreign tourist offices (MGTO) throughout the world were closed in early 1997 and consolidated with their embassies. Those continuing to operate in North America include the following:

United States: Chicago, IL (☎ **312/606-9252**); Houston, TX (☎ **713/ 772-2581**); Los Angeles, CA (☎ **213/351-2069,** fax 213/351-2074); Miami, FL (☎ **305/718-4091**); New York, NY (☎ **800/446-3942**); and the Mexican Embassy Tourism Delegate, 1911 Pennsylvania Ave., Washington, DC 20005 (☎ **202/728-1750**). The MGTO offices have been combined with Mexican Consulate offices in the same cities, providing one central source for official information on Mexico.

Canada: 1 Place Ville-Marie, Suite 1931, Montréal, QUEB, H3B 2C3 (☎ **514/871-1052**); 2 Bloor St. W., Suite 1502, Toronto, ON, M4W 3E2 (☎ **416/925-2753**); 999 W. Hastings, Suite 1110, Vancouver, BC, V6C 2W2 (☎ **604/669-2845**). Embassy office: 1500-45 O'Connor St Ottawa Ontario, Can K1P 1A4 (☎ **613/233-8988,** fax 613/235-9123).

STATE TOURISM DEVELOPMENT OFFICE   Two Mexican states have a tourism and trade development office in the United States: **Oaxaca and Tabasco States Convention and Visitors Bureau,** 7880 St. Felipe, Suite 130, Houston, TX 77063 (☎ **713/339-1880;** fax 713/339-1615).

ENTRY REQUIREMENTS

DOCUMENTS   All travelers to Mexico are required to present **proof of citizenship,** such as an original birth certificate with a raised seal, a valid passport, or naturalization papers. Those using a birth certificate should also have a current photo identification such as a driver's license or official ID. Those whose last name on the birth certificate is different from their current name (women using a married name, for example) should also bring a photo identification card *and* legal proof of the name change such as the *original* marriage license or certificate. This proof of citizenship may also be requested when you want to reenter either the United States or Mexico. Note that photocopies are *not* acceptable. When reentering the U.S. you must prove both your citizenship and your identification so always take a picture ID, like a driver's license or better yet, a valid passport. Birth certificates will enable you to enter Mexico, but alone, will not enable you to reenter the U.S.

Note: While the U.S. State Department endorses the entry requirements outlined above, some readers have reported problems trying to enter Mexico using only a birth certificate. To ensure against any needless delay at immigration, make sure you follow the requirements to the letter—the birth certificate must be the *original* version with the raised seal. Or avoid any potential problem by carrying your U.S. passport.

You must also carry a **Mexican Tourist Permit (FMT),** which is issued free of charge by Mexican border officials after proof of citizenship is accepted. The tourist permit is more important than a passport in Mexico, so guard it carefully. If you lose it, you may not be permitted to leave the country until you can replace it—a bureaucratic hassle that can take anywhere from a few hours to a week. (If you do lose your tourist permit, get a police report from local authorities indicating that your documents were stolen; having one *might* lessen the hassle of exiting the country without all your identification.)

A tourist permit can be issued for up to 180 days, although your stay south of the border may be shorter than that. Sometimes officials don't ask—they just stamp a time limit, so be sure to say "6 months" (or at least twice as long as you intend to stay). If you should decide to extend your stay, you may request that additional time be added to your permit from an official immigration office in Mexico.

Note that children under age 18 traveling without parents or with only one parent must have a notarized letter from the absent parent or parents authorizing the travel.

LOST DOCUMENTS To replace a **lost passport,** contact your embassy or nearest consular agent (see "Fast Facts: Mexico," below). You must establish a record of your citizenship and also fill out a form requesting another Mexican Tourist Permit if it, too, was lost. Without the **tourist permit** you can't leave the country, and without an affidavit affirming your passport request and citizenship, you may have problems at Customs when you get home. So it's important to clear everything up *before* trying to leave. Mexican Customs may, however, accept the police report of the loss of the tourist permit and allow you to leave.

CUSTOMS ALLOWANCES When you enter Mexico, Customs officials will be tolerant as long as you have no illegal drugs or firearms. You're allowed to bring in two cartons of cigarettes, or 50 cigars, plus a kilogram (2.2 lb.) of smoking tobacco; the liquor allowance is two 1-liter bottles of anything, wine or hard liquor; you are also allowed 12 rolls of film. A laptop computer, camera equipment, and sporting equipment (golf clubs, scuba gear, a bicycle) that could feasibly be used during your stay are also allowed. The underlying guideline is to not bring anything that looks like it's meant to be resold in Mexico.

When you reenter the **United States,** federal law allows you to bring in up to $400 in purchases duty-free every 30 days. The first $1,000 over the $400 allowance is taxed at 10%. You may bring in a carton (200) of cigarettes, 100 cigars, or 2 kilograms (4.4 lb.) of smoking tobacco, plus 1 liter of an alcoholic beverage (wine, beer, or spirits).

Canadian citizens are allowed $50 in purchases after a 24-hour absence from the country or $300 after a stay of 48 hours and $750 after a stay of 7 days or more. In addition, Canadian citizens may bring 200 cigarettes or 50 cigars plus 1 kilo (2.2 lb.) of chewing tobacco, and 1.5 liters of hard liquor or wine.

British travelers returning from outside the European Union are allowed to bring in £145 worth of goods, in addition to the following: up to 200 cigarettes, 50 cigars or 250 grams of tobacco; 2 liters of wine; 1 liter of liqueur greater than 22% alcohol by volume and 60cc/milliliters of perfume. If any item worth more than the limit of £145 is brought in, payment must be made on the full value, not just on the amount above £145.

Citizens of **New Zealand** are allowed to return with a combined value of up to NZ$1,000 in goods, duty-free.

GOING THROUGH CUSTOMS Mexican Customs inspection has been streamlined. At most points of entry, tourists are requested to press a button in front of what looks like a traffic signal, which alternates on touch between red and green signals. Green light and you go through without inspection; red light and your luggage or car may be inspected briefly or thoroughly. If you have an unusual amount of luggage or an oversized piece, you may be subject to inspection despite the traffic signal routine.

MONEY

CASH/CURRENCY The currency in Mexico is the Mexican **peso.** Paper currency comes in denominations of 20, 50, 100, 200, and 500 pesos. Coins come in denominations of 1, 2, 5, 10, and 20 pesos, and 20 and 50 **centavos** (100 centavos equal 1 peso). The current exchange rate for the U.S. dollar is around 10 pesos; at that rate, an item that costs 10 pesos would be equivalent to US$1.

Getting **change** continues to be a problem in Mexico. Small-denomination bills and coins are hard to come by, so start collecting them early in your trip and continue as you travel. Shopkeepers everywhere seem always to be out of change and small bills; that's doubly true in a market.

Many establishments that deal with tourists, especially in coastal resort areas, quote prices in dollars. To avoid confusion, they use the abbreviations "Dlls." for dollars and "M.N." (*moneda nacional,* or national currency) for pesos. All dollar equivalencies in this book were based on an exchange rate of 10 pesos per dollar.

EXCHANGING MONEY The rate of exchange fluctuates a tiny bit daily, so you probably are better off not exchanging too much of your currency at once. Don't forget, however, to have enough pesos to carry you over a weekend or Mexican holiday, when banks are closed. In general, avoid carrying the U.S. $100 bill, the bill most commonly counterfeited in Mexico, and therefore the most difficult to exchange, especially in smaller towns. Since small bills and coins in pesos are hard to come by in Mexico, the U.S. $1 bill is very useful for tipping.

The bottom line on exchanging money of all kinds: It pays to ask first and shop around. Banks pay the top rates.

Exchange houses (*casas de cambio*) are generally more convenient than banks since they have more locations and longer hours; the rate of exchange may be the same as a bank or only slightly lower. *Note:* Before leaving a bank or exchange-house window, always count your change in front of the teller before the next client steps up.

Money Matters

The **universal currency sign ($)** is used to indicate pesos in Mexico. The use of this symbol in this book, however, denotes U.S. currency.

Large airports have currency-exchange counters that often stay open whenever flights are arriving or departing. Though convenient, these generally do not offer the most favorable rates.

A hotel's exchange desk commonly pays less favorable rates than banks; however, when the currency is in a state of flux, higher-priced hotels are known to pay *higher* than bank rates, in their effort to attract dollars. The bottom line: it pays to shop around, but in almost all cases, you receive a better exchange by changing money first, then paying for goods or services, rather than by paying with dollars directly to an establishment.

BANKS & ATMS   Banks in Mexico are rapidly expanding and improving services. New hours tend to be from 9am until 5 or 6pm, with many open for at least a half day on Saturday, and some even offering limited hours on Sunday. The exchange of dollars, which used to be limited until noon, can now be accommodated anytime during business hours in the larger resorts and cities. Some, but not all, banks charge a service fee of about 1% to exchange traveler's checks. However, most purchases can be paid for directly with traveler's checks at the stated exchange rate of the establishment. Don't even bother with personal checks drawn on a U.S. bank—although theoretically they may be cashed, it only happens with weeks of delay, and the bank will wait for your check to clear before giving you your money.

Travelers to Mexico can also easily access money from **automatic teller machines (ATMs),** now available in most major cities and resort areas in Mexico. Universal bank cards (such as the Cirrus and PLUS systems) can be used, and this is a convenient way to withdraw money from your bank and avoid carrying too much with you at any time. There is often a service fee charged by your bank for each transaction, but the exchange rate is generally more favorable than one found at a currency house. Most machines offer Spanish/English menus and dispense pesos, but some offer the option of withdrawing dollars. Be sure to check the daily withdrawal limit before you depart, and ask your bank whether you need a new personal ID number. For Cirrus locations abroad, call ☎ **800/424-7787,** or check out MasterCard's Web site (**www.mastercard.com/atm/**). For PLUS usage abroad, call ☎ **800/843-7587,** or visit Visa's Web site (**www.visa.com/atms**).

TRAVELER'S CHECKS   Traveler's checks are readily accepted nearly everywhere, but they can be difficult to cash on a weekend or holiday or in an out-of-the-way place. Their best value is in replacement in case of theft. Frequently in Mexico, a bank or establishment will pay more for traveler's checks than for cash dollars.

CREDIT CARDS   You'll be able to charge most hotel, restaurant, and store purchases, as well as almost all airline tickets, on your credit card. You can get cash advances of several hundred dollars on your card, but there may be a wait of 20 minutes to 2 hours. You generally can't charge gasoline purchases in Mexico; however, with the new franchise system of Pemex stations taking hold, this may change as well. Visa ("Bancomer" in Mexico), MasterCard ("Carnet"), and American Express are the most accepted cards.

Creditcard charges will be made in pesos, then converted into dollars by the bank issuing the credit card. Generally you receive a favorable bank rate when paying by credit card. However, be aware that some establishments add a 5% to 7% surcharge when you pay with a credit card.

THEFT   Almost every credit card company has an emergency 800-number that you can call if your wallet or purse is stolen. They may be able to wire you a cash advance off your credit card immediately, and in many places, they can deliver an emergency credit card in a day or two. The issuing bank's 800-number is usually on the back of the credit card—though, of course, that doesn't help you much if the card was stolen. The toll-free information directory will provide the number if you dial ☎ **800/555-1212.** Citicorp Visa's U.S. emergency number is ☎ **800/336-8472.** American Express cardholders and traveler's check holders should call ☎ **800/221-7282** for all money emergencies. MasterCard holders should call ☎ **800/307-7309.**

If you opt to carry traveler's checks, be sure to keep a record of their serial numbers, separately from the checks, of course, so you're ensured a refund in just such an emergency.

Odds are that if your wallet is gone, the police won't be able to recover it for you. However, after you realize that it's gone and you cancel your credit cards, it is still worth informing them. Your credit card company or insurer may require a police report number. If you do lose your wallet anywhere outside Mexico City, before panicking, retrace your steps—you'll be surprised at how many honest people are in Mexico and it is likely that you'll find someone trying to find you to return your wallet.

2 When to Go

SEASONS   High season begins around December 20 and continues to Easter. It is certainly the best time to be in the Yucatán if you're here for calm, warm weather; snorkeling, diving, and fishing (the calmer weather means more clearer and more predictable seas); or to visit the ruins that dot the interior of the peninsula. Book well in advance if you plan to be in Cancún around the holidays.

Low season begins the day after Easter and continues to mid-December; during low season, prices may drop 20% to 50%. Increasingly in Cancún and along the Riviera Maya, demand by European visitors is creating a summer "high" season, with hotel rates approaching those charged in the winter months.

Generally speaking, Mexico's **dry season** runs from November through April, with the **rainy season** stretching from May through October. It isn't a problem if you're staying close to the beaches, but for those bent on road-tripping to Chichén-Itzá, Uxmal, or other sites, temperatures and humidity in the interior can be downright stifling from May through July. Later in the rainy season the frequency of **tropical storms** and **hurricanes** increases; such storms, of course, can put a crimp in your vacation. But they can cool off temperatures, making ruins climbing a real joy, accompanied by cool air and a slight wind. November is especially ideal for Yucatán travels.

Villahermosa is sultry and humid all the time. San Cristóbal de las Casas, at an elevation of 7,100 feet, is much cooler than the lowlands, and downright cold in winter.

Yucatán Calendar of Festivals & Special Events

January

- **New Year's Day (Año Nuevo).** National holiday. Parades, religious observances, parties, and fireworks welcome in the New Year everywhere. In traditional indigenous communities, new tribal leaders are inaugurated with colorful ceremonies rooted in the pre-Hispanic past. January 1.

- **Three Kings Day (Día de Reyes),** nationwide. Commemorates the Three Kings' bringing of gifts to the Christ Child. On this day, children receive gifts, much like the traditional gift giving that accompanies Christmas in the United States. Friends and families gather to share the *Rosca de Reyes,* a special cake. Inside the cake there is a small doll representing the Christ Child; whoever receives the doll in his or her piece must host a tamales-and-*atole* party the next month. January 6.

February

- **Candlemass (Día de la Candelaria),** nationwide. Music, dances, processions, food, and other festivities lead up to a blessing of seed and candles in a tradition that mixes pre-Hispanic and European traditions marking the end of winter. All those who attended the Three Kings Celebration reunite to share *atole* and tamales at a party hosted by the recipient of the doll found in the Rosca. February 2.

✪ **Carnaval.** Carnaval takes place the 3 days preceding Ash Wednesday and the beginning of Lent. It is celebrated with special gusto in Cozumel, where the celebration resembles Mardi Gras in New Orleans, with a festive atmosphere and parades. Transportation and hotels are packed, so it's best to make reservations well in advance and arrive a couple of days ahead of the beginning of celebrations. In 2001, the dates are from February 25 through 27.

- **Ash Wednesday.** The start of Lent and time of abstinence. It's a day of reverence nationwide, but some towns honor it with folk dancing and fairs. In 2001, the date is February 28.

March

- **Benito Juárez's Birthday.** National Holiday. Small hometown celebrations countrywide. March 21.
- **Spring Equinox,** Chichén-Itzá. On the first day of spring, the Temple of Kukulcan—Chichén-Itza's main pyramid—aligns with the sun and the shadow of the plumed serpent moves slowly from the top of the building down. When the shadow reaches the bottom, the body joins the carved stone snake's head at the base of the pyramid. According to ancient legend, at the moment that the serpent is whole, the earth is fertilized to assure a bountiful growing season. Visitors come from around the world to marvel at this sight, so advance arrangements are advisable. March 21. (The shadow can be seen from Mar 19 to 23.) Elsewhere, the equinox is celebrated with festivals and celebrations to welcome spring, in the custom of the ancient Mexicans, with dances and prayers to the elements and the four cardinal point, in order to renew their energy for the year. It's customary to wear white, with a red ribbon.

✪ **Holy Week.** Celebrates the last week in the life of Christ from Palm Sunday through Easter Sunday with somber religious processions almost nightly, spoofing of Judas, and reenactments of specific biblical events, plus food and craft fairs. Businesses close during this traditional week of Mexican national vacations.

If you plan on traveling to or around Mexico during Holy Week, make your reservations early. Airline seats on flights into and out of the country will be reserved months in advance. Buses to these towns or to almost anywhere in Mexico will be full, so try arriving on the Wednesday or Thursday before Good Friday. Easter Sunday is quiet. For 2001, April 8 through 14 is Holy Week, Easter Sunday is April 15, and the week following is a traditional vacation period.

May

- **Labor Day,** nationwide. Workers' parades countrywide and everything closes. May 1.
- **Holy Cross Day (Día de la Santa Cruz).** Workers place a cross on top of unfinished buildings and celebrate with food, bands, folk dancing, and fireworks around the work site. May 3.
- **Cinco de Mayo.** Puebla and nationwide. A national holiday that celebrates the defeat of the French at the Battle of Puebla. May 5.
- **Feast of San Isidro.** The patron saint of farmers is honored with a blessing of seeds and work animals. May 15.
- **Cancún Jazz Festival.** For dates and schedule information, call ☎ **800/ 44-MEXICO.**

June

- **Navy Day (Día de la Marina),** celebrated in all coastal towns with naval parades and fireworks. June 1.

✪ **Corpus Christi,** celebrated nationwide. Honors the Body of Christ (the Eucharist) with religious processions, masses, and food. Festivities include performances of *voladores* (flying pole dancers) beside the church and at the ruins of El Tajín. *Mulitas* (mules) handmade from dried corn husks and painted, often with a corn-husk rider, and sometimes accompanied by pairs of corn-husk dolls, are traditionally sold there on that day. Dates vary.

- **Día de San Pedro (St. Peter and St. Paul's Day),** nationwide. Celebrated wherever St. Peter is the patron saint, and honors anyone named Pedro or Peter. June 29.

August

✪ **Assumption of the Virgin Mary.** Celebrated throughout the country with special masses and in some places with processions. August 20 to 22.

September

- **Independence Day.** Celebrates Mexico's independence from Spain. A day of parades, picnics, and family reunions throughout the country. At 11pm on September 15, the president of Mexico gives the famous independence *grito* (shout) from the National Palace in Mexico City. At least half a million people are crowded into the *zócalo,* and the rest of the country watches the event on TV or participates in local celebrations, which mirror the festivities at the national level. The enormous military parade on September 16 starts at the *zócalo* and ends at the Independence Monument on Reforma. Tall buildings downtown are draped in the national colors—red, green, and white—and the *zócalo* is ablaze with lights. The schedule of events is exactly the same in every village, town, and city across Mexico. September 15 to 16.

- **Fall Equinox,** Chichén-Itzá. The same shadow play that occurs during the spring equinox repeats itself for the fall equinox. September 21 to 22.

October

- **Día de la Raza ("Ethnicity Day" or Columbus Day).** Commemorates the fusion of the Spanish and Mexican peoples. October 12.

November

✪ **Day of the Dead.** What's commonly called the Day of the Dead is actually 2 days, All Saints' Day—honoring saints and deceased children—and All Souls' Day, honoring deceased adults. Relatives gather at cemeteries countrywide, carrying candles and food, often spending the night beside the graves of loved ones. Weeks before, bakers begin producing bread formed in the shape of mummies or round loaves decorated with bread "bones." Decorated sugar skulls emblazoned with glittery names are sold everywhere. Many days ahead, homes and churches erect special altars laden with Day of the Dead bread, fruit, flowers, candles, favorite foods, and photographs of saints and of the deceased. On the 2 nights, children dress in costumes and masks, often carrying mock coffins and pumpkin lanterns, into which they expect money will be dropped, through the streets. November 1 to 2.

- **Revolution Day.** Commemorates the start of the Mexican Revolution in 1910 with parades, speeches, rodeos, and patriotic events. November 20.

○ **Feast of the Virgin of Guadalupe.** Throughout the country the patroness of Mexico is honored with religious processions, street fairs, dancing, fireworks, and masses. It is one of Mexico's most moving and beautiful displays of traditional culture. The Virgin of Guadalupe appeared to a young man, Juan Diego, in December 1531, on a hill near Mexico City. He convinced the bishop that he had seen the apparition by revealing his cloak, upon which the Virgin was emblazoned. It's customary for children to dress up as Juan Diego, wearing mustaches and red bandanas. One of the most famous and elaborate celebrations takes place at the Basílica of Guadalupe, north of Mexico City, where the Virgin appeared. But every village celebrates this day, often with processions of children carrying banners of the Virgin and with *charreadas* (rodeos), bicycle races, dancing, and fireworks. December 12.

- **Christmas Posadas.** On each of the 9 nights before Christmas, it's customary to reenact the Holy Family's search for an inn, with door-to-door candlelit processions in cities and villages nationwide. These are also hosted by most businesses and community organizations, taking the place of the northern tradition of a Christmas party. December 15 to 24.

- **Christmas.** Mexicans extend this celebration and often leave their jobs beginning 2 weeks before Christmas all the way through New Year's. Many businesses close, and resorts and hotels fill up. Significant celebrations take place on December 23.

- **New Year's Eve.** As in the rest of the world, New Year's Eve in Mexico is celebrated with parties, fireworks, and plenty of noise. December 31.

3 Active Vacations in the Yucatán

Mexico has numerous **golf** courses, especially in the resort areas; there are excellent ones in Cancún and Playa del Carmen.

Visitors can enjoy **tennis, waterskiing, surfing, bicycling,** and **horseback riding. Scuba diving** is excellent off the Yucatán's Caribbean coast, with Cozumel considered one of the top five dive spots in the world.

PARKS   Most of the national parks and nature reserves are understaffed or unstaffed. In addition to the reliable Mexican companies offering adventure trips (such as the **AMTAVE** members; see below), many U.S.-based companies also offer this kind of travel, with trips led by specialists.

OUTDOORS ORGANIZATIONS & TOUR OPERATORS   There's an active association in Mexico of eco- and adventure-tour operators called **AMTAVE** (Asociación Mexicana de Turismo de Aventura y Ecoturismo, A.C.). It publishes an annual catalog of participating firms, and its offerings must all meet certain criteria for security, quality, and training of the guides, as well as for sustainability of natural and cultural environments. For more information, contact the association (in Mexico City) at ☎/fax **5/663-5381,** e-mail: amtave@mexico.com; www.amtave.com.mx); ask for Marlene Ehrenberg or Daniel Martínez.

The Archaeological Conservancy, 5301 Central Ave. NE, Suite 1218, Albuquerque, NM 87108-1517 (☎ **505/266-1540,** www.americanarcheology. com, e-mail: archonn@nm.net), presents one trip to Mexico per year led by an expert, usually an archaeologist. The trips change from year to year and space is limited, so you must make reservations early in the year.

ATC Tours and Travel, calle 16 de Septiembre 16, 29200 San Cristóbal de las Casas, Chiapas (☎ **967/8-2550** or 967/8-2557; fax 967/8-3145, e-mail: adventours@atctours.com.mx), a Mexico-based tour operator with an excellent reputation, offers specialist-led trips primarily in southern Mexico. In addition to trips to the ruins of Palenque and Yaxchilán (extending into Belize and Guatemala by river, plane, and bus if desired), it also offers horseback tours to Chamula or Zinacantán, and day-trips to the ruins of Toniná around San Cristóbal de las Casas, Chiapas; birding in the rain forests of Chiapas and Guatemala (including in the El Triunfo Reserve of Chiapas where you can see the rare quetzal bird and orchids); hikes out to the shops and homes of native textile artists of the Chiapas highlands; and walks from the Lagos de Montebello in the Montes Azules Biosphere Reserve, with camping and canoeing. It can also prepare custom itineraries that center on whichever activities or areas interest you.

Culinary Adventures, 6023 Reid Dr. NW, Gig Harbor, WA 98335 (☎ **253/851-7676;** fax 253/851-9532), specializes in a short but special list of cooking tours in Mexico, featuring well-known cooks and traveling to particular regions known for excellent cuisine. The owner, Marilyn Tausend, is the co-author of *Mexico the Beautiful Cookbook,* and *Cocinas de la Familia* (Family Kitchens).

Far Flung Adventures, P.O. Box 377, Terlingua, TX 79852 (☎ **800/359-4138** or 915/371-2489; www.farflung.com), takes clients on specialist-led river trips combining rafting and camping at archeological sites.

Trek America, P.O. Box 189, Rockaway, NJ 07866 (☎ **800/221-0596** or 973/983-1144; fax 973/983-8551, www.trekamerica.com, e-mail: info@trekamerica.com), organizes lengthy, active trips that combine trekking, hiking, van transportation, and camping in the Yucatán, Chiapas, Oaxaca, the Copper Canyon, and Mexico's Pacific coast, and a trip that covers Mexico City, Teotihuacán, Taxco, Guadalajara, Puerto Vallarta, and Acapulco.

DIVING PACKAGES

In Cozumel, you may be able to save money by purchasing diving packages, which include the price of the hotel and a given number of dives. Many divers, however, save more money by staying in a cheaper hotel than a package calls for and booking dives directly with a diving concession. This method may be particularly practical in the fall, when stormy seas often preclude diving, and you therefore won't have to pay for unused dives. For more on diving off Cozumel Island, see chapter 4.

4 Health, Safety & Insurance

STAYING HEALTHY

COMMON AILMENTS   Travelers to certain regions of Mexico, such as **San Cristóbal de las Casas,** with an elevation of 7,100 feet, occasionally experience **elevation sickness,** which results from the relative lack of oxygen and the decrease in barometric pressure that characterizes high elevations (over 5,000 ft./1,500m). Symptoms include shortness of breath, fatigue, headache, insomnia, and even nausea. At high elevations it takes about 10 days to acquire the extra red blood corpuscles you need to adjust to the scarcity of oxygen. To help your body acclimate to the higher elevation, drink plenty of fluids, avoid alcoholic beverages, which tend to exaggerate conditions, and don't overexert yourself during the first few days. If you have heart or lung problems, talk to your doctor before going above 8,000 feet.

Antibiotics and other drugs that you'd need a prescription to buy in the U.S. are sold over-the-counter in Mexican pharmacies. Mexican pharmacies also have common over-the-counter cold, sinus, and allergy remedies, although not the broad selection we're accustomed to finding easily.

Mosquitoes and **gnats** are prevalent along the coast and in the Yucatán lowlands. Insect repellent (*repelente contra insectos*) is a must, and it's not always available in Mexico. If you'll be in these areas and are prone to bites, bring a repellent along that contains the active ingredient DEET. Avon's "Skin So Soft" also works extremely well. If you're sensitive to bites, pick up some antihistamine cream from a drugstore at home.

Most readers won't ever see a scorpion (*alacrán*). But if you're stung by one, go immediately to a doctor.

MORE SERIOUS DISEASES   You shouldn't be overly concerned about tropical diseases if you stay on the normal tourist routes and don't eat street food. However, both dengue fever and cholera have appeared in Mexico in recent years. Talk to your doctor, or a medical specialist in tropical diseases, about any precautions you should take. You can also get medical bulletins from the U.S. State Department and the Centers for Disease Control (see "Sources of Information," above). You can protect yourself by taking some simple precautions: watch what you eat and drink; don't swim in stagnant water (ponds, slow-moving rivers, or wells); and avoid mosquito bites by covering up, using repellent, and sleeping under mosquito netting. The most dangerous areas seem to be on Mexico's west coast, away from the big resorts, which are relatively safe.

EMERGENCY EVACUATION   For extreme medical emergencies, there's a service from the United States that will fly people to American hospitals: **Air-Evac,** a 24-hour air ambulance (☎ **888/554-9729,** or call collect 510/293-5968). You can also contact the service in Guadalajara (☎ **01-800/305-9400** or 3/616-9616 or 3/615-2471). There are several companies that offer air evacuation service; for a good list of companies refer to the U.S. State department Web site at **travel.state.gov/medical.html**.

SAFETY

I have lived and traveled in Mexico for almost a decade, have never had any serious trouble, and rarely feel suspicious of anyone or any situation. You will probably feel physically safer in most Mexican cities and villages than in any comparable place at home. However, crime in Mexico has received much attention in the North American press over the past two years. Many in Mexico feel this unfairly exaggerates the real dangers of traveling there, but it should be noted that crime is in fact on the rise, including taxi robberies, kidnappings, and highway carjackings. The most severe crime problems have been concentrated in Mexico City, where even long-time foreign residents will attest to the overall lack of security there, although it is finally showing signs of improving. See "Sources of Information" above for information on how to access the latest **U.S. State Department advisories.** Travelers should contact the agency for security information before traveling to **Chiapas.**

Precautions are necessary, but travelers should be realistic. When traveling any place in the world, common sense is essential. A good rule of thumb is that you can generally trust people whom you approach for help, assistance, or

What to Do if You Get Sick

It's called "travelers' diarrhea" or *turista,* the Spanish word for "tourist": the persistent diarrhea, often accompanied by fever, nausea, and vomiting, that used to attack many travelers to Mexico. Some in the United States call this "Montezuma's revenge," but you won't hear it referred to this way in Mexico. Widespread improvements in infrastructure, sanitation, and education have practically eliminated this ailment, especially in well-developed resort areas. Most travelers make a habit of drinking only bottled water, which also helps to protect against unfamiliar bacteria. In resort areas, and generally throughout Mexico, only purified ice is used. Doctors say it's not caused by just one "bug," but by a combination of consuming different foods and water, upsetting your schedule, being overtired, and experiencing the stresses of travel. A good high-potency (or "therapeutic") vitamin supplement, and even extra vitamin C help; yogurt is good for healthy digestion. If you do happen to come down with this ailment, nothing beats Pepto Bismol, readily available in Mexico.

How to Prevent It: The U.S. Public Health Service recommends the following measures for preventing travelers' diarrhea:

* *Drink only purified water.* This means tea, coffee, and other beverages made with boiled water; canned or bottled carbonated beverages and water; or beer and wine. Most restaurants with a large tourist clientele use only purified water and ice.

* *Choose food carefully.* In general, avoid salads, uncooked vegetables, and unpasteurized milk or milk products (including cheese). However, salads in a first-class restaurant, or one serving a lot of tourists, are generally safe to eat. Choose food that is freshly cooked and still hot. Peelable fruit is ideal. Don't eat undercooked meat, fish, or shellfish.

In addition, something as simple as clean hands can go a long way toward preventing *turista.*

Since **dehydration** can quickly become life threatening, the Public Health Service advises that you be especially careful to replace fluids and electrolytes (potassium, sodium, and the like) during a bout of diarrhea. Do this by drinking Pedialyte, a rehydration solution available at most Mexican pharmacies, or glasses of natural fruit juice (high in potassium) with a pinch of salt added. Or you can also try a glass of boiled pure water with a quarter teaspoon of sodium bicarbonate (baking soda) added.

directions—but be wary of anyone who approaches you offering the same. The more insistent they are, the more cautious you should be. The crime rate is on the whole much lower in Mexico than in most parts of the United States, and the nature of crimes in general is less violent—most crime is motivated by robbery or by jealousy. Random, violent, or serial crime is essentially unheard of in Mexico. You are much more likely to meet kind and helpful Mexicans than you are to encounter those set on thievery and deceit.

(See also "Emergencies" under "Fast Facts: Mexico," later in this chapter.)

CRIME, BRIBES & SCAMS

The areas covered by this book are not prone to extensive bribes, scams, robberies, or other malevolent crimes. However, you may encounter difficulties: with Customs officials at the Mérida airport, Mérida taxi drivers, and police officers on the outskirts of Mérida; along the lovely highway from Villaher-mosa through Escarcega to Xpuhil; with traffic police in Chetumal; as well as the occasional car thief in Cancún. Generally speaking there's no need to be overly guarded as you travel in the Yucatán. More than likely, anything lost will be returned to you. A good rule of thumb is that you can generally trust people whom you approach for help or directions, but you should be wary of anyone who approaches you offering the same. The more insistent someone is, the more cautious you should be.

For years Mexico was known as a place where bribes—called *propinas* (tips) or *mordidas* ("bites")—were expected; however, the country is rapidly changing. Frequently, offering a bribe today, especially to a police officer, is considered an insult, and it can land you in deeper trouble.

If you believe a **bribe** is being requested, here are a few tips on dealing with the situation. Even if you speak Spanish, don't utter a word of it to Mexican officials. That way you'll appear innocent, all the while understanding every word.

When you are crossing the border, should the person who inspects your car ask for a tip, you can ignore this request—but understand that the official may suddenly decide that a complete search of your belongings is in order. If faced with a situation where you feel you're being asked for a *propina,* how much should you offer? Usually $3 to $5 or the equivalent in pesos will do the trick. There's a number to **report irregularities with Customs officials** (☎ 01/800-001-4800 in Mexico). Your call will go to the office of the Comptroller and Administrative Development Secretariat (SECODAM); however, be fore-warned that most personnel do not speak English. Be sure you have some basic information—such as the name of the person who requested a bribe or acted in a rude manner, as well as the place, time, and day of the event.

Whatever you do, **avoid impoliteness;** under no circumstances should you insult a Latin American official. Mexico is ruled by extreme politeness, even in the face of adversity. In Mexico, *gringos* have a reputation for being loud and demanding. By adopting the local custom of excessive courtesy, you'll have greater success in negotiations of any kind. Stand your ground, but do it politely.

As you travel in Mexico, you may encounter several types of **scams,** which are typical throughout the world. One involves some sort of a **distraction** or feigned commotion. While your attention is diverted, a pickpocket makes a grab for your wallet. In another common scam, an **unaccompanied child** pretends to be lost and frightened and takes your hand for safety. Meanwhile the child, or an accomplice, manages to plunder your pockets. A third involves **confusing currency.** A shoe-shine boy, street musician, guide, or other indi-vidual might offer you a service for a price that seems reasonable—in pesos. When it comes time to pay, he or she tells you the price is in dollars, not pesos, and becomes very hostile if payment is not made. Be very clear on the price and currency when services are involved.

INSURANCE

There are three kinds of travel insurance: trip cancellation, medical, and lost luggage coverage. **Trip cancellation insurance** is a good idea if you have paid a large portion of your vacation expenses up front. The other two types of insurance, however, don't make sense for most travelers. Rule number one: check your existing policies before you buy any additional coverage.

Your existing health insurance should cover you if you get sick while on vacation (though if you belong to an HMO, you should check to see whether you are fully covered when away from home). If you need hospital treatment, most health insurance plans and HMOs will cover out-of-country hospital visits and procedures, at least to some extent. However, most make you pay the bills up front at the time of care, and you'll get a refund after you've returned and filed all the paperwork. Members of **Blue Cross/Blue Shield** can now use their cards at select hospitals in most major cities worldwide (☎ **800/810-BLUE** or www.bluecares.com/blue/bluecard/wwn for a list of hospitals). For independent travel health-insurance providers, see below.

Your homeowner's insurance should cover **stolen luggage.** The airlines are responsible for $2,500 on domestic flights if they lose your luggage; if you plan to carry anything more valuable than that, keep it in your carry-on bag.

The differences between travel assistance and insurance are often blurred, but in general the former offers on-the-spot assistance and 24-hour hotlines (mostly oriented toward medical problems), while the latter reimburses you for travel problems (medical, travel, or otherwise) after you have filed the paperwork. The coverage you should consider will depend on how much protection is already contained in your existing health insurance or other policies. Some credit- and charge-card companies may insure you against travel accidents if you buy plane, train, or bus tickets with their cards. Before purchasing additional insurance, read your policies and agreements over carefully. Call your insurers or credit/charge-card companies if you have any questions.

Some credit cards (American Express and certain gold and platinum Visa and MasterCards, for example) offer automatic flight insurance against death or dismemberment in case of an airplane crash.

If you'll be driving in Mexico, see "Getting There/By Car" and "Getting Around/By Car" below for information on **collision** and **damage** and **personal accident insurance.**

5 Tips for Travelers with Special Needs

FOR FAMILIES Children are considered the national treasure of Mexico, and Mexicans will warmly welcome and cater to your children. Where many parents were reluctant to bring young children into Mexico in the past, primarily due to health concerns, I can't think of a better place to introduce children to the exciting adventure of exploring a different culture. Some of the best introductions for children in Mexico is Cancún, with its array of theme parks and attractions. Hotels can often arrange for a baby-sitter. Some hotels in the moderate-to-luxury range have small playgrounds and pools for children and hire caretakers with special activity programs during the day. Few budget hotels offer these amenities.

Before leaving, you should check with your doctor to get advice on medications to take along. Disposable diapers cost about the same in Mexico but are of poorer quality. You can get Huggies Supreme and Pampers identical to the ones sold in the United States, but at a higher price. Gerber's baby foods are sold in many stores. Dry cereals, powdered formulas, baby bottles, and purified water are all easily available in mid-size and large cities or resorts.

Cribs, however, may present a problem; only the largest and most luxurious hotels provide them. However, rollaway beds to accommodate children staying in the room with parents are often available. Child seats or high chairs at restaurants are common, and most restaurants will go out of their way to accommodate the comfort of your child.

FOR PEOPLE WITH DISABILITIES   Mexico may seem like one giant obstacle course to travelers in wheelchairs or on crutches. At airports, you may encounter steep stairs before finding a well-hidden elevator or escalator—if one exists. Airlines will often arrange wheelchair assistance for passengers to the baggage area. Porters are generally available to help with luggage at airports and large bus stations, once you've cleared baggage claim.

In addition, escalators (and there aren't many in the country) are often out of operation. Stairs without handrails abound. Few rest rooms are equipped for travelers with disabilities, or when one is available, access to it may be via a narrow passage that won't accommodate a wheelchair or a person on crutches. Many deluxe hotels (the most expensive) now have rooms with baths for people with disabilities. Those traveling on a budget should stick with one-story hotels or hotels with elevators. Even so, there will probably still be obstacles somewhere. Generally speaking, no matter where you are, someone will lend a hand, although you may have to ask for it.

Few airports offer the luxury of boarding an airplane from the waiting room. You either descend stairs to a bus that ferries you to the waiting plane that's boarded by climbing stairs, or you walk across the airport tarmac to your plane and ascend the stairs. Deplaning presents the same problem in reverse.

FOR SENIORS   Mexico is a popular country for retirees. For decades, North Americans have been living indefinitely in Mexico by returning to the border and recrossing with a new tourist permit every 6 months. Mexican immigration officials have caught on, and now limit the maximum time in the country to six months within any year. This is to encourage even partial residents to comply with the proper documentation.

A very informative newsletter for prospective retirees is *AIM*, Apdo. Postal 31–70, 45050 Guadalajara, Jalisco, Mexico. It is well-written and candid. Subscriptions are $18 to the United States and $21 to Canada. Back issues are three for $5.

FOR GAY & LESBIAN TRAVELERS   Mexico is a conservative country, with deeply rooted Catholic religious traditions. Public displays of same-sex affection are rare and still considered shocking for men, especially outside of urban or resort areas. Women in Mexico frequently walk hand in hand, but anything more would cross the boundary of acceptability. However, gay and lesbian travelers are generally treated with respect and should not experience any harassment, assuming the appropriate regard is given to local culture and customs.

The International Gay & Lesbian Travel Association (IGLTA) (☎ **800/448-8550** or 954/776-2626; fax 954/776-3303; www.iglta.org) can provide helpful information and additional tips. The **Travel Alternative Group (TAG)** maintains a database and Gay-Friendly Accommodations Guide. For details, call (☎ **415/437-3800**, e-mail: info@mark8ing.com). **Arco Iris** is a gay-owned, full-service travel agency and tour operator specializing in Mexico packages and special group travel. Contact the agency by phone (☎ **800/795-5549**), or through its Web site: **www.freeyellow.com/members/arco/index.html**.

FOR SINGLES   Mexico may be an old favorite for romantic honeymoons, but it's also a great place to travel on your own without really being or feeling alone. Although offering an identical room rate regardless of single or double occupancy is slowly becoming a trend in Mexico, many of the hotels mentioned in this book still offer singles at lower rates.

Mexicans are very friendly, and it's easy to meet other foreigners. But if you don't like the idea of traveling alone, then try **Travel Companion Exchange,** P.O. Box 833, Amityville, NY 11701 (☎ **800/392-1256** or 516/454-0880; fax 516/454-0170), which brings prospective travelers together. Members complete a profile, then place an anonymous listing of their travel interests in the newsletter. Prospective traveling companions then make contact through the exchange. Membership costs $99 for 6 months or $159 for a year. It also offers an excellent booklet on avoiding theft and scams while traveling abroad, for $3.95.

FOR WOMEN   As a female traveling alone, I can tell you firsthand that I feel safer traveling in Mexico than in the United States. But I use the same common sense precautions I use traveling anywhere else in the world and am alert to what's going on around me.

Mexicans in general, and men in particular, are nosy about single travelers, especially women. If taxi drivers or anyone else with whom you don't want to become friendly asks about your marital status, family, etc., my advice is to make up a set of answers (regardless of the truth): "I'm married, traveling with friends, and I have three children."

Saying you are single and traveling alone may send out the wrong message about availability. Movies and television shows exported from the United States have created an image of sexually aggressive North American women. If bothered by someone, don't try to be polite—just leave or head into a public place.

6 Getting There

BY PLANE

The airline situation in Mexico is changing rapidly, with many new regional carriers offering scheduled service to areas previously not served. In addition to regularly scheduled service, charter service direct from U.S. cities to resorts is making Mexico more accessible. For information about saving money on air-fares using the Internet, see our Online Directory, page 43.

THE MAJOR INTERNATIONAL AIRLINES   The main airlines operating direct or nonstop flights from the United States to Cancún, Cozumel, and Mérida include **Aerocalifornia** (☎ 800/237-6225), **Aeromexico** (☎ 800/237-6639), **Air France** (☎ 800/237-2747), **American** (☎ 800/433-7300), **Continental** (☎ 800/231-0856), **Lacsa** (☎ 800/225-2272), **Mexicana** (☎ 800/531-7921), **Northwest** (☎ 800/225-2525), **United** (☎ 800/241-6522), and **USAirways** (☎ 800/428-4322).

BY CAR

Driving is not the cheapest way to get to Mexico, but it is the best way to see the country. Even so, you may think twice about taking your own car south of the border once you've pondered the bureaucracy that affects foreign drivers

CyberDeals for Net Surfers

A great way to find the cheapest fare is by using the Internet to do your searching for you. In addition to specialized travel Web sites, great last-minute deals are also available directly from the airlines, as well as from charter companies that offer discount package tours. For a more extensive rundown of the best sites to check out, refer to Frommer's Online Directory, page 43.

You must carry your temporary car-importation permit, tourist permit (see "Entry Requirements," above), and, if you purchased it, your proof of Mexican car insurance (see below) in the car at all times. The temporary car-importation permit papers will be issued for between 6 months to a year, while the tourist permit is usually issued for 30 days. It's a good idea also to overestimate the time you'll spend in Mexico, so that if something unforeseen happens and you have to (or want to) stay longer, you'll have avoided the hassle of getting your papers extended. Whatever you do, don't overstay either permit. Doing so invites heavy fines and/or confiscation of your vehicle, which will not be returned. Remember also that 6 months does not necessarily work out to be 180 days—be sure that you return before whichever expiration date comes first.

here. One option is to rent a car for touring around a specific region, once you arrive in Mexico. Rental cars in Mexico are now generally new, clean, and very well maintained. Although pricier than in the United States, discounts are often available for rentals of a week or longer, especially when arrangements are made in advance from the United States. (See "Car Rentals," below, for more details).

If, after reading the section that follows, you have any additional questions or you want to confirm the current rules, call your nearest Mexican consulate or Mexican Government Tourist Office. Although travel insurance companies are generally helpful, they may not have the most accurate information available. To check on road conditions or to get help with any travel emergency while in Mexico, call ☎ **01 800/903-9200,** or 5/250-0151 in Mexico City. Both numbers are staffed by English-speaking operators.

In addition, check with the **U.S. State Department** (see "Sources of Information," at the beginning of this chapter) for its warnings about dangerous driving areas.

CAR DOCUMENTS To drive your car into Mexico, you'll need a **temporary car-importation permit,** which is granted after you provide a strictly required list of documents (see below). The permit can be obtained either through Banco del Ejército (*Banjercito*) officials, who have a desk, booth, or office at the Mexican Customs (*Aduana*) building after you cross the border into Mexico. Insurance companies such as AAA and Sanborn's used to be able to issue this permit; however, they no longer are.

The following requirements for border crossing were accurate at press time:

- **A valid driver's license,** issued outside of Mexico.
- **Current, original car registration and a copy of the original car title.** If the registration or title is in more than one name and not all the named people are traveling with you, then a notarized letter from the absent person(s) authorizing use of the vehicle for the trip is required; have it ready just in case. The car registration and your credit card (see below) must be in the same name.
- **A valid international major credit card.** With a credit card, you are only required to pay a $16 car-importation fee. The credit card must be in the same name as the car registration. If you do not have a major credit card (Visa, Mastercard, American Express, or Diners Club) you will have to post a bond or make a deposit equal to the value of the vehicle. Check cards are not accepted.

- **Original immigration documentation.** This will either be your tourist permit (FMT), or the original immigration booklet, FM2 or FM3, if you hold this more permanent status.
- **A signed declaration promising to return to your country of origin with the vehicle.** This form (*Carta Promesa de Retorno*) is provided by AAA or Sanborn's before you go or by Banjercito officials at the border. There's no charge. The form does not stipulate that you must return through the same border entry you came through on your way south.
- **Temporary Importation Application.** Upon signing this form, you are stating that you are only temporarily importing the car for your personal use, and will not be selling the vehicle. This is to help regulate the entry and restrict the resale of unauthorized cars and trucks. Vehicles in the U.S. are much less expensive, and for years were brought into Mexico for resale.

If you receive your documentation at the border, Mexican officials will make two copies of everything and charge you for the copies. For up-to-the-minute information, a great source is the customs office in Nuevo Leon (Modulo de Importacion Temporal de Automoviles, Aduana Nuevo Leon) (☎ **52-8/712-2071**).

Important reminder: Someone else may drive the car, but the person (or relative of the person) whose name appears on the car-importation permit must *always* be in the car at the same time. (If stopped by police, a nonregistered family member driver driving without the registered driver must be prepared to prove familial relationship to the registered driver—no joke.) Violation of this rule makes the car subject to impoundment and the driver subject to imprisonment and/or a fine. You can only drive a car with foreign license plates if you have an international (non-Mexican) driver's license.

MEXICAN AUTO INSURANCE   Auto insurance is not legally required in Mexico. U.S. insurance is invalid in Mexico; to be insured in Mexico, you must purchase Mexican insurance. Any party involved in an accident who has no insurance may be sent to jail and his or her car impounded until all claims are settled. This is true even if you just drive across the border to spend the day. U.S. companies that broker Mexican insurance are commonly found at the border crossing, and several will quote daily rates.

Car insurance can also be purchased through **Sanborn's Mexico Insurance,** P.O. Box 52840, 2009 S. 10th, McAllen, TX 78505-2840 (☎ **956/686-0711;** fax 956/686-1417 in Texas or 800/638-9423 elsewhere in the U.S.). The company has offices at all of the border crossings in the United States. Its policies cost the same as the competition's do, but you get legal coverage (attorney and bail bonds if needed) and a detailed mile-by-mile guide for your proposed route. Most of Sanborn's border offices are open Monday through Friday, and a few are staffed on Saturday and Sunday. **AAA** auto club also sells insurance. Another insurance company with offices in California is Oscar Padilla Mexican Insurance Services (☎ **800/258-8600;** www.mexicaninsurance.com).

RETURNING TO THE UNITED STATES WITH YOUR CAR   The car papers you obtained when you entered Mexico *must* be returned when you cross back with your car or at some point within 180 days. (You can cross as many times as you wish within the 180 days.) If the documents aren't returned, heavy fines are imposed ($250 for each 15 days late), and your car may be impounded and confiscated or you may be jailed if you return to Mexico. You can only return the car documents to a Banjercito official on duty at the Mexican Customs (*Aduana*) building *before* you cross back into the United States. Some border cities have Banjercito officials on duty 24 hours a day, but others do not; some also do not have Sunday hours. On the U.S. side, Customs agents may or may not inspect your car from stem to stern.

BY SHIP

Numerous cruise lines serve the Mexican Caribbean. Possible trips might cruise from Miami to the Caribbean (which often includes stops in Cancún, Playa del Carmen, and Cozumel). Several cruise-tour specialists arrange substantial discounts on unsold cabins if you're willing to take off at the last minute. One such company is **The Cruise Line,** 150 NW 168 St. North Miami Beach, Miami, FL 33169 (☎ **800/777-0707,** or 305/521-2200).

BY BUS

Greyhound-Trailways (or its affiliates) offers service from around the United States to the Mexican border, where passengers disembark, cross the border, and buy a ticket for travel into the interior of Mexico. At many border crossings there are scheduled buses from the U.S. bus station to the Mexican bus station.

7 Getting Around

An important note: If your travel schedule depends on an important connection, say a plane trip between points, or a ferry or bus connection, use the telephone numbers in this book or other information resources mentioned here to find out if the connection you are depending on is still available. Although we've done our best to provide accurate information, transportation schedules can and do change.

BY PLANE

To fly from point to point within Mexico, you'll rely on Mexican airlines. Mexico has two privately owned large national carriers: **Mexicana** (☎ **800/366-5400,** toll-free inside Mexico), and **Aeromexico** (☎ **800/021-4000,** toll-free inside Mexico), in addition to several up-and-coming regional carriers. Mexicana and Aeromexico both offer extensive connections to the United States as well as within Mexico.

Several of the new regional carriers are operated by or can be booked through Mexicana or Aeromexico. Regional carriers are **Aerocaribe** (see Mexicana); **Aerolitoral** (see Aeromexico); and **Aero Mar** (see Mexicana). The regional carriers are expensive, but they go to difficult-to-reach places. In each applicable section of this book, we've mentioned regional carriers with all pertinent telephone numbers.

Because major airlines can book some regional carriers, read your ticket carefully to see if your connecting flight is on one of these smaller carriers—they may leave from a different airport or check in at a different counter.

AIRPORT TAXES Mexico charges an airport tax on all departures. Passengers leaving the country on an international departure pay $18—in dollars or the peso equivalent. It has become a common practice to include this departure tax in your ticket price, but double-check to make sure so you're not caught by surprise at the airport upon leaving. Taxes on each domestic departure you make within Mexico cost around $12.50, unless you're on a connecting flight and have already paid at the start of the flight, in which case you shouldn't be charged again.

Starting in May 1999, Mexico is also charging an additional $18 "tourism tax," the proceeds of which go into a tourism promotional fund. This may or may not be included in your ticket price, so be sure to set aside this amount in either dollars or pesos to pay at the airport upon departure.

RECONFIRMING FLIGHTS   Although Mexican airlines say it's not necessary to reconfirm a flight, it's still a good practice. To avoid getting bumped on popular, possibly overbooked flights, check in for an international flight the required hour-and-a-half in advance of travel.

BY CAR

Most Mexican roads are not up to U.S. standards of smoothness, hardness, width of curve, grade of hill, or safety marking, with the exception of the roads in and around Cancún. Driving at night is dangerous—the roads aren't good and are rarely lit; trucks, carts, pedestrians, and bicycles usually have no lights; and you can hit potholes, animals, rocks, dead ends, or bridges out with no warning.

The "spirited" style of Mexican driving sometimes requires super vision and reflexes. Be prepared for new customs, as when a truck driver flips on his left turn signal when there's not a crossroad for miles. He's probably telling you the road's clear ahead for you to pass—after all, he's in a better position to see than you are. Another custom that's very important to respect is **how to make a left turn.** Never turn left by stopping in the middle of a highway with your left signal on. Instead, pull off the highway onto the right shoulder, wait for traffic to clear, then proceed across the road.

GASOLINE   There's one government-owned brand of gas and one gasoline station name throughout the country—**Pemex** (Petroleras Mexicanas). There are two types of gas in Mexico: *magna,* an 87-octane unleaded gas, and the newer premium 93-octane. In Mexico, fuel and oil are sold by the liter, which is slightly more than a quart (40 liters equals about $10^1/_2$ gal.). There is a new trend toward franchise Pemex stations, many of which have bathroom facilities and convenience stores—a great improvement over the old ones. *Important note:* No credit cards are accepted for gas purchases; however, some of the new franchise stores are beginning to accept a type of new gas debit card. This is a new practice, and many gas station attendants may not yet know about it, or be a part of the program.

TOLL ROADS   Mexico charges some of the highest tolls in the world for its network of new toll roads; as a result, they are rarely used. Generally speaking, using the toll roads will cut your travel time between destinations. Older toll-free roads are generally in good condition but travel times tend to be longer, since they tend to be mountainous and clotted with slow-moving trucks.

BREAKDOWNS   If your car breaks down on the road, help might already be on the way. Radio-equipped green repair trucks operated by uniformed English-speaking officers patrol the major highways during daylight hours to aid motorists in trouble. These **"Green Angels"** will perform minor repairs and adjustments for free, but you pay for parts and materials.

Your best guide to repair shops is the Yellow Pages. For specific makes and shops that repair cars, look under "Automoviles y Camiones: Talleres de Reparación y Servicio"; auto-parts stores are listed under "Refacciones y Accesorios para Automoviles." To find a mechanic on the road, look for a sign that says TALLER MECÁNICO.

MINOR ACCIDENTS   When possible, many Mexicans drive away from minor accidents or try to make an immediate settlement, to avoid involving the police. If the police arrive while the involved persons are still at the scene, everyone may be locked in jail until blame is assessed. In any case, you have to settle up immediately, which may take days of red tape. Foreigners who don't speak fluent Spanish are at a distinct disadvantage when trying to explain their side of the event. Three steps may help the foreigner who doesn't wish to do as the Mexicans do: If you were in your own car, notify your Mexican insurance company, whose job it is to intervene on your behalf. If you were in a rental car, notify the rental company immediately and ask how to contact the nearest adjuster. (You did buy insurance with the rental, right?) Finally, if all else fails, ask to contact the nearest Green Angel, who may be able to explain to officials that you are covered by insurance. See also "Mexican Auto Insurance" in "Getting There," above.

CAR RENTALS   You'll get the best price if you reserve a car a week in advance in the United States. U.S. car-rental firms include **Avis** (☎ **800/ 331-1212** in the U.S., 800/TRY-AVIS in Canada), **Budget** (☎ **800/527-0700** in the U.S. and Canada), **Hertz** (☎ **800/654-3131** in the U.S. and Canada), and **National** (☎ **800/CAR-RENT** in the U.S. and Canada). For European travelers, **Kemwel Holiday Auto** (☎ **800/678-0678**) and **Auto Europe** (☎ **800/223-5555**) can arrange Mexican rentals, sometimes through other agencies. These and some local firms have offices in Mexico City and most other large Mexican cities. You'll find rental desks at airports, all major hotels, and many travel agencies.

Cars are easy to rent if you have a major credit card, are 25 or over, and have a valid driver's license and passport with you. Without a credit card you must leave a cash deposit, usually a big one. Rent-here/leave-there arrangements are usually simple to make but more costly.

Car-rental costs are high in Mexico because cars are more expensive here. The condition of rental cars has improved greatly over the years, however, and clean, comfortable, new cars are the norm. The basic cost of a 1-day rental of a Volkswagen Beetle, with unlimited mileage (but before 17% tax and $15 daily insurance), was $44 in Cancún, and $27 in Mérida. Renting by the week gives you a lower daily rate. Avis was offering a basic 7-day weekly rate for a VW Beetle (before tax or insurance) of $190 in Cancún, $160 in Mérida, and $225 in Mexico City. Prices may be considerably higher if you rent in these same cities around a major holiday.

Car-rental companies usually write up a credit-card charge in U.S. dollars.

Deductibles   Be careful—these vary greatly in Mexico; some are as high as $2,500, which comes out of your pocket immediately in case of car damage. Hertz's deductible is $1,000 on a VW Beetle; Avis's is $500 for the same car.

Insurance   Insurance is offered in two parts: **Collision and damage** insurance covers your car and others if the accident is your fault, and **personal accident** insurance covers you and anyone in your car. Read the fine print on the back of your rental agreement and note that insurance may be invalid if you have an accident while driving on an unpaved road.

Travel Tip

Little English is spoken at bus stations, so come prepared with your destination written down, then double-check the departure signs.

Damage   Always inspect your car carefully and note every damaged or missing item, no matter how minute, on your rental agreement, or you may be charged for it.

BY TAXI

Most airports and bus stations have *colectivo* (minibuses or minivans) or fixed-rate taxis to town or the hotel zone. The *colectivo* is always the least expensive way to go. Buy a special *colectivo* ticket from a booth that's usually located near the exit door of the main airport concourse.

Taxis are the preferred way to get around in almost all of the resort areas of Mexico. Short trips within towns are generally charged by preset zones, and are quite reasonable compared with U.S. rates. For longer trips, or excursions to nearby cities, taxis can generally be hired for around $10 to $15 per hour, or for a negotiated daily rate. Even drops to different destinations, say between Cancún and Playa del Carmen, can be arranged. A negotiated one-way price is usually much less than the cost of a rental car for a day, and service is much faster than traveling by bus. For anyone who is uncomfortable driving in Mexico, this is a convenient, comfortable alternative. An added bonus is that you have a Spanish-speaking person with you in case you run into any car or road trouble. Many taxi drivers speak at least some English. Your hotel can assist you with the arrangements.

BY BUS

Bus service in the Yucatán is beginning to catch up to the high standard seen elsewhere in Mexico. Buses are frequent, readily accessible, and can get you to almost anywhere you want to go. They're often the only way to get from large cities to other nearby cities and small villages. Don't hesitate to ask questions if you're confused about anything.

Dozens of Mexican companies operate large, air-conditioned, Greyhound-type buses between most cities. Travel class is generally labeled second (*segunda*), first (*primera*), and deluxe (*ejecutiva*), which is referred to by a variety of names. The deluxe buses often have fewer seats than regular buses, show videos en route, are air-conditioned, and have few stops; some have complimentary refreshments. Many run express from origin to the final destination. They are well worth the few dollars more that you'll pay. In rural areas, buses are often of the school-bus variety, with lots of local color.

Whenever possible, it's best to buy your reserved-seat ticket, often via a computerized system, a day in advance on many long-distance routes and especially before holidays. Schedules are fairly dependable, so be at the terminal on time for departure. Current information may be obtained from local bus stations. See the Appendix B for a list of helpful bus terms in Spanish.

8 The Pros & Cons of Package Tours

Say the words "package tour" and many people automatically feel as though they're being forced to choose: your money or your lifestyle. This isn't necessarily the case. Most Mexican packages let you have both your independence *and* your in-the-black bank-account balance. Package tours are not the same thing as escorted tours. They are simply a way of buying your airfare, accommodations, and other pieces of your trip (usually airport transfers, and sometimes meals and activities) at the same time.

For popular destinations like the Yucatán's beach resorts they're often the smart way to go, because they can save you a ton of money. In many cases, a package that includes airfare, hotel, and transportation to and from the airport will cost you less than just the hotel alone if you booked it yourself. That's because packages are sold in bulk to tour operators, who resell them to the public.

You can buy a package at any time of the year, but the best deals usually coincide with low season—May to early December—when room rates and airfares plunge. But packages vary widely. Some offer a better class of hotels than others. Some offer the same hotels for lower prices. Some offer flights on scheduled airlines while others book charters. In some packages, your choices of accommodations and travel days may be limited. Each destination usually has some packagers that are better than the rest because they buy in even bigger bulk. Not only can that mean better prices, but it can also mean more choices—a packager that just dabbles in Mexico may only have a half-dozen or so hotels for you to choose from, while a packager that focuses much of its energy on south-of-the-border vacations may have dozens of hotels to choose from, with a good selection in every price range.

WARNINGS

- **Read the fine print.** Make sure you know *exactly* what's included in the price you're being quoted, and what's not.
- **Don't compare Mayas and Aztecs.** When you're looking over different packagers, compare the deals that they're offering on similar properties. Most packagers can offer bigger savings on some hotels than others.
- **Know what you're getting yourself into—and if you can get yourself out of it.** Before you commit to a package, make sure you know how much flexibility you have.
- **Use your best judgment.** Stay away from fly-by-nights and shady packagers. Go with a reputable firm with a proven track record. This is where your travel agent can come in handy.

WHERE TO BROWSE

- For one-stop shopping on the Web, go to **www.vacationpackager.com**, an extensive search engine that'll link you up with more than 30 packagers offering Mexican beach vacations—and even let you custom design your own package.
- Check out **www.2travel.com** and find a page with links to a number of the big-name Mexico packagers, including several of the ones listed here.

PACKAGERS PACKIN' A PUNCH

- **Aeromexico Vacations** (☎ 800/245-8585; www.aeromexico.com): Year-round packages for Cancún and Cozumel. Aeromexico has a large selection of resorts in these destinations (39 in Cancún, 11 in Cozumel) in a variety of price ranges. The best deals are from Houston, Dallas, San Diego, Los Angeles, Miami, and New York, in that order.
- **American Airlines Vacations** (☎ 800/321-2121; www.americanair.com): American has year-round deals for Cancún and Cozumel. You don't have to fly with American if you can get a better deal on another airline; land-only packages include hotel, airport transfers, and hotel room tax. American's hubs to Mexico are Dallas/Fort Worth, Chicago, and Miami, so you're likely to get the best prices—and the most direct flights—if you live near those cities.
- **America West Vacations** (☎ 800-356-6611; www.americawest.com): Has deals to Cancún and Cozumel, mostly from its Phoenix gateway.

- **Apple Vacations** (☎ 800/365-2775; www.applevacations.com): Apple offers inclusive packages to all the beach resorts and has the largest choice of hotels: 48 in Cancún, and 17 in Cozumel. Scheduled carriers booked for the air portion include American, United, Mexicana, Delta, TWA, US Airways, AeroCalifornia, and Aeromexico. Apple perks include baggage handling and the services of an Apple representative at the major hotels.
- **Classic Custom Vacations** (☎ 800/221-3949): A new company that specializes in package vacations to Mexico's finest luxury resorts. It combines discounted first class and economy airfares on American, Continental, Mexicana, Alaska, America West, and Delta Airlines with stays at the most exclusive hotels in Cancun, Riviera Maya, Merida, and Cozumel. In many cases, these packages offer free meals, private airport transfers, and free upgrades as well.
- **Continental Vacations** (☎ 800/634-5555; www.flycontinental.com): The airline has year-round packages available to Cancún and Cozumel, and the best deals are from Houston; Newark, New Jersey; and Cleveland. You have to fly Continental.
- **Delta Vacations** (☎ 800/872-7786; www.delta-air.com): Has year-round packages to Cancún. Atlanta is the hub, so expect the best prices from there.
- **Friendly Holidays** (☎ 800/344-5687; www.friendlyholidays.com): This major player in the Mexico field is based in upstate New York, but also has offices in California and Houston, so it has the bases covered. It offers trips to Cancún and Cozumel. Although it doesn't have the largest variety of hotels from which to choose, the ones it works with are high quality. In addition, its Web site is very user-friendly, listing both a starting price for 3 nights' hotel room and a figure for air add-ons, so at least you have a rough idea of what your trip is likely to cost you.
- **Funjet Vacations** (bookable through travel agents, or, ☎ 800-558-3050; www.funjet.com): One of the largest vacation packagers in the United States, Funjet has packages to Cancún, Cozumel, and the Riviera Maya. You can choose a charter or fly on American, Continental, Delta, Aeromexico, USAirways, Alaska Air, TWA, or United.
- **GOGO Worldwide Vacations** (☎ 888/636-3942, www.gogowwv. com): Has trips to all the major beach destinations, including Cancún.
- **Mexicana Vacations (or MexSeaSun Vacations)** (☎ 800/531-9321; www.mexicana.com): Offers getaways to all the resorts buttressed by Mexicana's daily direct flights from Los Angeles to Cancún.
- **Pleasant Mexico Holidays** (☎ 800/448-3333; www.pleasantholidays. com): Another of the largest vacation packagers in the United States, with a total of 84 hotels in the most popular destinations including Cancún/Playa del Carmen and Cozumel. Car rentals are part of most packages traveling to Cancún and Cozumel.
- **TWA Vacations** (☎ 800/438-2929; www.twa.com): Runs year-round packages to Cancún from its St. Louis hub.

REGIONAL PACKAGERS

FROM THE EAST COAST **Liberty Travel** (☎ 888/271-1584; www. libertytravel.com), one of the biggest packagers in the Northeast, often runs a full-page add in the Sunday papers, with frequent Cancún specials. You won't get much in the way of service, but you will get a good deal.

FROM THE WEST COAST   Sunquest Holidays (☎ 800/357-2400 or 888/888-5028 for departures within 14 days) is one of the largest packagers for Mexico on the West Coast, arranging regular charters to Cancún and Cozumel from Los Angeles, paired with a large selection of hotels.

FROM THE SOUTHWEST   Town and Country (bookable through travel agents) packages regular deals to Cancún and Cozumel with America West from the airline's Phoenix and Las Vegas gateways.

RESORTS   The biggest hotel chains and resorts also sell packages. The Mexican-owned Fiesta Americana/Fiesta Inns, for example, run **Fiesta Break** deals that include airfare from New York, Los Angeles, Dallas, or Houston, airport transfers, optional meal plans, and more. In 2000, a high-season Fiesta Break package from Dallas to Cancún cost $214, based on double occupancy, and includes airfare, tax, transfers, and 3 nights in the Fiesta Americana Cancún. Call ☎ **800/9-BREAK-9** for details, or ☎ **800/FIESTA-1** for land-only packages.

Fast Facts: Mexico

Abbreviations   Dept. (apartments); Apdo. (post office box); Av. (*Avenida*; avenue); c/ (*calle*; street); Calz. (*Calzada*; boulevard). "C" on faucets stands for *caliente* (hot), and "F" stands for *fría* (cold). PB (*planta baja*) means ground floor, and most buildings count the next floor up as the first floor (1).

Business Hours   In general, businesses in larger cities are open between 9am and 7pm; in smaller towns many close between 2 and 4pm. Most are closed on Sunday. In resort areas it is common to find more stores open on Sundays, as well as extended business hours for shops, often until 8pm or even 10pm. Bank hours are Monday through Friday from 9 or 9:30am to 5 or 6pm. Increasingly, banks are offering Saturday hours for at least a half-day.

Cameras/Film   Film costs about the same as in the United States. Tourists wishing to use a video or still camera at any archaeological site in Mexico and at many museums operated by the Instituto de Antropología e Historia (INAH) will be required to pay $4 per video camera and/or still camera in their possession at each site or museum visited. Such fees are noted in the listings for specific sites and museums. Also, use of a tripod at any archaeological site in Mexico requires a permit from INAH. It's courteous to ask permission before photographing anyone, and is never considered polite to take photos inside a church in Mexico, whether or not a service is taking place. In some areas, such as around San Cristóbal de las Casas, there are other restrictions on photographing people and villages. Such restrictions are noted in specific cities, towns, and sites.

Customs   See "Visitor Information, Entry Requirements & Money," earlier in this chapter.

Doctors/Dentists   Every embassy and consulate is prepared to recommend local doctors and dentists with good training and modern equipment; some of the doctors and dentists even speak English. See the list of embassies and consulates under "Embassies/Consulates," below. Hotels with a large foreign clientele are often prepared to recommend English-speaking doctors. Almost all first-class hotels in Mexico have a doctor on call.

Drug Laws   To be blunt, don't use or possess illegal drugs in Mexico. Mexican officials have no tolerance for drug users, and jail is their solution, with very little hope of getting out until the sentence (usually a long one) is completed or heavy fines or bribes are paid. Remember, in Mexico the legal system assumes you are guilty until proven innocent. (*Important note:* It isn't uncommon to be befriended by a fellow user, only to be turned in by that "friend," who's collected a bounty.) Bring prescription drugs in their original containers. If possible, pack a copy of the original prescription with the generic name of the drug.

U.S. Customs officials are also on the lookout for diet drugs sold in Mexico but illegal in the U.S., possession of which could also land you in a U.S. jail. If you buy antibiotics over-the-counter (which you can do in Mexico)—say, for a sinus infection—and still have some left, you probably won't be hassled by U.S. Customs.

Drugstores   See "Pharmacies," below.

Electricity   The electrical system in Mexico is 110 volts AC (60 cycles), as in the United States and Canada. However, in reality it may cycle more slowly and overheat your appliances. To compensate, select a medium or low speed for hair dryers. Many older hotels still have electrical outlets for flat two-prong plugs; you'll need an adapter for any modern electrical apparatus that has an enlarged end on one prong or that has three prongs. Many first-class and deluxe hotels have the three-holed outlets (*trifásicos* in Spanish). Those that don't may have loan adapters, but to be sure, it's always better to carry your own.

Embassies/Consulates   They provide valuable lists of doctors and lawyers, as well as regulations concerning marriages in Mexico. Contrary to popular belief, your embassy cannot get you out of a Mexican jail, provide postal or banking services, or fly you home when you run out of money. Consular officers can provide you with advice on most matters and problems, however. Most countries have a representative embassy in Mexico City and many have consular offices or representatives in the provinces.

The Embassy of the **United States** in Mexico City is next to the Hotel María Isabel Sheraton at Paseo de la Reforma 305, at the corner of Río Danubio (☎ **5/209-9100**). There are consular agencies in Cancún (☎ **98/83-0272**) and Mérida (☎ **99/25-5011**).

The Embassy of **Australia** in Mexico City is located at Rubén Darío 55 Col. Polanco (☎ **5/531-5225**, fax 5/531-9552); it's open Monday through Friday from 9am to 1pm. (www.immi.gob.au; e-mail: dfat@ozemb.org.mx).

The Embassy of **Canada** in Mexico City is located at Schiller 529, in Polanco (☎ **5/724-7900**; www.canada.org.mx); it's open Monday through Friday from 9am to 1pm and 2 to 5pm (at other times the name of a duty officer is posted on the embassy door).

The Embassy of **New Zealand** in Mexico City is located at José Luis Lagrange 103, 10th floor, Col. Los Morales Polanco (☎ **5/281-5304** or 5/281/5486); it's open Monday through Thursday from 9am to 2pm and 3 to 5pm and Friday from 9am to 2pm (kiwimexico@compuserve.com.mx).

The Embassy of the **United Kingdom** in Mexico City is found in Río Lerma 71, Col. Cuauhtemoc (☎ **5/207-2089** or 5/207-7672); it's open Monday through Friday from 8:30am to 3:30pm (www.embajadabritanica.com.mx).

Irish and **South African** citizens should go to the British Consulate.

Emergencies The 24-hour **Tourist Help Line** in Mexico City is ☎ **800/903-9200,** or 5/250-0151. A tourist legal assistance office (Procuraduria del Turista) is located in Mexico City (☎ **5/625-8153** and 625-8154). Though the phones are frequently busy, it offers 24-hour service, and there is always an English-speaking person available.

Internet Access In large cities and resort areas a growing number of 5-star hotels offer business centers with Internet access. You'll also find cybercafes in destinations that are popular with expats and business travelers. Interestingly enough, it is also becoming more common to find an Internet outpost even in the most remote areas, as it is becoming the principal source of receiving and communicating information. Note that many ISPs will automatically cut off your Internet connection after a specified period of time (say, 10 minutes), because telephone lines are at a premium. Some Telmex offices also have free access Internet kiosks in their reception areas.

Legal Aid International Legal Defense Counsel, 111 S. 15th St., 24th Floor, Packard Building, Philadelphia, PA 19102 (☎ **215/977-9982**), is a law firm specializing in the legal difficulties of Americans abroad. See also "Embassies/Consulates" and "Emergencies," above.

Liquor Laws The legal drinking age in Mexico is 18; however, it is extremely rare that anyone will be asked for ID or denied purchase (often, children are sent to the stores to buy beer for their parents). Grocery stores sell everything from beer and wine to national and imported liquors. You can buy liquor 24 hours a day; but during major elections, dry laws often are enacted for as much as 72 hours in advance of the election—and those laws apply to foreign tourists as well as local residents. Mexico also does not have any 'open container' laws for transporting liquor in cars, but authorities are beginning to target drunk drivers more aggressively. It's a good idea to drive defensively.

It is not legal to drink in the street; however, many tourists do so. Use your better judgement—if you are getting too drunk you shouldn't drink in the street because you are more likely to get stopped by the police. As is the custom in Mexico, it is not so much what you do, it is how you do it.

Mail Postage for a postcard or letter is 59¢; it may arrive anywhere between 1 to 6 weeks later. A registered letter costs $1.90. Sending a package can be quite expensive—the Mexican Postal service charges $8 per kilo (or 2.20 lbs.)—and unreliable; it takes between 2 and 6 weeks, if indeed it arrives at all—packages are frequently lost within the Mexican postal system, although the situation has improved in recent years. The recommended way to send a package or important mail continues to be through Federal Express, DHL, UPS, or any other reputable international mail service.

Newspapers/Magazines Two English-language newspapers, the *News* and the *Mexico City Times,* are published in Mexico City, distributed nationally, and carry world news and commentaries, plus a calendar of the day's events, including concerts, art shows, and plays. Newspaper kiosks in larger Mexican cities will carry a selection of English-language magazines.

Pets Taking a pet into Mexico is easy, but requires a little preplanning. For travelers coming from the United States and Canada, your pet needs to be checked for health within 30 days before arrival in Mexico. Most veterinarians in major cities have the appropriate paperwork—an official health certificate, to be presented to Mexican Customs officials, which ensures the pet is up-to-date on its vaccinations. When you and your pet return from Mexico, the same type of paperwork will be required by U.S. Customs officials. If your stay extends beyond the 30-day time frame of your U.S.-issued certificate, you'll need to get an updated Certificate of Health issued by a veterinarian in Mexico that also states the condition of your pet, and the status of its vaccinations. To be certain of any last-minute changes in requirements, consult the Mexican Government Tourist Office nearest you (see "Visitor Information, Entry Requirements & Money," earlier in this chapter).

Pharmacies *Farmacias* will sell you just about anything you want, with a prescription or without one. Most pharmacies are open Monday through Saturday from 8am to 8pm. There are generally one or two 24-hour pharmacies now located in the major resort areas. Pharmacies take turns staying open during off-hours, so if you are in a smaller town and need to buy medicines after normal hours, ask for the *farmacia de turno*.

Police In Mexico City, police are to be suspected as frequently as they are to be trusted; however, you'll find many who are quite honest and helpful. In the rest of the country, especially in the tourist areas, the majority are very protective of international visitors.

Taxes There's a 15% IVA (value-added) tax on goods and services in most of Mexico, and it's supposed to be included in the posted price. This tax is 10% in Cancún and Cozumel. There is an exit tax of around $18 imposed on every foreigner leaving the country, usually included in the price of airline tickets.

Telephone/Fax Telephone area codes are gradually being changed all over the country. The change may affect the area code and first digit or only the area code. Some cities are even adding exchanges and changing whole numbers. Courtesy messages telling you that the number you dialed has been changed do not exist. You can call operator assistance for difficult-to-reach numbers. Many fax numbers are also regular telephone numbers; you have to ask whoever answers your call for the fax tone (*"tono de fax, por favor"*). Cellular phones are becoming more and more popular for small businesses in resort areas and smaller communities. To dial a cellular number inside the same area code, dial 044 and then the number. To dial the cellular phone from anywhere else in Mexico, first dial 01, and then the 8-digit number. To dial it from the U.S., just dial 011-52 plus the 8-digit number.

The **country code** for Mexico is **52.** For instructions on how to call Mexico from the United States, call the United States from Mexico, place calls within Mexico, or use a pay phone, consult "Telephones & Mail" in the Appendix, and the inside back cover of this book.

Time Zone Central standard time prevails throughout most of Mexico, and for all of the areas covered in this book. Mexico observes **daylight savings time.**

Tipping Most service employees in Mexico count on tips for the majority of their income—especially true for bellboys and waiters. Bellboys should receive the equivalent of 50¢ to $1 U.S. per bag; waiters generally receive 10% to 20% depending on the level of service. In Mexico, it is not customary to tip taxi drivers, unless they are hired by the hour or provide touring or other special services.

Water   Most hotels have decanters or bottles of purified water in the rooms, and the better hotels have either purified water from regular taps or special taps marked *agua purificada.* Some hotels will charge for in-room bottled water. Virtually any hotel, restaurant, or bar will bring you purified water if you specifically request it, but you'll usually be charged for it. Bottled purified water is sold widely at drugstores and grocery stores. Some popular brands are Santa Maria, Ciel, Agua Pura, and Pureza. Evian and Bonafont are widely available.

Planning Your Trip: An Online Directory

By Lynne Bairstow

Day by day, the Internet becomes more integrated into our lives—including the way we plan and book our travel. By early 2000, one in every ten trips was being booked online, a trend that's sure to accelerate.

The Internet not only provides a wealth of destination information, it gives you the chance to compare experiences with fellow travelers, ask experts for pre-trip advice, seek out discounted fares once only accessible to travel industry insiders, and stay in touch via e-mail while you're away. The instant communication and storehouse of information has revolutionized the way travel is researched, reserved, and realized.

The Frommer's Online Directory will help you take better advantage of the travel planning information available online, and is best used in conjunction with this book. Part 1 lists general Internet resources that can make any trip easier, such as sites for obtaining the best possible prices on airline tickets. In Part 2 you'll find some top online guides for the Yucatán, organized by town and region.

Please keep in mind that this is not a comprehensive list, but rather a discriminating selection to get you started. Recognition is given to sites based on their content value and ease of use and are not paid for—unlike some Web site rankings, which are based on payment. Finally, remember this is a press-time snapshot of leading Web sites—some undoubtedly will have evolved, changed, or moved by the time you read this.

1 Top Travel Planning Web Sites

While the Internet was once a conglomeration of sites for researching places to visit, several key companies have emerged that offer comprehensive travel planning and booking. In addition to the Frommer's Online site (see box, below), we list the other top online travel agencies below, along with some more specialized services.

WHY BOOK ONLINE?

Online agencies have come a long way over the past few years, now providing tips for finding the best fare, and giving you suggested dates or times to travel that yield the lowest price. Other sites even allow you to establish the price you're willing to pay, and they check the airlines' willingness to accept it. However, in some cases, these sites may not always yield the best price. Unlike a travel agent, they may not have access to charter flights offered by wholesalers.

Editor's Note: What You'll Find at the Frommer's Site

We highly recommend **Arthur Frommer's Budget Travel Online** (**www.frommers.com**) as an excellent travel planning resource. Of course, we're a little biased, but you'll find indispensable travel tips, reviews, monthly vacation giveaways, and online booking. Among the most popular features of this site is the regular "Ask the Expert" bulletin boards, which feature one of the Frommer's authors answering your questions via online postings.

Subscribe to Arthur Frommer's Daily Newsletter (**www.frommers.com/ newsletters**) to receive the latest travel bargains and inside travel secrets in your e-mailbox every day. You'll read daily headlines and articles from the dean of travel himself, highlighting last-minute deals on airfares, accommodations, cruises, and package vacations. You'll also find great travel advice by checking our Tip of the Day or Hot Spot of the Month.

Search our Destinations archive (**www.frommers.com/ destinations**) of more than 200 domestic and international destinations for great places to stay, tips for traveling there, and what to do while you're there. Once you've researched your trip, the online reservation system (**www.frommers.com/ booktravelnow**) takes you to Frommer's favorite sites for booking your vacation at affordable prices.

Online booking sites aren't the only places to reserve airline tickets—all major airlines have their own Web sites and often offer incentives—bonus frequent flyer miles or net-only discounts, for example—when you buy online or buy an e-ticket.

The new trend is toward conglomerated booking sites. By mid-2000 a consortium of U.S. and European-based airlines are planning to launch an as-yet unnamed Web site that will offer fares lower than those available through travel agents. United, Delta, Northwest, and Continental have initiated this effort, based on their success at selling airline seats at their own online sites.

The best of the travel planning sites are now highly personalized; they store your seating preferences, meal preferences, tentative itineraries, and credit-card information, allowing you to quickly plan trips or check agendas.

In many cases booking your trip online can be better than working with a travel agent. It gives you the widest variety of choices, control, and the 24-hour convenience of planning your trip when you choose. All you need is some time—and often a little patience—and you're likely to find the fun of online travel research will greatly enhance your trip.

WHO SHOULD BOOK ONLINE?

Online booking is best for travelers who want to know as much as possible about their travel options, those who have flexibility in their travel dates and are looking for the best price, and for bargain hunters driven by a good value, who are open-minded about where they travel.

One of the biggest successes in online travel for both passengers and airlines is the offer of last-minute specials, such as weekend deals or other Internet-only fares that must be purchased online. Another advantage is that you can cash in on incentives for booking online, such as rebates or bonus frequent flyer miles.

More people still look online than book online, partly due to fear of putting their credit card numbers out on the Net. Secure encryption coupled with increasing experience buying online have removed this fear for most travelers. To be sure you're in secure mode when you book online, look for a little icon of a key or a padlock at the bottom of your Web browser.

Business and other frequent travelers also have found numerous benefits in online booking, as the advances in mobile technology provide them with the ability to check flight status, change plans, or get specific directions from handheld computing devices, mobile phones and pagers. Some sites will even e-mail or page a passenger if his or her flight is delayed.

Online booking is increasingly able to accommodate complex itineraries, even for international travel. The pace of evolution on the Net is rapid, so you'll probably find additional features and advancements by the time you visit these sites. What the future holds for online travelers is increasing personalization, customization, and reaching out to you.

TRAVEL PLANNING & BOOKING SITES

Below are listings for the top sites for planning and booking travel. The following sites offer domestic and international flight, hotel, and rental car bookings, plus news, destination information, and deals on cruises and vacation packages. Free (one-time) registration is required for booking.

⊙ Expedia. **expedia.com**

Expedia is known as the fastest and most flexible online travel planner for booking flights, hotels, and rental cars. Features include a **Flight Price Matcher**, which allows your preferred airline to match an available fare with a competitor; a comprehensive **Fare Compare** area showing the differences in fare categories and airlines; and a **Fare Calendar** to help you plan your trip around the best possible fares. Its main limitation is that like many online databases, Expedia focuses on the major airlines and hotel chains, so don't expect to find many budget airlines or cozy B&Bs here.

Personalized features allow you to store your itineraries and receive weekly fare reports on favorite cities. You can also check on the status of flight arrivals and departures, and with MileageMinder, track all your frequent flyer accounts.

(*Note:* In early 2000, Expedia bought travelscape.com and vacationspot.com, and incorporated these sites into expedia.com.)

Travelocity (incorporates Preview Travel). **www.travelocity.com; (also incorporates www.previewtravel.com)**

Travelocity offers reservations and tickets for more than 400 airlines, plus reservations and purchase capabilities for more than 45,000 hotels and 50 car rental companies. An exclusive feature of the SABRE system used here is the **Low Fare Search Engine,** which automatically searches for the three lowest-priced itineraries based on a traveler's criteria. Last-minute deals and consolidator fares (provided by Travel Information Software Systems, or TISS) are included in the search. If you book with Travelocity, you can select specific seats for your flights with online seat maps and view diagrams of the most popular commercial aircraft. Their hotel finder provides street-level location maps and photos of selected hotels.

Online Directory

Airline Web Sites

Below are the Web sites for the major airlines serving Mexico. These sites offer schedules and flight booking, and most have pages where you can sign up for e-mail alerts for weekend deals and other late-breaking bargains.

Aeromexico. www.aeromexico.com
Alaska Airlines. www.alaskaair.com
America West. www.americawest.com
American Airlines. www.aa.com
Continental Airlines. www.continental.com
Delta. www.delta-air.com
Mexicana. www.mexicana.com
Northwest Airlines. www.nwa.com
TWA. www.twa.com
United Airlines. www.ual.com
USAirways. www.usairways.com

Travelocity features an inviting interface for booking trips, though the wealth of graphics involved can make the site somewhat slow to load, and any adjustment in desired trip planning means you'll need to completely start over.

This site also has some very cool tools. With the **Fare Watcher** e-mail feature, you can select up to five routes and you'll receive e-mail notices when the fare changes by $25 or more. If you own an alphanumeric pager with national access that can receive e-mail, Travelocity's **Flight Paging** can alert you if your flight is delayed. You can also access real-time departure and arrival information on any flight within the SABRE system.

Note to AOL Users: You can book flights, hotels, rental cars and cruises on AOL at keyword: Travel. The booking software is provided by Travelocity/Preview Travel and is similar to the Internet site. Use the AOL "Travelers Advantage" program to earn a 5% rebate on flights, hotel rooms and car rentals.

TRIP.com. www.trip.com

TRIP.com began as a site geared for business travelers, but its innovative features and highly personalized approach have broadened its appeal to leisure travelers as well. It is the leading travel site for those using mobile devices to access Internet travel information.

TRIP.com includes a trip planning function that provides the average and lowest fare for the route requested, in addition to the current available fare. An on-site "newsstand" features airfare sales and other travel specials. Among its most popular features are Flight TRACKER and intelliTRIP. **Flight TRACKER** allows users to track any commercial flight en route to its destination anywhere in the U.S., while accessing real-time FAA-based flight monitoring data. **intelli-TRIP** is a travel search tool that allows users to identify the best airline, hotel, and rental carfares in less than 90 seconds.

In addition, it offers e-mail notification of flight delays, city resource guides, currency converters, and a weekly e-mail newsletter of fare updates, travel tips, and traveler forums.

Yahoo! Travel. www.travel.yahoo.com

Yahoo! is currently the most popular of the Internet information portals, and its travel site is a comprehensive mix of online booking, daily travel news, and destination information. Its **Best Fares** area offers what it promises, and provides feedback on refining your search if you have flexibility in travel dates or times. There is also an active section of Message Boards for discussions on travel in general, and to specific destinations.

SPECIALTY TRAVEL SITES

Although the sites listed above provide the most comprehensive services, some travelers have specialized needs that are best met by a site that caters specifically to them.

For adventure travelers, **iExplore** (www.iexplore.com) is a great source for booking adventure and experiential travel, as well as for finding information on related services and products. The site combines the secure Internet booking functions with hands-on expertise and 24-hour live customer support by seasoned adventure travelers for those interested in trips off the beaten path. The company is a supporting member of the Ecotourism Society, and is committed to environmentally responsible travel worldwide.

Another excellent site for adventure travelers is **Away.com** (www.away.com), which features unique vacations for challenging the body, mind, and spirit. Trips may include cycling in the Loire Valley, an African Safari, or assisting in the excavation of a Mayan ruin. For those without the time for such an extended, exotic trip, offbeat weekend getaways are also available. Services include a customer service center staffed with experts to answer calls and e-mails, plus a network of over 1,000 pre-screened tour operators. Trips are categorized by cultural, adventure, and green travel. Away.com also offers a Daily Escape e-mail newsletter.

GORP (Great Outdoor Recreation Pages; www.gorp.com) has been a standard for adventure travelers since its founding in 1995 by outdoor enthusiasts Diane and Bill Greer. Tapping their own experiences, they created this Web site that offers the unique travel destinations and encourages active participation by fellow GORP visitors through the sophisticated menu of online forums, contests, and discussions.

For travelers who prefer more unique accommodations, **InnSite** (www.innsite.com) offers listings for inns and B&Bs in all 50 U.S. states and dozens of countries around the globe. (This site even includes a listing for a "floating hotel"—a 6-cabin barge—moored on Paris's Quai Henri IV.) Find an inn at your destination, have a look at images of the rooms, check prices and availability, and then send e-mail to the innkeeper if you have further questions. This is an extensive directory of bed and breakfast inns, but only includes listings if the proprietor submitted one (note that listings are free). The descriptions are written by the innkeepers, and many listings link to the inn's own site, where you can find more information and images.

Another good resource for mostly one-of-a-kind places in the U.S. and abroad is **Places to Stay** (www.placestostay.com), which focuses on resort accommodations.

"Have Kids, Still Travel!" is the motto of the **Family Travel Forum** (FTF; www.familytravelforum.com), a site dedicated to the ideals, promotion, and support of travel with children. FTF is supported by memberships, which are available in flexible prices ranging from a $2.95 monthly fee to a heftier, annual fee for more comprehensive services. Since no advertising is accepted, FTF provides its members with honest, unbiased information, informed advice and practical tips designed to make traveling with children a healthier, safer, hassle-free experience, not to mention a better value.

Online Directory

TOP VACATION PACKAGE SITES

Both **Expedia** and **Travelocity** (see above) offer excellent selections and searches for complete vacation packages. Travelers can search by destination and desired dates coupled with how much they are willing to spend. Travelocity has a valuable "Cruise Critic" function, to help would-be cruisers obtain firsthand accounts of the quality and details of a cruise from recent passengers.

Travel wholesalers, like **Apple Vacations** (**www.applevacations.com**) and **Funjet** (**www.funjet.com**), are also good starting points, but still require that the final booking be handled through a travel agent.

As travel agents tend to be more expert at sorting through the values in vacation packages, you might find **Vacation.com** (**www.vacation.com**) helpful in previewing packages and finding an appropriate agent to help you book the deal. This site represents a nationwide network of 9,800 local travel agencies that specialize in finding the best values in cruises, vacation packages, tours, and other leisure travel services. To find a Vacation.com member agency, enter your zip code and the Vacation.com Agency Finder will locate a nearby office.

LAST-MINUTE DEALS & OTHER ONLINE BARGAINS

There is nothing airlines hate more than flying with lots of empty seats. The Net has enabled airlines to offer last-minute bargains to entice travelers to fill those seats. Most of these are announced on Tuesday or Wednesday and are valid for travel the following weekend, but some can be booked weeks or months in advance. You can sign up for weekly e-mail alerts at airlines' sites (For Web sites of airlines, see "Airline Web Sites," below) or check sites that compile lists of these bargains, such as **Smarter Living** or **WebFlyer** (see below). To make it easier, visit a site that will round up all the deals and send them in one convenient weekly e-mail. But last-minute deals aren't the only online bargains; other sites can help you find value even if you haven't waited until the eleventh hour. Increasingly popular are services that let you name the price you're willing to pay for an air seat or vacation package, and travel auction sites.

Cheap Tickets. www.cheaptickets.com

Cheap Tickets has exclusive deals not available through more mainstream channels. One caveat about the Cheap Tickets site is that it will offer fare quotes for a route, and later show this fare is not valid for your dates of travel—most other Web sites, such as Expedia, consider your dates of travel before showing what fares are available. Despite its problems, Cheap Tickets can be worth the effort because its fares can be lower than those offered by its competitors.

✪ **1travel.com. www.1travel.com**

Here you'll find deals on domestic and international flights, cruises, hotels, and all-inclusive resorts such as Club Med. 1travel.com's **Saving Alert** compiles last-minute air deals so you don't have to scroll through multiple e-mail alerts. A feature called "Drive a little using low-fare airlines" helps map out strategies for using alternate airports to find lower fares. And **Farebeater** searches a database that includes published fares, consolidator bargains and special deals exclusive to 1travel.com. *Note:* The travel agencies listed by 1travel. com have paid for placement.

Bid for Travel. www.bidfortravel.com

Bid for Travel is another of the travel auction sites, similar to Priceline (see below), which are growing in popularity. In addition to airfares, Internet users can place a bid for vacation packages and hotels.

Go4less.com. www.go4less.com

Specializing in last-minute cruise and package deals, Go4less has some excellent offers. The Hot Deals section gives an alphabetical listing by destination of super discounted packages.

Moment's Notice. www.moments-notice.com

As the name suggests, Moment's Notice specializes in last-minute vacation and cruise deals. You can browse for free, but if you want to purchase a trip you have to join Moment's Notice, which costs $25. Go to World Wide Hot Deals for a complete list of special deals in international destinations.

✪ Priceline.com. travel.priceline.com

Even people who aren't familiar with many Web sites have heard about Priceline.com. Launched in 1998 with an ad campaign featuring William Shatner, Priceline lets you "name your price" for domestic and international airline tickets and hotel rooms. In other words, you select a route and dates, guarantee with a credit card, and make a bid for what you're willing to pay. If one of the airlines in Priceline's database has a fare lower than your bid, your credit card will automatically be charged for a ticket.

But you can't say when you want to fly—you have to accept any flight leaving between 6am and 10pm on the dates you selected, and you may have to make a stopover. No frequent flyer miles are awarded, and tickets are non-refundable and can't be exchanged for another flight. So if your plans change, you're out of luck. Priceline can be good for travelers who have to take off on short notice (and who are thus unable to qualify for advance purchase discounts). But be sure to shop around first, because if you overbid, you'll be required to purchase the ticket—and Priceline will pocket the difference between what it paid for the ticket and what you bid.

Priceline says that over 35% of all reasonable offers for domestic flights are being filled on the first try, with much higher fill rates on popular routes (New York to San Francisco, for example). It defines "reasonable" as not more than 30% below the lowest generally available advance-purchase fare for the same route.

Travelzoo.com. www.travelzoo.com

At this Internet portal, over 150 travel companies post special deals. It features a Top 20 list of the best deals on the site, selected by its editorial staff each Wednesday night. This list is also available via an e-mail list, free to those who sign up.

WebFlyer. www.webflyer.com

WebFlyer is a comprehensive online resource for frequent flyers and also has an excellent listing of last-minute air deals. Click on "Deal Watch" for a roundup of weekend deals on flights, hotels and rental cars from domestic and international suppliers.

Online Directory

Know When the Sales Start

While most people learn about last-minute weekend deals from e-mail dispatches, it can pay to check the airline sites to find out precisely when they post their special fares. Because deals are limited, they can vanish within hours, sometimes minutes—often before you even read your e-mail. An example: Southwest's specials are posted at 12:01am Tuesdays (Central time). So if you're looking for a cheap flight, stay up late and check Southwest's site to grab the best new deals.

ONLINE TRAVELER'S TOOLBOX

Veteran travelers usually carry some essential items to make their trips easier. Following is a selection of online tools to smooth your journey.

Visa ATM Locator. www.visa.com/pd/atm/

MasterCard ATM Locator. www.mastercard.com/atm

Find ATMs in hundreds of cities in the U.S. and around the world. Both include maps for some locations and both list airport ATM locations, some with maps. *Tip:* You'll usually get a better exchange rate using ATMs than exchanging traveler's checks at banks, but check in advance to see what kind of fees your bank will assess for using an overseas ATM.

CDC Travel Information. www.cdc.gov/travel/index.htm

Health advisories and recommendations for inoculations from the U.S. Centers for Disease Control. The CDC site is good for an overview, but it's best to consult your personal physician on required vaccinations or health precautions.

✪ **Foreign Languages for Travelers. www.travlang.com**

Learn basic terms in more than 70 languages and click on any underlined phrase to hear what it sounds like. (*Note:* free audio software and speakers are required.)

Intellicast. www.intellicast.com

Weather forecasts for all 50 states and cities around the world. Note that temperatures are in Celsius for many international destinations, so don't think you'll need that winter coat for your next trip to Athens.

✪ **Mapquest. www.mapquest.com**

This best of the mapping sites lets you choose a specific address or destination, and in seconds, it will return back a map and detailed directions. It really is easier than calling, asking, and writing down directions. The site also links to special travel deals and helpful sites.

Net Café Guide. www.netcafeguide.com/mapindex.htm

Locate Internet cafés at hundreds of locations around the globe. Catch up on your e-mail, log onto the Web and stay in touch with the home front, usually for just a few dollars per hour.

Travelers' Tales. www.travelerstales.com

Considered the best in compilations of travel literature, Travelers' Tales are an award-winning series of books grouped by destination (Mexico, France, China, etc.) or by theme (Love & Romance, Women in the Wild, The Adventure of Food). It's a new kind of travel book that offers a description of a place

Travel Discussion Sites

One of the best sources of travel information is word-of-mouth from someone who has just been there. Internet discussion groups are offering an unprecedented way for travelers around the globe to connect and share experiences. The **Frommer's Online** site (**www.frommers.com**) offers these message boards, and also areas where you can pose questions to the guidebook writers themselves, in its section, "Ask the Expert." **Yahoo! Travel, Expedia,** and **Travelocity** are other good sources of online travel discussion groups.

The granddaddy of specialized discussions on particular topics is **Usenet,** a collection of over 50,000 newsgroups. You'll find a comprehensive listing at **Deja News** (**www.dejanews.com/usenet/**), or at **www.liszt.com**.

Check E-mail at Internet Cafes While Traveling

Until a few years ago, most travelers who checked their e-mail while traveling carried a laptop—an expensive and often technologically problematic option. Thankfully, Web-based free e-mail programs have made it much easier to check your mail.

Just open an account at any one of the numerous "freemail" providers—the original leaders continue to be **Hotmail** (**hotmail.com**), **Excite** (**www.excite.com**), and **Yahoo! Mail** (**mail.yahoo.com**), though many are available. AOL users should check out **AOL Netmail**, and **USA.NET** (**www.usa.net**) comes highly recommended for functionality and security. You can find hints, tips and a mile-long list of freemail providers at **www.emailaddresses.com.**

Then, all you'll need to check your mail is a Web connection, easily available at Net cafes and copy shops around the world. After logging on, just call up your freemail's Internet address, enter your username and password and you'll have access to your mail. From these sites you can download all of your e-mail—even from office accounts—or your local or national Internet Service Provider address. There will be a section generally called "check other mail" that allows you to add the names of other e-mail servers.

Internet cafes have become ubiquitous, so for a few dollars an hour you'll be able to check your mail and send messages from virtually anywhere in the world. Interestingly, Internet cafes tend to be more common in very remote areas, where they may offer the best form of access for an entire community, especially if phone lines are difficult to obtain.

Online Directory

or type of journey through the experiences of many travelers. It makes for a perfect traveling companion.

Universal Currency Converter. www.xe.net/currency
See what your dollar or pound is worth in more than a hundred other countries.

**U.S. State Department Travel Warnings. travel.state.gov/
  travel_warnings.html**
Reports on places where health concerns or unrest might threaten U.S. travelers. Keep in mind that these warnings can be dated and conservative. You can also sign up to receive State Department briefings via e-mail.

Web Travel Secrets. www.web-travel-secrets.com
If this list leaves you yearning for more, Web Travel Secrets offers one of the best compilations around. It offers advice and tips on how to find the lowest prices for airlines, hotels, and cruises and also provides a comprehensive listing of links for airfare deals, airlines, booking engines, discount travel, resources, hotels, and travel magazines.

2 The Top Web Sites for Cancún, Cozumel & the Yucatán

The Internet can provide a wealth of destination-specific information, as well as the opportunity to chat online with other people who have recently visited the place you are considering. There are two basic types of sites that can help you sift through the maze of information to arrive at the truly useful: directories and search engines.

Directories function much the same way as a library, or the old-style card catalog. You can first narrow your request by selecting a category, then working your way down to the type of site or information you're most interested in. Note that a person will categorize every site listed in a directory, so although the listings may not include every possible page on the Internet, the chance for getting targeted information is much better. **Yahoo!** (www.yahoo.com) is the granddaddy of all search directories, but if your goal is finding sites with more detailed destination information, be sure to look for information under the category "Regional", rather than its "Travel" button, or you'll go to its reservation site.

Mexico Web (www.mexico.web.com.mx) is an online directory—in English and Spanish—that shamelessly copies the format of Yahoo!, but is forgiven, due to the wealth of sites it lists. It covers all destinations in Mexico as well as providing links to cultural, news, shopping, politics, and ecological sites. It's probably the most comprehensive listing of Web sites about Mexico available.

Search engines work by finding Web sites that match your request, based on "key words". If you enter, "Cancun", for example, theoretically a listing of all of the best sites containing information about Cancún will be returned to you. We know, however, that it isn't always so easy. Because of the imprecise nature of this process, sometimes a basic search can return literally thousands of options, many of them inappropriate. The more detailed and precise you can make your search, such as "Cancun Hotels", or "Akumal Diving", the more precise and worthwhile the results are bound to be. Among the best of the search engines are the following:

- **www.directhit.com**, will return your search findings, plus provide suggestions to narrow your search to the most accurate hit—for example, when you search for a place, it will return current weather, maps, vacation packages and other useful information.
- **www.excite.com**, loads current weather information and maps for any travel destinations you're searching information about.
- **www.hotbot.com**, offers not only fast, accurate search results, but links to travel planning sites, related books, and opportunities to write reviews.
- **www.search.com**, If you don't want to sift through multiple search pages, this one site pulls together the results from all of the top search sites.

CANCÚN

All About Cancun. www.cancunmx.com
Before taking off on a vacation every traveler has a few questions and, if Cancún is your destination, this site is a good place to start. There's a database of answers to the most commonly asked questions, called "The Online Experts." There is a specialized section for diving, plus a live chat area and copies of recent articles published about Cancún.

Surfers Beware

If you are not viewing an "official" site, sponsored by the Tourism or Visitor's Bureau, most of the listings will only include companies that have paid for space, so don't expect objective analysis like you find in this guidebook.

✪ Cancún Convention & Visitor's Bureau. **gocancun.com**
This official site of the Cancún Convention and Visitor's Bureau lists excellent information on events and area attractions. Both attractive and well-organized, it has a vacation planning and meeting planning area, plus special sections for travel agents and the press. Its hotel guide is one of the most complete available.

Cancún Online. **www.cancun.com**
This comprehensive guide has lots of information about things to do and see in Cancún, with most details provided by paying advertisers. Highlights include forums, live chat, property-swap, bulletin boards, plus information on local Internet access, news and events. You can even reserve a golf tee time or conduct wedding planning online. The essential information mostly consists of brochures slapped online. Still it can be useful for perusing images of lodgings, checking out restaurant's specialties, or printing coupons (typically for 10% off) for dining or golf.

✪ Cancún Travel Guide. **www.go2cancun.com**
This group specializing in online information about Mexico has put together an excellent resource for Cancún rentals, hotels, and area attractions. Note that only paying advertisers are listed, but you'll find most of the major players here. The alluring beach images and useful maps make this site worth visiting.

Mexico Web Cancún Chat. **www.mexicoweb.com/chats/cancun/**
This is one of the more active chats online specifically about Cancún. The users share inside information on everything from the cheapest beers to the quality of food at various all-inclusive resorts.

COZUMEL

✪ Cozumel.net. **www.cozumel.net**
This site is a cut above the typical dining/lodging/activities sites. Click on "About Cozumel" to find schedules for ferries and island-hop flights and to learn about the latest news. There's also a comprehensive listing on B&Bs and vacation home rentals, plus great info on diving, maps, and a chat room.

Cozumel Travel Planner. **go2cozumel.com**
A very well done guide to area businesses and attractions, by this online Mexico specialist.

Travel Notes. **travelnotes.cc**
This site boasts over 1,000 pages of information and photos on Cozumel island—with an emphasis on diving, deep sea fishing, and other water-bound activities.

Viva Cozumel. **viva-cozumel.com**
With weather forecasts, links to dive shops, and listings for restaurants and hotels, this site can come in handy—just don't expect objectivity; the businesses pay for space to advertise their wares. They do offer some Internet-only deals that can make a visit worthwhile.

ELSEWHERE IN THE YUCATÁN

Cancún South. **www.cancunsouth.com**
Billed as a guide for independent travelers, this site has itineraries and detailed driving instructions, plus tips of lodging and attractions for exploring the areas south of Cancún.

Diario Yucatán. **www.yucatan.com.mx**
A Spanish language newspaper serving the Yucatán region.

Ecotravels in Mexico. **www2.planeta.com/mader/ecotravel/mexico/mexico.html**
This site covers the whole country and has a nice section on the Yucatán about halfway down the page.

Kuartos.com. **kuartos.com**
A well-designed and easy-to-use site for finding hotels and making reservations throughout Cancún and the Mayan Riviera. Each hotel listing has a photo and detailed description (plus lowest rates), and allows you to check availability and make reservations. It also features super specials for selected properties.

✪ Maya: Portraits of a People. **www.nationalgeographic.com/explorer/maya/more.html**
A fascinating collection of articles from *National Geographic* and other sources.

Mayan Riviera Guide. **cancun.mayan-riviera.com**
From places to stay to maps to the area's cenotes (underground caves for diving) this site covers the extent of the Mayan Riviera, with specialized content for Cancún, Playa del Carmen, Akumal, Cozumel, Isla Mujeres, and Punte Bete. The more heavily trafficked areas have the best information, but the site is easy to navigate and has some great interactive maps.

Mayan Riviera Travel Guide. **xaac.com/playacar**
This site, though basic in design, offers information on some of the more remote and lesser traveled areas, including Tulum, Valladolid, and Ria Lagartos. It offers few images but excellent factual information.

Mexico's Yucatán Directory. **www.mexonline.com/yucatan.htm**
A nice roundup of vacation rentals, tour operators and information on the Mayan sites from MexOnline. For more information on Mexico's indigenous history, see the set of links on the Pre-Columbian page (www.mexonline.com/precolum.htm).

Mysterious Places: Chichén-Itzá. **www.mysteriousplaces.com/chichen_itza_page.html**
An illuminating photo tour of Chichén-Itzá's temples. See images of the Temple of the Warriors, the Nunnery, and the Observatory, among other ruins.

Palenque. **www.mpsnet.com.mx/mexico/chiapas/palenque.html**
The best part of this page is the photography. The images offer a sense of what awaits you at Palenque—you'll also find some basic visitor information.

Playa Magazine Online. **www.playadelcarmen.com**
This online version of the locally popular information guide offers plenty of tips, news, and tourist information for those bound for Playa del Carmen.

The Net Traveler. **www.thenettraveler.com**
This site specializes in information about the Yucatán, Quintana Roo (home state of Cancún), and Chiapas, as well as other areas in the old Mayan empire. Its information on archeological sites, as well as on diving in the region's caves and cenotes, is especially good.

✪ Yucatán Web. **www.yucatanweb.com**
An excellent all-around guide to the Yucatán including pages for Isla Mujeres, Playa del Carmen, Puerto Morelos and Punta Bete. Each sub-site has a map and tips for getting around, dining, lodging and more. You'll also find many links to sites for dive shops, hotels, etc.

Online Directory

Cancún 3

Simply stated, Cancún is the reason why most people travel to Mexico. The sheer number of annual travelers to Cancún underscores the magnetic appeal of this resort on Mexico's eastern coast, with almost 3 million people visiting this enticing beach resort annually, most of them on their first trip to this country. The reasons are both numerous and obvious.

Cancún offers an unrivaled combination of high-quality accommodations, dreamy beaches, a wide diversity of shopping, dining, nightlife, and activities nearby, with most offered at exceptional values with easy air access. There is also the added lure of ancient cultures »evident in all directions, and a growing number of eco-oriented theme parks.

No doubt about it—Cancún is the peak of Caribbean splendor with translucent turquoise waters and powdery white-sand beaches, coupled with coastal areas of great natural beauty. But Cancún is also a modern mega-resort. Even a traveler feeling apprehensive about visiting foreign soil will feel completely at home and at ease here. English is spoken, dollars are accepted, roads are well paved, and lawns are manicured. Malls are the mode for shopping and dining, and you would swear some hotels are larger than a small town. Travelers feel comfortable in Cancún. You do not need to spend a day getting your bearings, as you immediately see familiar names for dining, shopping, nightclubbing, and sleeping.

You may have heard that in 1974 a team of Mexican government computer analysts picked Cancún for tourism development for its ideal mix of elements to attract travelers—they were right on. It's actually an island, a 14-mile long sliver of land connected to the Mexican mainland by two bridges and separated from it by the expansive Nichupté lagoon. (Cancún means Golden Snake in the Mayan language.)

In addition to attractions of its own, Cancún is a convenient distance from the more traditional resorts of **Isla Mujeres, Playa del Carmen,** and **Cozumel** and the **Maya ruins** at Tulum, Chichén-Itzá, and Cobá. All are within driving distance for a day-trip.

You will run out of vacation days before you run out of things to do in Cancún. Snorkeling, jet-skiing, jungle tours, and visits to ancient Maya ruins or modern ecological theme parks are among the most popular diversions. There are a dozen malls with name-brand and duty-free shops (with better-than-U.S.-priced European goods), plus over 350 restaurants and nightclubs. Over 24,000 hotel rooms in the area offer something for every taste and every budget.

Cancún's luxury hotels have pools so spectacular you may find it tempting to remain poolside, but don't. Set aside some time to simply gaze into the ocean and wriggle your toes in the fine, brilliantly white sand. This is, after all, what put Cancún on the map.

Highlighting both the country's breathtaking natural beauty and the depth of its thousand-year-old history, Cancún perfectly showcases Mexico, and has become its calling card to world travelers.

1 Orientation

GETTING THERE

BY PLANE If this is not your first trip to Cancún, you'll notice the airport continues to undergo expansion, adding a new terminal and second runway in 1999. **Aeromexico** (☎ **800/237-6639** in the U.S., 01/800-021-4000 toll-free within Mexico, or 9/884-1186 in Cancún; www.aeromexico.com) offers direct service from Atlanta, Houston, Miami, and New York, plus connecting service via Mexico City from Dallas, Los Angeles, and San Diego. **Mexicana** (☎ **800/531-7921** from the U.S., 91/800-36654 toll-free within Mexico, 9/887-4444 or 9/886-0124 in Cancún; www.mexicana.com.mx) flies in from Chicago, Denver, Guadalajara, Los Angeles, Oakland, San Antonio, San Francisco, and San Jose via Mexico City, with nonstop service from Miami and New York. In addition to these carriers, many charter companies —such as Apple Vacations, Funjet, and Friendly Holidays—travel to Cancún, and these package tours make up at much as 60 percent of the arrivals here by U.S. visitors (see "The Pros & Cons of Packaged Tours" in chapter 2).

Regional carrier **Aerocozumel** (☎ **9/884-2000,** affiliated with Mexicana) flies from Cozumel, Havana, Belize, Mexico City, Merida, Chetumal, and other points within Mexico, as well as to Miami, Chicago, and Oakland. The regional airline **Aviateca** (☎ **800/327-9832** in the U.S.; 9/884-3938) flies from Cancún to Mérida, Villahermosa, Tuxtla, Gutiérrez, Guatemala City, and Flores (near Tikal).

You'll want to confirm departure times for flights back to the U.S.; here are the Cancún airport numbers of the major international carriers: American (☎ 9/883-4461; www.aa.com), Continental (☎ 9/886-0006; www.flycontinental.com), and Northwest (☎ 9/886-0044 or 9/886-0046; www.nwa.com).

Most major car-rental firms have outlets at the airport, so if you're renting a car, consider picking it up and dropping it off at the airport to save on airport-transportation costs. Another way to save money is to arrange for the rental before you leave home. If you wait until you arrive, the daily cost of a rental car will be around $65 to $75 for a VW Beetle. Major rental services include Avis (☎ 800/331-1212 in the U.S., or 9/883-0803; www.avis.com); Budget (☎ 800/527-0700 in the U.S., 9/884-4812 or fax: 9/884-5011); Dollar (☎ 800/800-4000 or 9/886-0159); National (☎ 800/328-4567 in the U.S., or 9/886-4493; www.nationalcar.com); and Hertz (☎ 800/654-3131 in the U.S. and Canada, or 9/884-4692; www.hertz.com). The Hotel Zone is 6¹/₂ miles, or about a 20-minute drive from the airport along wide, well-paved roads.

Rates for a private taxi from the airport are around $20 to downtown Cancun, or $35–$40 to the Hotel Zone, depending on your destination. Special vans (*colectivos*) run from Cancún's international airport into town. Tickets are purchased from the booth to the far right as you exit the building, and cost about $8. There's minibus

Downtown Cancún

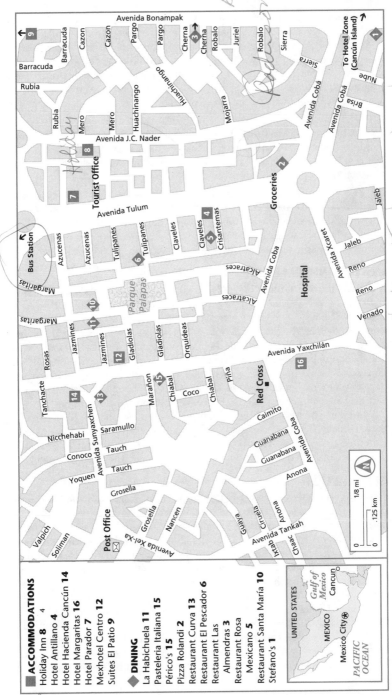

■ ACCOMMODATIONS
Holiday Inn **8** **4**
Hotel Antillano **4**
Hotel Hacienda Cancún **14**
Hotel Margaritas **16**
Hotel Parador **7**
Mexhotel Centro **12**
Suites El Patio **9**

◆ DINING
La Habichuela **11**
Pastelería Italiana **15**
Périco's **15**
Pizza Rolandi **2**
Restaurant Curva **13**
Restaurant El Pescador **6**
Restaurant Las
  Almendras **3**
Restaurant Rosa
  Mexicano **5**
Restaurant Santa María **10**
Stefano's **1**

57

transportation from the airport to the Puerto Juárez passenger ferry that takes you to Isla Mujeres that costs $9.50. A private taxi can also be hired, for about $40.

There is no *colectivo* service returning to the airport from Ciudad Cancún or the Zona Hotelera, so you'll have to hire a taxi, but you'll find the rate will be much less than your trip from the airport. The reason for this is that only federally chartered taxis may take fares from the airport, but any taxi may bring passengers to the airport. Ask at your hotel what the fare should be, but expect to pay only half what you were charged from the airport to your hotel.

BY CAR   From Mérida or Campeche, take Highway 180 east to Cancún. This is mostly a winding, two-lane road, which branches off into the express toll road 180D between Izamal and Nuevo Xcan. Nuevo Xcan is approximately 26 miles from Cancún. Mérida is about 52 miles away, or a 3¹/₂-hour drive.

BY BUS   Cancún's **ADO bus terminal** (☎ **9/884-4804** or 9/884-4352) is in downtown Ciudad Cancún at the intersection of Avenidas Tulum and Uxmal. All out-of-town buses arrive here. Buses run to Playa del Carmen, Tulum, Chichén-Itzá, and other nearby beach and archaeological zones, as well as to other points within Mexico. For package deals to popular destinations, see "Road Trips from Cancun," below.

VISITOR INFORMATION

The **State Tourism Office** (☎ 9/884-8073) is centrally located downtown on the east side of avenida Tulum 26 next to Banco Inverlat, immediately left of the Ayuntamiento Benito Juárez building between Avenidas Cobá and Uxmal. It's open daily from 9am to 9pm. A second tourist information office, the Conventions and Visitors Bureau (☎ **9/884-6531** or 9/884-3438), is located on avenida Cobá at avenida Tulum, next to Pizza Rolandi, and is open Monday through Friday from 9am to 8pm. Hotels and their rates are listed at each office, as are ferry schedules. For information prior to your arrival in Cancún, call ☎ **800-CANCUN-8** toll free from the U.S., or visit the Convention Bureau's Web site, **www.gocancun.com**.

Pick up free copies of the monthly *Cancún Tips* booklet and a seasonal tabloid of the same name. Both are useful and have fine maps. The publications are owned by the same people who own the Captain's Cove restaurants, a couple of sightseeing boats, and time-share hotels, so the information, though good, is not completely unbiased.

CITY LAYOUT

There are really two Cancúns: **Isla Cancún** (Cancún Island) and **Ciudad Cancún** (Cancún City). The latter, on the mainland, has restaurants, shops, and less-expensive hotels, as well as all the other establishments that make life function—pharmacies, dentists, automotive shops, banks, travel and airline agencies, car-rental firms—all within an area about 9 blocks square. The city's main thoroughfare is **avenida Tulum.** Heading south, avenida Tulum becomes the highway to the airport and to Tulum and Chetumal; heading north, it intersects the highway to Mérida and the road to Puerto Juárez and the Isla Mujeres ferries.

The famed **Zona Hotelera** (also called the **Zona Turística**) stretches out along Isla Cancún, a sandy strip 14 miles long, shaped like a "7." It's joined to the mainland by the Playa Linda bridge at the north end, and Punta Nizuc bridge at the southern end. Between the two areas lies Laguna Nichupté. Avenida Cobá from Cancún City becomes Paseo Kukulkán, the island's main traffic artery. Cancún's international airport is just inland from the south end of the island.

FINDING AN ADDRESS   The street-numbering system is a holdover from Cancún's early days. Addresses are still given by the number of the building lot and by the *manzana* (block) or *supermanzana* (group of city blocks). The city is still relatively small, and the downtown section can easily be covered on foot.

On the island, addresses are given by kilometer number on Paseo Kukulkán or by reference to some well-known location. In Cancún, streets are named after famous Mayan cities. Chichén Itzá, Tulum, and Uxmal are the names of the boulevards in Cancún, as well as nearby archeological sites.

GETTING AROUND

BY TAXI   Taxi prices in Cancún are clearly set by zone, although keeping track of what's in which zone can take some doing. In late 1999, taxi rates within the hotel zone increased to a minimum fare of $5 per ride, making it one of the most expensive taxis areas in Mexico. In addition, you'll find that the taxis operating in the Cancún Hotel Zone feel perfectly justified in having a discriminatory pricing structure: Local residents pay about half of what tourists pay, and guests at higher priced hotels pay about double what budget hotel guests are charged—these are all established by the taxi union. Rates should be posted outside of your hotel; however, if you have a question, all taxi drivers are required to have an official rate card in their taxi, though it's generally in Spanish.

Within the downtown area the cost is about $1.50 per cab ride (not per person); within any other zone, now $5. Between two zones will also cost $5, and if you cross two zones that'll cost $7.50. Settle on a price in advance, or check at your hotel, where destinations and prices are generally posted. Trips to the airport from most zones cost $14. Taxis can also be rented for $18 per hour for travel around the city and Hotel Zone, but this rate can generally be negotiated to $10–$12. If you want to hire a taxi to take you to Chichén-Itzá or along the Riviera Maya, expect to pay about $30 per hour, as they feel they are also providing guide services.

BY BUS   Bus travel within Cancún continues to improve, and is increasingly the most popular way of getting around. Most buses cost 45¢. In town, almost everything is within walking distance. Ruta 1 and Ruta 2 ("Hoteles") city buses travel frequently from the mainland to the beaches along avenida Tulum (the main street) and all the way to Punta Nizuc at the far end of the Zona Hotelera on Isla Cancún. Ruta 8 buses go to Puerto Juárez/Punta Sam for ferries to Isla Mujeres. They stop on the east side of avenida Tulum. Both these city buses operate between 6am and 10pm daily. Beware of private buses along the same route; they charge far more than the public ones. The public buses have the fare amount painted on the front; at the time of publication the fare was $4.50 pesos (45¢).

BY MOPED   Mopeds are a convenient but dangerous way to cruise around through the very congested traffic. Rentals start at $25 for a day. A credit-card voucher is required as security for the moped. You should receive a crash helmet (it's the law) and instructions on how to lock the wheels when you park. Read the fine print on the back of the rental agreement regarding liability for repairs or replacement in case of accident, theft, or vandalism.

Fast Facts: Cancún

American Express   The local office is located at avenida Tulum 208 and Agua (☎ **9/884-1999** or 9/884-6942; www.americanexpress.com/mex/) and is open Monday through Friday from 9am to 2pm and 4 to 6pm, and Saturday from 9am to 1pm. It's 1 block past the Plaza México.

Area Code The telephone area code is **9.**

Climate It's hot but not overwhelmingly humid. The rainy season is May through October. August through October is the hurricane season, which brings erratic weather. November through February is generally sunny, but can also be cloudy, windy, somewhat rainy, and even cool, so a sweater is handy, as is rain protection.

Consulates The **U.S. Consular Agent** is located in the Playa Caracol 2, 3rd level, no. 320–323, km 8.5 boulevard Kukulkán (☎ **9/883-0272**). The office is open Monday through Friday from 9am to 1pm and 3 to 6pm. The **Canadian** Consulate is located in the Plaza México 312 (☎ **9/883-3360**). The office is open Monday through Friday from 9am to 5pm. The **United Kingdom** has a consular office in Cancún (☎ **9/881-0100**, ext. 63815; fax: 9/885-1225; e-mail: information@britishconsulatecancun.com). Irish, Australian, and New Zealand citizens should be referred to their embassies in Mexico City.

Crime Car break-ins are just about the only crime, and they happen frequently, especially around the shopping centers in the Zona Hotelera. VW Beetles and Golfs are frequent targets.

Currency Exchange Most banks are downtown along avenida Tulum and are usually open Monday through Friday from 9:30am to 5pm, and many now have automatic teller machines for after-hour cash withdrawals. In the Hotel Zone you'll find banks in the Plaza Kukulkán and next to the convention center. There are also many *casas de cambio* (exchange houses). Downtown merchants are eager to change cash dollars, but island stores don't offer very good exchange rates. Avoid changing money at the airport as you arrive, especially at the first exchange booth you see—its rates are less favorable than any in town or others farther inside the airport concourse.

Drugstores Next to the Hotel Caribe Internacional, **Farmacia Canto,** avenida Yaxchilán 36, at Sunyaxchen (☎ **9/884-9330**), is open 24 hours. American Express, MasterCard, and Visa are accepted.

Emergencies To report an emergency, dial ☎ **06,** which is supposed to be similar to 911 emergency service in the United States. For first aid, the **Cruz Roja** (Red Cross; ☎ **9/884-1616,** fax 9/884-7466) is open 24 hours on avenida Yaxchilán between Avenidas Xcaret and Labná, next to the Telmex building. **Total Assist,** a small nine-room emergency hospital with English-speaking doctors at Claveles 5, SM 22, at avenida Tulum (☎ **9/884-1058** or 9/884-1092; e-mail: htotal@qroo1.telmex.net.mx), is also open 24 hours. American Express, MasterCard, and Visa are accepted. Desk staff may have limited English. There is also an Air Ambulance service available, by calling ☎ **800-305-9400,** (toll free within Mexico. *Urgencias* means "Emergencies."

Internet Access **C@ncunet,** located in a kiosk on the 2nd floor of Plaza Kukulkán, Km. 13 Paseo Kukulkán, offers Internet access for $4 for 15 minutes, or $16 per hour, from 10am to 10pm (☎ **9/885-0055**). In downtown Cancún, **Sybcom** offers Internet access for $3.80 per hour, $2 for 30 minutes, or $1 for 15 minutes. They are located in the Plaza Alconde, Local 2, at Ave. Náder, just in front of Clinica AMAT (☎ **9/884-6807**), and are open from 8am to 11pm, Monday through Saturday.

Luggage Storage/Lockers Hotels will generally tag and store excess luggage while you travel elsewhere.

Newspapers/Magazines   For English-language newspapers and books, go to **Fama** on avenida Tulum between Tulipanes and Claveles (☎ **9/884-6586**), open daily from 8am to 10pm, with a new upstairs coffee shop. American Express, MasterCard, and Visa are accepted. Most hotel gift shops and news-stands also carry English-language magazines, and the English-language Mexican newspapers.

Police   To reach the **police** (Seguridad Pública), dial ☎ **9/884-1913** or 9/884-2342. The ***Procuraduría del Consumidor*** (consumer protection agency) is opposite the Social Security Hospital at avenida Cobá 9–11, located upstairs from the Fenix drugstore. It's open Monday through Saturday, 9am to 3pm, ☎ **9/ 884-2634** or 9/884-2701.

Post Office   The **main post office** is at the intersection of Avenidas Sunyax-chen and Xel-Ha (☎ **9/884-1418**). It's open Monday through Friday from 8am to 5pm and Saturday from 9am to 12pm.

Safety   There is very little crime in Cancún. People are generally safe late at night in tourist areas; just use ordinary common sense. As at any other beach resort, don't take money or valuables to the beach. See "Crime," above.

   Swimming on the Caribbean side presents a danger from undertow. See "The Beaches" in "Beaches & Water Sports," below, for flag warnings.

Seasons   Technically, high season is December 15 to Easter; low season is May through July, and October 1 through December 15, when prices are reduced 10% to 30%. Some hotels are starting to charge high-season rates between July and September, when travel is high for Mexican national, European, and school-holiday visitors, although they may be less than in winter months. There's a short low season in January just after the Christmas–New Year's holiday.

Special Events   The annual **Cancun Jazz Festival,** featuring internationally known musicians, is held each year over the U.S. Memorial Day weekend, in late-May. The Cancún Marathon takes place each December, and attracts world-class athletes, as well as numerous amateur competitors. Additional information is available through the Convention and Visitors Bureau.

Telephones   The phone system for Cancún changed in July 1999. The area code is now **9** (it was 98)**.** All local numbers now have seven digits instead of six, and all numbers begin with 8. If a number is written 98/84-1234, when in Cancún you must dial 884-1234.

2 Where to Stay

Island hotels are stacked along the beach like dominoes, almost all of them offering clean, modern facilities. Extravagance is the byword in the more recently built hotels, many of which are awash in a sea of marble and glass. Some hotels, however, while exclusive, affect a more relaxed attitude. The water is placid on the upper end of the island facing Bahía de Mujeres, while beaches lining the long side of the island facing the Caribbean are subject to choppier water and crashing waves on windy days. (For more information on swimming safety, see "Beaches & Water Sports," later in this chapter.) Be aware that the farther south you go on the island, the longer it takes (20 to 30 min. in traffic) to get back to the "action spots," which are primarily between the Plaza Flamingo and Punta Cancún on the island and along avenida Tulum on the mainland.

Almost all major hotel chains are represented on Cancún Island, so this list can be viewed as a representative summary, with a select number of notable places to stay. The reality is that Cancún is so popular as a "package" destination from the U.S. that price and special deals are often the deciding factor for those traveling here (see "The Pros & Cons of Packaged Tours" in chapter 2). Ciudad Cancún offers independently owned, smaller, and less expensive stays. Prices are lower here during the off-season (April through November). For condo, home, and villa rentals, as an alternative to hotel stays, check with **Cancun Hideaways,** a company specializing in luxury properties, downtown apartments, and condos—many offered at prices much lower than comparable hotel stays. Owner Maggie Rodriguez, a former resident of Cancun, has made this niche market her specialty. You can preview her offerings at **www. cancun-hideaways.com.**

The hotel listings in this chapter begin on Cancún Island and finish in Cancún City, where bargain lodgings are available. Parking is available at all island hotels.

CANCÚN ISLAND
VERY EXPENSIVE

Hilton Cancún Beach & Golf Resort. Km 17 Paseo Kukulkán, Retorno Lacandones, 77500 Cancún, Q. Roo. ☎ **800/228-3000** in the U.S., or 9/881-8000. Fax 9/881-8080. www.hiltoncancun.com.mx. E-mail: reservations@hiltoncancun.com 426 units. A/C MINIBAR TV TEL. High-season standard rooms $300–$380 double; Beach Club rooms $380–$580 double; suite $480–$530. Low-season standard rooms $220–$300; Beach Club $300–$500; suite $400–$450. AE, DC, MC, V.

Grand, expansive, and fully equipped, this is a true resort in every sense of the word. If your motto is ""the bigger the better," then this is the place for you. The Hilton Cancun, which was formerly opened in 1994 as the Caesar Park Resort, changed to the Hilton in December 1999. It is situated on 250 acres of prime Cancún beachfront property with two restaurants, seven interconnected pools, an 18-hole par-72 golf course across the street, and a location that gives every room a sea view. Like the sprawling resort, rooms are grandly spacious and immaculately decorated in a minimalist style. Marble floors and bathrooms throughout are softened with area rugs and pale furnishings. All rooms have sea views and some have both sea and lagoon views. Other amenities in each luxurious room include robes, house shoes, hair dryers, and safe-deposit boxes. Suites have coffeemakers. Beach Club guests enjoy nightly cocktails and each Tuesday a manager's cocktail party on the patio. The elegant Beach Club rooms are set off from the main hotel in two- and three-story buildings (no elevators) and have their own check-in and concierge service. The hotel is especially appealing to golfers, as it's one of only two hotels in Cancun with an on-site course (the other is the Mélia, with an 18-hole executive course).

Important Note on Hotel Prices

Cancún's hotels, even in budget and moderately priced hotels, generally set their rates in dollars, so they are immune to any swings in the peso. Travel agents and wholesalers always have air/hotel packages available, and Sunday papers often advertise inventory-clearing packages at prices much lower than the rates listed here. There are also numerous all-inclusive properties in Cancún, which allow you to take a fixed-cost vacation, if this is what you're looking for. Note that the price quoted to you when you call a hotel's reservation number from the United States may not include Cancún's 12% tax. Prices can vary considerably at different times of the year, so it pays to consult a travel agent or shop around.

Isla Cancún (Zona Hotelera)

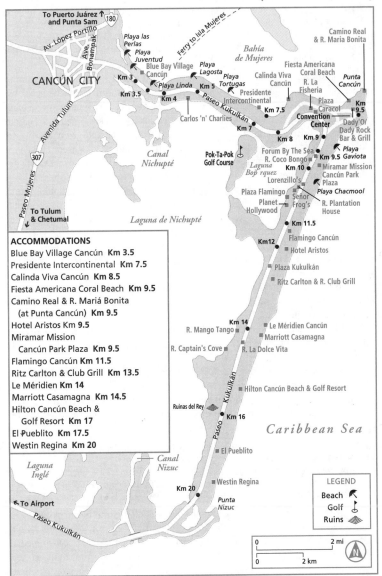

To Puerto Juárez ↑
and Punta Sam
180

Ferry to Isla Mujeres

Av. López Portillo

Ave. Bonampak

CANCÚN CITY

Avenida Tulum

307

Paseo Mujeres

To Tulum
& Chetumal

Playa las
Perlas
Playa
Juventud
Blue Bay Village
Cancún Km 3
Playa Linda
Km 3.5
Km 4
Carlos 'n' Charlies

Playa
Lagosta Km 5
Playa
Tortugas
Presidente
Intercontinental

Bahía
de Mujeres

Calinda Viva
Cancún

Fiesta Americana
Coral Beach
R. La
Fisheria

Camino Real
& R. Maria Bonita

Punta
Cancún

Plaza
Caracol Km
9.5
Convention
Center
Dady'O/
Dady Rock
Bar & Grill

Km 7.5
Km 7
Km 8 Km 9

Paseo Kukulkán

Canal
Nichupté

Pok-Ta-Pok
Golf Course

Laguna de Nichupté

Laguna
Nichupté
Bop rquez

Forum By The Sea
R. Coco Bongó
Lorenzillo's
Plaza Flamingo
Planet
Hollywood
Señor
Frog's

Playa
Gaviota Km 9.5
Miramar Mission
Cancún Park
Plaza
Playa Chacmool
R. Plantation
House
Km 10

Km 11.5

Km12
Flamingo Cancún
Hotel Aristos

Plaza Kukulkán

Ritz Carlton & R. Club Grill

Km 14
R. Mango Tango
R. Captain's Cove
R. La Dolce Vita
Le Méridien Cancún
Marriott Casamagna

Paseo Kukulkán

Hilton Cancún Beach & Golf Resort

Ruinas del Rey
Km 16

El Pueblito

Canal
Nizuc

Laguna
Inglé

To Airport

Paseo Kukulkán

Km 20
Westin Regina
Punta
Nizuc

Caribbean Sea

ACCOMMODATIONS

Blue Bay Village Cancún **Km 3.5**
Presidente Intercontinental **Km 7.5**
Calinda Viva Cancún **Km 8.5**
Fiesta Americana Coral Beach **Km 9.5**
Camino Real & R. Mariá Bonita
  (at Punta Cancún) **Km 9.5**
Hotel Aristos **Km 9.5**
Miramar Mission
  Cancún Park Plaza **Km 9.5**
Flamingo Cancún **Km 11.5**
Ritz Carlton & Club Grill **Km 13.5**
Le Méridien **Km 14**
Marriott Casamagna **Km 14.5**
Hilton Cancún Beach &
  Golf Resort **Km 17**
El Pueblito **Km 17.5**
Westin Regina **Km 20**

LEGEND
Beach
Golf
Ruins

0   2 mi
0   2 km
N

Dining: Spices Restaurant serves the cuisines of Mexico, Argentina, and Italy, while **Sirenita** offers selections of Japanese and seafood cuisine.

Amenities: 18-hole, par-72 golf course; seven interconnected swimming pools with a swim-up bar; two whirlpools; two lighted tennis courts; water-sports center; large fully equipped gym with daily aerobics; massage; sauna. A Kids Club is part of the gym program. Greens fee is $86 for 18 holes for guests and $106 for nonguests; carts cost $22. Laundry and room service, ice machine on each floor, concierge, tour desk, beauty salon, gift shop and boutiques, golf clinic, car rental.

Fiesta Americana Grand Coral Beach. Km 9.5 Paseo Kukulkán, 77500 Cancún, Q. Roo. ☎ **800/343-7821** in the U.S., or 9/881-3200. Fax 9/881-3263. E-mail: coralbus@cancun. rce.com.mx, bcenter1@fiestaamericana.com.mx. 602 units. A/C MINIBAR TV TEL. High season $328–$555 double, Club Floors $529–$650 double, Caribbean Suite $875. Low season $222–$424 double, Club Floors $381–$504 double, Caribbean Suite $695. AE, MC, V.

This sophisticated, spectacular hotel, which opened in 1991, has a lot to recommend it: perfect location, gracious service, grand public areas, and a full range of water sports, beach activities, and indoor tennis. It's enormous in a Mexican way and grandly European in its lavish halls and lobby. It's embellished with elegant dark-green granite from France, deep-red granite from South Africa, black-and-green marble from Guatemala, beige marble from Mexico, a canopy of stained glass from Guadalajara, and hardwood floors from Texas. The elegance seeps into the guestrooms, which are decorated with more marble, area rugs, and tasteful Mexican decorations. All rooms have balconies facing the ocean. Master suites are enormous, with double vanities, dressing room, bathrobes, whirlpool bathtubs, and large terraces; all rooms have hair dryers. Two concierge floors feature daily continental breakfast and evening cocktails, and a 24-hour reception-cashier. Two junior suites are equipped for guests with disabilities.

The hotel's great Punta Cancún location (opposite the convention center, and within walking distance of shopping centers and restaurants) has the advantage of facing the beach to the north, meaning the surf is calm and perfect for swimming. This is an ideal choice for any type of traveler who is looking to be at the heart of all that Cancún has to offer.

Dining/Diversions: The five-star **La Jolla** serves Mexican fare; the **Coral Reef** offers seafood and international cuisine; and there's a casual pool dining area. There are five bars.

Amenities: A 660-foot-long free-form swimming pool; swim-up bars; 1,000 feet of beach; three indoor tennis courts with stadium seating; gymnasium with weights, sauna, and massage; water-sport rentals on the beach; business center; tennis pro shop; fashion and spa boutiques; beauty and barber shops; laundry and room service; travel agency; car rental; massage.

✪ **Le Méridien Cancún.** Retorno del Rey Km 14, Zona Hotelera, 77500, Cancún, Q. Roo. ☎ **800/543-4300** in the U.S., or 9/881-2200. Fax 9/881-2201. www.meridencancun. com.mx, www.lemeridien-hotels.com. E-mail: reservaciones@meridiencancun.com.mx. 213 rooms. A/C, TV, TEL, MINIBAR. High season $290 standard, $450 suite. Low season $220 standard, $350 suite. Ask for special spa packages. AE, DC, MC, V. Free parking.

Of all of the luxury properties in Cancun, Le Méridien is the most inviting, with a refined yet welcoming sense of personal service. From the intimate lobby and reception area, to the most outstanding concierge service in Cancún, guests feel immediately pampered upon arrival. The hotel itself is smaller than others, and is more an elegant boutique hotel than an immense resort—a feeling those who are overstressed by activity at home are certain to welcome. The decor throughout the rooms and common areas is one of understated elegance, with cool color combinations of white and varying hues of Caribbean blue and golden tones, set off by rich wood accents. It's both classy and comforting, not overdone. Rooms are generous in size, and most have small balconies overlooking the pool, with a view to the ocean. There's a small sitting area, functional desk, and armoire that houses the satellite TV and minibar; plus a very large marble bath with separate tub and glassed-in shower. The hotel attracts many Europeans, as well as younger, sophisticated travelers, and is ideal for a second honeymoon or romantic break.

Certainly, a highlight of—or even a reason to book—a stay here is time spent at the Spa del Mar, one of Mexico's finest and most complete European spa facilities, with two levels and over 15,000 square feet of services dedicated your body and soul. A complete fitness center with extensive cardio and weight machines is found on the upper level. The Spa is located below, comprised of a health snack bar, full-service salon, and 14 treatment rooms, as well as separate men's and women's steam rooms, saunas, Jacuzzis, cold plunge pool, inhalation rooms, tranquility rooms, lockers, and changing areas.

You may need that health club if you fully enjoy the gourmet restaurant Cote Sud with its specialties based on Mediterranean and Provençal cuisines. The menu is simply delicious—not pretentious.

An added attraction is that Le Méridien welcomes the small pets of guests, with prior reservation.

Dining/Diversions: Two restaurants: Le St. Trop casual beachside dining, specializing in grilled foods, and Cote Sud, serving exquisite Mediterranean cuisine. The Lobby bar and lounge is a comfortable place for drinks, with comfy, oversized sofas and seating areas.

Amenities: Spa del Mar, a fully equipped European spa and fitness center. Three cascading swimming pools and a Jacuzzi lay between the Spa and beach, backed by two championship tennis courts. Cushioned lounges, shade umbrellas, a massage *palapa*, and water sports equipment are all available on the beach. A supervised children's program features the Penguin Clubhouse, play equipment, and wading pool. The business center offers Internet access, along with traditional business services.

✪ **Ritz-Carlton Hotel.** Retorno del Rey #36, off Km 13.5 Paseo Kukulkán, 77500 Cancún, Q. Roo. ☎ **800/241-3333** in the U.S. and Canada, or 9/885-0808. Fax 9/881-0815. E-mail: ritzbc@cancun.com.mx or mmaya@rc-cancun.com. www.ritzcarlton.com. 365 units. A/C MINIBAR TV TEL. High season $349–$475 double; $389–$850 Club floors, $499–$559 suites. Low season $189–$279 double; $295–$429 Club floors, $309–$409 suites. AE, MC, V. Free guarded parking.

On 7½ acres, the nine-story Ritz-Carlton has set the standard for excellence in Cancún and in Mexico. It is easily the island's most elegant hotel and a member of Leading Hotels of the World. The hotel has won countless recognition and accolades for its impeccable service and stunning decor of stained glass, marble, and lush carpets. Fresh flowers are placed throughout the property. It's the place to stay for those who want to feel pampered and indulged.

The spacious guest rooms are as sumptuous as the public areas. All rooms have safe-deposit boxes, electronic locks, and twice-daily maid service. Suites are large, and some have a private dressing area, two TVs, balconies, and 1½ bathrooms. In all rooms, marble bathrooms have telephones, separate tubs and showers, lighted makeup mirrors, scales, robes, and hair dryers. Floors 8 and 9 are for Ritz-Carlton Club members and offer guests special amenities, including five mini-meals a day, private butler service, and Hermés bath products. The hotel fronts a 1,200-foot white-sand beach, and all rooms overlook the ocean, pool, and tropical gardens. Special packages for golfing, spa, and weekend getaways are worth exploring.

Dining/Diversions: Of the five exceedingly stylish restaurants, **The Club Grill,** a fashionable English pub, is one of the best restaurants in the city (See "Where to Dine," below), offering grilled specialties, nightly entertainment, and a dance floor. The **Caribe Bar and Grill** is open for snacks during pool hours. The **Lobby Lounge** opens at 5pm daily offering tea and, later, live music between 7:30 and 11pm. This bar was the original home of proper tequila tastings, and features one of the world's most extensive menus of fine tequilas, plus Cuban cigars.

Amenities: On the beach, deluxe cabanas for two, with thickly cushioned lounges, are available just in front of the two connecting swimming pools (heated during the winter months), with Jacuzzis. For play, there are three lighted tennis courts and a fully equipped gym and spa with Universal weight training and cardiovascular equipment, personal trainers, steam, sauna, facial, and massage services. A Ritz Kids program offers supervised activities for children. Rounding out the offerings are a pharmacy/gift shop, exclusive shopping arcade, and beauty and barbershops. Laundry and dry cleaning, 24-hour room service, travel agency, and concierge are also available.

EXPENSIVE

✪ Camino Real Cancún. Av. Kukulkán, 77500 Punta Cancún (Apdo. Postal 14), Cancún, Q. Roo. ☎ **800/722-6466** in the U.S., or 9/883-0100. Fax 9/883-1730. E-mail: crcunin@mail. caribe.net.mx. www.caminoreal.com/cancun. 389 units. A/C MINIBAR TV TEL. High season standard $275 double, Camino Real Club $230–$320 double; $1,600 suite. Low season standard $195 double, Camino Real Club $230 double, $1,320 suite. AE, DC, MC, V. Daily fee for guarded parking adjacent to hotel.

On 4 acres right at the tip of Punta Cancún, the Camino Real is among the island's most appealing places to stay. The architecture is trademark Camino Real style—contemporary and sleek, with strategic angles. Rooms were recently remodeled in a rustic Mexican style, still elegantly outfitted with pink breccia-marble floors, and pleasing, bright colors. Some rooms in the new 18-story Camino Real Club have an elegant Mexican decor, while standard rooms in this section are much like rooms in the rest of the resort. Master suites have expansive views, large dining tables for four, and hot tubs on the balconies. Camino Real Club guests receive a complimentary full breakfast daily in the Beach Club lobby, as well as complimentary cocktails and snacks there each evening. Lower priced rooms have lagoon views. While the setting is sophisticated, the hotel is also very welcoming to children, as it is a favored name within Mexico, where vacations are synonymous with family.

Dining/Diversions: Three restaurants include a seafood-specialties restaurant; indoor casual dining with flame-broiled meat; and an elegant evening-only restaurant featuring Mexican cuisine. The more casual restaurant features a children's menu. There's an Italian night on Wednesday and a Mexican Grill Party on Friday. The lobby bar features Mexican music nightly from 5:30 to 7:30pm, and the sea-view **Azucar Disco** swings into action Monday through Saturday at 9:30pm.

Amenities: Freshwater pool, private saltwater lagoon with sea turtles and tropical fish, private beach, sailing pier, water-sports center. There are also three lighted tennis courts, beach volleyball, boutiques, gift shops, barber and beauty shops, state-of-the-art fitness center with steam bath, laundry and room service, travel agency, car rental, in-room safe-deposit boxes, baby-sitting (with advance notice), medical service, 24-hour room service, and massages.

Marriott Casamagna. Km 14.5 Paseo Kukulkán, 77500 Cancún, Q. Roo. ☎ **800/228-9290** in the U.S., or 9/881-2000. Fax 9/881-2071. E-mail: cancunmarriott@infosel.net.mx. www.marriott.com. 450 units. A/C MINIBAR TV TEL. High season $225–$254 double; $350 suite. Low season $139–$160 double; $300 suite. Ask about available packages. AE, CB, MC, V.

This is quintessential Marriott—those who are familiar with the chain's standards will feel at home here and appreciate the hotel's attention to detailed service. Entering through a half-circle of Roman columns, you pass through a domed foyer to a wide, lavishly marbled 44-foot-high lobby filled with plants and shallow pools. Guest rooms have contemporary furnishings, tiled floors, and ceiling fans; most have balconies. All suites occupy corners and have enormous terraces, ocean views, and TVs in both the living room and the bedroom. All rooms are very well maintained, and are equipped with safe deposit boxes and hair dryers. The hotel caters to family travelers with specially priced packages (up to two children can stay free with parents), and the Club Amigos supervised children's program. Look for a more deluxe offering from Marriott, the 450-room luxury **JW Cancun,** to open on the beach next to the CasaMagna in mid-2000. Its hallmark promises to a 20,000-square-foot Spa and Fitness Center.

Dining/Diversions: The hotel has five restaurants: La Capilla overlooks the pool and ocean and features an international menu; La Isla serves light snacks and beverages poolside; the Bahia Club offers the same fare, only served on the beach; the recently remodeled Mikado offers Japanese and Thai cuisine; and Champions' serves American-style food accompanied by televised sports. The lobby bar features nightly Mariachi music.

Amenities: Beach; swimming pool; two lighted tennis courts; health club with saunas, whirlpool, aerobics, and juice bar; beauty and barber shop; massage and facials available; laundry and room service; travel agency; car rental.

Presidente Inter-Continental Cancún. Km 7.5 Av. Kukulkán, 77500 Cancún, Q. Roo. ☎ **800/327-0200** in the U.S., or 9/883-0200. Fax 9/883-2515. E-mail: cunhc@interconti. com. www.interconti.com. 99 units. A/C TV TEL. High season $240–$300 double. Low season $190–$230 double. AE, MC, V. Ask about special promotional packages.

On the island's best beach facing the placid Bahía de Mujeres, the Presidente's location is reason enough to stay here, and it's just a 2-minute walk to Cancun's championship Pok-Ta-Pok Golf Club. Cool and spacious, the Presidente sports a postmodern design with lavish marble and wicker accents and a strong use of color. Guests have a choice of two double beds or one king-size bed. All rooms have tastefully simple unfinished pine furniture and in-room safes. Sixteen rooms on the first floor have patios with outdoor whirlpool tubs. The club floors offer private balconies, robes, magnified makeup mirrors, complimentary continental breakfast, evening drinks and canapés, 1 hour free use of the tennis court, complimentary use of the fitness club, and use of a private key-activated elevator. Two rooms are available for guests with disabilities and two floors are reserved for nonsmokers. The expansive pool has a pyramid-shaped waterfall, and is surrounded by cushioned lounge chairs. Coming from Cancún City, you'll reach the Presidente on the left side of the street before you get to Punta Cancún. For it's ambiance, I feel the Presidente is an ideal choice for a romantic getaway, or for couples who enjoy indulging in the sports of golf, tennis, or shopping.

Dining: The fine-dining Mediterraneo restaurant features foods from France, Greece, Italy, Spain, and Morocco. El Caribeño, a three-level *palapa* restaurant by the beach and pool, serves all meals, but specializes in seafood. Frutas y Flores is an informal coffee shop. Room service is available 24 hours, and complimentary coffee is served with your wake-up call.

Amenities: Two landscaped swimming pools with a waterfall, whirlpools, fitness center, a great beach fronting the calm Bahía de Mujeres, lighted tennis courts, water-sports equipment rental, marina, laundry and room service, travel agency, car rental.

✪ **Westin Regina Cancún.** Km 20 Paseo Kukulkán, 77500 Cancún, Q. Roo. ☎ **800/ 228-3000** in the U.S., or 9/885-0086. Fax 9/885-0296. Tel 800/524-5405 inside Mexico. www.westin.com. E-mail: westin@sybcom.com. 293 units. A/C MINIBAR TV TEL. High season $285–$450 double. Low season $180–$299 double. AE, MC, V, DC.

The strikingly austere but grand and beautiful architecture, impressive with its elegant use of stone and marble, is the stamp of leading Latin American architect Ricardo Legorreta. The hotel is divided into two sections, the main hotel and the more exclusive six-story hot-pink tower section. Standard rooms are unusually large and beautifully furnished with cool, contemporary furniture. Those on the sixth floor have balconies, and first-floor rooms have terraces. Rooms in the tower all have ocean or lagoon views, extensive use of marble, furniture with Olinalá lacquer accents, Berber carpet area rugs, oak tables and chairs, and terraces with lounge chairs. It's important to note that this hotel is a 15- to 20-minute ride from the "action" strip that lies between the Plaza Flamingo and Punta Cancún, so it's a better choice for those who want to relish a little more seclusion than Cancún typically offers. However, it is easy to join the action when so inclined—buses stop in front and taxis are readily available.

Dining/Diversions: There are two restaurants—**Arrecifes** for elegant dining on seafood and Italian cuisine, and **El Palmar** for casual dining—and two bars.

Amenities: Five swimming pools; three whirlpools; beach; two lighted tennis courts; gymnasium with Stairmaster, bicycle, weights, aerobics, sauna, steam, and massage; pharmacy/gifts; boutiques; beauty and barber shop; laundry and room service; baby-sitting; concierge; travel agency; car rental; purified tap water; and ice machine on each floor.

MODERATE

✪ **Blue Bay Getaway Cancún.** Km 3.5 Paseo Kukulkán, 77500 Cancún, Q. Roo. ☎ **800/ BLUE-BAY** in the U.S., or 9/883-0344. Fax 9/883-0904. www.bluebayresorts.com. E-mail: cancun@bluebayresorts.com or bbayreservas@infosel.net.mx. 216 units. A/C TV TEL. High season $280 double. Low season $180 double. Rates are all-inclusive (room, food, beverages, and activities). AE, MC, V. Free parking.

Blue Bay Getaway Cancún is a spirited yet relaxing all-inclusive resort for adults only, and favored by young adults. Surrounded by acres of tropical gardens, it's ideally located at the northern end of the Hotel Zone close to the major shopping plazas, restaurants, and nightlife, with a terrific beach with calm waters for swimming. Comfortable, clean, and modern, guests have a choice of rooms in two sections: the central building features 72 rooms decorated in rustic wood, the main lobby, administrative offices, restaurants, and Tequila Sunrise bar. The remaining nine buildings offer guests 148 rooms, featuring a colorful Mexican decor with lagoon, garden, and ocean views available. Nonsmoking rooms and wheelchair-accessible rooms are available upon request. All rooms feature satellite TV, private bathrooms with showers, and direct-dial phone. Safe-deposit boxes are available for an extra charge, as is dry-cleaning and laundry service. Blue Bay allows guests to use the amenities and facilities at their sister resort, the Blue Bay Club and Marina (a resort for families), located just outside of Ciudad Cancún, near the ferry to Isla Mujeres. There's a free bus and boat shuttle service provided between both Blue Bay resorts.

Keeping guests active is the obvious objective here, with two swimming pools, four Jacuzzis, windsurfing, kayaks, catamarans, boogie boards, complimentary snorkeling and scuba lessons in the swimming pool, a marina, an exercise room with daily aerobics classes, tennis court, bicycles, and a game room with pool and Ping-Pong tables.

All meals and drinks are included with the room price, served at one of four restaurants. Among them, **El Embarcadero** is an ocean-view restaurant serving buffet-style international cuisine. **La Lagarta** features natural, healthful breakfasts and a "snack bar" menu during the day, then an à la carte Italian menu for dinner. Its four bars include a video bar and disco. In addition, there are theme-night dinners, nightly shows, and live entertainment in its outdoor theater with capacity for 150 guests.

Calinda Viva Cancún. Km 8.5 Paseo Kukulkán, 77500 Cancún, Q. Roo. ☎ **800/221-2222** in the U.S., or 9/883-0800. Fax: 9/883-2087. 216 units. A/C TV TEL. High season $145–$250 double. Low season $138–$158 double. AE, MC, V. Free parking.

From the street, this hotel looks like a blockhouse, but on the ocean side you'll find a small but pretty patio garden and Cancún's best beach for safe swimming. Its location is ideal, close to all the shops and restaurants clustered near Punta Cancún and the Convention Center. You have a choice of rooms with either lagoon or ocean views. The rooms are large and undistinguished in decor, but comfortable, with marble floors and either two double beds or a king-size bed. Several studios with kitchenette are available upon request. Facilities include one swimming pool for adults and one for children, two lighted tennis courts, water-sports equipment rental, and a marina. The main restaurant is open for all meals. Two others, both beside the pool, serve drinks and light meals. They're joined by three bars. This hotel also offers non-smoking areas and wheelchair access.

El Pueblito. Km 17.5 Paseo Kukulkán, 77500 Cancún, Q. Roo. ☎ **9/885-0422** or 9/885-0797. Fax 9/885-2066. E-mail: pueblitoreservations@acnet.net. 340 units. A/C TV TEL. High season $280 double, all-inclusive. Low season $240 double, all-inclusive. AE, MC, V. Free parking.

Consistent renovations and upgrades and a changeover to an all-inclusive concept has made this hotel more appealing than ever, an another exceptional all-inclusive value. Dwarfed by its ostentatious neighbors, the El Pueblito lobby resembles a traditional Mexican hacienda, with several three-story buildings (no elevators) terraced in a V-shape down a gentle hillside toward the sea. A meandering swimming pool with waterfalls runs between the two series of buildings. Rooms are very large in size, and have all been repainted and restyled with modern rattan furnishings, travertine marble floors, and large bathrooms. An additional 100 rooms were just added this year. All have either a balcony or terrace, facing the pool or sea. Three restaurants and two bars, plus a lobby cafe are on the grounds, serving a constant flow of buffet-style meals and snacks. There's also the choice of a nightly theme party, complete with entertainment. Adult activities include aerobics, cooking classes, tennis, volleyball, and non-motorized water sports. Minigolf and a water slide, plus a full program of kid's activities, make this an ideal place for families with children. Baby-sitting services are also available for $10 per hour. The hotel is located towards the southern end of the island past the Hilton Resort.

✪ **Flamingo Cancún.** Km 11.5 Bvld. Kukulkán, 77500 Cancún, Q. Roo. ☎ **9/883-1544.** Fax 9/883-1029. www.mexicoweb.com/flamingo. E-mail flamicun@grool.prodigy.net.mx. 221 units. A/C TV TEL. High season $170 double. Low season $120 double. AE, MC, V. Free, unguarded parking across the street in the Plaza Flamingos.

The Flamingo seems to have been inspired by the dramatic, slope-sided architecture of the Camino Real, but it's considerably smaller—and less expensive. The clean, comfortable, and modern guest rooms have minibars and balconies. Guest room entrances border a courtyard facing the interior swimming pools and *palapa* pool bar—a second pool with a sundeck overlooks the ocean. A colorful open-air restaurant faces the courtyard pool, plus there's another beach restaurant, Albatros. Dive and snorkeling gear are available for rent at their marina, and there's a new, small gym. The Flamingo is in the heart of the island hotel district, opposite the Flamingo Shopping Center and close to other hotels, shopping centers, and restaurants. The two restaurants and snack bar are open daily, and a lobby bar and pool bar offer libations. Live music is performed nightly in the lobby bar. It's a friendly, accommodating choice for families.

Miramar Misión Cancún Park Plaza. Km 9.5 Av. Kukulkán, 77500 Zona Hotelera Cancún, Q. Roo. ☎ **800/215-1333** in the U.S., or 9/883-1755. Fax 9/883-1136. www.misionpark. com.mx. E-mail: miramar@sybcom.com. 266 units. A/C MINIBAR TV TEL. High season $250. Low season $190 double. AE, MC, V.

Each of the ingeniously designed rooms has partial views of the lagoon and ocean. Public spaces throughout the hotel have lots of dark wood, cream-beige stucco, red tile, and pastel accents. There's a large, rectangular swimming pool that extends through the hotel and down to the beach, with built-in, submerged sun-chairs. There's also a newly added oversized Jacuzzi (the largest in Cancun!), sundeck, and snack bar on the 7th floor roof. Rooms are on the small side but bright and comfortable, with a small balcony, bamboo furniture, and tropical-colored bedspreads; bathrooms have polished limestone vanities. In-room amenities include hair dryers and safe-deposit boxes.

Three restaurants serve Mexican and international cuisine. There's live music nightly in the lobby bar, and a bar by the pool serves guests during pool hours. A nightclub, Batacha, also has live music for dancing from 9pm to 4am Tuesday through Sunday.

INEXPENSIVE

Hotel Aristos. Km 12 ave. Kukulkán, 77500 Cancun Q. Roo. ☎ **800/527-4786** in the U.S., or 9/883-0011. E-mail: aristos@cancun.com.mx. 245 units. A/C TV TEL. High season $120 double. Low season $100 double. All-inclusive option for 3 meals and drinks, add $36 daily. AE, MC, V. Free, unguarded parking.

This was one of the island's first hotels, and continues to welcome repeat guests, especially European and senior travelers. Rooms are in the process of all being remodeled, with upgraded wood furnishings and decor. Though small, they are very clean and cool, with red-tile floors and small balconies. All rooms face either the Caribbean or the *paseo* and lagoon; the best views (and no noise from the *paseo*) face the Caribbean side. The hotel has one restaurant and several bars, and offers room and laundry service, cable TV, a travel agency, and baby-sitting service. The central pool overlooks the ocean with a wide stretch of beach one level below the pool and lobby. A new *palapa* section adjoining the pool is being added. You'll also find a marina with watersports equipment and two lighted tennis courts. Beware of spring break here, when the hotel rocks with loud music poolside all day. They do, however, wisely separate the spring-breakers into their own section of the hotel, facing the Paseo, and reserve the beach-facing rooms for other guests.

CANCÚN CITY
MODERATE

✪ **Holiday Inn Cancún.** Av. Nader #1, SM2, Centro,77500, Cancún, Q. Roo. ☎ **9/ 887-4455.** Fax 9/884-7954. www.iminet.com/mexico/200e5.html. E-mail: hic@mail. sybcom.com. 248 units. A/C, TV, TEL. High season $125 standard, $140 Jr. suite. Low season $105 standard, $126 Jr. suite. AE, MC, V.

This is the nicest hotel in downtown Cancún, and one of the very best values in the area. Resembling a Mexican Hacienda, rooms are set off from a large rotunda-style lobby, lush gardens, and a pleasant pool area. This hotel offers all the expected comforts of a chain like Holiday Inn, yet in an atmosphere that is decidedly Mexican in its hospitality. Rooms have views of the garden, the pool, or the street, and feature a small sitting area and balcony. All rooms have Talavera tile inlays and brightly colored fabric accents, along with in-room safe, electric coffee maker, hair dryer, iron, and ironing board. Bathrooms have a combination tub and shower. There are two restaurants: El Patio, by the pool, opens only for breakfast, while El Granero serves breakfast, lunch, and dinner. There's also a lively lobby bar. The ample-sized pool has an adjoining bar and separate wading area for children. For the more active, there's a small gym with a sauna and tennis courts. Additional on-site services include a travel agency, beauty shop, car rental, and tobacco and gift shop. Guests of the Holiday Inn may enjoy the facilities of the Melía Cancún Beach Club, with complimentary shuttle service. The hotel is located right behind the State Government building, in walking distance to downtown Cancun dining and shopping.

INEXPENSIVE

Hotel Antillano. Ave. Claveles 1 (corner with Ave. Tulum), 77500 Cancún, Q. Roo. ☎ **9/884-1532.** Fax 9/884-1878. www.hotelantillano.com. E-mail: antillano@mpsnet. com.mx. 48 units. A/C TV TEL. High season $60 double. Low season $52 double. AE, MC, V.

A quiet and very clean choice, Hotel Antillano is close to the Ciudad Cancún bus terminal. Rooms overlook either avenida Tulum, the side streets, or the interior lawn and pool, with the latter being the most desirable since they are quieter. Each room has coordinated furnishings, one or two double beds, a sink area separate from the bathroom, red-tile floors, and a small TV. There's a small bar to one side of the reception area and a travel agency in the lobby. The hotel offers guests use of its beach club on the island. Baby-sitting can be arranged. To find it from Tulum, walk west on Claveles a half block; it's opposite the Restaurant Rosa Mexicana. Parking is on the street.

✪ **Hotel Hacienda Cancún.** Sunyaxchen 39-40, 77500 Cancún, Q. Roo. ☎ **9/884-3672.** Fax 9/884-1208. E-mail: hhda@cancun.com.mx. 35 units. A/C TV TEL. High season $45 double. Low season $38 double. MC, V.

This extremely pleasing little hotel is a great value. The facade has been remodeled to look like a hacienda, and all rooms were refurbished in 1998, with new floors and rustic, Mexican furnishings. The guest rooms are clean and very comfortable; all have two double beds and windows (but no views), and safe-deposit boxes. There's a nice small pool and cafe under a shaded *palapa* in the back. To find it from avenida Yaxchilán, turn west on Sunyaxchen; it's on your right next to the Hotel Caribe International, opposite 100% Natural. Parking is on the street.

✪ **Hotel Margaritas.** Av. Yaxchilán #41, SM22, Centro, 77500, Cancún, Q. Roo. ☎ **9/884-9333** or 01800/711-1531. Fax 9/884-1324. 100 rooms. A/C, TV, TEL. High season $65 double. Low season $45 double. AE, MC, V.

Located in downtown Cancún, this four-story hotel with elevator is comfortable and unpretentious, offering one of the best values in Cancún. Rooms have white tile floors, are exceptionally clean and bright, pleasantly decorated, and each has a small balcony. There are soft-drink vending machines in each floor. There is an attractive pool surrounded by lounge chairs, with a wading section for children. Adjacent to the peach marble lobby lies an al fresco dining area and restaurant that serves breakfast, lunch, and dinner. Specialties are Mexican food and pizzas baked in a wood oven, and room service is also available. The hotel offers laundry service, money exchange, and complimentary safety deposit boxes. Special services include medical service, gift shop, travel agency, baby-sitters, and meeting rooms.

Hotel Parador. Av. Tulum 26, 77500 Cancún, Q. Roo. ☎ **9/884-1043** or 9/884-1310. Fax 9/884-9712. 66 units. A/C TV TEL. High season $52 double. Low season $38 double. Ask about promotional rates. MC, V.

One of the most popular downtown hotels, the three-story Parador is conveniently located. Guestrooms are arranged around two long, narrow garden courtyards leading back to a pool (with separate children's pool) and grassy sunning area. The rooms are modern, each with two double beds, a shower, and cable TV. Help yourself to bottled drinking water in the hall. There's a restaurant/bar, and it's next to Pop's restaurant, almost at the corner of Uxmal. Street parking is limited.

Mexhotel Centro. Yaxchilán 31, SM 22, Cancún, Q. Roo.77500 ☎ **9/884-3078.** Fax 884-3478 in the U.S. or 9/884-3478. 80 units. A/C TV TEL. High season $80 double. Low season $48 double. AE, MC, V.

The Mexhotel Centro has the warmth and style of a small hacienda when entering from the back; on the street side, it's been incorporated into a small shopping mall. The three stories of rooms (with elevator) front a lovely palm-shaded pool area with comfortable tables and chairs and a restaurant. Standard rooms are extra clean with muted decor, two double beds framed with wrought-iron headboards, large tile bathrooms with separate sinks, desks, and over-bed reading lights. Although prices may seem high for the location, privileges at the beach and pool facilities at its sister resort in the Hotel Zone make it a great bargain (there's an extra charge for transportation, but it's close to the bus route). The hotel is between Jazmines and Gladiolas, kitty-corner from Périco's.

Suites El Patio. Av. Bonampak #51 and Cereza, SM2A, Centro, 775000, Cancún, Q. Roo. ☎ **9/884-3500.** Fax 9/884-3540. www.cancun-suites.com. E-mail: cancun@cancun-suites. com. 18 units. A/C, FAN. $50 double. Ask for discounts for longer stays. AE, V, MC.

Many of the guests at this small hotel stay for up to a month, for the combination of its excellent value and warm hospitality. This European-style guesthouse caters to those travelers looking for more of the area's culture. You won't find any bars, pools, or loud parties in this place; what you will find is excellent service and impeccable accommodations. Rooms face the plant-filled interior courtyard, dotted with groupings of wrought iron chairs and tables. Each room has a slightly different decor and set of amenities, but all have white tile floors and rustic wood furnishings in their various configurations. All rooms have in-room safety boxes and ceiling fans, and non-smoking rooms are available. Some have light kitchenette facilities, and there's also a common kitchen area with purified water and a cooler for stocking your own supplies. There is a public phone in the entranceway, and if you request it they can arrange for a cellular phone in your room. A small restaurant serves breakfast and dinner, and a game and TV room has a large screen cable TV, library stocked with books on Mexican culture, backgammon, cards, and board games. It offers special packages with lodging and Spanish lessons, and discounts for longer stays.

3 Where to Dine

The restaurant scene in Cancún is dominated by U.S.-based franchise chains—which really need no introduction. These include Hard Rock Cafe, Planet Hollywood, Rainforest Cafe, Tony Roma's, TGI Fridays, Ruth's Chris Steak House, and the gamut of fast-food burger places. The restaurants listed here are either locally owned, one-of-a-kind restaurants, or exceptional selections at area hotels, many with live music as an accompaniment to the dining experience.

One unique way to combine dinner with sightseeing is aboard the **Lobster Dinner Cruise** (☎ **9/883-1488,** 9/883-3268). Cruising around the tranquil, turquoise waters of the lagoon, passengers feast on lobster dinners accompanied by wine. Cost is $64.50 per person, and the cruise departs daily from the Royal Yacht Club & Marina. There are two departures: the sunset dinner cruise leaves at 4pm during winter months, 5pm during the summer; while the moonlight cruise leaves at 7:30pm during the winter, and 8:30pm during the summer.

CANCÚN ISLAND
VERY EXPENSIVE

✪ **Club Grill.** Ritz-Carlton Hotel, Km 13.5 Paseo Kukulkán. ☎ **9/885-0808.** Reservations required. Main courses $11–$40. AE, DC, MC, V. Tues–Sun 7–11pm. INTERNATIONAL.

Cancún's most elegant and stylish restaurant is also its most delicious. Even rival restaurateurs give it an envious thumbs up. The gracious service starts as you enter the anteroom with its comfortable couches and chairs and selection of fine tequilas and Cuban cigars. It continues into the candlelit dining room with padded side chairs and tables shimmering with silver and crystal. Under the trained eye of chef de cuisine John Patrick Gray, elegant plates of peppered scallops, truffles, and potatoes in tequila sauce, grilled lamb, or mixed grill arrive without feeling rushed after the appetizer. The restaurant has both smoking and nonsmoking sections (a rarity in Mexico). A band plays romantic music for dancing from 8pm on. This is the place for that truly special night out. A dress code is enforced: no sandals or tennis shoes, and gentlemen must wear long pants.

The Plantation House. Km10.5 Paseo Kukulkán, Zona Hotelera, 77500, Cancún, Q. Roo. ☎ **9/885-1455**, 9/883-1433, or 9/883-2120. Reservations recommended. Soups $6–$12. Main courses $13–$35. AE, MC, V. Daily 5pm–12:30am. CARIBBEAN/FRENCH.

This casually elegant, pale yellow and blue clapboard restaurant overlooking Nichupté lagoon takes you back to the time when the Caribbean first became infused with European tastes and culinary talents. The decor combines island-style colonial charm with elegant touches of precious woods, fines crystal, sterling silver cutlery, and porcelain dinnerware. For starters, try their signature tartar of poached shrimp with lemon juice and olive oil, or a creamy crabmeat soup. Move on to the main event, which may consist of classic Veal Wellington in a puff pastry with duck paté, fish fillet crusted in spices and herbs and topped with a vanilla sauce, or lobster medallions in a mango sauce. An outstanding wine list and piano music make this restaurant ideal for a memorable dinner.

EXPENSIVE

Captain's Cove. Km 15 Paseo Kukulkán. ☎ **9/885-0016.** Main courses $16–$20; breakfast buffet $7.95. AE, MC, V. Daily 7am–11pm. INTERNATIONAL/SEAFOOD.

Though it sits almost at the end of Paseo Kukulkán, far from everything, the Captain's Cove continues to pack customers into its several dining levels. Diners face big open windows overlooking the lagoon and Royal Yacht Club Marina. For breakfast there's an all-you-can-eat buffet. Main courses of steak and seafood are the norm at lunch and dinner, and there's a menu catering especially to children. For dessert there are flaming coffees, crêpes, and key lime pie. The restaurant is on the lagoon side opposite the Omni Hotel.

✪ **La Dolce Vita.** Km 14.6 Paseo Kukulkán. ☎ **9/885-0150** or 9/885-0161. Fax 9/85-05-90. www.cancun.com/dining/dolce. E-mail: dolcevita@sybcom.com. Reservations required for dinner. Main courses $9–$29. AE, MC, V. Daily noon–midnight. ITALIAN/SEAFOOD.

Prepare to dine on some the best Italian food in Mexico here. Now at its new location on the lagoon, and opposite the Marriott Casamagna, the casually elegant La Dolce Vita is even more pleasant and popular than its old garden location downtown, with a choice of dining in air-conditioned comfort, or on an open-air terrace with a view of the lagoon. Appetizers include pâté of quail liver and carpaccio in vinaigrette, or mushrooms provençcal. They specialize in homemade pastas combined with fresh seafood. You can order green tagliolini with lobster medallions, linguine with clams or seafood, or rigatoni Mexican-style (with chorizo, mushrooms, and chives) as a main course, or as an appetizer for half-price. Other main courses include veal with morels, fresh salmon with cream sauce, spinach linguini with medallions of lobster and shrimp in a white wine sauce, and fresh fish served in a variety of sauces. New choices include vegetarian lasagna and grilled, whole lobster. Dinner is accompanied by live jazz from 7pm to 11:30pm, Mondays through Saturdays.

La Fisheria. Plaza Caracol, Shopping Center 2nd floor, ☎ **9/883-1395.** Main courses $6.50–$21. AE, MC, V. Daily 11am–12am. SEAFOOD.

Patrons find a lot to choose from at this restaurant overlooking boulevard Kukulkán and the lagoon. The expansive menu includes shark fingers with a jalapeño dip, grouper fillet stuffed with seafood in a lobster sauce, Acapulco-style *ceviche* (in a tomato sauce), New England clam chowder, steamed mussels, grilled red snapper with pasta—you get the idea. The menu changes daily, but there's always *tikin xik,* that great Yucatecan grilled fish marinated in *achiote* sauce. And for those not inclined toward seafood, a wood-burning oven pizza might do, or perhaps one of the grilled chicken or beef dishes. A non-smoking section has just been added.

✪ **Lorenzillo's.** Km 10.5 Paseo Kukulkán. ☎ **9/883-1254.** www.lorenzillos.com. E-mail: lorenzillos@mail.sybcom.com. Main courses $8–$50. Reservations recommended. AE, MC, V. Daily 12:00pm–11:30pm. SEAFOOD. Free parking.

Live lobster is the overwhelming favorite here, and part of the appeal is selecting your "dinner" out of the giant lobster tank. Lorenzillo's sits on the lagoon under a giant *palapa* roof. A dock leads down to the main dining area, and when that's packed (which is often), a wharf-side bar handles the overflow. In addition to lobster—which comes grilled, steamed, or stuffed—good bets are the shrimp stuffed with cheese and wrapped in bacon, the Admiral's fillet coated in toasted almonds and a light mustard sauce, or the seafood-stuffed squid. Desserts include the tempting Martinique: Belgian chocolate with hazelnuts, almonds, and pecans, served with vanilla ice cream. There's a festive, friendly atmosphere, and children are very welcome. A personal favorite, I never miss a lobster stop here when I'm in Cancun.

Mango Tango. Km 14.2 Paseo Kukulkán, opposite the Ritz-Carlton. ☎ **9/885-0303.** Main courses $10–$16; dinner show $35–$38. Reservations recommended. AE, MC, V. Daily 2pm–2am. INTERNATIONAL.

Mango Tango's made a name for itself with its sizzling floor shows and live reggae music(see "Cancún After Dark," below), but its kitchen is deserving of attention as well. Try the peel-your-own shrimp, Argentine-style grilled meat with chimichurri sauce, and other grilled specialties. The Mango Tango Salad has shrimp, chicken, avocado, red onion, tomato, and mushrooms served on mango slices. Entrees include Mango Tango rice with seafood and fried bananas. The Creole gumbo comes with lobster, shrimp, and squid, and a new coconut and mango cake is a deserving finish to the meal. The beauty of dining here is that you can stay and enjoy one of the currently hot night spots in Cancún.

✪ **María Bonita.** Hotel Camino Real, Punta Cancún. ☎ **9/883-0100,** ext. 8060 or 8061. Main courses $25–$31. Reservations recommended. AE, DC, MC, V. Daily 6:30–11:45pm. REGIONAL/MEXICAN/NOUVELLE MEXICAN.

Enjoy Mexico at its very best—its music, food, and atmosphere—in a stylish setting that captures the essence of the country. Overlooking the water, the interior is divided by cuisine—**La Cantina Jalisco** includes an open, colorful Mexican kitchen (with pots and pans on the wall) and tequila bar (with more than 50 different tequilas); the **Salón Michoacán** in the center features that state's cuisine; and the **Patio Oaxaca** on the lower level offers Oaxacan fare. The menu also includes the best of Mexico's other cuisines, as excellently prepared as you'll find them anywhere, with a few international dishes thrown in for variety. While you dine, you'll be serenaded by trios, marimba music, jarocho, and the ever-enchanting mariachis. The different peppers used in sauces and preparation are explained on the front of the menu, and each dish is marked for its heat quotient (from zero to two chiles). A nice starter is the Mitla salad, which has Oaxaca cheese slices (the state is known for its excellent cheese) dribbled with a little olive oil and a coriander dressing. The stuffed chile "La Doña"—a poblano pepper (mildly hot) filled with lobster and *huitlacoche,* in a cream sauce—comes as either an appetizer or a main course and is wonderful. The restaurant is to the left of the hotel entrance and is entered from the street.

Savio's. Plaza Caracol. ☎/fax **9/883-2085.** Main courses $8.25–$20. AE, MC, V. Daily 10am–midnight. ITALIAN.

Savio's, in stylish black and white with tile floors and green marble-topped tables, is on two levels, and faces Paseo Kukulkán through two stories of awning-shaded windows. Its bar is always crowded with patrons sipping everything from cappuccino to imported beer. Repeat diners look forward to large fresh salads and richly flavored, subtly herbed Italian dishes. The ravioli stuffed with ricotta and spinach is served in a delicious tomato sauce.

CANCÚN CITY
EXPENSIVE

La Habichuela. Margaritas 25. ☎ **9/884-3158.** kukulcan@qroo1.telmex.net.mx. Reservations recommended in high season. Main courses $10–$32. AE, MC, V. Daily 12pm–midnight. GOURMET SEAFOOD/CARIBBEAN/MEXICAN. Free parking.

In a garden setting with tables covered in pink-and-white linens and soft music playing in the background, this restaurant is ideal for a romantic evening. For an all-out culinary adventure, try *habichuela* (string bean) soup; shrimp in any number of sauces including Jamaican *tamarindo,* tequila, and a ginger and mushroom combination; and the Maya coffee with *xtabentun* (a strong, sweet, anise-based liquor). The grilled seafood and steaks are excellent as well, but this is a good place to try a Mexican specialty such as enchiladas Suizas or *tampiqueña*–style (thinly sliced, marinated, and grilled) beef. For something totally divine, try the "Cocobichuela," which is lobster and shrimp in a curry sauce served in a coconut shell and topped with fruit.

✪ **Perico's.** Yaxchilán 61. ☎ **9/884-3152.** Main courses $9–$20. AE, MC, V. Daily 1pm–1am. MEXICAN/SEAFOOD/STEAKS.

Perico's has colorful murals that almost dance off the walls, a bar area overhung with baskets and saddles for bar stools, colorfully bedecked leather tables and chairs, and accommodating waiters; it's always booming and festive. The extensive menu offers well-prepared steak, seafood, and traditional Mexican dishes for moderate rates (except lobster). This is a place not only to eat and drink but to let loose and join in the fun, so don't be surprised if everybody drops their forks and dons huge Mexican sombreros to shimmy and snake in a conga dance around the dining room. It's fun whether or not you join in, but definitely not the place for that romantic evening alone. There's marimba music from 7:30 to 9:30pm, and mariachis from 9:30pm to midnight. This is a popular spot, so expect a crowd.

MODERATE

✪ **Restaurant El Pescador.** Tulipanes 28, off Av. Tulum. ☎ **9/884-2673.** Fax 9/884-3639. Main courses $9–$50; Mexican plates $5–$9. AE, MC, V. Daily 11am–11pm. SEAFOOD.

Locals all seem to agree, this is the best spot for fresh seafood in Cancún. There's often a line at this restaurant, which serves well-prepared fresh seafood in its street-side patio and upstairs venue overlooking Tulipanes. Feast on shrimp cocktail, conch, octopus, Creole-style shrimp (*camarones à la criolla*), charcoal-broiled lobster, and stone crabs. *Zarzuela* is a combination seafood plate cooked in white wine and garlic. There's a

Mexican specialty menu as well. Another branch, **La Mesa del Pescador,** is in the Plaza Kukulkán on Cancún Island and is open the same hours, but is more expensive.

Restaurant Rosa Mexicano. Claveles 4. ☎ **9/884-6313.** Fax 9/884-2371. Reservations recommended for parties of 6 or more. Main courses $6–$12; lobster $25. AE, MC, V. Daily 5–11pm. MEXICAN HAUTE.

This beautiful little place has candlelit tables and a plant-filled patio in back, and it's almost always packed. Colorful paper banners and piñatas hang from the ceiling, efficient waiters wear bow ties and cummerbunds color-themed to the Mexican flag, and a trio plays romantic Mexican music nightly. The menu features "refined" Mexican specialties. Try the *pollo almendro,* which is chicken covered in a cream sauce sprinkled with ground almonds, or the pork baked in a banana leaf with a sauce of oranges, lime, chile ancho, and garlic. The steak *tampiqueño* is a huge platter that comes with guacamole salad, quesadillas, beans, salad, and rice.

INEXPENSIVE

Pizza Rolandi. Cobá 12. ☎ **9/884-4047.** Fax 9/884-3994. Pasta $5–$8; pizza and main courses $5–$14. www.rolandi.com. E-mail: grupo.rolandi@mail.caribe.net.mx. AE, MC, V. Daily 12:30pm–midnight. ITALIAN.

At this shaded outdoor patio restaurant you can choose from almost two dozen different wood-oven pizzas and a full selection of spaghetti, calzones, Italian-style chicken and beef, and desserts. There's a full bar list as well. There's another Pizza Rolandi in Isla Mujeres at 110 avenida Hidalgo (☎ **9/877-0430**) with the same food and prices. It's open Monday through Sunday from 11am to 11pm. Both have become standards for dependably good casual fare in Cancun.

✪ **Restaurant Los Almendros.** Av. Bonampak and Sayil. ☎ **9/887-1332.** Main courses $4–$7. Daily 11am–10pm. AE, V, MC. YUCATECAN.

To steep yourself in Yucatecan cuisine and music, head directly to this large, colorful, air-conditioned restaurant. Readers have written to say they ate here almost exclusively, since the food and service are good and the illustrated menu, with color pictures of dishes, makes ordering easy. Some of the regional specialties include lime soup, *poc chuc* (a marinated, barbecue-style pork), chicken or pork *pibil* (a sweet and spicy, shredded meat), and such appetizers as *panuchos* (soft fried tortillas with refried beans and either shredded turkey or pork *pibil*—a type of barbecue sauce in which the meat is cooked). The *combinado* Yucateco is a sampler of four typically Yucatecan main courses: chicken, *poc chuc,* sausage, and *escabeche* (onions marinated in vinegar and a sour orange sauce). It's located opposite the bullring.

Restaurant Santa María. Azucenas at Parque Palapas. ☎ **9/884-3158.** Fax 9/887-1716. Main courses $3.50–$9; tacos 75¢–$5. AE, V, MC. Daily 5pm–1am. MEXICAN.

The open-air Santa María restaurant is a clean, gaily decked-out place to sample authentic Mexican food. It's cool and breezy, with patio dining that's open on two sides, and furnished with leather tables and chairs covered in multicolored cloths. A bowl of *frijoles de olla* and an order of beefsteak tacos will fill you up for a low price. You may want to try the tortilla soup or enchiladas, or go for one of its specialty grilled U.S.–cut steaks, order of fajitas, ribs, or grilled seafood, all of which arrive with a baked potato. New offerings include traditional Yucatecan dishes.

Stefano's. Bonampak 177. ☎ **9/887-9964.** Main courses $6–$9; pizza $5.75–$9.75. AE, MC, V. Daily, 12pm–1am. ITALIAN/PIZZA/PASTA.

It began primarily as a "local" restaurant, but now Stefano's, which serves Italian food with a few Mexican accents, is equally popular with tourists. On the menu you'll find ravioli stuffed with *huitlacoche;* rigatoni in tequila sauce; and seafood with chile peppers, nestled proudly alongside the Stefano special pizza, made with fresh tomato, cheese, and pesto, or their three-cheese and shrimp pizza. It offers a vegetarian pizza, calzones stuffed with spinach, mozzarella, and tomato sauce, and other options for non-meat eaters. For dessert the ricotta strudel is something out of the ordinary, or else try the tiramisu. There are lots of different coffees and mixed drinks as well, plus an expanded wine list.

COFFEE & PASTRIES

Pasteleria Italiana. Av. Yaxchilán 67-D, SM 25, near Sunyaxchen. ☎ **9/884-0796.** Pastries $1.75–$2.25; ice cream $2; coffee $1–$2. AE. Mon–Sat 9am–11pm; Sun 1–9pm. COFFEE/PASTRIES/ICE CREAM.

More a casual neighborhood coffeehouse than a place aimed at tourists, this shady little respite has been doing business here since 1977. You'll spot it by the white awning that covers the small outdoor, plant-filled table area. Inside are refrigerated cases of tarts and scrumptious-looking cakes, ready to be carried away in their entirety or by the piece. The coffeehouse is in the same block as Perico's, between Maraño and Chiabal.

4 Beaches, Water Sports & Boat Tours

THE BEACHES   The best stretches of beach are dominated by the big hotels. All of Mexico's beaches are public property, so you can use the beach of any hotel by walking through the lobby, or by accessing them from the beach. Be especially careful on beaches fronting the open Caribbean, where the undertow can be quite strong. By contrast, the waters of Mujeres Bay (Bahía de Mujeres) at the north end of the island are usually calm, and ideal for swimming. Get to know Cancún's water-safety pennant system, and make sure to check the flag at any beach or hotel before entering the water. Here's how it goes:

- **White**   Excellent
- **Green**   Normal conditions (safe)
- **Yellow**   Changeable, uncertain (use caution)
- **Black or red**   Unsafe; use the swimming pool instead!

In the Caribbean, storms can arrive and conditions can change from safe to unsafe in a matter of minutes, so be alert: If you see dark clouds heading your way, head to shore and wait until the storm passes.

Playa Tortuga (Turtle Beach), Playa Langosta (Lobster Beach), Playa Linda (Pretty Beach), and Playa Las Perlas (Beach of the Pearls) are some of the public beaches. At most beaches, in addition to swimming you can rent a sailboard and take lessons, ride a Parasail, or partake in a variety of water sports. There's a small but beautiful portion of public beach on Playa Caracol, by the Xcaret Terminal. Both of these face the calm waters of Bahía de Mujeres and for that reason are preferable to those facing the Caribbean.

WATER SPORTS   Many beachside hotels offer water-sports concessions that include rental of rubber rafts, kayaks, and snorkeling equipment. On the calm Nichupte Lagoon are outlets for renting **sailboats, jet-skis, Windsurfers,** and **water skis.** Prices vary and are often negotiable, so check around.

For windsurfing, go to the Playa Tortuga public beach, where there's a **Wind-surfing School** (no phone) with equipment for rent.

DEEP-SEA FISHING   You can arrange a day of **deep-sea fishing** at one of the numerous piers or travel agencies for around $200 to $360 for 4 hours, $420 for

6 hours, and $520 for 8 hours for up to 4 people. Marinas will sometimes assist in putting a group together. Charters include a captain, a first mate, bait, gear, and beverages. Rates are lower if you depart from Isla Mujeres or from Cozumel Island, and frankly, the fishing is better closer to these departure points.

SNORKELING AND SCUBA   Known for its shallow reefs, dazzling color, and diversity of life, Cancún is one of the best places in the world for beginning **scuba diving.** Punta Nizuc is the northern tip of the Great Mesoamerican Reef (Gran Arrecife Maya), the largest reef in the western hemisphere, and one of the largest in the world. In addition to the sea life present along this reef system, several sunken boats add a variety of dive options. Inland, a series of caverns and wellsprings, known as *cenotes,* are fascinating venues for the more experienced diver. Drift diving is the norm here, with popular dives going to the reefs at **El Garrafón** and the **Cave of the Sleeping Sharks.**

Resort courses that teach the basics of diving—enough to make shallow dives and slowly ease your way into this underwater world of unimaginable beauty—are offered in a variety of hotels. Scuba trips run around $60 for two-tank dives at nearby reefs, $100 and up for locations farther out. **Scuba Cancún,** km 5 Paseo Kukulkán, on the lagoon side offers a 4-hour resort course for $60 (☎ **9/883-1011;** fax 9/884-2336; www.scubacancun.com.mx, e-mail: scuba@cancun.com.mx. Phone reservations also available in the evenings from 7:30 to 10:30pm using the fax line). Full certification takes 4 to 5 days and costs around $345. They're open from 8:30am to 8pm, and accept major credit cards. The largest operator is **Aquaworld** (☎ **9/885-2288** or 9/883-3007, www.aquaworld.com.mx, e-mail: info@aquaworld.com.mx; located across from the Meliá Cancún at km 15.2 Paseo Kukulkán), offering resort courses and diving from their man-made anchored dive platform, Paradise Island. Its **Sub See Explorer** is a submarine-style boat with picture windows that hang beneath the surface. The boat doesn't actually submerge—it's more an updated version of the glass-bottom boat concept—but it does provide nondivers with a look at life beneath the sea. They are open 24 hours a day, and also accept all major credit cards. **Scuba Cancún** also offers diving trips to 20 nearby reefs, including Cuevones at 30 feet and the open ocean at 30 to 60 feet (offered in good weather only). The average dive is around 35 feet. One-tank dives cost $55, and two-tank dives cost $60.50. Discounts apply if you bring your own equipment. Dives usually start around 9am and return by 2:15pm. Snorkeling trips cost $27.50 and leave every afternoon after 2pm for shallow reefs about a 20-minute boat ride away.

Besides **snorkeling** at **Garrafón National Park** (see "Boating Excursions," below), travel agencies offer an all-day excursion to the natural wildlife habitat of **Isla Contoy,** which usually includes time for snorkeling. This island, located an hour-and-a-half past Isla Mujeres, is a major nesting area for birds, and is a treat for true nature lovers. Only two boats hold permits for excursions there, which depart at 9am and return by 5pm. The price of $60 includes drinks and snorkeling equipment.

JET-SKI TOURS   The popular **Jungle Cruise** is offered by several companies and takes you by jet-ski or WaveRunner through Cancún's lagoon and mangrove estuaries out into the Caribbean Sea and a shallow reef. The excursion runs about $2^1/_2$ hours (you drive your own boat), and is priced from $35 to $40, with snorkeling and beverages included. Some of the motorized miniboats seat one person behind the other, others seat you side-by-side.

The operators and names of boats offering excursions change often. The popular **Aquaworld** (☎ **9/885-2288,** km 15.2 Paseo Kukulkán) calls theirs the Jungle Tour, charges $38.50 for the $2^1/_2$ hour excursion, which includes 45 minutes of snorkeling time. They even give you a free snorkel, but they do have the less-desirable seating configuration of one-behind-the-other—meaning the person in back gets a great view of the driver's head. Departures are 9am, 12pm, and 2:30pm daily. To find out what's available when you're there, check with a local travel agent or hotel tour desk; they should have a wide range of options. You can also go to the Playa Linda Pier either a day ahead or the day of your intended outing and buy your own ticket for trips on the Nautibus or to Isla Mujeres. If you go on the day of your trip, arrive at the pier around 8:45am, since most boats leave by 9 or 9:30am.

BOATING EXCURSIONS

ISLA MUJERES   The island of **Isla Mujeres,** just 10 miles offshore, is one of the most pleasant day-trips from Cancún. At one end is **El Garrafón National Underwater Park,** which is excellent for snorkeling. At the other end is a captivating village with small shops, restaurants, and hotels, and **Playa Norte,** the island's best beach. If you're looking for relaxation and can spare the time, the island is worth several days.

There are four ways to get there: by frequent **public ferry** from Puerto Juárez, which takes between 15 and 45 minutes; by a **shuttle boat** from Playa Linda or Playa Tortuga—an hour-long ride, with irregular service; by the **Watertaxi** (more expensive, but faster), next to the Xcaret Terminal; and by one of the daylong **pleasure-boat trips,** most of which leave from the Playa Linda pier.

The inexpensive Puerto Juárez **public ferries** are just a few miles from downtown Cancún. From Cancún City, take the Ruta 8 bus on avenida Tulum to Puerto Juárez. The fast ferry (15-minute ride) costs $2 per person; the 45-minute boat is a bargain at less than $1. Departures are every half-hour from 6am to 8:30am, then every 15 minutes until 8:30pm. Upon arrival, the ferry docks in downtown Isla Mujeres by all the shops, restaurants, hotels, and Norte beach. You'll need a taxi to get to Garrafón Park at the other end of the island. You can stay as long as you like on the island (even overnight) and return by ferry, but be sure to ask about the time of the last returning ferry—don't depend on the posted hours.

Pleasure-boat cruises to Isla Mujeres are a favorite pastime here. Modern motor yachts, catamarans, trimarans, and even old-time sloops—more than 25 boats a day—take swimmers, sunners, snorkelers, and shoppers out into the translucent waters. Some tours include a snorkeling stop at Garrafón, lunch on the beach, and a short time for shopping in downtown Isla Mujeres. Most leave at 9:30 or 10am, last about 5 or 6 hours, and include continental breakfast, lunch, and rental of snorkel gear. Others, particularly the sunset and night cruises, go to beaches away from town for pseudo-pirate shows, and include a lobster dinner or Mexican buffet. If you want to actually see Isla Mujeres, go on a morning cruise, or go on your own using the public ferry at Puerto Juárez mentioned above. Prices for the day-cruises run around $45 per person.

Other excursions go to the **reefs** in glass-bottom boats, so you can have a near-scuba-diving experience and see many colorful fish. However, the reefs are some distance from the shore and impossible to reach on windy days with choppy seas. They've also suffered from overvisitation, and their condition is far from pristine. The glass-bottomed **Nautibus** ($25 adults, $12.40 children; ☎ 9/883-3552 or 9/883-2119) has been around for years. The morning and afternoon trips (9:30am, 11am, 12pm, and 2pm) in a glass-bottom boat from the Playa Linda Pier to the Chitale coral reef to see colorful fish take about 1 hour and 20 minutes, with around 50 minutes of it in transit. The **Atlantis Submarine** takes you even closer to the sub-aquatic action. Departures vary, depending on weather conditions. Prices range from $44 to $65, depending on the length of the trip. Still other boat excursions visit **Isla**

Contoy, a **national bird sanctuary** that's well worth the time. If you are planning to spend time in Isla Mujeres, the Contoy trip is easier and more pleasurable to take from there.

5 Outdoor Activities & Attractions

OUTDOOR ACTIVITIES

DOLPHIN SWIMS   On Isla Mujeres, you have the opportunity to swim with dolphins at **Dolphin Discovery** (☎ **9/883-0779,** fax 9/883-0722; www.dolphindiscovery. com, e-mail: splashcn@qroo.telmex.net.mx). Each session lasts 1 hour, with an educational introduction followed by 30 minutes of swim time. Price is $119, with transportation to Isla Mujeres an additional $15. Advanced reservations are required, as capacity is limited each day. Assigned swimming times are 9am, 11am, 1pm, or 3pm, and you must arrive 1 hour prior to your time.

GOLF & TENNIS   The 18-hole **Club de Golf Cancún** (☎ **9/883-0871,** e-mail: poktapok@sybcom.com), also known as the Pok-Ta-Pok Club, was designed by Robert Trent Jones, Sr., and is located on the northern leg of the island. Greens fees run $95 per 18 holes, with clubs renting for $18, shoes for $12, and a caddy priced at $20 per bag. The club is open daily; American Express, MasterCard, and Visa are accepted. It also has tennis courts available for play. The **Melía Cancún** (☎ **9/ 881-1100**) offers a 9-hole, executive course; the fee is $25, and the club is open daily from 8am to 4pm. American Express, Mastercard, and Visa are accepted. The **Hilton Cancun Golf & Beach Resort** (☎ **9/881-8016,** fax 9/881-8084) has its own championship 18-hole, par-72 course designed around the "Ruinas Del Rey." Greens fees for the public are $106 for 18 holes, $70 for 9 holes; Hilton Cancun guests pay $86 for 18 holes and $53 for 9, which includes a golf cart. Golf clubs and shoes are available for rent as well, and the club is open daily from 6am to 6pm.

There's also the **Mini Golf Palace,** located at km 14.5 Paseo Kukulkán, that offers a more compact version of the game for all ages. It's open from 11am to 10pm daily, ☎ **9/885-0533.**

HORSEBACK RIDING   Rancho Loma Bonita (☎ **9/887-5465** or 9/887-5423) is Cancún's most popular option for horseback riding. Five-hour packages are available that include 2 hours of riding to caves, *cenotes*—spring-fed, underground caves, lagoons, Mayan ruins, and along the Caribbean coast, plus a Donkey Polo game and some time for relaxing on the beach. It also has a new four-wheel ATV ride for $45, on the same route as the horseback tour. Located about 30 minutes south, the price of $55 includes transportation to the ranch, riding, soft drinks, and lunch, plus guide and insurance. American Express, MasterCard, and Visa are accepted.

IN-LINE SKATING   You can rent in-line skates outside Plaza Las Glorias Hotel and in front of Playa Caracol, where the valet parking is located. The jogging track that runs parallel to paseo Kukulkán along the hotel zone is well-maintained and safe.

ATTRACTIONS

A MUSEUM   To the right side of the entrance to the Cancún Convention Center is the **Museo Arqueológico de Cancún** (☎ **9/883-0305,** mac98@qroo1.telmex.net.mx), a small but interesting museum with relics from archaeological sites around the state. Admission is $1.50 (free on Sun and holidays); the hours are Tuesday through Sunday from 9am to 7pm.

BULLFIGHTS   Cancún has a small bullring (☎ **9/884-8372,** bull@qroo1.telmex. net.mx) near the northern (town) end of Paseo Kukulkán opposite the Restaurant Los

Almendros. Bullfights are held every Wednesday at 3:30pm during the winter tourist season. There are usually four bulls, and the spectacle begins with a folkloric dance exhibition, followed by a performance of the Charros (Mexico's sombrero-wearing cowboys). Travel agencies in Cancún sell tickets: $30 for adults, with children admitted free of charge; seating is by general admission. AE, V, MC, also accepted.

HELICOPTER TOURS   Panoramic helicopter flights allow you to see the complete overview of this island paradise and surrounding areas. Both day and evening flights are available, as are tours to the Ruins and south along the Riviera Maya. **Heli Data** offers customized tours, with hourly rates depending upon the length of flight and time of day. Hotel pick up is provided. For details, call ☎ **9/883-3104.**

6 Shopping

Despite the surrounding natural splendor, shopping has become one of the favored activities in Cancún. It is known throughout Mexico for its diverse array of shops and festival malls that cater to a large number of international tourists. Tourists arriving from the United States may find apparel more expensive in Cancún, but the selection is much broader than in other Mexican resorts. There are numerous duty-free shops that offer excellent value on European goods, the largest being **UltraFemme** (☎ **9/884-1402** or 9/885-0804), specializing in imported cosmetics, perfumes, and fine jewelry and watches. Its downtown Cancún location on Avenida Tulum, Supermanzana 25, offers lower prices than its locations in Plaza Caracol, Kukulkán Plaza, Plaza Mayafair, Flamingo Plaza, or at the international airport.

Handcrafts and other *artesanía* works are more limited and more expensive in Cancún than in other regions of Mexico, since they are not produced here. They are available, though; there are several **open-air crafts markets** easily visible on avenida Tulum in Cancún City and near the convention center in the Hotel Zone. One of the biggest is **Coral Negro** (located at paseo Kukulkán, km 9.5 ☎ **9/883-0758,** fax: 9/883-0758), open daily from 7am to 11pm. Located inside is a small restaurant, Xtabentun, that serves Yucatecan food, and Slices Pizza, that metamorphoses into a disco each evening from 9pm to 11pm.

The main venue for shopping in Cancún is the **mall**—not quite as grand as its U.S. counterpart, but close. All of Cancún's malls are air-conditioned, sleek, and sophisticated, with most located on avenida Kukulkán between km 7 and km 12. Everything from fine crystal and silver to designer clothing and decorative objects can be found, along with numerous restaurants and clubs. Stores are generally open daily from 10am to 10pm, with clubs and restaurants remaining open much later. Here's a brief rundown on the malls and some of the shops they contain.

Inside the **Plaza Kukulkán** (☎ **9/885-2200,** www.kukulcanplaza.com) you'll find the largest selection—over 300—of shops, restaurants, and entertainment. There's a branch of Banco Serfin, OK Maguey Cantina Grill, a movie theater with U.S. movies, an Internet access kiosk, Tikal, a shop with Guatemalan textile clothing, several crafts stores, a liquor store, several bathing-suit specialty stores, record and tape outlets, a leather goods store (including shoes and sandals), and a store specializing in silver from Taxco. A new Fashion Gallery, which features designer clothing, has been added. In the food court are a number of U.S. franchise restaurants, including Ruth's Chris Steakhouse, plus one featuring specialty coffee. For entertainment, there's a bowling alley, Q-Zar laser game pavilion, and video game arcade. There's a large indoor parking garage. They're open from 10am to 10pm, and 10am to 11pm during high season. They'll provide handicapped assistance upon request, and have wheelchairs, strollers, and lockers available at the information desk.

Planet Hollywood anchors the **Plaza Flamingo** (☎ 9/883-2945), but inside you'll also pass branches of Bancrecer, Subway, and La Casa del Habano for Cuban cigars.

The long-standing **Plaza Caracol** (☎ 9/883-1038) holds Cartier jewelry, Guess, Waterford Crystal, Señor Frog clothing, Samsonite luggage, Gucci, and La Fisheria restaurant.

Maya Fair Plaza/Centro Comercial Maya Fair, frequently called "Mayfair" (☎ 9/883-2801), is the oldest mall, with a lively open-bricked center with open-air restaurants and bars such as Tequila Sunrise, and several stores selling silver, leather, and crafts.

The entertainment-oriented **Forum by the Sea** (avenida Kukulkán, km 9, ☎ 9/883-4425),has shops including Tommy Hilfiger, Levi's, Diesel, Swatch, and Harley Davidson, but most people come here for the food and fun, choosing from Hard Rock Cafe, Coco Bongo, Rainforest Cafe, Beer Factory, Cambalache, Sushi-ito, Zandunga, and Santa Fe Beer Factory, plus an extensive food court. It's open from 10am to midnight (bars remain open later).

The newest and most intriguing is the **La Isla Shopping Village** (km 12.5 Paseo Kukulkán; ☎ 9/883-5025; www.cancunshoppingmalls.com), an open air festival mall that looks like a small village, where walkways lined with shops and restaurants criss-cross over little canals. It also has a "riverwalk" alongside the Nichupte Lagoon, and an interactive aquarium and dolphin swim facility (planned to open in mid-2000). Shops include Zara clothing, Bennetton, Guess, Swatch, H. Stern, Ultra Femme, and the first **Warner Brothers Studio** store in Mexico. Dining choices include **Johnny Rockets, The Food Court** (not actually a "food court," but an Anderson's restaurant), and the beautiful Mexican restaurant, **La Casa de los Margaritas**. There's also a first-run movie theatre, video arcade, and several nightclubs, including **Max-O's** and **Alebrejes**. It's located across from the Sheraton, on the lagoon side of the street.

7 Cancún After Dark

One of Cancún's main draws is its active nightlife. The hottest centers of action are the **Centro Comercial Mayfair, Forum by the Sea,** and the new **La Isla Village.** Hotels also compete with happy-hour entertainment and special drink prices to entice visitors and guests from other resorts. (Lobby bar–hopping at sunset is one great way to plan next year's vacation.)

THE CLUB & MUSIC SCENE

Clubbing in Cancún, still called discoing here, is a favorite part of the vacation experience, and can go on each night until the sun rises over that incredibly blue sea. Several of the big hotels have nightclubs, usually a disco, or entertain in their lobby bars with live music. At discos, expect to pay a cover charge of $10 to $20 per person, and $5 to $8 for a drink. Some of the higher-priced discos include an open bar or live entertainment.

Numerous restaurants, such as **Carlos 'n' Charlie's, Planet Hollywood, Hard Rock Cafe, Señor Frog's, TGI Friday's,** and **Iguana Wana,** double as nighttime party spots; offering wildish fun at a fraction of the prices of more costly discos.

The most refined and upscale of all Cancún's nightly gathering spots is the **Lobby Lounge** at the **Ritz-Carlton Hotel** (☎ 9/885-0808), with live dance music and a list of over 120 premium tequilas for tasting or sipping.

Azúcar Bar Caribeño (☎ 9/883-0441), adjacent to the Hotel Camino Real, offers spicy tropical salsa, meringue, and bolero dancing, with bands from Cuba, Jamaica, and the Dominican Republic; it's open Monday through Saturday from 9:30pm to 4am.

La Boom (km 3.5 Paseo Kukulkán, ☎ **9/883-1152,** fax: 9/883-1458, laboom@ mail.sybcom.com), has two sections: on one side is a video bar, and on the other is a bilevel disco with cranking music. Both sides are air-conditioned. Each night there's a special deal going on: no cover, free bar, ladies' night, bikini night. Popular with early twenty–somethings, it's open nightly from 10pm to 6am. A sound-and-light show begins at 11:30pm in the disco. The cover varies for the disco and the bar depending on the night—most nights ladies are free, and men pay covers that vary between $10 and $20 with open bar.

Carlos 'n' Charlie's (km 4.5, Paseo Kukulkán, ☎ **9/883-0846**), is a reliable place to find both good food and packed frat house–type entertainment in the evenings. There's a dance floor to go along with the live music that starts nightly around 8:30pm. A cover charge kicks in if you're not planning to eat. It's open daily from 11am to 2am.

With recorded music, **Carlos O'Brian's** (Tulum 107, SM 22, ☎ **9/884-1659**) is only slightly tamer than other Carlos Anderson restaurants/nightspots in town (Señor Frog and Carlos 'n' Charlie's). It's open daily from 10am to 12:30am.

Christine's, at the Hotel Krystal on the island (☎ **9/883-1793**), has been around for years, with its signature laser-light shows, infused oxygen, and large video screens, but has been overtaken by hipper clubs. It still maintains a dress code of no shorts or jeans, and opens at 9:30pm nightly. American Express, MasterCard, and Visa are accepted.

Currently one of the consistently hottest spots in town is **Coco Bongo** (in Forum by the Sea, km. 9.5 Paseo Kukulkán; ☎ **9/883-5061**), whose main appeal is that with no formal dance floor, you can dance anywhere you can find the space—and that includes on the tables, on the bar, or even on the stage with the live band! The music alternates between Caribbean, salsa, techno, and classics from the '70s and '80s. It draws a young, hip crowd.

Also sizzling is the new club **Liquid** (☎ **9/883-1302**), a sister club of the Miami Beach club of the same name. A more sleek, sophisticated, and intimate (relatively speaking) club, it has stunning light shows, and features techno and alternative music. It's located at Km 9 Paseo Kukulkán, in The Party Center, next to the Convention Center, and is open from 10pm to 5am . . . but those in the know don't even think of going until after midnight.

Dady'O (km 9.5, Paseo Kukulkán, ☎ **9/883-3333**), is a highly favored rave with frequent long lines. It opens nightly at 9:30pm, and generally charges a cover of $15.

Dady Rock Bar and Grill (km 9.5, Paseo Kukulkán, ☎ **9/883-1626**), the off- spring of Dady'O, opens early (7pm) and goes as long as any other nightspot, offering a new twist on entertainment, with a combination of live bands and DJ-orchestrated music, along with an open bar, full meals, a buffet, and dancing.

Hard Rock Cafe (in Plaza Lagunas Mall and Forum by the Sea, ☎ **9/883-3269** or 9/883-2024, www.hardrock.com) entertains with a live band at 10:30pm every night except Wednesday. At other times you get lively recorded music to munch by— the menu combines the most popular foods from American and Mexican cultures. It's open daily from 11am to 2am.

Planet Hollywood (Flamingo Shopping Center, km 11, Paseo Kukulkán, ☎ **9/ 885-3044,** www.planethollywood.com) is the still-popular brainchild of Sylvester Stallone, Bruce Willis, and Arnold Schwarzenegger. It's both a restaurant and night- time music/dance spot with mega-decibel live music. It's open daily from 11am to 2am. American Express, MasterCard, and Visa are accepted.

Sports Wagering

This form of entertainment seems to be sweeping Mexico's resorts. TV screens mounted around the room of **Sports Bar LF Caliente** (☎ **9/883-3704,** located on km 3.5 Paseo Kukulkán, across from La Boom disco), shows all the action in race-track, football, soccer, and so on in a bar/lounge setting. It's open 11am to 1am. No credit cards.

THE PERFORMING ARTS

Nightly performances of the **Ballet Folklórico de Cancún** (☎ **9/881-0400,** ext. 193 or 194) are held at the Cancún Convention Center. Tickets are sold between 8am and 9pm at a booth just as you enter the Convention Center. Dinner is available before the show. Dinner-show guests pay around $46, and arrive at 6:30pm for drinks, which are followed by dinner at 7pm, and the show at 8pm. The price includes an open bar, dinner, show, tax, and tip. You can also pay $28 and pass on dinner. For this price you'll enjoy the show and an open bar, and you'll need to arrive by 7:30pm. Ask if any discounts are available. American Express, MasterCard, and Visa accepted. The show is Monday–Saturday. Several hotels host **Mexican fiesta nights,** including a buffet dinner and a folkloric dance show; admission, including dinner, ranges from $35 to $50. In the Costa Blanca shopping center, **El Mexicano** restaurant (☎ **9/884-4207**) hosts a tropical dinner show every night as well as live music for dancing. The entertainment alternates each night with mariachis entertaining off-and-on from 7 to 11pm and a folkloric show from 8 to 9:30pm.

You can also get in the party mood at ✪ **Mango Tango** (km 14, Paseo Kukulkán, ☎ **9/885-0303**), a lagoon-side restaurant/dinner-show establishment. Diners can choose from two levels, one nearer the music and the other overlooking it all. Music is loud and varied, but mainly features reggae or salsa. The 1-hour-and-20-minute dinner show begins at 8:30pm nightly and costs $38. At 9:30pm live reggae music begins. If you're not dining but come just for the music and drinks, a $10 cover charge applies. It's opposite the Ritz Carlton.

For something that mingles tourists with the locals, head for the downtown **Parque de las Palapas** (the main park) for *Noches Caribeños,* where live tropical music is provided at no charge for anyone who wants to listen and dance. Performances begin at 7:30pm on Sundays, and sometimes there are performances on Fridays and Saturdays, but the calendar varies.

8 Day-Trips: Archaeological Sites & Eco-Theme Parks

One of the best ways to spend a vacation day is by exploring the nearby archeological ruins or one the new ecological theme parks near Cancún. Within easy driving distance are historical and natural treasures, unlike any you've likely encountered before. Cancún can be a perfect base for day- or overnight trips or the starting point for a longer exploration.

Organized day-trips are popular and easy to book through any travel agent in town, or you can plan a journey on your own via bus or rental car. Greenline (☎ **9/883-4545**) buses offer packages (*paquetes*) to popular nearby destinations. The package to **Chichén-Itzá** departs at 8:30am and includes the round-trip air-conditioned bus ride, with video, for the 3-hour trip, entry to the ruins, 2 hours at the ruins, and lunch. The tour returns to Cancún by 7:30pm; cost is $59.

Price Tour (☎9/883-2016) offers day trips to **Cozumel,** that depart at 8am and return by 6:30pm, and include round-trip, air-conditioned bus transportation to and from Playa del Carmen and the ferry ticket to and from Cozumel. The trips cost $45.

The Maya ruins to the south at **Tulum** or **Cobá** should be your first goal, then perhaps the *caleta* (cove) of **Xel-Ha** or the day-trip to **Xcaret.** If you're going south, consider staying a night or two on the island of **Cozumel** or at one of the budget resorts on the **Tulum coast** or **Punta Allen,** south of the Tulum ruins. **Isla Mujeres** is an easy day-trip off mainland Cancún. Although I don't recommend it, by driving fast or catching the right buses you can go inland to **Chichén Itzá,** explore the ruins, and return in a day, but it's much better to spend at least 2 days seeing Chichén Itzá, Mérida, and Uxmal.

ARCHAEOLOGICAL SITES

TULUM   A popular day-excursion combines a visit to the ruins at Tulum with the ecological water park, Xel-Ha (see below). Ancient Tulum is a stunning site—and my personal favorite of all the ruins—poised on a rocky hill overlooking the transparent, turquoise Caribbean Sea. It's not the largest or most important of the Mayan ruins in this area, but it's the only one by the sea, which makes it the most visually impressive, in my opinion. Intriguing carvings and reliefs decorate the well-preserved structures, which date back to between the 12th and 16th centuries A.D., in the Post-classic period.

The site is surrounded by a wall on three sides, which explains the name ("Tulum" means fence, trench, or wall). Its ancient name is believed to have been *Záma,* a derivative of the Maya word for morning, or dawn, and sunrise at Tulum is certainly dramatic. The wall is believed to have been constructed after the original buildings to protect the interior religious altars from a growing number of invaders. It is considered to have been principally a place of worship, but members of the upper classes later took up residence here to take advantage of the protective wall. Between the two most dramatic structures—the Castle and the Temple of the Wind—lies Tulum Cove. A small inlet with a beach of fine, white sand, it was a point of departure for Mayan trading vessels in ancient times. Today, it's a playground for tourists, and you can enjoy a refreshing swim there. Entrance to the site without a tour is $2; use of video camera requires a $4 permit.

RUINAS DEL REY   Cancún has its own **Mayan ruins**—a small site that's less impressive than the ruins at Tulum, Cobá, or Chichén-Itzá. Mayan fishermen built this small ceremonial center and settlement very early in the history of Maya culture. It was then abandoned, to be resettled again near the end of the Post-classic period, not long before the arrival of the conquistadors. The platforms of numerous small temples are visible amid the banana plants, papayas, and wildflowers. The Hilton Cancún hotel golf course has been built around the ruins, but there is a separate entrance for sightseers. You'll find the ruins about 13 miles from town, at the southern reaches of the Zona Hotelera, almost to Punta Nizuc. Look for the Hilton hotel on the left (east), then the ruins on the right (west). Admission is $4.50 (free on Sundays and holidays); the hours are daily from 8am to 5pm (☎ 9/884-8073).

ECO-THEME PARKS AND RESERVES

The popularity of Xcaret and Xel-Ha has inspired a growing number of entrepreneurs to ride the wave of interest in ecological and adventure theme parks. Be aware that "theme park" more than "ecological" is the operative phrase, and also the newer parks of Aktun Chen, Tres Ríos, and Xpu-Ha are—so far—are less commercial and more focused on nature than their predecessors. Included below are also several true reserves, which have less in the way of facilities, but offer an authentic encounter with the natural beauty of the region.

AKTUN CHEN   This park, consisting of a spectacular 5,000-year-old grotto and an abundance of wildlife, is the first time above-the-ground cave systems in the Yucatan have been open to the public. The name means "cave with an underground river inside," and the main cave of three is more than 600 yards long, with a magnificent vault. Discreet illumination and easy walking paths make visiting the caves more comfortable, without appearing to alter them much from their natural state. The caves contain thousands of stalactites, stalagmites, and sculpted rock formations, along with a 40-foot-deep cenote with clear blue water. Akun Chen was once underwater itself, and fossilized shells and fish embedded in the limestone are visible as you walk along the paths. Caves are an integral part of the region's geography and geology, and knowledgeable guides take you around while providing explanations of what you see, as well as mini-history lessons in the Maya's association with these caves. Tours have no set times—guides are available to take you when you arrive—and groups are kept to a maximum of 20 people. Surrounding the caves are nature trails throughout the 988-acre park, where spottings of deer, spider monkeys, iguanas, and wild turkeys are common. A small informal restaurant and gift shop are also on site.

It's easy to travel by yourself to Aktun Chen; from Cancún, travel south along Highway 307 (the road to Tulum). Just past the turn-off for Akumal a sign on the right side of the highway indicates the turn-off to Aktun-Chen; from there, it's a 3-kilometer drive west along a smooth, but unpaved road. Travel time from Cancún is about an hour, and the park is open from 8am until dark. The entry fee of $12 includes the services of a guide (no phone).

EL EDEN RESERVA ECOLÓGICA   Established in 1990, this is a privately owned 500,000-acre reserve dedicated to research for biological conservation in Mexico. Only 30 miles northwest of Cancún, it takes around 2 hours to reach the center of this reserve deep in the jungle. It's intended as an overnight (or more) excursion for people who want to know more about the biological diversity of the peninsula. Within the reserve, or near to it, marine grasslands, mangrove swamps, rain forests, savannas, wetlands, and sand dunes are found, as well as evidence of archaeological sites and at least 205 different species of birds, plus orchids, bromeliads, and cacti. Among the local animals are the spider monkey, jaguar, cougar, deer, and ocelot. The "ecoscientific" tours offered include naturalist-led bird-watching, animal tracking, star gazing, spotlight surveys for nocturnal wildlife, and exploration of *cenotes* and Mayan ruins. Comfortable, basic accommodations are provided. Tours include transportation from Cancún, 1 or 2 nights accommodation at La Savanna Research Station, meals, nightly cocktail, guided nature walks, and tours. The tours cost $235 to $315 depending on the length of stay, with a fee of $90 per extra night. American Express is accepted. Contact: **Ecocolors** (Camarón 32 SM 27, ☎ **9/884-3667,** Fax 9/884-9580, www. cancun.com.mx, www.iminet.com/mexico/eden.html, e-mail:ecoco@cancun.com.mx). Ecocolors specializes in ecologically oriented tours around the Cancún area.

SIAN KA'AN BIOSPHERE RESERVE   About 80 miles south of Cancún, this 1.3-million-acre area was set aside in 1986 to preserve a region of tropical forests, savannas, mangroves, canals, lagoons, bays, *cenotes,* and coral reefs, all of which are home to hundreds of birds and land and marine animals. The Friends of Sian Ka'an, a nonprofit group based in Cancún, offers biologist-escorted day-trips (weather permitting) from the **Cabañas Ana y José** just south of the Tulum ruins. Trips take place Monday through Saturday for $58 per person using their vehicle or $48 per person if you drive yourself. The price includes chips and soft drinks, round-trip van transportation to the reserve from the Cabañas, a guided boat/birding trip through one of the reserve's lagoons, and use of binoculars. Tours can accommodate up to 18 people. Trips start from the Cabañas at 9am and return there around 3pm. For reservations, contact Amigos de Sian Ka'an (Crepúsculo 18, and Amanecer, Supermanzana 44, Manzana 13 Residencial Alborada. ☎ **9/848-2136,** 9/848-1618, 9/848-1593, 9/884-9583; fax 9/848-1618) in Cancún. Office hours are 9am to 3pm and 6 to 8pm.

TRES RÍOS   This eco/adventure park is actually a nature reserve, located on more than 150 acres of land, that offers guests a beautiful natural area for kayaking, canoeing, snorkeling, horseback riding, or biking along jungle trails. It's definitely less commercial than the other eco-theme parks, and is essentially just a great natural area for participating in these activities. Located just 25 minutes south of Cancún, there is an entrance fee of $19 for adults and $12 for children, which includes canoe trips, the use of bikes, kayaks, and snorkeling equipment, as well as the use of hammocks and beach chairs once you tire yourself out. Extra charges apply for scuba diving, horseback riding, and other extended, guided tours through the preserve and its estuary. Tres Ríos also has rest room facilities, showers, and a convenience store. A half-day Kayak Express tour to Tres Ríos is sold in most Cancún travel agencies. Priced at $39, it includes admission to the park and its activities, plus round-trip transportation, lunch, and two non-alcoholic drinks. Call ☎ **9/887-4977** in Cancún for details and reservations. The park is open daily from 9am to 6pm.

XCARET: A DEVELOPED NATURE PARK   Six-and-a-half miles south of Playa del Carmen (and 50 miles south of Cancún) is the turnoff to Xcaret (pronounced *ish-car-et*), a specially built ecological and archaeological theme park that is one of the area's most popular tourist attractions. Xcaret has become almost a reason in itself to visit Cancún. It's the closest thing to Disneyland you'll find in Mexico, with myriad attractions in one location, most of them participatory. It's open Monday through Saturday from 8:30am to 8pm and Sunday from 8:30am to 5:30pm. Everywhere you look in Cancún are signs advertising Xcaret or someone handing you a leaflet about it. It even has its own bus terminal to take tourists from Cancún at regular intervals, and it has added an evening extravaganza. Plan to spend a full day here.

Xcaret may celebrate Mother Nature, but its builders rearranged quite a bit of her handiwork in completing it. If you're looking for a place to escape the commercialism of Cancún, this may not be it; it's relatively expensive and may even be very crowded, thus diminishing the advertised "natural" experience. Children, however, love it, and the jungle setting and palm-lined beaches are beautiful. Once past the entrance booths (built to resemble small Mayan temples) you'll find pathways that meander around bathing coves, the snorkeling lagoon, and the remains of a group of real Mayan temples. You'll have access to swimming beaches; limestone tunnels to snorkel through; marked palm-lined pathways; a wild-bird breeding aviary; a *charro* exhibition; horseback riding; scuba diving; a botanical garden and nursery; a sea turtle nursery where the turtles are released after their 1st year; a pavilion showcasing regional butterflies; a tropical aquarium, where visitors can touch underwater creatures such as manta rays, starfish, and octopi; and a "Dolphinarium," where visitors (on a first-come, first-served basis) can swim with the dolphins for an extra charge of $80.

Another attraction at Xcaret is a replica of the ancient Mayan game, Pok-ta-pok, where six "warriors" bounce around a 9-pound ball with their hips. The Seawalker is a watersport designed for nonswimmers. By donning a special suit and helmet with a connected air pump, you can walk on the ocean floor or examine a coral reef in a small bay.

There is also a visitor center with lockers, first aid, and gifts. Visitors aren't allowed to bring in food or drinks, so you're limited to the rather high-priced restaurants on site. No personal radios are allowed, and you must remove all suntan lotion if you swim in the lagoon to avoid poisoning the lagoon habitat.

The admission price of $39 per person entitles you to all the facilities—boats, life jackets, and snorkeling equipment for the underwater tunnel and lagoon, and lounge chairs and other facilities. Other attractions, such as snorkeling at $22, horseback riding at $39, scuba diving at $45 for certified divers and $65 for a resort course, and the Dolphin Swim at $80, cost extra. There may be more visitors than equipment (such as beach chairs), so bring a beach towel and your own snorkeling gear. Travel agencies in Cancún offer day-trips to Xcaret, departing at 8am and returning at 6pm, for $65 for adults ($45 for children), including transportation, admission, and a guide. You can also buy a ticket to the park at the **Xcaret Terminal** (☎ **9/883-0654** or 9/883-3143), next to the Hotel Fiesta Americana Coral Beach on Cancún Island. "Xcaret Day and Night" includes round-trip transportation from Cancún, a *charreada* festival, lighted pathways to Maya ruins, dinner, and a folkloric show for $69 for adults and $45 for children age 5 to 11; age 5 and under are free. Buses leave the terminal at 9 and 10am daily, with the "Day and Night" tour returning at 9:30pm.

XEL-HA   The Caribbean coast of the Yucatán is carved by the sea into hundreds of small *caletas,* or coves, that form the perfect habitat for tropical marine life, both flora and fauna. Many *caletas* remain undiscovered and pristine along the coast, but Xel-Ha, 8 miles south of Akumal, is enjoyed daily by throngs of snorkelers and scuba divers, who come to luxuriate in its warm waters and swim among its brilliant fish. Xel-Ha (shell-*hah*) is a swimmers' paradise, with no threat of undertow or pollution. It's a beautiful, completely calm cove that's a perfect place to bring kids for their first snorkeling experience. Experienced snorkelers may be disappointed, as the crowds here seem to have driven out the living coral and many of the fish. (You can find more abundant marine life and avoid an admission charge by going to Akumal, among other spots.)

The entrance to Xel-Ha (☎ **9/884-9422;** www.xelha.com.mx) is a half mile from the highway. Admission is $19 per adult and $11.50 for children age 5 to 12 (children under age 5 are free), and includes use of inner tubes, life vest, and shuttle train to the river. You can also choose an all-inclusive option for admission, equipment, food, and beverages for $43 for adults and $30 for children. It's open daily from 8:30am to 5pm, offers free parking with admission, and accepts American Express, MasterCard, and Visa. Once in the 10-acre park, you can rent snorkeling equipment and an underwater camera, but you may also bring your own. Food and beverage service, changing rooms, showers, and other facilities are all available. Platforms have been constructed that allow decent sea-life viewing for non-snorkelers.

In addition, it offers "snuba," a clever invention that combines snorkeling and scuba. Snuba is a shallow water diving system that places conventional scuba tanks on secure rafts that float at surface level; the "snuba-diver" breathes normally through a mouthpiece, which is part of a long air hose attached to the tank above. This enables a swimmer to go as deep as 20 feet below the surface, and stay down for as long as an hour or more. It's a great transition to scuba, and many divers may even enjoy it, as it leaves you remarkably unencumbered by equipment.

When you swim, be careful to observe the "swim here" and "no swimming" signs. The greatest variety of fish can be seen right near the ropes marking off the no-swimming areas, and near any groups of rocks. An interactive dolphin attraction has been added, with a 45-minute swim, costing $55, or an educational program for $30.

Reservations should be made at least 24 hours in advance for one of the 4-daily options: 9:30am, 12:30pm, 2pm, or 3:15pm.

Just south of the Xel-Ha turnoff on the west side of the highway, don't miss the ruins of **ancient Xel-Ha.** You'll likely be the only one there as you walk over limestone rocks and through the tangle of trees, vines, and palms. There is a huge, deep, dark *cenote* to one side, a temple palace with tumbled-down columns, a jaguar group, and a conserved temple group. A covered *palapa* on one pyramid guards a partially preserved mural. Admission is $2.50.

Xel-Ha is close to the ruins at **Tulum** (see above), and makes for a good place for a dip when you've finished climbing these Maya ruins. You can even make the short 8-mile hop north from Tulum to Xel-Ha by public bus. When you get off at the junction for Tulum, ask the restaurant owner when the next buses come by, otherwise you may have to wait as long as 2 hours on the highway.

XPU-HA   This is another eco-park in the same vein as Xcaret and Xel-Ha—it offers a range of activities that center on yet another of the exquisite coves along the Riviera Maya—the coastal area that extends south from Cancún to Chetumal. The difference lies in that, along with the eco-tour trend, Xpu-Ha capitalizes on another travel trend—the all-inclusive concept. One entrance price of $59 includes round-trip transportation from Cancún, beverages, snacks, a choice of tours (bicycle, snorkel, or cultural), plus sports equipment and the use of lockers, showers, and facilities. The fee is $10 less if you do not use their transportation. It's located 50 miles south of Cancún, off the road to Tulum. Once at Xpu-Ha (pronounced shpoo-ha), you can snorkel or dive; relax on the white-sand beach—commonly in a hammock strung between palms; explore the sheltered Aviary, with toucans, macaws, and other tropical birds; or kayak through mangrove-lined lagoons. Xpu-Ha is considered to have one of the most diverse environments in North America, and also is home to protected species including crocodiles, sea turtles, native deer, and snakes. Only 3% of the total 91.5 acres has been developed to build the access road and install rest room facilities, showers, services, and snack bars, so there is plenty of nature to enjoy. It seems to attract a younger, more energetic crowd. The park opens at 8am and closes at dark (☎ 9/885-0020).

4 Isla Mujeres, Cozumel & the Riviera Maya

A Mexican friend of mine reminded me that the Mayas never settled in Cancún. "The original inhabitants always choose the best places to live," he reasoned, pointing to neighboring Cozumel, Tulum, Isla Mujeres, and other sites along the Yucatán coastline. Each of these holds remnants of ancient settlements in addition to many modern attractions.

In fact, those who shun the highly stylized, rather Americanized ways of Cancún will find that these and other stops in the Yucatán offer abundant natural pleasures, authentic experiences, and a relaxed charm. They're so close to the easy air access of Cancún, yet miles away in mood and matter.

The **Quintana Roo** Caribbean coast, dubbed the "Riviera Maya," stretches south from Cancún all the way to Chetumal. It's 230 miles of powdery white-sand beaches, scrubby jungle, and crystal-clear lagoons full of coral and colorful fish. Along this coastline—and the islands off the peninsula—are a few places worthy of being designated "resorts," as well as a handful of inexpensive hideaways. Over the past 2 years, it has attracted a lot of attention from developers and is rapidly evolving into a destination dotted with "eco-tourism resorts,"— perhaps an oxymoron, but marketable, nonetheless. Some treasured spots on both the Punta Allen Peninsula and the Majahual Peninsula also merit attention.

Many travelers only become acquainted with these areas after an initial stay in Cancún, venturing out on day-trips that take them sailing over to Isla Mujeres, down the Caribbean coast to Tulum, or exploring the reefs off Cozumel. Their next trip often concentrates on one or more of these smaller towns.

EXPLORING MEXICO'S CARIBBEAN COAST

ISLA MUJERES   A day trip to Isla Mujeres on a party boat is one of the most popular excursions from Cancún. This fish-shaped island is located just 8 miles northeast of Cancún. It's a quick boat ride away, allowing ample time to get a taste of the peaceful pace of life here. But to fully explore the small village of shops and cafes, relax at the broad, tranquil Playa Norte, or snorkel or dive El Garrafón Reef (a national underwater park), more time is needed. Overnight accommodations range from rustic to offbeat chic on this small island where relaxation rules.

Passenger ferries go to Isla Mujeres from Puerto Juárez near Cancún, and car ferries leave from Punta Sam, also near Cancún. More expensive passenger ferries, with less frequent departures, leave from the Playa Linda pier on Cancún Island.

1 Isla Mujeres

10 miles (16km) N of Cancún

Isla Mujeres (Island of Women) is a casual, laid-back reprive from the conspicuously commercialized action of Cancún, visible across a narrow channel. Just 5 miles long and 2¹/₂ miles wide, it's known as the best value in the Caribbean, assuming you favor a slow and easy-going vacation pace, and prefer simplicity to pretense.

This is an island of white-sand beaches and turquoise waters, complemented by a town filled with Caribbean-colored clapboard houses and rustic, open-air restaurants specializing in the bounty of the sea. Hotels are clean and comfortable, but if you're looking for lots of action or opulence, you'll be happier in Cancún. A few recent additions in accommodations on Isla Mujeres are now providing more luxurious choices, but still maintain a decidedly casual atmosphere.

Francisco Hernández de Córdoba gave the island its name when he landed there in 1517, upon seeing figurines of partially clad females along the shore. These are now believed to have been offerings to the Mayan goddess of fertility and the moon, Ixchel. Their presence is an indication that the island was sacred to the Maya.

At midday, suntanned visitors hang out in open-air cafes and stroll streets lined with frantic souvenir vendors. Calling out for attention to their bargain-priced wares, they give a carnival atmosphere to the hours when tour-boat traffic is at its peak. Befitting the size of the island, most of the traffic consists of golf carts, *motos* (also called mopeds), and bicycles. Once the tour boats leave, however, Isla Mujeres reverts back to its more typical, tranquil way of life, where taking a *siesta* in a hammock is a favored pastime.

Days in "Isla"—as the locals call it—can alternate between adventurous activity and absolute repose. Trips to the Isla Contoy bird sanctuary are popular, as are the excellent diving, fishing, and snorkeling—in 1998 the island's coral coast was made part of Mexico's new Marine National Park. The island and several of its traditional hotels attract regular gatherings of yoga practitioners. In the evenings most people find the slow, casual pace one of the island's biggest draws. The cool night breeze is a perfect accompaniment to casual open-air dining and drinking in small street-side restaurants. Most people pack it in as early as 9 or 10pm, when most of the businesses close. Those in search of a party, however, will find kindred souls at the bars on Playa Norte that stay open late.

ESSENTIALS

GETTING THERE & DEPARTING   Puerto Juárez (☎ 9/877-0618), just north of Cancún, is the dock for the passenger ferries to Isla Mujeres. The *Caribbean Queen* makes the 45-minute trip many times daily, and costs just under $2. The newer, air-conditioned *Caribbean Express* makes the trip in 20 minutes, has storage space for luggage, and costs about $3, running every hour on the half hour between 6:30am and 8:30pm. Pay at the ticket office, or if the ferry is about to leave, you can pay aboard. Note: Upon arrival by taxi or bus to Puerto Juárez, be wary of pirate "guides" who offer advice and tell you either the ferry is cancelled or that it's several hours until the next ferry. They'll offer the services of a private "lancha" (small boat) for about $40—but it's nothing but a scam. Small boats are available, and on a co-op basis are priced at $10 to $22 for a one-way fare, based on number of passengers. They take about

50 minutes for the trip over, and are not recommended on days with rough seas. Check with the clearly visible ticket office for information—it is the only accurate source.

Taxi fares are now posted by the street where the taxis park; be sure to check the rate before agreeing to a taxi for the ride back to Cancún. Rates generally run $9 to $12 depending upon your final destination. Moped and bicycle rentals are also readily available as you depart the ferryboat. This small complex also has public rest rooms, luggage storage, a snack bar, and souvenir shops.

Isla Mujeres is so small that a vehicle isn't necessary, but if you're taking one, you'll use the **Punta Sam** port a little beyond Puerto Juárez. The ferry runs the 40-minute trip five or six times daily between 8am and 8pm, all year except in bad weather. Times are generally as follows: Cancún to Isla, 8am, 11am, 2:45pm, 5:30pm, and 8:15pm, with returns from Isla to Cancún at 6:30am, 9:30am, 12:45pm, 4:15pm, and 7:15pm; however, you should check with the tourist office in Cancún to verify this schedule. Cars should arrive an hour in advance of the ferry departure to register for a place in line and pay the posted fee, which varies depending on weight and type of vehicle. The sole gas pump in Isla is found at the intersection of Ave. Rueda Medina and Abasolo St., just northwest of the ferry docks.

There are also ferries to Isla Mujeres from the **Playa Linda,** known as the Embarcadero pier in Cancún, but they're less frequent and more expensive than those from Puerto Juárez. The Playa Linda ferries simply don't run if there isn't a crowd. A **Water Taxi** (☎ **9/886-4270** or 9/886-4847; e-mail: asterix1@prodigy.net.mx) to Isla Mujeres operates from Playa Caracol, between the Fiesta Americana Coral Beach Hotel and the Xcaret terminal on the island, with prices about the same as those from Playa Linda, and about four times the cost of the public ferries from Puerto Juárez. Scheduled departures are 9 and 11am and 1 and 3pm with returns from Isla Mujeres at 10am, noon, 2pm, and 5pm. Adult fares are $13.50, kids ages 3 to 12 are half-price, and those under age 3 ride free.

To get to either Puerto Juárez or Punta Sam **from Cancún,** take any Ruta 8 city bus from avenida Tulum. If you're coming from Mérida, you can either fly to Cancún and then proceed to Puerto Juárez, or you can take a bus directly from the Mérida bus station to Puerto Juárez. **From Cozumel,** you can either fly to Cancún (there are daily flights) or take a ferry to Playa del Carmen (see the Cozumel section below for details), where you can travel to Puerto Juárez.

Arriving: Ferries arrive at the ferry dock (☎ **9/877-0065**) in the center of town. The main road that passes in front of the ferry dock is Avenida Rueda Medina. Most hotels are close by. Tricycle taxis are the least expensive and most fun way to get to your hotel; you and your luggage pile in the open carriage compartment while the "driver" peddles through the streets. Regular taxis are always lined up in a parking lot to the right of the pier, with their rates posted. If someone on the ferry offers to arrange a taxi for you, politely decline, unless you'd like some help with your luggage down the short pier—it just means an extra, unnecessary tip for them.

VISITOR INFORMATION   The **City Tourist Office** (☎/fax **9/877-0767**) is located on Ave. Rueda Medina, in front of the pier. It's open Monday through Friday from 8am to 9pm, and Saturday and Sunday from 9am to 2pm. Also look for *Islander,* a free publication with history, local information, advertisements, and event listings (if any).

ISLAND LAYOUT   Isla Mujeres is about 5 miles long and 2¹/₂ miles wide, with the town located at the northern tip of the island. "Downtown" is a compact 4 blocks by

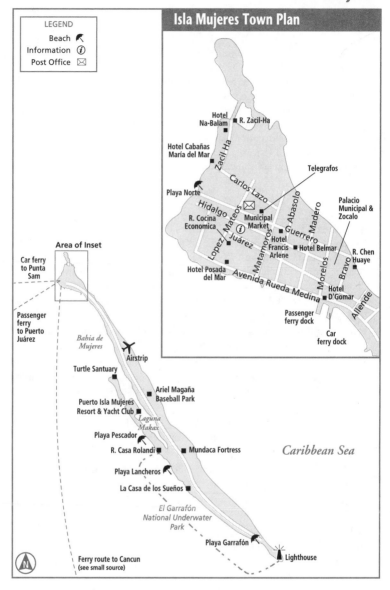

Isla Mujeres Town Plan

LEGEND
Beach 🏖
Information ⓘ
Post Office ✉

Hotel Na-Balam
R. Zacil-Ha
Zacil Ha
Hotel Cabañas María del Mar
Carlos Lazo
Telegrafos
Playa Norte
Hidalgo
Palacio Municipal & Zocalo
R. Cocina Economica
Municipal Market
Abasolo
Madero
López / Mateos
Juárez
Guerrero
Hotel Francis Arlene
Hotel Belmar
R. Chen Huaye
Matamoros
Morelos
Bravo
Hotel Posada del Mar
Avenida Rueda Medina
Hotel D'Gomar
Allende
Passenger ferry dock
Car ferry dock

Area of Inset

Car ferry to Punta Sam

Passenger ferry to Puerto Juárez

Bahia de Mujeres

Airstrip
Turtle Sanctuary
Ariel Magaña Baseball Park
Puerto Isla Mujeres Resort & Yacht Club
Laguna Makax
Playa Pescador
R. Casa Rolandi
Mundaca Fortress
Caribbean Sea
Playa Lancheros
La Casa de los Sueños
El Garrafón National Underwater Park
Playa Garrafón
Lighthouse
N
Ferry route to Cancun (see small source)

6 blocks, so it's very easy to get around. The **ferry docks** (☎ **9/877-0065**) are right at the center of town, within walking distance of most hotels, restaurants, and shops. The street running along the waterfront is avenida **Rueda Medina,** commonly called the **malecón.** The **market** (Mercado Municipal) is by the post office on **calle Guerrero,** an inland street at the north edge of town, which, like most streets in the town, is unmarked.

GETTING AROUND   A popular form of transportation on Isla Mujeres is the electric **golf cart,** available for rent at many hotels for $10 per hour or $40 per day.

El Sol Golf Cart Rental will deliver one to you, ☎ 9/877-0068, or you can visit them at Ave. Francisco Madero 5, if you're just visiting for the day. The golf carts don't go more than 20 miles per hour, but they're fun. Anyway, on Isla Mujeres you aren't there to hurry. Many people enjoy touring the island by **"moto,"** the local sobriquet for motorized bikes and scooters. Fully automatic versions are available for around $20 per day or $5 per hour. They come with seats for one person, but some are large enough for two. There's only one main road with a couple of offshoots, so you won't get lost. Be aware that the rental price does not include insurance, and any injury to yourself or the vehicle will come out of your pocket. **Bicycles** are also available for rent at some hotels for $2 per hour or $5 per day, including a basket and lock.

If you prefer to use a taxi, rates are about $1 for trips within the downtown area, or $4 for a trip to the southern end of Isla. You can also rent them for about $10 per hour.

Fast Facts: Isla Mujeres

Area Code   The area code of Isla Mujeres is **9.** The first three digits (to accommodate the new dialing system) for all telephone numbers on the island have been changed from 872 to 877. In Islas this new dialing system is not in full working order yet, so there are some numbers that still work when you dial only the last five digits. Keep that in mind when you try to make local calls while in Isla. If dialing seven digits gets you a recording, simply hang up and try dialing the last five digits of the phone number.

Consumer Protection   The local branch of **Profeco** protection agency has a local phone number, ☎ **9/877-0126.**

Currency Exchange   Isla Mujeras has numerous *Casas de Cambios,* or money exchanges, that you can easily spot along the main streets. Most of the hotels listed here provide this service for their guests, although often at rates slightly lower than the commercial enterprises.

Hospital   The **Hospital de la Armada** is on Av. Rueda Medina at Ojon P. Blanco (☎ **9/877-0001**). It's a half mile south of the town center.

Internet Access   CompuIsla, Abasolo 11, between Medina and Juárez streets (☎ **9/877-0898**), offers Internet access for $4 per hour Monday through Friday from 8am to 10pm, Saturday from 9am to 4pm.

Pharmacy   Isla Mujeres Farmacía has the best selection of perscription and over-the-counter medicines. It's located on Calle Benito Juárez, between Morelos and Bravo, across from Van Cleef & Arpels.

Post Office/Telegraph Office   The post office (☎ **9/877-0085**), or *correo,* is located on calle Guerrero #12, at the corner with López Matéos, near the market. It's open Monday through Friday, from 9am to 4pm.

Taxis   Call for a taxi at ☎ **9/877-0066.**

Telephone   Ladatel phones accepting coins and prepaid phone cards are found at the plaza and throughout town.

Tourist Seasons   Isla Mujeres's tourist season (when hotel rates are higher) is a bit different from that of other places in Mexico. High season runs December through May, a month longer than in Cancún; some hotels raise their rates in August and some hotels raise their rates beginning in mid-November. Low season is June through mid-November.

BEACHES & WATER SPORTS

THE BEACHES   The most popular beach in town used to be called Playa Cocoteros ("Cocos" for short). Then, in 1988, Hurricane Gilbert destroyed the coconut palms on the beach. Gradually, the name has changed to **Playa Norte,** referring to the long stretch of beach that extends around the northern tip of the island, to your left as you get off the boat. This is a truly splendid beach—a wide stretch of fine white sand and calm, translucent, turquoise-blue water. Topless sunbathing is permitted. The beach is easily reached on foot from the ferry and from all downtown hotels. Water-sports equipment, beach umbrellas, and lounge chairs are available for rent. Those in front of restaurants usually cost nothing if you use the restaurant as your headquarters for drinks and food. New palms are sprouting all over Playa Norte, and it won't be long before it deserves to get its old name back.

Garrafón National Park is known best as a snorkeling area, but there is a nice stretch of beach on either side of the park. **Playa Lancheros** is on the Caribbean side of Laguna Makax. Local buses go to Lancheros, then turn inland and return to downtown. The beach at Playa Lancheros is nice, but the few restaurants there are high-priced.

WATER SPORTS   Swimming   Wide Playa Norte is the best swimming beach, with Playa Lancheros second. There are no lifeguards on duty on Isla Mujeres, and the system of water-safety flags used in Cancún and Cozumel isn't used here.

SNORKELING   By far the most popular place to snorkel is **Garrafón National Park.** It is located at the southern end of the island, where you'll see numerous schools of colorful fish. The well-equipped park has beach chairs, changing rooms, rental lockers, showers, and a snack bar. Once a public national underwater park, in late 1999 it was concessioned to, and is now operated by, the same people who operate Xel Ha, south of Cancún. Public facilities have been improved, and two restaurant-bars have been added. Admission is $10 for adults and $6 for children. (AE, MC, and V are accepted). Day-trip packages from Cancun are now also available, priced at $29 and up, including round-trip transportation (☎ **9/884-9422** in Cancún, and 9/877-0890 at the park).

Also good for snorkeling is the **Manchones Reef,** which is just offshore and reached by boat, where a bronze cross was installed in 1994.

Another excellent location is around the lighthouse (*el faro*) in the **Bahía de Mujeres** at the southern tip of the island, where the water is about 6 feet deep. Boatmen will take you for around $20 per person if you have your own snorkeling equipment or $25 if you use theirs.

DIVING   Several dive shops have opened on the island, most offering the same trips. The traditional dive center is **Buzos de México,** on Rueda Medina at Morelos (no phone), next to the boat cooperative. Certification is available (5 to 6 days for $350), as are resort courses ($80 with three dives), and all dives are led by certified dive masters. **Bahía Dive Shop,** on Rueda Medina 166, across from the car-ferry dock (☎ **9/877-0340**), is a full-service shop with dive equipment for sale or rent and resort and certification classes. They are open daily from 9am to 7pm, and accept Visa and MasterCard only. Another respected dive shop is **Coral Scuba Center** (☎ **9/ 877-0061** or 9/877-0769), located at Matamoros 13A and Rueda Medina. They offer discounted prices for those who bring their own gear, and also have rental bungalows available for short-term and long-term stays.

Cuevas de los Tiburones (Caves of the Sleeping Sharks) is Isla's most famous dive site and costs $70–$80 for a two-tank dive at a depth of 70 to 80 feet (only advisable for experienced divers). There are actually two places to see the sleeping sharks: the Cuevas de Tiburones and **La Punta.** A storm collapsed the arch that was featured in a Jacques Cousteau film showing the sleeping sharks, but the caves are still there. Sharks have no gills, and so must constantly move to receive the oxygen they need. (Remember the line in *Annie Hall* equating relationships to sharks: "They must constantly move forward or die"?) The phenomenon here is that the high salinity and lack of carbon monoxide in the caves, combined with strong and steady currents, allow the sharks to receive the oxygen they need without moving. Your chance of actually seeing sleeping sharks, by the way, is about one in four; fewer sharks are present than in the past. The best time to see them is January through March.

Other dive sites include a wreck 9km (14.4 miles) offshore; Banderas reef, between Isla Mujeres and Cancún, where there's always a strong current; Tabos reef on the eastern shore; and Manchones reef, 1km (1.6 miles) off the southeastern tip of the island, where the water is 15 to 35 feet deep. Another underwater site, "The Cross of the Bay," is close to Manchones reef. A bronze cross, weighing one ton and 39 feet high, was placed in the water between Manchones and Isla in 1994, as a memorial to those who have lost their lives at sea. The best season for diving is from June through August, when the water is calm.

In May of 1999, a shrimp boat suffering engine failure ran aground on a portion of a large coral reef, located just north of Isla. A section of the reef suffered significant damage, and officials are trying to place buoys in the area in an effort to steer as much traffic as possible away from this damaged area.

FISHING   To arrange a day of fishing, ask at the **Sociedad Cooperativa Turística** (the boatmen's cooperative) located on Avenida Rueda Medina (no phone), next to Mexico Divers and Las Brisas restaurant, or the travel agency mentioned below, under "A Visit to Isla Contoy." The cost can be shared with four to six others and includes lunch and drinks. Captain Tony Martínez (☎ 9/877-0274) also arranges fishing trips aboard his *lancha,* **Marinonis,** with advanced reservations recommended. All year you'll find bonito, mackerel, kingfish, and amberjack. Sailfish and sharks (hammerhead, bull, nurse, lemon, and tiger) are in good supply in April and May. In winter, larger grouper and jewfish are prevalent. Four hours of fishing close to shore costs around $150; 8 hours farther out goes for $240. The cooperative is open Monday through Saturday from 8am to 1pm and 5 to 8pm, and Sunday from 7:30 to 10am and 6 to 8pm.

YOGA   Increasingly, Isla is becoming known as a great place to combine a relaxing beach vacation with various types of yoga practice and instruction. The impetus for this trend began at **NaBalam Beach Hotel** (☎ 9/877-0279, www.nabalam.com), where yoga classes are offered under its large poolside *palapa,* complete with yoga mats and props. The classes, which take place Monday through Friday from 8:30 to 10am, are free to guests, or $10 per class to visitors. NaBalam is also the site of frequent yoga instruction vacations, featuring respected yoga teachers, and a more extensive practice schedule.

Yoga classes are also available at the **Casa de la Cultura,** on Ave. Guerrero, between Abasolo and Madero streets. The schedule changes, so call them at ☎ 9/877-0639. They are open Monday through Saturday from 9am to 1pm, and 4pm to 8pm. They also offer dance classes, drawing classes, and a book exchange that's the closest thing to a library on Isla.

MORE ATTRACTIONS

DOLPHIN DISCOVERY   You can swim with live dolphins in this enclosure, located on Treasure Island, on the side of Isla Mujeres that faces Cancún. Swims take place in groups of six people with two dolphins and one trainer. First, swimmers listen to an educational video and spend time in the water with the trainer and the dolphins before enjoying 15 minutes of free swimming time with them. Reservations are recommended, and you must arrive an hour prior to your assigned swimming time, at 9am, 11am, 1pm, or 3pm. Make your reservations at ☎ **9/8770-207,** or in Cancún at ☎ 98/83-0779. Additional information is available at www.dolphindiscovery.com. Cost is $119 per person, plus $15 if round-trip transportation from Cancún is required.

A TURTLE SANCTUARY   A worthwhile outing on the island is to this reserve dedicated to preserving Caribbean sea turtles and to educating the public about them.

As recently as 20 years ago fishermen converged on the island nightly from May through September waiting for these monster-size turtles to lumber ashore to deposit their Ping Pong ball–shaped eggs. Totally vulnerable once they begin laying their eggs, and exhausted when they have finished, the turtles were easily captured and slaughtered for their highly prized meat, shell, and eggs. Then a concerned fisherman, Gonzalez Cahle Maldonado, began convincing others to spare at least the eggs, which he protected. It was a start. Following his lead, the fishing secretariat founded this **Centro de Investigaciones** 10 years ago; it's funded by both the government and private donations. Since then at least 28,000 turtles have been released and every year local schoolchildren participate in the event, thus planting the notion of protecting the turtles for a new generation of islanders.

Six different species of sea turtles nest on Isla Mujeres. An adult green turtle, the most abundant species, measures 4 to 5 feet in length and can weigh as much as 450 pounds when grown. At the center, visitors walk through the indoor and outdoor turtle pool areas, where the creatures paddle around. The turtles are separated by age, from newly hatched up to 1 year. Besides protecting the turtles that nest on Isla Mujeres of their own accord, the program also captures turtles at sea, brings them to enclosed compounds to mate, and later frees them to nest on Isla Mujeres after they have been tagged. People who come here usually end up staying at least an hour, especially if they opt for the guided tour, which I recommend. The sanctuary is on a piece of land separated from the island by Bahía de Mujeres and Laguna Makax; you'll need a taxi to get there. Admission is $1; the shelter is open daily from 9am to 5pm. For more information call ☎ **9/877-0595.**

A MAYA RUIN   Just beyond the lighthouse, at the southern end of the island, is a pile of stones that formed a small Maya pyramid before Hurricane Gilbert struck in 1988. Believed to have been an observatory built to the moon and fertility goddess Ixchel, it's been reduced to more or less a rocky heap. The location, on a lofty bluff overlooking the sea, is still worth seeing. It is believed that Mayan women traveled here on annual pilgrimages to seek Ixchel's blessings of fertility. If you're at Garrafón National Park and want to walk, it's not too far. Turn right from Garrafón. When you see the lighthouse, turn toward it down the rocky path.

A PIRATE'S FORTRESS   The Fortress of Mundaca is about 2^1/$_2$ miles in the same direction as Garrafón, about a half mile to the left. The fortress was built by a slave trader who claimed to have been the pirate Mundaca Marecheaga. In the early 19th century he arrived at Isla Mujeres and proceeded to set up a blissful paradise in a pretty, shady spot, while making money selling slaves to Cuba and Belize. According to island lore, he decided to settle down and build this hacienda after being captivated by the charms of an island girl. However, she reputedly spurned his affections and married another islander, leaving him heartbroken and alone on Isla Mujeres. Admission is $1.50, and the fortress is open daily, from 10am to 6pm.

A VISIT TO ISLA CONTOY   If at all possible, plan to visit this pristine uninhabited island, 19 miles by boat from Isla Mujeres, that was set aside as a national wildlife reserve in 1981. The oddly shaped 3.8-mile-long island is covered in lush vegetation and harbors 70 species of birds as well as a host of marine and animal life. Bird species that nest on the island include pelicans, brown boobies, frigates, egrets, terns, and cormorants. Flocks of flamingos arrive in April. June, July, and August are good months to spot turtles that bury their eggs in the sand at night. Most excursions troll for fish (which will be your lunch), anchor en route for a snorkeling expedition, and skirt the island at a leisurely pace for close viewing of the birds without disturbing the habitat, then pull ashore. While the captain prepares lunch, visitors can swim, sun, follow the nature trails, and visit the fine nature museum. For a while the island was closed to visitors, but it's reopened now after rules for its use and safety were agreed to by fishermen and those bringing visitors. The trip from Isla Mujeres takes about 45 minutes one way, more if the waves are choppy. Because of the tight-knit boatmen's cooperative, prices for this excursion are the same everywhere: $30. You can buy a ticket at the **Sociedad Cooperativa Turística** located on avenida Rueda Medina (next to Mexico Divers and Las Brisas restaurant), or at one of several travel agencies, such as **La Isleña,** on Morelos between Medina and Juárez (☎ **9/877-0578**). La Isleña is open daily from 7:30am to 9:30pm and is a good source for tourist information. Contoy trips leave at 8:30am and return around 4pm. Their price is $40 for adults and $20 for children. Major credit cards are accepted.

Three types of boats go to Contoy. Small boats have one motor and seat eight or nine people. Medium-size boats have two motors and hold 10. Large boats have a toilet and hold 16 passengers. Most boats have a sun cover. The first two types are being phased out in favor of larger, better boats. Boat captains should respect the cooperative's regulations regarding capacity and should have enough life jackets to go around. Snorkeling equipment is usually included in the price, but double-check that before heading out. On the island, there is a small government museum with rest room facilities.

SHOPPING

Shopping is a casual activity here. There are only a few shops of any sophistication. Otherwise you are bombarded by shop owners, especially on Hidalgo, selling Saltillo rugs, onyx, silver, Guatemalan clothing, blown glassware, masks, folk art, beach paraphernalia, and T-shirts in abundance. Prices are lower here than in Cancún or Cozumel, but with the overeager sellers, bargaining is necessary to avoid paying too much.

The one treasure you're likely to take back is a piece of fine jewelry—Isla is known for its excellent, duty-free prices on gemstones, and handcrafted work made to order. Diamonds, emeralds, sapphires, and rubies can be purchased as loose stones, then mounted while you're off exploring the island. The superbly crafted gold, silver, and gems are available at very competitive prices in the workshops near the central plaza. The stones are also available in the rough. **Van Cleef & Arpels** (☎ **9/877-0331**) has a store here, with a broad selection of jewelry at competitive prices. Located at the corner of Morelos and Juárez streets, it's easily the largest store in Isla, open daily from 9am to 9pm, and accepts all major credit cards.

The new **Martin Good Gallery** opened in 1999 in the Casa de los Sueños B&B, at the southern end of the island (Carretera al Garrafón s/n, ☎ **9/877-0651;** fax 9/877-0708). It's easily the finest gallery in the entire Cancun/Isla area, and offers high-quality original paintings and sculptures by local artists, as well as some contemporary Mexican masters, such as Jose Luis Cuevas. During high season, it offers occasional cocktail receptions for exhibition openings. It's open 10:30am to 3:30pm, Monday through Saturday, and by appointment at other times.

WHERE TO STAY

There are plenty of hotels in all price ranges on Isla Mujeres. Rates are at their peak during high season, which is the most expensive and most crowded time to go. Elizabeth Wenger of **Four Seasons Travel** in Montello, Wisconsin (☎ **800/ 552-4550**), specializes in Mexico travel and books a lot of hotels in Isla Mujeres particularly. Her service is invaluable in high season when hotel occupancy is high. For those interested in private home rentals or longer term stays, contact **Mundaca Travel and Real Estate** in Isla Mujeres (☎ **9/877-0025;** fax 9/877-0076; www.mundacatravel.com).

In the last few years, Isla has seen the emergence of several smaller but decidedly upscale places to stay. For anyone wanting the proximity and ease of arrival that Cancún offers—but not its excesses—you should seriously consider these new options in Isla Mujeres, where a trip to the mainland is less than an hour if you do choose to enjoy its shopping or dining.

VERY EXPENSIVE

✪ **La Casa de los Sueños.** Carretera Garrafón s/n, 77400 Isla Mujeres, Q. Roo. ☎ **800/ 551-2558** in the U.S., or 9/877-0651. Fax 9/877-0708. www.lossuenos.com. E-mail: info@ lossuenos.com. 10 units. A/C FAN TV. High season $250–$375 double. Low season $215–$335 double. Rates include breakfast. MC, V.

This "house of dreams" is easily Isla Mujeres' most sophisticated property, originally built as a private residence. Luckily for us, it opened in early 1998 as an upscale, adults-only B&B. Its location on the southern end of the island, adjacent to El Garrafón National Park, makes it ideal for snorkeling and diving enthusiasts. The captivating design features vivid sherbet-colored walls—think watermelon, lime, blueberry—and a sculpted architecture. There's a large, open interior courtyard, tropical gardens, and an infinity pool that melts into the cool Caribbean waters. All rooms have balconies or terraces and face west, offering stunning views of the sunset and the night lights of Cancún. In addition, the rooms—which have names like "Serenity," "Passion," and "Love"—also have satellite TV, large, marble bathrooms, and luxury amenities. There's a small *palapa*-shaded lounge area with a wooden sun terrace overlooking the water, a private boat dock, and complimentary use of snorkeling equipment, kayaks, and bikes for sightseeing around the island. Geared to a healthful, stress-free vacation, the B&B forbids smoking and encourages casual dress and no shoes. Meditation areas and daily massage services are also available. Private boat transportation from Cancún to the B&B's dock can be arranged on request.

Dining/Diversions: Each morning, coffee, juice, and fruit are delivered to your room, at a requested hour. The well-equipped kitchen and dining area serves full American breakfasts, included in the rates, plus light lunches, upon request, for an extra charge. There's also an honor-system bar in the courtyard reception area for refreshments.

Amenities: Swimming pool, meditation areas, massage service, yoga and reiki classes (must be scheduled in advance), free use of bikes, sun terrace, boat dock, diving, and snorkeling available. A telephone is available at the office, for messages.

✪ **Hotel Villa Rolandi Gourmet & Beach Club.** Fracc. Lagunamar SM 7 Mza. 75 L 15 & 16, 77400 Isla Mujeres, Q. Roo, ☎ **9/877-0700,** fax 9/877-0100. www.rolandi.com. E-mail: rolandi@rolandi.com. 20 units. A/C MINIBAR TV TEL. High season $310, double. Low season $229, double. Rates include round-trip transportation from the Cancun airport, daily continental breakfast, and à la carte lunch or dinner in the on-site restaurant. AE, MC, V.

The newest hotel in Isla is adding to the island's options for guests who enjoy its tranquility—but also like being pampered. Villa Rolandi is an exceptional value, with luxurious, high-quality rooms styled in a Mediterranean decor that offer every conceivable amenity. Each of the 20, oversized suites has an ocean view and either a large terrace or balcony with a full-size private Jacuzzi—whose water is changed with each guest's arrival. Floors are made of stone, and ceilings are vaulted. TVs offer satellite music and movies, phones are cordless, and rooms all have a sophisticated in-room sound system, safe, and servi-bar. There's a recessed seating area that extends out to the balcony or terrace. Bathrooms are large, and tastefully decorated in deep-hued Tikal marble. The stained glassed-in shower has dual shower heads, stereo speakers, jet options, and even converts into a steam room.

Gourmet dining is an integral part of a stay at Villa Rolandi, its owner being the Swiss-born restaurateur who made a name for himself with his family of Rolandi restaurants on Isla Mujeres and in Cancún. The gourmet Casa Rolandi restaurant and bar overlooks the Caribbean, and has a colorful dining area as well as more casual, open-air terrace seating for drinks or light snacks. It serves seafood, Swiss, and northern Italian specialties, including its famed wood-burning-oven pizzas, and homemade pastas—especially notable is the shrimp scampi. There's also live music each night at sunset, and a selection of over 80 premium tequilas.

This intimate hideaway with highly personalized service is ideal for honeymooners, who receive a complementary bottle of domestic champagne upon arrival, when notified in advance. Only children over age 13 are welcome. Transportation from the Playa Linda dock in Cancún to the dock at Villa Rolandi is by their private catamaran yacht, *Cocoon*, and is included in the price of your stay.

Dining/Diversions: The onsite restaurant, Casa Rolandi, is of the regionally renowned Rolandi restaurant family, and serves lunch and dinner. Continental breakfast is delivered to your suite in a safe box at a pre-appointed hour, and à la carte lunch or dinner is included daily in the room price. A large wooden terrace bar overlooks the channel between Isla and Cancún, a perfect place for enjoying a sunset cocktail. Twenty-four-hour room service is also available.

Amenities: The infinity pool has a cascading waterfall that ends in a little pool on their small private beach. A fitness center offers a complete selection of basic work out equipment, and also has an open-air massage area. The concierge service can arrange diving, snorkeling, or fishing trips, or any other desired tour services. Round-trip transportation from Cancún airport is included.

Puerto Isla Mujeres Resort & Yacht Club. Puerto de Abrigo Laguna Macax, 77400 Isla Mujeres, Q. Roo, (reservation address: Km 4.5 Paseo Kukulcán, 77500 Cancún, Q. Roo). ☎ **800/960-ISLA** in the U.S., 9/877-0413, 9/877-0330, or 98/83-1228 in Cancún. www.puertoisla.com. E-mail: isla@cancun.rce.com.mx. 24 units. A/C MINIBAR TV TEL. High season $195–$250 suite, $350 villa. Low season $145–$190 suite, $275 villa. Rates include transportation from office in Playa Linda and daily continental breakfast. AE, MC, V.

The concept here—an exclusive glide-up yachting/sailing resort—is unique not only to Isla Mujeres, but also to most of Mexico. Facing an undeveloped portion of the glass-smooth, mangrove-edged Macax Lagoon, Puerto Isla Mujeres is a collection of modern suites and villas with sloping white-stucco walls and red-tile roofs spread across spacious palm-filled grounds. Beautifully designed with Scandinavian and Mediterranean elements, guest quarters feature tile, wood-beam ceilings, natural teak wood and marble accents, televisions with VCR, stereos with CD changer, safe deposit boxes, and living areas. Suites have a large, comfortable living area with minibar on a lower level, with the bedroom set above it, loft-style. Villas have two bedrooms upstairs with a full bathroom and a small bathroom downstairs with a shower. Each villa also features a small stylish kitchen area with dishwasher, microwave, refrigerator, and coffeemaker. A whirlpool is on the upper patio off the master bedroom. Nightly turndown service leaves the next day's weather forecast on the pillow beside the requisite chocolate. The daily continental breakfast arrives early each morning in a discreet little cubbyhole in the wall. The beach club, with refreshments, is a water-taxi ride across the lagoon on a beautiful stretch of beach. A staff biologist can answer questions about birds and water life on Isla Mujeres.

Dining: Two restaurants, one indoor and one poolside.

Amenities: Nearby beach club, free-form swimming pool with swim-up bar. On-site spa offers complete massage services. Transportation is offered from the Cancún office at Playa Linda by boat to Isla Mujeres, plus there's a full-service marina with 60 slips for 30- to 60-foot vessels, short- and long-term dockage in the area's only designated hurricane shelter, fueling station, charter yachts and sailboats, and sailing school. Mopeds, golf carts, bikes, and water-sports equipment for rent, and video and CD library. Laundry and room service.

EXPENSIVE

Hotel Na Balam. Zazil Ha 118, 77400 Isla Mujeres, Q. Roo. ☎ **9/877-0279.** Fax 9/877-0446. www.nabalam.com. E-mail: nabalam@cancun.rce.com.mx; nabalam@nabalam.com. 31 units. A/C FAN. High season $150–170 suite. Low season $112 suite. Ask about special weekly and monthly rates. AE, MC, V. Free unguarded parking.

Increasingly, Na Balam is becoming known as a haven for yoga students or those interested in a more introspective vacation. This popular, two-story hotel near the end of Norte Beach has comfortable rooms on a quiet, ideally located portion of the beach. Rooms are in three sections, with some facing the beach and others across the street in a garden setting with a swimming pool. All rooms have either a terrace or a balcony, with hammocks. Each spacious suite contains a king or two double beds, a seating area, and folk-art decorations. Though other rooms are newer, the older section is well kept, with a bottom-floor patio facing the peaceful, palm-filled, sandy inner yard and Norte Beach. There are also facilities for small meetings, and an on-site travel agency. From Monday through Friday yoga classes are offered from 8:30 to 10am; complimentary for guests, or $10 per class for non-guests. There's a new Internet room, with access billed at $10 per hour. They also offer in-room massage service. To find the hotel from the pier, walk 5 blocks to López Mateos; turn right and walk 4 blocks to Lazo (the last street). Turn left and walk to the sandy road parallel to the beach and turn right. The hotel is half a block farther.

Dining/Diversions: The restaurant, **Zazil Ha,** is one of the island's most popular (see "Where to Dine," below), serving Mexican and Caribbean cuisine, seafood, and vegetarian specialties. There are two bars—one adjacent to the restaurant and one on the beach. The beachside bar serves a selection of natural juices, and is known as one of the most popular spots for sunset watching during the evenings.

Amenities: Swimming pool and beach; diving and snorkeling trips available; mopeds, golf carts, and bikes for rent; library, rec room with TV and VCR, and Ping-Pong tables. A new Internet room has been added. Salon services including massage, manicures, pedicures, and facials, along with yoga classes. Laundry, baby-sitting, and in-room massage for an additional charge.

MODERATE

Hotel Cabañas María del Mar. Av. Arq. Carlos Lazo 1, 77400 Isla Mujeres, Q. Roo. ☎ **800/ 223-5695** in the U.S., or 9/877-0179. Fax 9/877-0213 or 9/877-0156. 73 units. A/C. High season $100–$130 double. Low season $50–$80 double. Rates include continental breakfast. MC, V.

A good choice, the Cabañas María del Mar is located on Playa Norte, a half block from the Hotel Nabalam. The older two-story section behind the reception area and beyond the garden offers nicely outfitted rooms facing the beach, all with two single or double beds, refrigerators, and balconies strung with hammocks and ocean views. New bathroom fixtures and mini-fridges have been added. Eleven single-story cabañas closer to the reception and pool were all completely remodeled in late 1999, in a rustic Mexican style, with new bathroom fixtures and the addition of a mini-fridge. The newest addition, **El Castillo,** is across the street, built over and beside Buho's restaurant. It contains all "deluxe" rooms, but some are larger than others; the five rooms on the ground floor all have large patios. Upstairs rooms have small balconies. All have ocean views, blue-and-white tile floors, and tile baths, and are outfitted in colonial-style furniture. There's a small pool in the garden. The owners also have a bus for tours and a boat for rent, as well as golf-cart and *moto* (motorized bikes or scooters) rental.

To get here from the pier, walk left 1 block, then turn right on Matamoros. After 4 blocks, turn left on Lazo, the last street. The hotel is at the end of the block.

INEXPENSIVE

Hotel Belmar. Av. Hidalgo 110, 77400 Isla Mujeres, Q. Roo. ☎ **9/877-0430.** Fax 9/877-0429. hotel.belmar@mail.caribe.net.mx. 11 units. A/C TV TEL. High season $56–$90 double. Low season $28–$45 double. AE, MC, V.

Situated above Pizza Rolandi (consider the restaurant noise), this hotel is run by the same people who serve up those wood-oven pizzas. Each of the simple but stylish rooms comes with two twin or double beds and tile accents. Prices are high for no views, but the rooms are very pleasant. On the other hand, this is one of the few island hotels with televisions (bringing in U.S. channels) in the room, plus it offers laundry and room service from noon to 11:30pm. There is a large colonial-decorated suite with Jacuzzi and a patio. The hotel is between Madero and Abasolo, 3¹/₂ blocks from the passenger-ferry pier.

Hotel D'Gomar. Rueda Medina 150, 77400 Isla Mujeres, Q. Roo. ☎ **9/877-0541.** 16 units. A/C. High season $25–$40 double. Low season $15–$30 double. No credit cards.

Completely remodeled in 1999—inside and out—you can hardly beat this hotel for comfort at reasonable prices. Rooms—each with two double beds—have new mattresses, drapes, and a paint job, and bathrooms have been re-tiled with new fixtures added. A wall of windows offers great breezes and picture views. The higher prices are for air-conditioning, which is hardly needed with fantastic breezes and ceiling fans. The only drawback is that there are five stories and no elevator. But it's conveniently located kitty-corner (look right) from the ferry pier, with exceptional rooftop views. The name of the hotel is the most visible sign on the "skyline."

✪ **Hotel Francis Arlene.** Guerrero 7, 77400 Isla Mujeres, Q. Roo. ☎ /fax **9/877-0310;** 9/877-0861. 26 units. A/C (in 14 units) or FAN. High season $45–$50 double; Low season $38–$42 double (higher prices are for rooms with A/C). No credit cards.

The Magaña family operates this neat little two-story inn, built around a small shady courtyard. You'll notice the tidy cream-and-white facade of the building from the street. Some of the rooms have ocean views, and each year they are all remodeled or updated. They are clean and comfortable, with tile floors, all-tile bathrooms, and a very homey feel to them. Each downstairs room has a coffeemaker, refrigerator, and stove; each upstairs room comes with a refrigerator and toaster. Some have either a balcony or a patio. Safe deposit boxes, telephone, and money exchange are available at the front desk, and in-room massage service is available. This hotel is very popular with families and senior travelers, and welcomes many repeat guests. Rates are substantially better if quoted in pesos and are reflected above. In dollars they are 15% to 20% higher. It's 5¹/₂ blocks inland from the ferry pier, between Abasolo and Matamoros.

Hotel Posada del Mar. Av. Rueda Medina 15 A, 77400 Isla Mujeres, Q. Roo. ☎ **800/ 544-3005** in the U.S., or 9/877-0044. Fax 9/877-0266. www.mexhotels.com/psd.html. E-mail: hposada@cancun.rce.com.mx. 43 units. A/C TEL. High season $57–$67 double. Low season $40–$45 double. AE, MC, V.

Simply furnished, quiet, and comfortable, this long-established hotel faces the water and a wide beach 3 blocks north of the ferry pier, and it has one of the few swimming pools on the island. The ample-sized rooms are in either a three-story building or one-story bungalow units. For the spacious quality of the rooms and the location, this is among the best values on the island. A wide, seldom-used but appealing stretch of Playa Norte is across the street, where watersports equipment is available for rent. A great, casual *palapa*-style bar and a lovely pool are set on the back lawn, and the restaurant **Pinguino** (see "Where to Dine," below) is by the sidewalk at the front of the property. This is probably the best choice in Isla for families, and children under age 12 stay free of charge with paying adults. From the pier, go left for 4 blocks; the hotel is on the right.

WHERE TO DINE

The **Municipal Market,** next door to the telegraph office and post office on avenida Guerrero, has several little food stands operated by obliging and hard-working women. At the **Panadería La Reyna,** at Madero and Juárez, you can pick up inexpensive sweet bread, muffins, cookies, and yogurt. It's open Monday through Saturday from 7am to 9:30pm.

As in the rest of Mexico, a **cocina económica** restaurant literally means "economic kitchen." Usually aimed at the local population, these are great places to find good food at rock-bottom prices. That's especially so on Isla Mujeres, where you'll find several, most of which feature delicious regional specialties.

MODERATE

Las Palapas Chimbo's. Norte Beach. No phone. Sandwiches and fruit $2–$3.50; seafood $5–$8. No credit cards. Daily 8am–12am. SEAFOOD.

If you're looking for a beachside *palapa*-covered restaurant where you can wiggle your toes in the sand while relishing fresh seafood, this is the best of them. Locals recommend it as their favorite on Norte Beach. Try the delicious fried fish (a whole one), which comes with rice, beans, and tortillas. You'll notice the bandstand and dance floor that's been added to the middle of the restaurant, and especially the sex-hunk posters all over the ceiling—that is, when you aren't gazing at the beach and the Caribbean. Chimbo's becomes a lively bar and dance club at night, drawing a crowd of drinkers and dancers (see "Isla Mujeres After Dark," below). To find it from the pier, walk left to the end of the malecón, then right onto the Playa Norte; it's about half a block on the right.

Pinguino. In the Hotel Posada del Mar, Av. Rueda Medina 15. ☎ **9/877-0878.** Main courses $3.75–$6.75; daily special $6, all-you-can-eat buffets, $4. AE, MC, V. Daily 7am–10pm; bar open to midnight. MEXICAN/SEAFOOD.

The best seats on the waterfront are on the deck of this restaurant/bar, especially in late evening when islanders and tourists arrive to dance and party. This is the place to feast on lobster—you'll get a beautifully presented, large, sublimely fresh lobster tail with a choice of butter, garlic, and secret sauces. The grilled seafood platter is spectacular, and fajitas and barbecue ribs are also popular. Breakfasts include fresh fruit, yogurt, and granola or sizable platters of eggs, served with homemade wheat bread. Both free parking and non-smoking areas are available. Pinguino is in front of the hotel, 3 blocks west of the ferry pier.

✪ **Pizza Rolandi.** Av. Hidalgo #10. ☎ **9/877-0430.** Main courses $3.50–$12. AE, V, MC. Daily 11am–11:30pm. ITALIAN/SEAFOOD.

Practically an institution in Isla, you're bound to dine at least one night at Rolandi's. The plate-sized pizzas or calzones are likely to lure you with their exotic ingredients— including lobster, black mushrooms, pineapple, or roquefort cheese, as well as more traditional tomatoes, olives, basil, and salami. The wood-burning oven provides the signature flavor to its pizzas, as well as to its baked chicken, roast beef, or mixed seafood casserole with lobster. Its extensive menu also offers a selection of salads and light appetizers, as well as an ample array of pasta dishes, steaks, fish, and scrumptious deserts. The setting is the open courtyard of the Hotel Belmar, with a porch over-looking the action on Hidalgo Street. It's 3¹/₂ blocks inland from the pier, between Madero and Abasolo.

✪ **Zazil Ha.** At the Hotel Na Balam, Norte Beach. ☎ **9/877-0279.** Fax 9/877-0446. Main courses $8–$15. AE, MC, V. Daily 7:30am–10:30am, 12:30–3:30pm, and 7–10pm. CARIBBEAN/INTERNATIONAL.

At this restaurant you can enjoy some of the island's best food while sitting at tables on the sand among palms and gardens. The serene environment is enhanced by the food—terrific pasta with garlic, shrimp in tequila sauce, fajitas, seafood pasta, and delicious molé enchiladas. New Caribbean specialties include cracked conch, coconut sailfish, jerked chicken, and stuffed squid. The new vegetarian menu is complemented by a selection of fresh juices, and there's even a special menu for those participating in yoga retreats. Between the set hours for meals you can have all sorts of enticing food, such as vegetable and fruit drinks, tacos and sandwiches, *ceviche,* and terrific nachos. It's likely you'll stake this place out for several meals before you leave. It's at the end of Playa Norte and almost at the end of calle Zazil Ha.

INEXPENSIVE

Cafecito. Calle Matamoros 42 Corner of Juárez. ☎ **9/877-0438.** Crepes $2.10–$4.20; breakfast $2.50–$4.50; main courses $4.80–$7.50. No credit cards. Daily 8am to 2pm. High Season Friday–Wednesday 5:30pm to 10:30 or 11:30 depending on the season. CREPES/ ICE CREAM/COFFEE/FRUIT DRINKS.

Sabina and Luis Rivera own this cute, Caribbean-blue corner restaurant where you can begin the day with flavorful coffee and a croissant and cream cheese, or end it with a hot-fudge sundae. Terrific crêpes are served with yogurt, ice cream, fresh fruit, or chocolate sauces, as well as ham and cheese. The two-page ice-cream menu satisfies most any craving, even one for waffles with ice cream and fruit. The three-course fixed-price dinner starts with soup, then a main course such as fish or curried shrimp with rice and salad, followed by dessert. It's 4 blocks from the pier at the corner of Juárez and Matamoros.

✪ **Chen Huaye.** Bravo 6. No phone. Main courses $2.25–$7. No credit cards. Wed–Mon 9am–11pm. YUCATECAN MEXICAN/HOME COOKING.

The Juan Garrido Trejo family owns this large lunchroom where tourists and locals find a variety of pleasing dishes at equally pleasing prices. Light meals include empanadas, Yucatecan *salbutes, panuchos,* and quesadillas. The *tamal colado,* or *tamal horneado,* are a daily special; *tamales* stuffed with chicken and baked in a banana leaf. Main courses might include breaded pork chops, chicken in adobado, or fried chicken. The name, by the way, is Maya for "only here." It's between Guerrero and Juárez; you'll recognize it by the wagon wheel in front.

Cocina Económica Carmelita. calle Juárez 14. No phone. Main dishes $3.50–$6, $3 daily lunch special. No credit cards. Mon–Sat 12:30–3pm; Dec–Mar also open for dinner, 4–8pm. MEXICAN/HOME COOKING.

Few tourists find their way to this tiny restaurant, but locals know they can get a filling, inexpensive, home-cooked meal prepared by Carmelita in the back kitchen and served by her husband at the three cloth-covered tables in the front room of their home. Two or three comida corridas are available each day and are served until they run out. They begin with the soup of the day and include a fruit water drink (*agua fresca*). Common selections include paella or *cochinita pibil,* and fish-stuffed chiles. Menu specialties include chicken in molé sauce, pork cutlet in a spicy sauce, or breaded shrimp. For fancier tastes, they have the least expensive lobster—served grilled or in a garlic sauce—in town, at $13 for an ample portion. It's 2 blocks from the passenger-ferry pier, between Bravo and Allende.

ISLA MUJERES AFTER DARK

Those in a party mood by day's end might want to start out at the beach bar of the **Hotel Na Balam** on Playa Norte, which hosts a crowd until around midnight. On Saturday and Sunday there's live music here between 4 and 7pm. **Las Palapas Chimbo's** restaurant on the beach becomes a jammin' dance joint with a live band from 9pm until whenever. Farther along the same stretch of beach, **Buho's**, the restaurant/beach bar of the Cabañas María del Mar, has its moments as a popular, low-key hangout. **Pinguino** in the Hotel Posada del Mar offers a convivial late-night hangout, where a band plays nightly during high season from 9pm to midnight. Near Matéos and Hidalgo, the new KoKo Nuts caters to a younger crowd, with alternative music for late night dancing.

2 Cozumel

44 miles (70km) SE of Cancún

Cozumel is the original Caribbean destination in Mexico, a top cruise-ship port of call in the Americas, and one of the world's top five dive destinations. Despite all this acclaim, Cozumel remains a laid-back island with an easy-going outlook and the kind of hospitality for which Mexicans are famous.

The largest island in the Mexican Caribbean, it is located just 12 miles offshore from Playa del Carmen, a 45-minute, $7 ferry ride away. The name comes from the Maya word Cuzamil, meaning "land of the swallows." Today, it remains the home of two species of birds found nowhere else: the Cozumel vireo and the Cozumel thrasher. Only 3% developed, this 28-mile-long, 11-mile-wide island still has vast stretches of pristine jungle and uninhabited shoreline. The only town is San Miguel de Cozumel, usually just called San Miguel.

The island offers all the components of a good vacation: excellent snorkeling and scuba diving, sailing and water sports, expensive resorts and modest hotels, international restaurants and local taco joints, and even a Maya ruin or two. Due to the influx of cruise visitors, shopping is extensive, with many duty-free stores selling jewelry, perfumes, and designer wares. If after a while you do get restless, the ancient Maya city of **Tulum,** the lagoons of **Xel-Ha** and **Xcaret,** or the nearby village of **Playa del Carmen** provide convenient and interesting excursions.

During pre-Hispanic times, the island was one of three important ceremonial centers (Izamal and Chichén-Itzá were the other two). Maya women would travel the 12 miles by boat to the island at least once in their life to worship the goddess of fertility, Ixchel. More than 40 sites containing shrines remain around the island today, and archaeologists still uncover the small dolls customarily offered in the fertility ceremony.

Salt and honey, trade products produced on the island, further linked Cozumel with the mainland; they were brought ashore at the ruins we know today as Tulum. The site was occupied when Hernán Cortez landed here in 1519. Before his own boat docked,

Cortez's men sacked the town and took the chief's wife and children captive. According to Bernal Díaz del Castillo's account, all were returned. Diego de Landa's account
says Cortez converted the Indians and replaced their sacred Maya figures with a cross
and a statue of Mary in the main temple at Cozumel.

After the Spanish Conquest, the island was an important port; but foreign diseases
decimated the population, and by 1570 it was almost uninhabited. The inhabitants
returned later, but the War of the Castes in the 1800s severely curtailed Cozumel's
trade. Cozumel continued its economic rollercoaster after the Caste War as a small commercial seaport. In the mid-1950s Cozumel's fame as a diving destination began to grow,
and development of the island followed that of Cancún beginning in the mid-1970s.

ESSENTIALS
GETTING THERE & DEPARTING
BY PLANE   **Aerocozumel,** a Mexicana affiliate, has numerous flights to and from
Cancún and Mérida. **Mexicana** flies from Mexico City.

Here are some telephone numbers for confirming departures to and from Cozumel:
Aerocozumel (☎ **9/872-3456,** or 9/884-2002 in Cancún); **Continental** (☎ **800/
231-0856** in the U.S., or 9/872-0487 in Cozumel); and **Mexicana** (☎ **800/531-7921**
in the U.S.; 01-800-502-2000 in Mexico; 9/872-0157 or 9/872-2945 at the airport;
fax 9/872-2945).

Only *colectivo* vans are available from the airport into town, costing around $6.
Taxis from town to the airport will run $8 to $12.

BY FERRY   There are passenger ferries to/from Playa del Carmen, and a car/
passenger ferry to/from Puerto Morelos. The former are run by **Water Jet Service**
(☎ **9/872-1508** or 9/872-1588) and make the trip between Cozumel and Playa del
Carmen in 45 minutes. The trip costs $7 one-way, and the boat is enclosed and air-
conditioned, with cushioned seats, bar service, and video entertainment. Departures
are almost hourly from 5am to 11pm. In Playa del Carmen, the ferry dock is 1½
blocks from the main square and from the bus station; in Cozumel, the ferries depart
from the main pier. Since schedules change frequently, be sure to double-check them
at the docks, especially the time of the last ferry back if that's the one you intend to
use. Storage lockers are available at the Cozumel dock for $2 per day.

The car/passenger ferry to Cozumel from Puerto Morelos (20 miles north of Playa
del Carmen) takes longer and is less frequent. For those who are considering taking a
car, be aware that in Cozumel you're better off without one; parking is difficult. I
would leave the car in Playa del Carmen and take the passenger ferry. If you need a
car, you can get a rental on the island. If you must take your car over, the terminus in
Puerto Morelos (☎ **9/871-0008**) is very easy to find. The car-ferry schedule is subject
to change, so double-check it before arriving in Puerto Morelos. The ferry leaves daily
at 5:30am, 10:30am, and 4pm. On Sundays the last trips are sometimes canceled. The
crossing takes approximately 2½ hours. Cargo takes precedence over private cars.
Officials suggest that camper drivers stay overnight in the parking lot to be first in line
for tickets. In any case, *always arrive at least 3 hours in advance of the ferry's departure
to purchase a ticket and to get in line.*

When returning to Puerto Morelos from Cozumel, the ferry departs from the international cruise-ship pier at 8am, 1:30pm, and 7pm daily. Get in line about 3 hours
before departure, and double-check the schedule by calling ☎ **9/872-0950.** The fare is
$45 per car and driver (more for campers) and $5 per extra passenger. People wanting
to go as passengers will find the Playa del Carmen ferry more convenient.

Cozumel Island

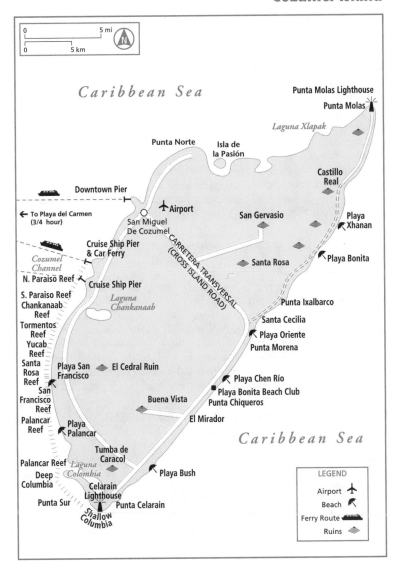

Caribbean Sea

5 mi

5 km

N

Punta Molas Lighthouse

Punta Molas

Laguna Xlapak

Punta Norte

Isla de
la Pasión

Castillo
Real

Downtown Pier

Airport

San Gervasio

Playa
Xhanan

← To Playa del Carmen
(3/4 hour)

San Miguel
De Cozumel

Playa Bonita

*Cozumel
Channel*

Cruise Ship Pier
& Car Ferry

CARRETERA TRANSVERSAL
(CROSS ISLAND ROAD)

Santa Rosa

N. Paraiso Reef

Cruise Ship Pier

Punta Ixalbarco

S. Paraiso Reef
Chankanaab
Reef

*Laguna
Chankanaab*

Santa Cecilia

Playa Oriente

Tormentos
Reef
Yucab
Reef

Punta Morena

Santa
Rosa
Reef

Playa San
Francisco

El Cedral Ruin

San
Francisco
Reef

Playa Chen Río

Playa Bonita Beach Club
Punta Chiqueros

Buena Vista

Palancar
Reef

Playa
Palancar

El Mirador

Caribbean Sea

Tumba de
Caracol

Palancar Reef
Deep
Columbia

*Laguna
Colombia*

Playa Bush

LEGEND

Celarain
Lighthouse

Airport ✈

Punta Sur

Punta Celarain

Beach 🏄

*Shallow
Columbia*

Ferry Route 🚢

Ruins 🔺

ORIENTATION

ARRIVING Cozumel's **airport** is immediately north of downtown. **Aero Transportes** *colectivo* vans at the airport provide transportation into town and to the north and south hotel zones. Buy your ticket as you exit the terminal. Passenger ferries arrive in Cozumel at the dock opposite the town's main square. The car ferry docks at the Inter-national Pier, which is south of town near the hotels La Ceiba and Sol Caribe. Cruise ships also dock at the International Pier and at a newer pier called Puerto Maya, about a mile further south (with a third pier under construction and controversy). The construction of **Puerto Maya** also stirred controversy because it was built over North

Paradise Reef—the reef with the best shore diving and snorkeling. Dive operators, the town, and ecological preservation activists from around the world protested the building of this pier, without success.

VISITOR INFORMATION   The **State Tourism Office** (☎/fax **9/872-0972**) is located on the second floor of the Plaza del Sol commercial building facing the central plaza and is open daily from 8am to 4pm.

CITY LAYOUT   San Miguel's main waterfront street is called **avenida Rafael Melgar,** running along the western shore of the island. The town is laid out on a grid, with avenidas running north and south, calles running east and west. The exception is **avenida Juárez,** which runs from the passenger-ferry dock through the main square and inland. Juárez divides the town into northern and southern halves.

Heading inland from the dock along Juárez, you'll find that the avenidas you cross are numbered by fives: 5 avenida, 10 avenida, 15 avenida. North of Av. Juárez, calles have even numbers: 2 Norte, 4 Norte, 6 Norte. South of Juárez, calles have odd numbers: 1 Sur (also called Adolfo Salas), 3 Sur, 5 Sur.

ISLAND LAYOUT   The island is cut in half by one road, which runs past the airport and the ruins of San Gervasio to the almost uninhabited southern coast of the island. The northern part of the island has no paved roads. It's scattered with small, badly ruined Maya sites, from the age when "Cuzamil" was a land sacred to the moon goddess Ixchel. San Gervasio is accessible by motor scooter and car.

The most inexpensive hotels are in the town of San Miguel. Moderate to expensive accommodations are north and south of town. Many cater to divers. South of the city is **Chankanaab National Park,** centered on the beautiful lagoon of the same name. Beyond Chankanaab are **Playa Palancar** and, offshore, the **Palancar Reef** (*arrecife*). At the southern tip of the island are **Punta Celarain** and the lighthouse.

The eastern, seaward shore of the island is mostly surf beach, beautiful for walking but dangerous for swimming.

GETTING AROUND   You can walk to most destinations in town. However, getting to outlying hotels and beaches, including the Chankanaab Lagoon, requires a taxi or rental car.

Car rentals are roughly the same price as on the mainland, depending on demand. Renting a small car costs less than renting two mopeds. International rental agencies have counters in the airport, or rentals can be arranged by your hotel tour desk or any local travel agency. See "By Car" under "Getting Around" in chapter 2 for specifics.

Moped rentals are all over the village and cost about $30 for 24 hours, but terms and prices vary. Carefully inspect the actual moped you'll be renting to see that all the gizmos are in good shape: horn, light, starter, seat, mirror. And be sure to note all damage to the moped on the rental agreement. Most important, read the fine print on the back of the rental agreement, which states that you are not insured, you are responsible for paying for any damage to the bike (or for all of it if it's stolen or demolished), and must stay on paved roads. It's illegal to ride a moped without a helmet (subject to a $25 fine).

Taxis: Here are a few sample fares: Island tour, $60; town to southern hotel zone, $5 to $8; town to northern hotels, $4 to $5; to Chankanaab from town, $6. Call

Be Streetwise _____

North/south streets have the right of way, and traffic doesn't slow down or stop.

☎ **9/872-0236** for taxi pickup. Fares on the island are fixed with little variation and not generally open to negotiation.

Fast Facts: Cozumel

American Express   The local representative is Fiesta Cozumel, calle 11 no. 598 (☎ **9/872-0725**).

Area Code   The telephone area code is **9.**

Climate   From October to December there can be strong winds all over the Yucatán, as well as some rain. In Cozumel, wind conditions in November and December can make diving dangerous. May to September is the rainy season.

Diving   If you intend to dive, remember to bring proof of your diver's certification. Underwater currents can be very strong here, and many of the reef drops are quite steep, making them excellent sites for experienced divers, but they can be too challenging for novice divers.

Internet access   There are a number of cyber cafes in and about the main square; of these, the **Internet Café** at the corner of calle 1 Sur and Av. 10 offered the cheapest rates and no minimum charge. Hours are from 9am to 11pm Monday to Saturday. There are a couple of other places around the corner on Av. 10 if you can't get on a computer there. Another option is **Coffee Net** at Av. Rafael Melgar #798 near the intersection with calle 11 sur (☎ **9/872-6394**). It's larger and keeps the same hours as the Internet Café.

Post Office   The post office (*correo*) is on avenida Rafael Melgar at calle 7 Sur, at the southern edge of town; it's open Monday to Friday from 9am to 6pm and Saturday from 9am to noon.

Recompression Chamber   There are three recompression chambers (*cámaras de recompresión*). One is on calle 5 Sur, 1 block off Melgar between Melgar and avenida 5 Sur (☎ **9/872-2387** or 9/872-1848). Normal hours are 8am–1pm and 4pm–8pm. The 24-hour emergencies number is ☎ **9/872-1430.** Another one is the **Hyperbaric Center of Cozumel,** ☎ **9/872-3070.**

Seasons   High season is Christmas to Easter, and in August.

EXPLORING THE ISLAND

For **diving and snorkeling** it's best to go directly to the recommended shops below. For **island tours, ruins tours** on and off the island, **glass-bottom boat tours, fiesta nights, fishing,** and other activities, I recommend the travel agency **InterMar Cozumel Viajes,** calle 2 Norte, 101-B between avenidas 5 and 10 (☎ **9/872-1098;** fax 9/872-0895; e-mail: intermar@cozumel.com.mx). The office is close to the main plaza between avenidas 5 and 10 Norte. But many activities you can do on your own without purchasing a tour.

WATER SPORTS

BOAT TRIPS   Boat trips are a popular pastime on Cozumel. Some excursions include snorkeling and scuba diving or a stop at a beach with lunch. Various types of tours are offered, including rides in glass-bottom boats for around $30. These usually start at 9am and end at 1pm and include beer and soft drinks.

Mardi Gras

Carnaval (Mardi Gras) is Cozumel's most colorful fiesta. It begins the Thursday before Ash Wednesday with daytime street dancing and nighttime parades on Thursday, Saturday, and Monday (the best).

FISHING The best months for fishing are April to September, when the catch includes blue and white marlin, sailfish, tarpon, swordfish, dorado, wahoo, tuna, and red snapper. Fishing costs $450 for six people all day or $80 to $85 per person for a half day for four people.

SCUBA DIVING Cozumel is Mexico's dive capital and one of the world's premier dive destinations. Don't forget to bring your dive card or you'll be out of luck. And if you bring your dive log, too, all the better. Various establishments on the island rent scuba gear—tanks, regulators with pressure gauge, buoyancy compensators, weight belts, masks, snorkels, and fins, but they all ask to see documentation that you're a diver. Many will also arrange a half-day boat expedition, complete with lunch, for a set price—usually around $40. Sign up the day before if you're interested. A two-tank morning dive costs around $50; some shops are now offering an additional afternoon one-tank dive for $9 for those who took the morning dives, or $25 for a one-tank dive. However, if you're a dedicated diver, you may save by buying a diving package that includes air transportation, hotel, and usually two dives a day. Cozumel is such a popular dive destination that it has over 60 dive operators and 3 recompression chambers on the island (see "Fast Facts: Cozumel," above).

The underwater wonders of the famous **Palancar Reef** are offshore from the beach of the same name. From the car-ferry pier south to Punta Celarain are more than 20 miles of offshore reefs. In the blue depths, divers find caves and canyons, small and large colorful fish, and an enormous variety of sea coral. The **Santa Rosa Reef** is famous for its depth, sea life, coral, and sponges. **San Francisco Reef,** off the beach by the same name south of town, has a drop-off wall, but it's still fairly shallow, with fascinating sea life. The **Chankanaab Reef,** where divers are joined by schools of tropical fish, is close to the shore by the national park of the same name. It's shallow and good for novice divers. South of Chankanaab along the eastern road, **Yucab Reef** has beautiful coral.

Numerous vessels on the island operate daily diving and snorkeling tours, so if you aren't traveling on a prearranged dive package, the best plan is to shop around and sign up for one of those. Of Cozumel's many dive shops, two are among the top: Bill Horn's **Aqua Safari,** in front of the Aqua Safari Inn and next to the Vista del Mar Hotel on Melgar at calle 5 (☎ **9/872-0101;** fax 9/872-0661); and in the Hotel Plaza Las Glorias (☎ **9/872-3362** or 9/872-2422) is a PADI five-star instructor center, with full equipment and parts, a good selection of books, and its own pier just across the street. They're on the Internet at www.aquasafari.com. **Dive House,** on the main plaza (☎ **9/872-1953;** fax 9/872-0368), offers PADI and NAUI SSI instruction. Both shops offer morning, afternoon, and night dives.

You can save money by renting your gear at a beach shop, such as the two mentioned above, and diving from shore. The shops at the Plaza Las Glorias and La Ceiba hotels are good for shore diving. It costs about $6 to rent one tank and weights; extra charges apply for regulator, BC, mask, and fins. The dives from shore are only worthwhile from San Francisco beach, Chankanaab, and La Ceiba beach. Even then it's a lot of work to haul your own gear. The sites are much better in the depths offshore, and it really is a lot easier to take a boat.

San Miguel de Cozumel

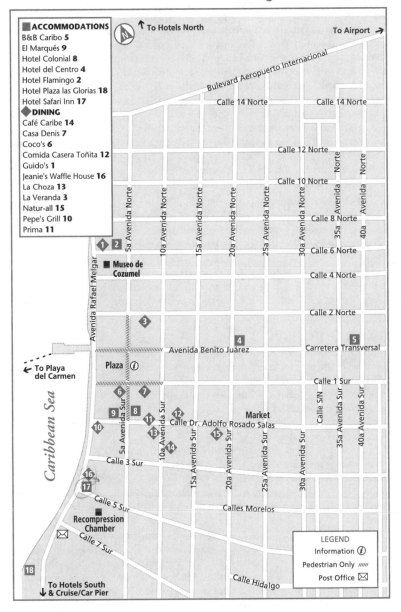

ACCOMMODATIONS
B&B Caribo **5**
El Marqués **9**
Hotel Colonial **8**
Hotel del Centro **4**
Hotel Flamingo **2**
Hotel Plaza las Glorias **18**
Hotel Safari Inn **17**

DINING
Café Caribe **14**
Casa Denis **7**
Coco's **6**
Comida Casera Toñita **12**
Guido's **1**
Jeanie's Waffle House **16**
La Choza **13**
La Veranda **3**
Natur-all **15**
Pepe's Grill **10**
Prima **11**

To Hotels North
To Airport
Bulevard Aeropuerto Internacional
Calle 14 Norte
Calle 12 Norte
Calle 10 Norte
Calle 8 Norte
Calle 6 Norte
Calle 4 Norte
Calle 2 Norte
Carretera Transversal
5a Avenida Norte
10a Avenida Norte
15a Avenida Norte
20a Avenida Norte
25a Avenida Norte
30a Avenida Norte
35a Avenida
40a Avenida
Norte

Museo de Cozumel
Avenida Rafael Melgar
Avenida Benito Juárez
Plaza
To Playa del Carmen
Caribbean Sea
Calle 1 Sur
Market
Calle Dr. Adolfo Rosado Salas
Calle SJN
35a Avenida Sur
40a Avenida Sur
5a Avenida Sur
10a Avenida Sur
15a Avenida Sur
20a Avenida Sur
25a Avenida Sur
30a Avenida Sur
Calle 3 Sur
Calle 5 Sur
Calles Morelos
Recompression Chamber
Calle 7 Sur
Calle Hidalgo
To Hotels South & Cruise/Car Pier

LEGEND
Information (i)
Pedestrian Only //////
Post Office ✉

A new twist in underwater Yucatán is **cenote diving** and **snorkeling.** The penin-sula's underground *cenotes* (say-*noh*-tehs) or sinkholes, which were sacred to the Maya, lead to a vast system of underground caverns. Here, the gently flowing water is so clear divers appear to be floating on air through caves that look just like those on dry land, complete with stalactites and stalagmites, plus tropical fish, eels, and turtles. The caverns were formed millions of years ago during the last two glacial eras, but only in recent years has this other world been opened to certified divers. The experienced cave divers/owners of **Yucatech Expeditions** (☎/fax **9/872-5659;** e-mail: yucatech@ cozumel.czm.com.mx), offer this unique experience five times weekly from Playa del Carmen (you take the ferry with your gear and they meet you with vans there). *Cenotes* are 30 to 45 minutes from Playa and a dive in each *cenote* lasts around 45 minutes. Snorkelers paddle around the *cenotes,* while divers explore the depths. Dives are within the daylight zone, about 130 feet into the caverns and no more than 60 feet deep. There's plenty of natural light. Company owner Germán Yañez Mendoza inspects diving credentials carefully and has a list of requirements divers must meet before cave diving is permitted. They also offer the equivalent of a resort course in cave diving and a full cave-diving course. A snorkeling trip to two *cenotes* runs around $65, while a two-*cenote* dive costs around $130, including transportation from Cozumel, tanks, weights, food, and drinks (beers only after the dives).

SNORKELING   Anyone who can swim can snorkel. Rental of the snorkel (breathing pipe), goggles, and flippers should cost only about $4 for half a day; a 2-hour snorkeling trip costs $15. The brilliantly colored tropical fish provide a dazzling show. **Chankanaab Park** is one of the best places to go on your own for an abundant fish show.

Agency-arranged **snorkeling excursions** cost around $40 for a 10am to 3pm trip that includes snorkeling at three different reefs, lunch, beer, and soft drinks. Two-hour snorkeling trips through the dive shops recommended above cost $15 and usually leave around 2:30pm.

A TOUR OF THE ISLAND

Travel agencies can book you on a group tour of the island for around $44, depending on whether the tour includes lunch and a stop for snorkeling. A taxi driver charges $60 for a 4-hour tour. A 4-hour horseback tour of the island's interior to the ruins and jungle costs $60; call **Rancho Buenavista** (☎ **9/872-1537** or 9/872-4374). The trip leaves from the InterMar Viajes travel agency mentioned above (call for schedule information). You can also easily rent a motorbike or car for half a day to take you around; see above under "Getting Around."

North of town, along avenida Rafael Melgar (which becomes Carretera Pilar), you'll pass a yacht marina and a string of Cozumel's first hotels, as well as some new condominiums. A few of the hotels have nice beaches. This road ends just past the hotels; you can then backtrack to the transversal road that cuts across the island from west (the town side) to east and links up with the eastern highway that brings you back to town.

The more interesting route begins by going south of town on Melgar (which becomes Costera Sur or Carretera a Chankanaab) past the Hotel Barracuda and Sol Caribe. After about 3 miles you'll see a sign pointing left down an unpaved road a short distance to the Rancho San Manuel, where you can rent horses. There are only seven horses here, but a guide and soft drink are included in the price. Rides cost $20 per hour. It's open daily from 8am to 4pm.

About 5 miles south of town you'll come to the Crowne Princess and La Ceiba hotels and also the dock for car ferries to Puerto Morelos. Go snorkeling in the water by the Hotel La Ceiba and you might spot a sunken airplane put there for an underwater movie. Offshore, from here to the tip of the island at Punta Celarain, 20 miles away, is the Underwater National Park, so designated to protect the reef from damage by visitors. Dive masters warn not to touch or destroy the underwater growth.

CHANKANAAB NATIONAL PARK

This park is the pride of many islanders. Chankanaab means "little sea," which refers to a beautiful land-locked pool connected to the sea through an underground tunnel— a sort of ocean in miniature. Snorkeling in this natural aquarium is not permited, but the park includes a lovely beach for sunbathing and snorkeling. It's best to arrive early to stake out a chair and *palapa* before the cruise-ship crowd arrives. Likewise, the snorkeling is best before noon. There are rest rooms, lockers, a gift shop, several snack huts, a restaurant, and a snorkeling-gear-rental palapa. You can also swim with dolphins here. The cost is $119 per person. Call ☎ **9/872-6605** for information and reservations.

Surrounding the lagoon is a botanical garden with shady paths and 351 species of tropical and subtropical plants from 22 countries and 451 species from Cozumel. Several Maya structures have been re-created within the gardens to give visitors an idea of Maya life in a jungle setting. There's a small natural history museum as well. Admission to the park costs $7; it's open daily from 8am to 5pm.

THE BEACHES

Ten miles past the Chankanaab National Park, you'll come to **Playa San Francisco** and, south of it, **Playa Palancar.** Besides the beach at Chankanaab Lagoon, they're Cozumel's best beaches. Food (usually overpriced) and equipment rentals are available. On the east side of the island, the **Playa Bonita Beach Club,** near Playa Chiqueros, has water sports and windsurfing-equipment rentals. The restaurant is open daily from 10am to 5pm.

PUNTA CELARAIN   After Playa San Francisco, you plow through the jungle on a straight road for miles until you're 17$^{1}/_{2}$ miles from town. Finally, you emerge near the southern reaches of the island on the east coast. The lighthouse you see in the distance is at Punta Celarain, the island's southernmost tip. The sand track is unsuitable for motorbikes, but in a car you can drive to the lighthouse in about 25 minutes.

THE EASTERN SHORE   The road along the east coast of the island is wonderful. There are views of the sea, the rocky shore, and the pounding surf. On the land side are little farms and forests. Exotic birds take flight as you approach, and monstrous (but harmless) iguanas skitter off into the undergrowth.

Most of the east coast is unsafe for swimming because the surf can create a deadly undertow. There are always cars pulled off along the road here, with the occupants spending the day on the golden beach dotted with limestone formations, but not in the churning waters. Three restaurants catering to tourists are along this part of the coast, complete with sombrero-clad iguanas for picture companions.

Halfway up the east coast, the paved eastern road meets the paved transversal road (which passes the ruins of San Gervasio) back to town, 9$^{1}/_{2}$ miles away. The east-coast road ends when it turns into the transversal, petering out to a narrow track of sandy road by a nice restaurant in front of the Chen Río Beach; vehicles, even motorbikes, will get stuck on the sand road. If you're a bird-watcher, leave your vehicle on the highway here and walk straight down the sandy road. Go slowly and quietly and, at the least, you'll spot many herons and egrets in the lagoon on the left that parallels the path. Much farther on are Maya ruins.

OTHER ATTRACTIONS

MAYA RUINS   One of the most popular island excursions is to **San Gervasio** (100 B.C. to A.D. 1600). A road leads there from the airport, or you can continue on the eastern part of the island following the paved transversal road. The worn sign to the ruins is easy to miss, but the turnoff (left) is about halfway between town and the eastern coast. Stop at the entrance gate and pay the $1 road-use fee. Go straight ahead over the potholed road to the ruins about 2 miles farther and pay the $4 to enter; camera permits cost $4 for each still or video camera you want to bring in. A small tourist center at the entrance has cold drinks and snacks for sale.

When it comes to Cozumel's Maya remains, getting there is most of the fun, and you should do it for the mystique and for the trip, not for the size or scale of the ruins. The buildings, though preserved, are crudely made and would not be much of a tourist attraction if they were not the island's only cleared and accessible ruins. More significant than beautiful, the site was once an important ceremonial center where the Maya gathered, coming even from the mainland. The important deity here was Ixchel, known as the goddess of weaving, women, childbirth, pilgrims, the moon, and medicine. Although you won't see any representations of her at San Gervasio today, Bruce Hunter, in his *Guide to Ancient Maya Ruins,* writes that priests hid behind a large pottery statue of her and became the voice of the goddess, speaking to pilgrims and answering their petitions. She was the wife of Itzamná, the sun god, and as such, preeminent among all Maya gods.

Tour guides charge $10 for a tour for one to six people. A better option is to find a copy of the green booklet *San Gervasio,* sold at local checkout counters or bookstores, and tour the site on your own. Seeing it takes 30 minutes. Taxi drivers offer a tour to the ruins for about $25; the driver will wait for you outside the ruins.

PARQUE ARQUEOLÓGICO   This park contains reproductions of many of Mexico's important archaeological treasures, including the 4-foot-high Olmec head and the Chaac-Mool seen at Chichén-Itzá. A Maya couple demonstrates the lifestyle of the Maya in a *nah,* or thatch-roofed oval home. The park is a nice addition to the island's cultural attractions and is well worth visiting, but wear bug repellent before you begin exploring. The park is open daily from 8am to 6pm; admission is $2.50. To get there, turn left on the unmarked road across from the International Pier, off Costera Sur, just south of the La Ceiba hotel, then left on avenida 65 Sur and follow the signs.

A HISTORY MUSEUM   The **Museo de la Isla de Cozumel,** on avenida Melgar between calles 4 and 6 Norte (☎ **9/872-1475**), is more than just a nice place to spend a rainy hour. On the first floor an excellent exhibit showcases endangered species, the origin of the island, and its present-day topography and plant and animal life, including an explanation of coral formation. Upstairs, showrooms feature the history of the town, artifacts from the island's pre-Hispanic sites, and colonial-era cannons, swords, and ship paraphernalia. It's open daily from 9am to 5pm. Admission is $3; guided tours in English are free. There's a rooftop restaurant open long hours.

TRIPS TO THE MAINLAND

PLAYA DEL CARMEN & XCARET   Going on your own to the nearby seaside village of **Playa del Carmen** and the **Xcaret** nature park is as easy as a quick ferry ride from Cozumel (for ferry information, see "Getting There & Departing," above). Playa del Carmen is covered in detail later in this chapter. Cozumel travel agencies offer a Xcaret tour that includes the ferry fee, transportation to the park, and the admission fee for $68.

CHICHÉN-ITZÁ, TULUM & COBÁ   Travel agencies can arrange day-trips to the fascinating ruins of **Chichén-Itzá** either by air or by bus. Since the ruins of **Tulum,** overlooking the Caribbean, and **Cobá,** in a dense jungle setting, are closer, they cost less to visit. These cities are quite a contrast to Chichén-Itzá. Cobá is a grandiose city spread out beside a lake within a remote jungle setting, while Tulum is smaller and more compact, and right on the beach. Neither has been restored to the same extent as Chichén-Itzá. A trip to both Cobá and Tulum begins at 9am and returns around 6pm.

SHOPPING

Shopping has evolved from the ubiquitous T-shirt shops into stores that now feature expensive resort wear, silver jewelry, and decorative art. Most stores are on avenida Melgar; the best shops for high-quality Mexican folk art are **Los Cinco Soles, Talavera,** and **Playa del Angel.** Prices for serapes, T-shirts, and the like are less expensive on the side streets off Melgar.

If you want to pick up some Mexican tapes and CDs, head to **Discoteca Hollywood,** at Juárez 421 (☎ **9/872-4090**); it's open Monday to Saturday from 9am to 10pm. Billing itself as the "Paradise of the Cassette," this store stocks a large selection.

WHERE TO STAY

Cozumel's hotels are in three separate locations: in the **central town,** and along the coast to the **north** and **south** of town. The older resorts, most of which are expensive, line the beaches and coral and limestone outcroppings north and south of town; the budget establishments are in the central part of town. *Note:* There's a **central reservations number** for many (not all) of the island's hotels (☎ 800/327-2254 in the U.S. and Canada). As an alternative to a hotel, **Cozumel Vacation Villas and Condos,** av. 10 Sur no. 124, 77600 Cozumel, Q. Roo (☎ **800/224-5551** in the U.S., 9/872-0729, or 9/872-1375; e-mail: info@cozumel-villas.com), offers a wide range of accommodations and prices.

Because Cozumel is such a big destination for divers, there are numerous options that cater to this specialty market. Some are for serious, no-frills divers who only want a good bed and a hot shower for after the dive. These hotels usually don't have a pool or restaurant. There are others that are a little more upscale, often on the beach, that offer complete dive services in addition to rooms and facilities. The remaining properties are for divers traveling with non-divers.

NORTH OF TOWN

I'll start with the northernmost hotels, then cover those in town and finish with the southern hotel zone. **Carretera Santa Pilar** or San Juan is the name of Melgar's northern extension, so just take Melgar north and all the hotels are lined up in close proximity to each other on the Santa Pilar Beach, a short distance from town and the airport.

Very Expensive

Hotel El Cozumeleño Beach Resort. Carretera Santa Pilar Km 4.5 (Apdo. Postal 53), 77600 Cozumel, Q. Roo. ☎ **9/872-0050** or 9/872-0049. Fax 9/872-0381. 250 units. A/C TEL TV. High season $310–$330 double; low season $200–240 double. All inclusive. AE, MC, V.

There are busy hotels and there are quiet ones. Mark this one down as a busy one. The large lobby is a flurry of motion and sound: activities coordinators rushing about, groups gathering for a trip somewhere, people making inquiries about the game room, etc. The Cozumeleño all-inclusive resort is for people who want an active vacation with plenty to do. It has one of the few bits of beach that exist on this stretch of coast and a lovely patio area. The owners have recently more than doubled the number of rooms in the hotel and have added to the amenities. The rooms in the old part are large, much longer than they are wide; rooms in the new part are smaller, but their shape allows for a less awkward arrangment of furniture. All the rooms look out over the sea. The glassed-in dining room also gives a view of the sea. The sandy beach here is small (although it has more beach than most of the hotels on the stretch), but the pool area is large and attractive, with shade *palapas* and many amenities.

Dining/Diversions: Two restaurants, one by the beach and pool and the other indoors, serve all three meals. For drinks, there's a karaoke bar, and there's a swim-up bar.

Amenities: Three pools (one for children, one with a roof, Jacuzzi, and swim-up bar), tennis court, water-sports equipment, 19-hole miniature golf course, two game rooms, gym, and diving center. Laundry and room service, travel agency, auto and moped rental.

Expensive

✪ **Playa Azul.** Carretera San Juan Km 4, 77600 Cozumel, Q. Roo. ☎ **9/872-0199** or 9/872-0043. Fax 9/872-0110. www.playa-azul.com E-mail: playazul@cozumel.com.mx. 50 units. A/C, TEL. High season $168 double, $224 suite. Low season $130 double, $195 suite. AE, MC, V. Free parking.

This hotel caters to those who seek lodging that's conducive to relaxing—the background commotion heard in the busier hotels is not present here, and the service has a personal feel to it. Rooms are spacious and decorated with a taste for simplicity and elegance; all come with either a king or two double beds, with suites offering two convertible single sofas in the separate living room area. All rooms come with a view of the sea, and most with terraces and balconies. There's a second-floor lobby with pool table and video room, plus a library. The beach area has shade *palapas,* plus a private dock for dive boat pick-ups. In-room safety deposit boxes, small refrigerators, and extra-large bathrooms are added features. There are also four master suites that come with in-room Jacuzzis.

Dining/Diversions: The **Playa Azul** restaurant specializes in seafood and Mexican cuisine and offers indoor or patio dining; there's room service available from 7am to 11pm. The beachfront *palapa* bar is open from 9am to 6pm.

Amenities: Beachfront pool with water-sports equipment; atrium lounge with video room and satellite TV. Laundry, dry cleaning, gift shop, room service, scooter and car rental. Massage service available.

Sol Cabañas del Caribe. Carretera Santa Pilar Km 4.5 (Apdo. Postal 9), 77600 Cozumel, Q. Roo. ☎ **888/341-5993** in the U.S., 9/872-0017, or 9/872-0072. Fax 9/872-1599. www.mexicoweb.com.travel/coz203.html. E-mail: paradisu@cozumel.com.mx. 48 units. A/C. High season $246 double. Low season $100 double. Dive and honeymoon packages available. AE, MC, V. Free secured parking.

Built in two sections, the hotel gives you two choices of room styles. Standard rooms in the two-story section adjacent to the lobby all face the water and are decorated in Southwest shades of apricot and blue. All have small sitting areas and either a porch or balcony. The one-story bungalow/cabaña section has a similar decor, but rooms are a little smaller and have patios on the beach.

Dining: The main restaurant is in a glassed-in terrace by the water, and there's a poolside spot for snacks.

Amenities: Swimming pool; water-sports equipment for rent including sailboats, jetskis, and diving, snorkeling, and windsurfing equipment; pharmacy; gift shop; travel agency.

Moderate

Hotel Fontán. Carretera San Juan Km 2.5, 77600 Cozumel, Q. Roo. ☎ **800/221-6509** in the U.S., or 9/872-0300. Fax 9/872-0105. 48 units. A/C TV TEL. High season $100–$150 double. Low season $90–$120 double. AE, MC, V. Free parking.

This hotel is an excellent value for your money. Rooms on all four floors of the newly remodeled hotel have private balconies; most have ocean views. Bathrooms all have showers. There's a nice pool and Jacuzzi by the beach (held up by a retaining wall), surrounded by lounge chairs. There's a restaurant/bar, plus a dock for water sports. A scuba shop is located on site, and kayaks and mountain bikes are available for use by hotel guests. Its Restaurant Jard'n Maya is open daily from 7am to 10:30pm.

IN TOWN

Very Expensive

✪ Hotel Plaza Las Glorias. Av. Rafael Melgar Km 1.5, 77600 Cozumel, Q. Roo. ☎ **800/ 342-AMIGO** in the U.S., or 9/872-2000. Fax 9/872-1937. E-mail: hplgcoz@sidek.com.mx. 170 units. A/C MINIBAR TV TEL. High season $330 double. Low season $209 double. AE, MC, V. Free parking.

This all-suite hotel offers the top-notch amenities of the expensive hotels farther out, but it's within 5 blocks of town. Beyond the expansive, lively lobby bar is the pool, with a swim-up bar, a multilevel deck, a shored-up beach, and the ocean. Most of the large, pleasantly furnished rooms have marble floors and separate sunken living rooms. All come with balconies or terraces facing the water. Standard in-room amenities include hair dryers, purified tap water, and in-room safety deposit boxes.

Dining/Diversions: There's a buffet at breakfast. The main restaurant features different specialties nightly. All meals are served outdoors under a *palapa* (weather permitting), and the popular lobby bar features a large-screen TV that brings in major sports events. In high season there's often live entertainment (soft music) and a happy hour with two-for-one drinks between 5 and 7pm.

Amenities: Swimming pool with Jacuzzi and swim-up bar by the beach, diving pier, organized pool games, recreational director, travel agency, concierge. Laundry and room service, travel agency, car rental, shopping arcade, and fully equipped dive shop with PADI and NAUI certification available.

Moderate

B&B Caribo. Av. Juárez 799, 77600 Cozumel, Q. Roo. ☎ **800/830-5558** in the U.S., or ☎ /fax 9/872-3195. www.visit-caribo.com 12 units. A/C. High season $60 double, $80 apartment; Low season $40 double; $50 apartment. Rates include full breakfast. AE, DISC, MC, V.

The owners of this B&B will make you feel right at home, and the lodging is quite comfortable. Nine neatly decorated, cheerful rooms come with cool tile floors, white furniture, blue bedspreads, and big bottles of purified drinking water. The three apartments come with small kitchens. Most rooms have a double and a single bed. There are a number of common rooms and a rooftop terrace. Breakfasts are elaborate, and the cooking is good. There is also a television/computer room with e-mail service. To find the Caribo from the plaza, walk 6¹/₂ blocks inland on Juárez; it will be a smartly painted blue-and-white house on the left.

✪ Hotel Flamingo. Calle 6 Nte. no. 81, 77600 Cozumel, Q. Roo. ☎ **800/806-1601** in the U.S. or fax 9/872-1264. www.hotelflamingo.com. 22 units. A/C. High season $55–$77 double. Low season $36–$45 double. AE, MC, V.

The Flamingo offers one of the best values in Cozumel and caters mostly to divers looking for extra-clean, basic accommodations. The Flamingo has three floors of quiet rooms, a grassy inner courtyard, rooftop terrace, and very helpful new management. Second- and third-story rooms are spacious. All have white tile floors and new bathroom fixtures; the higher prices are for rooms with air-conditioning, telephone, and cable TV. Rooms in the front of the building have balconies overlooking the street. All have two double beds. A penthouse suite comes with a full kitchen and sleeps up to six.

Trade paperbacks are by the reception desk, and there's a TV and complimentary coffee in the lobby. Special dive packages are available, and Spanish lessons are taught at the hotel. To find it, walk 5 blocks north on Melgar from the plaza and turn right on calle 6; the hotel is on the left between Melgar and avenida 5. Street parking is available.

Inexpensive

Hotel Colonial. Av. 5 Sur no. 9 (Apdo. Postal 286), 77600 Cozumel, Q. Roo. ☎ **9/872-0209,** 9/872-4034, or 9/872-0506. Fax 9/872-1387. 28 units. A/C TV TEL. High season $65 studio, $80 suite; low season $55 studio, $70 suite. AE, MC, V.

Across the street from the El Marqués hotel is a collection of shops and this pleasant four-story hotel, with an elevator. It's a good deal for the money, especially if you like to spread out. The lobby is far back past the shops. You get a quiet, spacious, furnished studio or a one-bedroom apartment with red-tile floors on the first floor; second- and third-floor rooms have kitchenettes. Studios come with refrigerators. And there's free coffee and sweet bread in the morning. The street is closed to traffic. From the plaza, walk a half block south on avenida 5 Sur; the hotel is on the left.

Hotel del Centro. Av. Juárez 501, 77600 Cozumel, Q. Roo. ☎ **9/872-5471.** Fax 9/872-0299. E-mail: hcentro@cozumel.com.mx. 14 units. A/C TV. High season $60 double. Low season $50 double. Suite for 4 w/kitchen $100. Discounts for weekly stays. No credit cards.

Although this new, surprisingly stylish hotel is located 6 long blocks from the water-front, it's a good bargain. The rooms are small, but modern and extra-clean, with decorative details, TV, and two double beds. Several suites with kitchenettes are also available. The rooms surround a garden courtyard with an oval pool framed by com-fortable lounge chairs and a restaurant/bar.

Hotel El Marqués. Av. 5 Sur no. 180, 77600 Cozumel, Q. Roo. ☎ **9/872-0677.** Fax 9/872-0537. 39 units. A/C. High season $49 double. Low season $38 double. Discounts for 3 or more nights if paying in cash. MC, V.

Step back into the 1960s in these sunny rooms with gold trim and Formica-marble countertops, French provincial overtones, gray-and-white tile floors, and two double beds. The junior suites have refrigerators; full suites have refrigerators, stoves, and sitting areas. Third-floor rooms have good views. The staff is friendly, and the price is right. To find it from the plaza, turn right (south) on avenida 5 Sur; the hotel is near the corner of Salas, on the right up the stairs next to Coco's restaurant.

✪ **Hotel Safari Inn.** Av. Melgar at calle 5 Sur (Apdo. Postal 41), 77600 Cozumel, Q. Roo. ☎ **9/872-0101.** Fax 9/872-0661. E-mail: dive@aquasafari.com. 12 units. A/C. $44 double. MC, V.

This pleasant budget hotel has a great location for divers: It's in town, above and behind the Aqua Safari Dive Shop. Natural colors and stucco pervade the interior of this three-story (no elevator) choice. The huge rooms come with firm beds, built-in sofas, and tiled floors. The hotel caters to divers and offers some good dive packages through its dive shop, Aqua Safari, one of the most reputable on the island. To find it from the pier, turn right (south) and walk 3 1/2 blocks on Melgar; the hotel is on your left facing the Caribbean at the corner of calle 5 Sur.

SOUTH OF TOWN

The hotels to the south of town tend to be more spread out and farther from town than the hotels to the north. Those farthest away are all-inclusive properties. The beaches along this part of the coast are slightly better than those to the north, but all the hotels have swimming pools and piers from which you can snorkle, and all of them accommodate divers. To get to these properties head south on Av. Melgar, which then becomes the coastal road **Costera Sur** (also called **Carretera a Chankanaab**).

Very Expensive

☉ Presidente Inter-Continental Cozumel. Costera Sur Km 6, 77600 Cozumel, Q. Roo.
☎ **800/327-0200** in the U.S., or 9/872-0322. Fax 9/872-1360. www.interconti.com.
253 units. A/C MINIBAR TV TEL. High season $300–$390 double (does not include rates for
Dec. 19–Jan. 1, when prices are very high). Low season $260–$340 double. Discounts and
packages available. AE, CB, DC, MC, V. Free parking.

This is Cozumel's finest hotel in terms of situation, on-site amenities, and service.
Palatial in scale, modern in style, the Presidente spreads across a long stretch of coast
with only distant hotels for neighbors. Rooms come in four categories distributed
among four buildings (two to five stories tall). Standard rooms come with a view of
the garden, superior rooms a view of the ocean. Deluxe ocean fronts and beach fronts
are more expensive, being larger and having spacious balconies or terraces (the main
difference is that the beach fronts are at ground level and the ocean fronts are on the
second floor. Non-smoking rooms are all on the fourth level of the main building, and
two rooms are set aside for guests with disabilities. There is plenty of sandy beach area
dotted with palm trees on the beautifully kept grounds.

Dining/Diversions: The **Arrecife** restaurant serves international specialties and is
open daily from 6pm to midnight. **Caribeño,** by the pool and beach, is open from
7am to 7pm. There are three bars, including a pool bar, and 24-hour room service. It
offers a special in-room dining option for deluxe beachfront rooms, and will set up
your private patio for a romantic dinner, complete with serenading trio.

Amenities: Swimming pool, two tennis courts, gym, massage service, transportation, water-sports equipment rental, dive shop and dive-boat pier, children's activities
program, pharmacy, boutiques. Laundry and room service, travel agency, concierge,
car, and motorbike rental.

Expensive

La Ceiba Beach Hotel. Costera Sur Km 4.5 (Apdo. Postal 284), 77600 Cozumel, Q. Roo.
☎ **800/435-3240** in the U.S., or 9/872-0844. Fax 9/872-0065. 112 units. A/C TV TEL. High
season $155–$200 double. Low season $122–$155 double. Diving packages available.
AE, MC, V. Free parking.

Across from the Crown Paradisse Sol Caribe, on the beach side of the road, La Ceiba
is named for the lofty and majestic tropical tree that was sacred to the Maya. It's a
popular hotel with divers, and the large lobby seems to always be bustling with guests.
The guest rooms, while not necessarily outfitted in the latest style, are nicely furnished,
large, and comfortable; all have ocean views and balconies. The swimming pool is only
steps from the beach.

The emphasis here is on water sports, particularly scuba diving, and if this is your
passion, be sure to ask about the special dive packages when you call for reservations.
Diving is available right from the hotel beachfront.

Dining: The **Galleon Bar/Restaurant,** off the lobby, has walls shaped like an old
ship and is open for all meals. **Chopaloca,** by the beach, is open daily from early
morning until almost midnight.

Amenities: Two swimming pools and hot tub by the beach with outdoor Jacuzzi;
tennis court; gym and sauna; water sports; dive shop and dive-boat pier; roped-off area
for snorkeling. Laundry and room service, travel agency.

WHERE TO DINE

Zermatt (☎ **9/872-1384**), a terrific little bakery, is located on avenida 5 at calle 4
Norte. On calle 2 Norte, half a block in from the waterfront, is the **Panificadora
Cozumel,** excellent for a do-it-yourself breakfast or for picnic supplies. It's open from
6am to 9pm daily.

VERY EXPENSIVE

Pepe's Grill. Av. Rafael Melgar at Salas. ☎ **9/872-0213.** Reservations recommended. Main courses $15–$35; children's menu $6.50. AE, MC, V. Daily 5–11:30pm. GRILLED SPECIALTIES.

Pepe's started the grilled-food tradition in Cozumel and continues as a popular trendsetter with low lights, soft music, attentive waiters, and excellent food; the perpetual crowd is here for a reason. The menu is extensive, with flame-broiled specialties such as beef filet Singapore and shrimp Bahamas. The children's menu offers breaded shrimp and fried chicken. For dessert try the cajeta crêpes.

EXPENSIVE

✪ **Lobster House (Cabaña del Pescador).** Km 4 Carretera Pilar. No Phone. Lobster sold by weight, $10–$30. No credit cards. Daily 6–10:30pm. LOBSTER.

If you do something well, then concentrate on that and forget the rest. This is obviously the house rule here, as the only item on the menu is their lobster dinner, served one way—boiled with just a hint of spices accompanied by sides of rice, vegetables, melted butter, and bread. I have to agree; for me it's the only way to eat lobster. The price of dinner is determined by the weight of the lobster you select, with side dishes provided at no charge. Dark wooden tables lit with candles lend a cozy, inviting atmosphere, surrounded by tropical gardens, fountains, and a small pond, complete with ducks. The owner Fernando welcomes you warmly, and will even send you next door to his brother's excellent Mexican food restaurant, El Guacamayo, if you must have something other than lobster. The Lobster House is located across from the Playa Azul hotel.

MODERATE

El Moro. 75 BIS Nte. 124. ☎ **9/872-3029.** Main courses $5–$12. MC, V. Fri–Wed 1–11pm; closed Thurs. REGIONAL.

Crowds flock to El Moro for its wonderfully prepared food and service, but not the decor, which is orange, orange, orange, and formica. And it's away from everything; a taxi is a must, costing around $1.50 one-way. But all misgivings will disappear as soon as you taste something (and especially if you sip on one of their giant, wallop-packing margaritas). The *pollo* Ticuleño, a specialty from the town of Ticul, is a rib-sticking, delicious, layered plate of smooth tomato sauce, mashed potatoes, crispy baked corn tortilla, and batter-fried chicken breast, all topped with shredded cheese and green peas. Besides the regional food, other specialties of Mexico include enchiladas and seafood prepared many ways, plus grilled steaks, sandwiches, and, of course, nachos. El Moro is 12¹/₂ blocks inland from Melgar between calles 2 and 4 Norte.

La Choza. Salas 198 at av. 10 Sur. ☎ **9/872-0958.** Breakfast $3.50; main courses $8–$16. AE, MC, V. Daily 7:30am–11pm. YUCATECAN/MEXICAN.

The filled tables looking out the big open-air windows on the corner of Salas and avenida 10 Sur announce that this is a favorite of both tourists and locals alike. It looks like a big Maya house with white stucco walls and a thatched roof. Platters of chiles stuffed with shrimp, *pollo en relleno negro* (chicken in a blackened pepper sauce), *puerco entomatado* (pork stew), and beefsteak in a poblano pepper sauce are among the specialties.

✪ **La Veranda.** Calle 4 Nte. ☎ **9/872-4132.** Reservations recommended in high season. Main courses $6–$16. MC, V. Daily 6pm–1am. SEAFOOD/INTERNATIONAL.

Nothing here is quite what you expect. La Veranda is in a new building that's architecturally like the old island frame houses with cut-out wood trim. It's a stylish restaurant with cloth-covered tables, good service, and terrific crispy fresh salads, curried chicken,

You Paid What?

47,000 hotels, 700 airlines,
50 rental car companies. And a few
million ways to save money.

Travelocity.com
A Sabre Company

Go Virtually Anywhere.

AOL Keyword: Travel

Will you have enough stories to tell your grandchildren?

Yahoo! Travel

large seafood platters, roast-beef sandwiches, fajitas, stir-fried vegetables, steaks, and an enormous Mexican combo including roasted chicken, rice, beans, guacamole, an enchilada, and a quesadilla. You can dine inside or on the veranda or patio in back overlooking the shaded garden. In the main room, casual couches and conversational areas are great for leisurely drinking, chatting, card playing, backgammon, or watching ESPN, CNN, WGN Chicago, or sporting events (the television is played at low volume). The gracious owners, Anibal and Mercedes de Iturbide, are almost always on hand. To get there from the plaza turn left (north) on avenida 5 Norte, walk 2 blocks, and turn right on calle 4 Norte; it's behind Zermatt bakery, on your right midway up the block.

✪ **Prima.** Calle Salas 109. ☎ **9/872-4242.** Pizzas $5–$9; pastas $8–$15; steaks $13–$20. AE, MC, V. Daily 4–11pm. ITALIAN.

One of the few good Italian restaurants in Mexico, Prima gets better every year. Everything is fresh—the pastas, vegetables, and sourdough pizza. Owner Albert Domínguez grows most of the vegetables in his local hydroponic garden. The menu changes daily and specializes in northern Italian seafood dishes. It might include shrimp scampi, fettuccine with pesto, and lobster and crab ravioli with cream sauce. The fettuccine Alfredo is wonderful, as are the puff-pastry garlic "bread" and crispy house salad. Steaks are USDA choice. Dining is upstairs on the breezy terrace. Next door is **Habanas Co.** with cigars and liquors. To get to either place from the pier, turn right (south) on Melgar and walk 2 blocks to calle 5 Sur and turn left. Prima is visible on your left between avenidas 5 and 10 Sur. Hotel delivery is available.

Guido's. Av. Melgar, between calles 6 and 8 Nte. ☎ **9/872-0946.** Main courses $8–$13; daily specials $5–$13. AE, MC, V. Mon–Sat 11am–11pm; Sun 5–11pm. ITALIAN.

This inviting interior garden, with deck chairs and glossy wood tables, is a restful place in daytime and a romantic, candlelit night spot. The specialty here (as in their branches in Isla Mujeres and Cancún) is wood-oven–baked pizzas. But for a change, look for pasta prepared five ways and the weekly specials, which may be a special appetizer of sea bass carpaccio, pizza, pasta, or fish with an Italian twist. To get there from the pier, turn left (north) on Melgar and walk 4 blocks; it's on your right.

INEXPENSIVE

✪ **Café Caribe.** Av. 10 Sur 215. ☎ **9/872-3621.** Coffee and pastries $1–$4. No credit cards. Mon–Sat 8am–1pm and 6–10:30pm. PASTRIES & COFFEE.

This cute little cafe behind a facade of fuchsia and dark green may become your favorite place to start the day, finish it, or spend time in between. You'll find ice cream, milk shakes, fresh cheesecake and carrot cake, waffles, bagels, croissants, and biscuits filled with cheese and cream, ham and cheese, or butter and marmalade. Nine different coffees are served, including Cuban, cappuccino, espresso, and Irish. To get there from the plaza, turn right (south) on avenida 5 Sur, walk 1 block and turn left on calle Salas, then right on avenida 10; it's on your left.

Casa Denis. Calle 1 Sur no. 267. ☎ **9/872-0067.** Breakfast $2–$4; main courses $4.75–$12. No credit cards. Mon–Sat 7am–11pm. REGIONAL/INTERNATIONAL.

This yellow wooden house holds a great home-style Mexican restaurant. Small tables are scattered outside on the pedestrian-only street and in two rooms separated by a foyer filled with family photos. More tables are set in the back on the shady patio. You can make a light meal from *empanadas* filled with potatoes, cheese, or fish, or go for the full *comida* of fried grouper, rice, and beans. Or better yet, try one of the regional specialties such as *pollo* pibil or pork brochette seasoned with the subtle flavor of achiote. Groups of four or more can request a special meal in advance. To get there from the plaza, walk a half-block inland up calle 1 Sur; it's on your right.

Coco's. Av. 5 Sur no. 180, at the corner of calle Salas. ☎ **9/872-0241.** Breakfast $3–$5.75. No credit cards. Tues–Sun 7am–noon. Closed the last 2 weeks of Sept. and the first week of Oct. MEXICAN/AMERICAN.

Tended by owners Terri and Daniel Ocejo, Coco's is clean and welcoming to the tourist, right down to the free coffee refills. Plan to indulge in stateside favorites like hash browns, corn flakes and bananas, gigantic blueberry muffins, cinnamon rolls, and cream-stuffed rolls. Mexican specialties include *huevos rancheros, huevos à la mexicana,* and eggs scrambled with chiles and covered with melted cheese. A gift section at the front includes gourmet coffee, local honey, bottles of hot peppers, chocolate, *rompope,* and vanilla. To get there from the plaza, turn right (south) on avenida 5 Sur. Coco's is on your right beside the entrance to the Hotel El Marqués.

Comida Casera Toñita. Calle Salas 265, between calles 10 and 15 Nte. ☎ **9/872-0401.** Breakfast $1.75–$3; main courses $3.75–$7; daily specials $3; fruit drinks $1.75. No credit cards. Mon–Sat 8am–6pm. HOME-STYLE YUCATECAN.

The owners have taken the living room of their home and made it into a comfortable dining room complete with filled bookshelves and classical music playing in the background. Whole fried fish, fish fillet, fried chicken, and beefsteak prepared to order are on the regular menu. Daily specials give you a chance to taste authentic regional food, including *pollo à la naranja,* chicken *mole, pollo en escabeche,* and pork chops with achiote seasoning. To reach Toñita's, walk south from the plaza on avenida 5 Sur for 1 block, then turn left on calle Salas and walk east $1^1/_2$ blocks; the restaurant is on your left.

Natur-all. Calle Rosado Salas 352. ☎ **9/872-5560.** Breakfast $1.75–$3.25; salads and sandwiches $1.55–$3; fruit and vegetable juices 95¢–$1.55. No credit cards. Wed–Mon 7am–5pm, Sun closes at 2:30pm. FRUIT/SANDWICHES.

The sweet smell of fruit will greet you as you enter Frutas Selectas, the downstairs grocery store specializing in fresh fruit. Upstairs is this cheery restaurant overlooking the street. A good place to go for light meals, it offers juices, smoothies, yogurt, veggie sandwiches, a salad bar, baked potatoes with toppings, and pastries. From the plaza, turn right and walk 1 block south on avenida 5 Sur, then turn left on calle Salas and walk 3 blocks east. It's on your right between 15th and 20th Norte.

Jeanie's Waffle House. Av. Melgar. ☎ **9/872-4145.** Waffles $3.15–$6; breakfast $3.25–$4; main courses $5–$9. No credit cards. Mon–Sat 6am–10pm, Sun 6am–noon. BREAKFAST/DESSERTS/MEXICAN.

Tables are often full since the Waffle House has far more business than it has space. The name is a bit misleading since you can order much more than waffles. You can also have breakfast anytime. Jeanie De Lille, the island's premier pastry chef, bakes crisp, light waffles and serves them in many ways, including the waffle ranchero with eggs and salsa, the waffle Benedict with eggs and hollandaise sauce, and waffles with whipped cream and chocolate. Hash browns, homemade breads, and great coffee are other reasons to drop in for breakfast mornings and evenings. The menu has been expanded to include fried fish and pasta, and there is a full bar. On Melgar, 4 blocks south of the plaza between the Aqua Safari and the Hotel Vista del Mar.

COZUMEL AFTER DARK

Cozumel is a town frequented by divers and other active visitors who play hard all day and wind down at night. The nightlife scene is low key and usually peaks in the early evening. The exception to this is the cruise-ship crowd. People sit in outdoor cafes around the *zócalo* (plaza) enjoying the cool night breezes until the restaurants close. **Carlos 'n' Charlie's,** the **Hard Rock Cafe,** and a couple of other bars are grouped together along Av. Melgar on the north side of the main plaza. They are among the liveliest and most predictable places in town. **Joe's Lobster Pub** on avenida 5 between Juárez and calle 2 Norte is the most happening place for live music, primarily reggae and salsa. Other specialty bars include the **Hog's Breath Saloon,** imported from Key West, and located on the main highway across from the international Pier; and **Scruffy Murphy's Irish Pub** on Rosado Salas, between Avenidas 10 and 15.

3 Puerto Morelos & Environs

21 miles (34km) S of Cancún

Development has largely passed by Puerto Morelos. It remains a quiet place—perfect for a relaxed vacation of lying about the beach and reading a book, with perhaps the occasional foray into a water sport or two. The beaches are not the best for swimming because there is a prominent reef offshore that shelters the shoals and beaches from waves. Without surf, a lot of sea grass grows on the bottom and washes up on the beach. But the water is as clear as anywhere along the coast, and if a little sea grass doesn't bother you, you'll find this place to be a cozy spot. Because of this same reef, there is good snorkeling and good kayaking. Another great thing about this place is that it has a large English-language bookstore. If you've forgotten your reading material, you can drop by here even if your eventual destination is farther down the coast. In pre-Columbian times, Maya women would depart from here on their pilgrimages to Cozumel to pay homage to the goddess of fertility. Nowadays, it serves as the terminus for the car ferry.

ESSENTIALS

GETTING THERE   By Car   Drive south from Cancún along Highway 307 to the km 31 marker, there's a large sign pointing the way to Puerto Morelos.

BY BUS   Buses going from Cancún to Tulum and Playa del Carmen usually stop here, but be sure to ask in Cancún if your bus makes the Puerto Morelos stop. **By the Puerto Morelos–Cozumel Car Ferry**   The dock (☎ 9/871-0008), the largest establishment in town, is very easy to find. See the Cozumel section above for details on the car ferry schedule, but several points bear repeating here: The schedule may change, so double-check it before arriving, and always arrive at least 3 hours in advance of the ferry's departure to purchase a ticket and to get in line. If not traveling by car, take the pedestrian ferry from Playa del Carmen.

EXPLORING IN & AROUND PUERTO MORELOS

Puerto Morelos attracts people who seek seaside relaxation without the crowds and high prices. There are a couple of good restaurants, a good pizzeria, an English-language bookstore, two dive shops, and recreational fishing boats. The bookstore, **Alma Libre,** has more English-language books than any in the Yucatan. Hours are from Tuesday to Saturday 10am–1pm and 6–9pm (e-mail: casamaya@yahoo.com). It's on the main square. Also on the main square is **Sub Aqua Explorers** (☎ 9/871-0078; fax 9/871-0027), a good dive shop that also arranges fishing trips. More than 15 dive sites are nearby and many are close to shore. A two-tank dive costs around $60 and night dives $55. Two hours of fishing costs around $80 and snorkeling excursions run around $5.

If you are traveling by car, there are a couple of worthwhile stops along Highway 307 on the way to Puerto Morelos from Cancún. **Croco Cun,** a zoological park where crocodiles are raised, is one of the most interesting attractions in the area—don't be put off by the comical name. This is not a zoo in the grand style, but it has interesting exhibits of crocodiles in all stages of development, as well as animals of nearly all the species that once roamed the Yucatán Peninsula. The snake exhibit is fascinating, though it may make you think twice about roaming the jungle. The rattlesnakes and boa constrictors are particularly intimidating, and the tarantulas are downright enormous. Children enjoy the guides' enthusiastic tours and are entranced by the spider monkeys and wild pigs. Wear plenty of bug repellent and allow an hour or two for the tour, followed by a cool drink in the restaurant. Croco Cun is open daily from 8:30am to 5:30pm. Admission is $5, and free for children under age 6. The park is at km 31 on Highway 307.

About half a mile before Puerto Morelos is the 150-acre **Jardín Botánico Dr. Alfredo Barrera,** opened in 1990 and named after the biologist who studied the *selva* (a common geographical term meaning "tropical evergreen broadleaf forest"). A natural, protected showcase for native plants and animals, it's open Tuesday to Sunday from 9am to 4pm. Admission is $3.75.

The park is divided into six parts: an **epiphyte area** (plants that grow on others); **Maya ruins;** an **ethnographic area,** with a furnished hut and typical garden; a **chiclero camp,** about the once-thriving *chicle* (chewing gum) industry; a **nature park,** where wild vegetation is preserved; and **mangroves.** Wandering along the marked paths, you'll see that the dense jungle of plants and trees is named and labeled in English and Spanish. Each sign has the plant's scientific and common names, use of the plant, and the geographic areas where it is found in the wild. It's rich in bird and animal life, too, but to catch a glimpse of something you'll have to move quietly and listen carefully.

WHERE TO STAY & DINE

Most of the lodging here is provided by small establishments; the only resort-like property is the Caribbean Reef Club, a clothing-optional hotel that caters to groups. It has some lovely facilities, including what the brochure describes as "a pulsating party Jacuzzi." Enough said.

Hacienda Morelos. Av. Rafael E. Melgar Lote 5, 77580 Puerto Morelos, Q. Roo. ☎/fax **9/ 871-0015.** 15 units A/C. $65–$85. AE. Free enclosed parking.

A small hotel on the water with pleasant rooms and good prices. Simple rooms are spacious and comfortable. All have an ocean view. Most come with a kitchenette and two double beds. The hotel has a small pool, and a Johnny Cairo's restaurant.

Johnny Cairo's. Av. Rafael E. Melgar (in the Hacienda Morelos hotel). ☎ **9/871-0449.** Main courses $6–$14. MC, V. Daily 1–10pm. CONTEMPORARY.

This restaurant is run by former chefs for the Ritz-Carlton in Cancún. Part of the menu has a Caribbean flavor to it, and many dishes are well-known favorites that have been tweaked in one direction or another—thus the "contemporary." But the cooks know how to put together a good menu. Also benefiting the restaurant is its location over the water, making it a very pleasant place to dine.

Los Pelícanos. On the ocean side behind and to the right of the zócalo. ☎ **9/871-0014.** Main courses $5–$16; lobster $25. MC, V. Daily 10am–10pm. SEAFOOD.

You'll notice the inviting restaurant down a block to the right of the plaza on the street paralleling the ocean. Select a table inside under the *palapa* or outside on the terrace (wear mosquito repellent in the evenings). From the terrace you have an easy view of

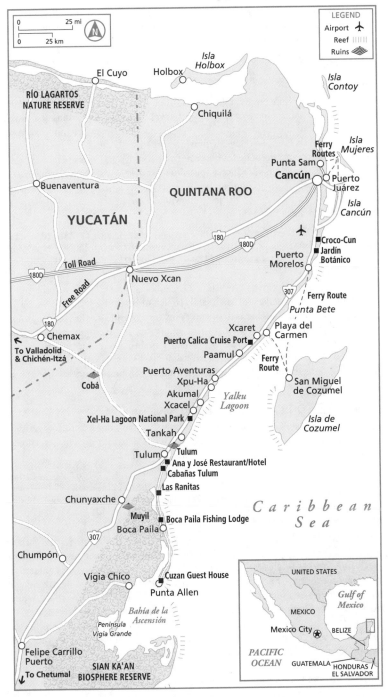

The Yucatán's Upper Caribbean Coast

pelicans swooping around the dock. The seafood menu has many offerings, from *ceviche* to conch prepared three ways to shrimp, lobster, and fish. There's grilled chicken and steak for those who don't want seafood.

Posada Amor. Apdo. Postal 806, 77580 Cancún, Q. Roo. ☎ **9/871-0033.** 18 units (9 with bathroom). $30 double with bathroom; $35 for a room with 4 beds and bathroom. No credit cards.

The simple, cheery little rooms at the Posada Amor, with screens and mosquito netting, are plain but adequate (and overpriced for what you receive). They're clustered around a patio in back of the restaurant. The Posada's restaurant is newly remodeled, rustic, and quaint like an English cottage, with whitewashed walls, small shuttered windows, and open rafters, and decorated with primitive paintings and flowers on each table. The food is tasty, with many regional specialties, sandwiches, and a *comida corrida* for $6. It's open daily from 7:30am to 10pm. To get here, when you enter town, turn right; with the town square on the left, follow the main street leading to the ferry; the hotel is about a block down on the right.

Rancho Libertad. Dom. Conocido, 77580 Puerto Morelos, Q. Roo. ☎ **888/305-5225** in the U.S. and Canada or 9/871-0181. www.rancholibertad.com. 12 units. High season $75–$65; low season $55–$45. No credit cards. Rates include continental breakfast, use of snorkel equipment and bicycles.

Just beyond the town center, right before the Caribbean Reef Club, is a cluster of two-story buildings with *palapa* roofs on a sandy stretch of beach. Each room comes with a porch area, a queen, a double bed, or two twins suspended from the ceiling, a couple of chairs, a small table, a private bath with hot water, and plenty of drinking water. Second-story rooms go for more than first-story rooms. There is a large *palapa* with sandy floor for a common area, and a dive shop next door. Guests have the use of a large refrigerator. Breakfast buffet includes fruit, cereal, bread, and yogurt. Massage service available.

EN ROUTE TO PLAYA DEL CARMEN

From Puerto Morelos, Playa del Carmen is only 20 miles, but before you get there, you'll pass a couple of places that make for nice beach destinations. The best choice is the upscale La Posada del Capitán Laffite, described below.

La Posada del Capitán Lafitte. Carretera Cancún–Tulum Km 62, 77710 Playa del Carmen, Q. Roo. ☎ **800/538-6802** in the U.S. and Canada, or 9/873-0214. Fax 9/873-0212. www.mexicoholiday.com. 62 units. High season $200 double. Low season $120 double. Christmas and New Year's are higher. Minimum 3- or 5-night stay. Rates include breakfast and dinner. MC, V. Free guarded parking.

Fifteen miles from Puerto Morelos you'll see a large sign on the left for the entrance to La Posada del Capitán Lafitte. A mile from the highway, down a rough dirt road, you'll come upon a lovely seaside retreat on a solitary stretch of sandy beach. Here you can enjoy the feeling of being on a private, nearly deserted island, while still enjoying all the amenities of a relaxing vacation. The numerous bungalows stretch out along a powdery white beach with space enough between them for luxurious separation. The one- and two-story white stucco bungalows hold between 1 and 4 units each. They are smallish but very comfortable, with tile floors, small, tiled bathrooms, either two double or one king-size bed, and an oceanfront porch. Twenty-nine bungalows have air-conditioning; the rest have fans. There's 24-hour electricity. If you wish, coffee can be served in the room as early as 6:30am. Guests can participate during summer in a turtle patrol of nearby beaches where green and loggerhead turtles nest. Divers from North America make up a sizable portion of the clientele here, as well as repeat visitors who come annually just for the peace and quiet. The hotel offers transportation service to and from the Cancún airport for $50 dollars per person, minimum of two passengers.

Dining/Diversions: One restaurant takes care of all meals, and the chef will prepare your catch. There's also a poolside bar and swinging-chair bar.

Amenities: You'll find a large raised swimming pool and sunning deck, well-equipped game room, and excellent dive shop with PADI instruction. Laundry and room service, and travel agency.

One and a half miles farther south are some economical lodgings on a beach just a few miles north of Playa del Carmen. The access road is marked by a sign that says PUNTA BETE. It is rough in places, but in a short amount of time you arrive at the water along a lightly populated stretch of beach. The road forks off in a couple of places and you'll see signs for *cabañas* pointing you in one direction or another. Of course, the word "cabañas" conjures up visions of idyllic native-style dwellings with thatched roofs, etc., but as often as not on the Yucatecan coast, it is employed to mean plain, unimaginative cement cubes. This is mostly the case here—Spartan (yet comfortable) and inexpensive dwellings at $30 to $40 per double. One of these places is **Cabañas Bahía Xcalacoco,** which has four to six *cabañas* and is run by a Mexican and American couple (Apdo. Postal 176, 77710 Playa del Carmen, Q. Roo).

If you come here between July and October, you can walk the beach at night to watch for **turtles** lumbering ashore to lay their eggs, or watch the eggs hatch and the tiny, vulnerable turtles scurry to the ocean.

4 Playa del Carmen

20 miles (32km) SW of Puerto Morelos, 44 miles (70km) SW of Cancún, 6.5 miles (10.5km) N of Xcaret, 8 miles (13km) N of Puerto Calica

Playa del Carmen is a small town that is growing quickly. It lies on one of the best stretches of beach on the coast and is perfect for enjoying the simple (and perhaps the best) pleasures of a seaside vacation—taking in the sun and the sea air while working your toes into soft, white sand; cooling down with a swim in clear, cool blue water; and strolling leisurely and aimlessly down the beach while listening to the sound of waves and feeling the light touch of tropical breezes.

The town itself (at least, my favorite part of it) has a casual, comfortable simplicity about it. The local architecture has deliberately adopted elements of native building—rustic clapboard walls, thatched roofs, lots of tropical foliage, irregular shapes and angles, and a ramshackle, unplanned look to many structures. All of this reflects the toned-down approach to tourism adopted by the locals.

Playa attracts a lot of people in their 20s and 30s. They come from far and wide; you'll hear snippets of several European languages while taking an evening stroll down the pedestrian-only avenida 5. Most come looking for a comfortable beach vacation, but not in the mode of all-inclusive resorts, time-shares, and other features of modern tourism. Here you will find the opposite of this, that rare combination of simplicity (in the form of a small town that can easily be crossed on foot) and variety (in terms of the many imaginative and one-of-a-kind restaurants and stores where you can enjoy a good meal and a drink or where you can pick up an unusual artifact for a friend back home). It is this aspect of cosmopolitan village and counter-culture getaway that makes Playa so different from the rest of the coast. The strong European influence has made topless sunbathing (nominally against the law in Mexico) a nonchalantly accepted practice anywhere there's a beach. Playa, however, is changing. How it will change in the end is anyone's guess, but in the last several years a few large, mainstream resorts have moved in, and a golf course has been constructed.

There is another reason for considering Playa as a destination: Its location is central to much of the Caribbean coast. From here it's easy to shoot out to Cozumel on the ferry, take land transportation south to the nature parks, the ruins at Tulum, and Cobá, or head north to Cancún.

ESSENTIALS

GETTING THERE & DEPARTING   **By Air**   When making your reservations, remember that it's easier and cheaper to get to Playa from Cozumel's airport than from Cancún's.

BY CAR   The turnoff to Playa del Carmen from Highway 307 is plainly marked, and you'll arrive on the town's widest street, avenida Principal, also known as avenida Benito Juárez (not that there's a street sign to that effect).

BY THE PLAYA DEL CARMEN–COZUMEL PASSENGER FERRY   See the Cozumel section "Getting There & Departing" above, for details.

BY TAXI   Taxi fares from the Cancún airport are high—about $60 one-way, but they're the fastest, most immediate form of travel. *Colectivos* from the Cancún airport can reduce this to about $30. Returning to the airport, there is a service offering shared taxi rides for $14 per person. Check at your hotel or at the Caribe Maya restaurant on avenida 5 at calle 8 for information and reservations.

BY BUS   The bus station in Playa del Carmen is on the corner of avenida Principal (the main street) and avenida 5.

Buses travel to and from Cancún with regularity, as well as to Xcaret, Tulum, Chetumal, Chichén-Itzá, and Mérida.

ORIENTATION

ARRIVING   The ferry dock in Playa del Carmen is 1 1/2 blocks from the main square and within walking distance of hotels. **Buses** arrive along avenida Principal, a short distance from hotels, restaurants, and the ferry pier. **Tricycle taxis** are the only vehicles allowed between the bus stations and avenida 5 and the ferry. A number of these efficient taxis meet each bus and ferry and can transport you and your luggage to almost any hotel in town. The New Puerto Calica cruise pier is almost 8 miles south of Playa del Carmen; Playa taxis meet each ship.

CITY LAYOUT   Villagers know and use street names, but few street signs exist. The main street, **avenida Principal,** also known as avenida Benito Juárez, leads to the *zócalo* from Highway 307. As it does so, it crosses several numbered avenues that run parallel to the beach, all of which are multiples of five. Avenida 5, 1 block before the beach, is closed to traffic from the *zócalo* to calle 6. On this avenue are many restaurants and shops. Almost all the town is north and west of the *zócalo.* Immediately south is the ferry pier and the Continental Playacar Hotel. This is the southern edge of town. Beyond this is the airstrip and the golf course development called Playacar, with several resort hotels.

Fast Facts: Playa del Carmen

Area Code   The telephone area code is **9.**

Doctor   Dr. E. Medina Peniche speaks English and can be reached around the clock at ☎ 9/873-0134.

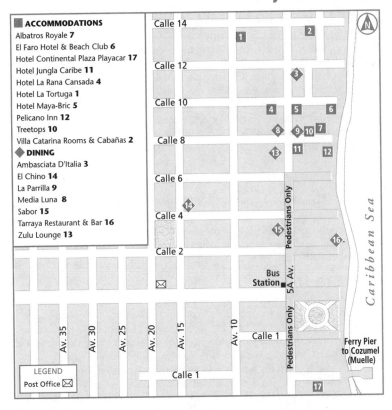

ACCOMMODATIONS
Albatros Royale **7**
El Faro Hotel & Beach Club **6**
Hotel Continental Plaza Playacar **17**
Hotel Jungla Caribe **11**
Hotel La Rana Cansada **4**
Hotel La Tortuga **1**
Hotel Maya-Bric **5**
Pelican Inn **12**
Treetops **10**
Villa Catarina Rooms & Cabañas **2**

DINING
Ambasciata D'Italia **3**
El Chino **14**
La Parrilla **9**
Media Luna **8**
Sabor **15**
Tarraya Restaurant & Bar **16**
Zulu Lounge **13**

Internet   I found the speediest connections at the Atomic Internet Café on calle 8 between avenidas 5 and 10: open daily from 9am to 11pm. But there are others, too, of which Cyberia, at the corner of calle 4 and avenida 15, wins the award for best name.

Money Exchange   There are several banks in Playa with automatic teller machines, and several money-exchange houses. Several are located close to the pier, or along avenida 5 at calle 8.

Parking   Because of the pedestrian-only blocks and increasing population and popularity of Playa, parking close to hotels has become more difficult. The most accessible parking lot is the Estacionamiento Mexico at the corner of avenida Principal and avenida 10, open daily 24 hours; the fee is $1.25 per hour and $8 per day. There's also a 24-hour lot just a block from the pier, where you can leave your car while you cross over to Cozumel.

Pharmacy   The Farmacia del Carmen (☎ 9/873-2330) on Av. Juárez between avenidas 5 and 10 is open 24 hours.

Post Office   The post office is on avenida Principal 3 blocks north of the plaza, on the right past the Hotel Playa del Carmen and the launderette.

Seasons   High season is August and from December to Easter. Low season is all other months, but November is becoming somewhat popular.

WHAT TO SEE & DO IN PLAYA

Playa is for relaxing. But beyond that, the island of **Cozumel** is a $7, 45-minute ferry ride away; **Tulum, Xel-Ha, and Xcaret** are easy excursions. Avenida 5 is lined with dozens of trendy, small shops selling imported batik clothing, Guatemalan fabric clothing, premium tequilas, Cuban cigars, masks, pottery, hammocks, and a few T-shirts. There's even a couple of tattoo parlors in the mix.

Reef diving can be arranged through **Tank-Ha Dive Center** (☎/fax **9/873-0302;** fax 9/873-1355; www.mayanriviera.com/diving/tankha; e-mail: tankha@playadelcarmen. com). The friendly owner, Alberto Leonard, came to Playa by way of Madrid, and is now offering cave and *cenote* diving excursions. You can also book his trips at the Hotel Maya Bric and at the Royal Albatross. Snorkeling trips cost $25 and include soft drinks and equipment. Two-tank dive trips are $55; resort courses are available for $65 with PDIC and PADI instructors.

An 18-hole championship **golf course** (☎ **9/873-0624**), designed by Robert Von Hagge, is open adjacent to the Continental Plaza Playacar. Greens fees are $99 (includes golf cart), caddie $20, club rental $20, and the price includes tax. Two **tennis** courts are also available at the club. If your hotel is a member of the golf club, greens fees may be reduced to as low as $20.

WHERE TO STAY

Staying in one of the small hotels in Playa can be more fun than staying in one of the resorts outside of town. Don't hesitate to stay in a place that's not on the beach—the town life here is much of the fun, and staying on the beach in Playa has its disadvantages, in particular the noise produced by a couple of beachside bars. Beaches are public property in Mexico, and you can lay out your towel anywhere you like without anyone bothering you. If you really want a quiet room on the beach, consider the Shangri-La Caribe, listed below. It's on the outskirts of town far from the bars but within walking distance of downtown. As for the all-inclusive properties, the **Porto Real** (☎ **9/ 881-7325**; www.real.com.mx) has the best location (for nongolfers). It's on the northern fringe of town, while the others are strung out well south of town, in the Playacar development.

VERY EXPENSIVE

Continental Plaza Playacar. Av. Espíritu Santo, Frac. Playacar, 77710 Playa del Carmen, Q. Roo ☎ **800/88-CONTI** in the U.S., or 9/873-0100. Fax 9/873-0105. E-mail: hcpply@ sidek.com.mx. 180 units. A/C MINIBAR TV TEL. High season $235–$328 double. Ask about off-season rates and special packages. AE, DC, MC, V.

The village's most upscale resort hotel opened in 1991 a block from the *zócalo*. The entrance to this five-story, pale-pink hotel leads you through a wide marble lobby beyond which you see the meandering pool with swim-up bar and the beach. The large, well-furnished rooms all have in-room safety deposit boxes, purified tap water, tile floors, large bathrooms, wet bars with refrigerators, and balconies. All but 13 have a view of the sea. To find it from the ferry pier, turn left when you get off the ferry and follow the road a short distance until you see the Playacar sign. If you're driving in, turn right at the last street before the main street dead-ends and you'll see signs to the hotel about 2 blocks ahead.

Dining/Diversions: La Pérgola, with pool, beach, and ocean view, serves international food daily for breakfast and dinner. **La Sirena** is the poolside restaurant. The stylish and welcoming lobby bar is open between 6pm and 1am daily.

Amenities: Oceanside pool with swim-up bar, water-sports equipment, one tennis court. Laundry and room service, baby-sitting, gift shop and boutiques, travel agency, and tours to nearby archaeological zones and lagoons.

EXPENSIVE

✪ **El Faro Hotel and Beach Club.** On the beach at calle 10 Nte., 77710 Playa del Carmen, Q. Roo. ☎ **888/243-7413** from the U.S., or 9/873-0970. Fax 9/873-0968. www. hotelfaro.com. 100 units. High season $155–$260 double. Low season $120–$215 double. Rates include breakfast. AE, MC, V. Limited free guarded parking available.

Rooms and suites are spread out on a large property graced by tall palms and tropical gardens fronting 75 meters of sandy beachfront. A small but stunning pool (heated in winter months) has islands of palms inside, and is bordered by cushioned lounges and a *palapa* bar. The entire property has a cool, clean feel to it, with its white-and-cream stucco exterior. The spacious rooms, in two-story buildings, have clay-tile floors, marble baths, and either one king or two double beds. Decor is Mexican folk art with rustic wood furnishings. All rooms have a large balcony or terrace; most have some view of the sea. Rates vary according to the dominant view—garden, sea, or beachfront—the size of the room, and the time of year. The property has many ecologically friendly extras that you can't see—the owners use solar heat and recycled water to maintain their lovely gardens. Also on the property is a lighthouse that actually functions as such.

Dining/Diversions: The restaurant offers Mexican and International food and is open until 6pm. *Palapa* poolside bar is open 8am to 8pm.

Amenities: Swimming pool, beach, massage services, free guarded parking. European spa services are in the process of being added.

✪ **Shangri-La Caribe.** Calle 38 (Apdo. Postal 253), 77710 Playa del Carmen, Q. Roo. ☎ **800/538-6802** in the U.S. or Canada, or 9/873-0611. Fax 9/873-0500. www. mexicoholiday.com. 85 units. High season $200 ocean-view double; $240 beachfront double. Low season $150 ocean-view double; $190 beachfront double. Rates include breakfast and dinner. Book well in advance during high season. MC, V. Free guarded parking.

This property consists of two-story, thatched bungalows spread out across an excellent beach. Accommodations come with a patio or terrace complete with hammock. Most come with two double beds, but a few have a king size. Windows are screened, and a ceiling fan circulates the breeze. Prices get higher the closer you get to the beach. Though you're very close to Playa del Carmen, hotel guests are almost the only ones using the beach, and the feeling is one of being many relaxing miles from civilization. The turn-off to the hotel is before Juárez—look for a Volkswagen dealership and a huge sign for the Shangri-La Caribe. A mile of paved road leads to the hotel.

Dining/Diversions: Two indoor restaurants serve breakfast and dinner, a poolside grill serves lunch. The bar is open long hours.

Amenities: The large inviting pool is surrounded by a sundeck. The absence of coral on the beach makes it an ideal place for windsurfing and swimming, not for snorkeling. The **Cyan-Ha Diving Center** on the premises offers diving, snorkeling, and fishing trips, and equipment rental for these sports. Horse rental, car rental, and bus or taxi tours to nearby lagoons and to Tulum, Cobá, and Chichén-Itzá.

MODERATE

Albatros Royale. Calle 8 (Apdo. Postal 31), 77710 Playa del Carmen, Q. Roo. ☎ **800/ 538-6802** in the U.S. and Canada, or 9/873-0001. 31 units. High season $85 double. Low season $58–$68 double. Rates include breakfast. MC, V.

This sister hotel to the neighboring Pelícano Inn rises up on a narrow bit of land facing the beach. The two stories of rooms all have tile floors, tile bathrooms with marble vanities and showers, balconies or porches, and most have ocean views. Most have two double beds, but seven have queen-size beds. Breakfast is taken almost next door at the Pelícano Inn. To get here from the corner of avenida 5 and calle 8 (where you'll see the Rincón del Sol center), turn toward the water on calle 8; it's midway down the block on your left. Street parking is scarce.

Hotel Jungla Caribe. Av. 5 Nte. at calle 8, 77710 Playa del Carmen, Q. Roo. ☎/fax **9/ 873-0650.** 25 units. TV. High season $60–$80 double; $95–$100 suite. Low season 30% off high-season prices. AE, MC, V.

Located right in the heart of the 5th Avenue action, "La Jungla" is an imaginative place, with highly stylized decor that mixes neoclassical with Robinson Crusoe. Its character is perfectly in keeping with the quirkiness of the town. Rolf Albrecht, the builder of the hotel, envisioned space and comfort for guests, so even the standard rooms are expansive, with gray-and-black marble floors, the occasional Roman column, and large bathrooms. Fifteen of the rooms are suites. The "tower" section of suites is connected to the hotel by a catwalk. There's an attractive pool in the courtyard beneath a giant Ramón tree. Eight rooms come without A/C, as is the case with the lowest priced double.

La Tortuga. Av. 10 no. 732, entre calles 12 and 14, 77710 Playa del Carmen, Q. Roo. ☎/fax **9/873-1484.** E-mail: hotel_la_tortuga@bigfoot.com. 33 units. A/C MINIBAR TV TEL. High season $95 double, $115 suite. Low season $75 double, $95 suite. AE, MC, V. Rates include continental or American breakfast.

A lovely two-story hotel built in the tropical style with thatched roof and rustic architectural elements, its rooms lack nothing in the way of comfort. These come with balconies or terraces facing lovely garden courtyards. Most rooms come with a king-size bed, but you can get one with two queens. The bathrooms are large, and the suites come with Jacuzzis. There are two pools and a poolside bar, with a grassy area surrounding it to take in the sun. Room service is available from the neighboring Tucan Restaurant. It's located 3 blocks off the beach.

INEXPENSIVE

Hotel Maya-Bric. Av. 5 Nte., 77710 Playa del Carmen, Q. Roo. ☎/fax **9/873-2041;** fax 9/873-0011. www.xaaac.com/playacar/mayabric.htm. E-mail: mayabric@playa.com.mx. 29 units. High season $35–$60 double. MC, V. 6% commission charged for using credit cards. Free guarded parking.

Centrally located, this two-story inn offers basic accommodation in clean rooms, each with two double beds with fairly firm mattresses; some have ocean views. The building frames a small pool where guests gather for card games and conversation. The Maya-Bric is frequented by loyal guests who return annually. The gates are locked at night, and only guests are allowed to enter. Higher prices are for air-conditioning, available in 16 rooms. The on-site dive shop, **Tank-Ha** (see "What to See & Do in Playa," above), rents diving and snorkeling gear and arranges trips to the reefs.

La Rana Cansada. Calle 10 #132, 77710 Playa del Carmen, Q. Roo. ☎/fax **9/873-0389.** E-mail: ranacansada@hotmail.com. 15 units. High season $45 double. Low season $35 double. No credit cards.

The "Tired Frog" reminds me of one of those small, quiet inns that you occasionally find in small towns in Mexico. There's an air of provincial domesticity to the place. Rooms surround a pretty courtyard with a little stone fountain. Hammocks are strung on the covered porch outside the rooms. Some rooms have concrete ceilings and others a thatched roof, but all have well-screened doors and windows and are painted in attractive colors. Two rooms have air conditioning. Paperbacks are available at the front desk. It's 1¹/₂ blocks inland from the beach. The hotel is between 5th and 10th avenues, 1¹/₂ blocks from the beach.

Treetops. Calle 8 s/n, 77710 Playa del Carmen, Q. Roo. ☎/fax **9/873-0351.** www. treetopshotel.com. E-mail: treetops@prodigy.net.mx. 17 units. High season $45–$78 double. Low season $35–$65 double. Rates include continental breakfast. MC, V.

This two-story hotel with a couple of bungalows linked by stone pathways is set in a small patch of undisturbed jungle with its own *cenote* and swimming pool. The bungalows are rustic but comfortable and come with small charms like thatched roofs and rock walls. The new rooms, in the main building, have air-conditioning, fans, refrigerators, and either balconies or patios. The restaurant offers a short menu of charcoal-broiled hot dogs and hamburgers (with U.S. beef), club sandwiches, home-made potato salad, Tex-Mex chili, and tacos. The **Sailorman's Pub,** on the right of the reception, is a good place to go for an evening drink and to meet fellow travelers. The bar is open daily from 3pm to midnight. Happy hour is from 6 to 8pm. There's satellite TV broadcasting U.S. channels in the reception area and bar. The hotel is half a block from the beach, half a block from avenida 5.

✪ **Villa Catarina Rooms & Cabañas.** Calle Privada Nte. between 12 and 14, 77710 Playa del Carmen, Q. Roo. ☎ **9/873-0970.** Fax 9/873-0968. 28 units. High season $50–$75 double. Low season $35–$55 double. MC, V.

Hammocks are stretched in front of each of the stylishly rustic rooms and *cabañas* here, nestled in a grove of palms and fruit trees. Each of the clean, well-furnished rooms has one or two double beds on wooden bases, with brick or wood floors. Some units have a small loft for reading and relaxing; others have *palapa* roofs or terraces. Furnishings and Mexican folk art decorations add a great touch that's uncommon for hotels in this price range. Bathrooms are detailed with colorful tiles, and some of the larger rooms have sitting areas. There's good cross-ventilation through well-screened windows. Complimentary coffee is available every morning. There's limited street parking. Be sure to specify this hotel when making reservations or they'll think you're calling about El Faro.

WHERE TO DINE

Restaurants are constantly opening and closing in Playa. Most restaurants do not take reservations and there seems to be little trouble getting a table.

EXPENSIVE

Ambasciata D'Italia. Av. 5 at calle 12. ☎ **9/873-0553.** Main courses $8–$15. AE, MC, V. Daily 7pm–midnight. ITALIAN.

The predominately Italian crowd filling the tables here is a telling sign that the food is authentic and delicious. Entrees cover a range of homemade pasta and northern Italian specialties, with seafood prominently featured. There's an admirable selection of wines and they serve exceptional espresso. The ambiance is lively and sophisticated.

✪ **La Parrilla.** Av. 5 at calle 8. ☎ **9/873-0687.** Main courses $6.25–$25. AE, MC, V. Daily noon–2am. MEXICAN/GRILL.

One of the most popular restaurants in town, it has an open-air dining area where the aroma of grilling meat permeates the air. The huge chicken fajitas come with plenty of homemade tortillas and beans, and if you want to feast on lobster, this is one place to do it. Side dishes such as guacamole, quesadillas, and tortilla soup are well prepared. Enchiladas and other Mexican standards are also on the menu. The tables fill quickly in the evening, but there are smaller bar tables set out in the plaza's courtyards, where you can wait.

MODERATE

El Chino. Calle 4 between Av. 10 and 15. ☎ **9/873-0015.** Breakfast $2.25–$3.50; main courses $5–$10. No credit cards. Daily 8am–11pm. YUCATECAN/MEXICAN.

Despite its name, there's not a Chinese dish on the menu. But locals highly recommend this place. Slightly off the popular row of restaurants on avenida 5, it doesn't try to impress tourists with its decor. But its simplicity is charming with tile floors and plastic-covered, polished wood tables beneath a large *palapa* roof and whirring ceiling fans. They offer a standard breakfast menu, plus you can order freshly blended fruit drinks. Main courses include such regional favorites as *poc chuc*, chicken *pibil*, and Ticul-style fish, plus chicken and shrimp *brochettes*. Other selections are lobster and shrimp crêpes, fajitas, and *ceviche*.

✪ **Media Luna.** Av. 5, between calles 8 and 10. No phone. Breakfast $3–$7; main courses $7–$12, sandwich with a salad $4–$6. No credit cards. Daily 7:30am–11:30pm. VEGETARIAN/ SEAFOOD.

The food here is outstanding; the owner-chef has come up with an eclectic menu that favors grilled seafood, sautées, and pasta dishes with inventive combinations of ingredients. Everything I had was quite fresh and prepared beautifully, taking its inspiration from various culinary traditions—Italian, Mexican, Japanese. The restaurant also makes sandwiches and salads, black bean quesadillas, and crêpes. The restaurant is open on two sides and is decorated in a modern rustic fashion in muted flesh tones.

Ronny's. On the beach, at calle 6. ☎ **9/873-0997.** Buffet breakfast $6; main courses $3–$30. AE, MC, V. Buffet breakfast daily 7–11am; lunch daily 11:30am–6pm (happy hour noon–1pm and 4–6pm). MEXICAN/AMERICAN.

Located on the beach, this is a good place to while away some hours munching and people-watching. The food is dependably good. The breakfast buffet is all-you-can-eat, so arrive hungry. Apart from breakfast you have a choice of fajitas, peel-your-own Cajun-flavored shrimp with U.S.-style tartar and shrimp sauce, hamburgers, hot dogs, quesadillas, pastries, ice cream, beer, wine, and coffee. From avenida Principal, walk 4 blocks north on avenida 5, turn right half a block on calle 8 to a marked Pelican Inn pathway, and turn right, or go to the beach and turn right; the hotel/restaurant is on the beach.

Zulu Lounge. Av. 5, between calles 6 and 8. ☎ **9/873-0056.** Main courses $4–$9. AE. Daily 5:30–11:30pm. THAI/VEGETARIAN.

Inspired by Thai flavors and decor, this fetching restaurant offers a casual, relaxing space for dining on flavorful food. Broken tile–topped tables add a Mexican touch to the smartly decorated interior accented by bamboo and Thai fabrics. Asian jazz and techno music underscores the hip ambiance and plays a little louder in the back room, where there's a couple of pool tables and a few rooms for rent. Standard Thai favorites include Pad Thai and vegetarian spring rolls. Their yellow curry is invitingly spicy. Most dishes are prepared with your choice of seafood, chicken, beef, or vegetarian. Full bar service and excellent espresso drinks are available.

INEXPENSIVE

Sabor. Av. 5 between calles 2 and 4. No phone. Yogurt and granola $1.50–$2.75; sandwiches $2–$3; vegetarian plates $2.25–$4; pastries 95¢–$1.50. No credit cards. Daily 8am–10:30pm. BAKERY/HEALTH FOOD.

A patio that's always full of patrons attests to the popularity of this modest restaurant. The list of hot and cold drinks includes espresso and cappuccino, café frappé, hot chocolate, tea, and fruit and vegetable drinks. Sabor now has Blue Bell ice cream (a favorite of Texans) and light vegetarian meals. Try a cup of something with a slice of pie and watch village life stroll by.

✪ **Tarraya Restaurant/Bar.** Calle 2 Nte. at the beach. ☎ **9/873-2040.** Main courses $4–$7; whole fish $8 per kilo. No credit cards. Daily noon–9pm. SEAFOOD.

"The restaurant that was born with the town," proclaims the sign. This is also the restaurant local : 6/28/2005 mend as the best for seafood. It's right on the beach, with the water practically ions. Since the owners are fishermen, the fish is so fresh it's T food hut doesn't look like much, but here you can have you several methods. If you haven't tried the Yucatecan specialty, Tik-n- he a good place to do so. Tarraya is on the beach, opposite the basketball court.

PLAYA DEL CARMEN AFTER DARK

It seems like everyone in town is out on avenida 5 or on the square until 10 or 11pm; there's pleasant strolling, meals and drinks at streetside cafes, shops to browse, and a few bars with live music. On the main square, there's a second-story bar with Latin music (mostly recorded, sometimes live) called **Cocodrilo's.** Down by the ferry dock is a **Señor Frog's,** which seems a bit out of place in Playa, dishing out its patented mix of thumping dance music, Jell-O shots, and frat-house antics; on the beach at 4th street. On the beach there's **Captain Tutiz,** which is designed like a pirate ship, has a large bar area, dance floor, and live entertainment nightly, and the beachside bar at the **Blue Parrot,** which seems to draw most of the European and American expatriate community for jazz. The **bar** at the Treetops hotel always has a congenial crowd gathered around the bar and television until midnight.

5 Highway 307 from Xcaret to Xel-Ha

South of Playa del Carmen, after you pass most of the Playacar development, you'll find a succession of commercial nature parks, planned resort communities, and for now, anyway, a few rustic beach hideaways and unspoiled coves. From north to south, this section covers in the following order Xcaret, Paamul, Puerto Aventuras, Xpu-Ha, Akumal, and Xel-Ha. Puerto Calica, the new cruise-ship pier, is $2^1/_2$ miles south of Xcaret and 8 miles south of Playa del Carmen.

Of the fledgling resorts south of Playa del Carmen, **Akumal** is one of the most attractive and welcoming, with comfortable hotels and bungalows that line two beautiful bays. **Puerto Aventuras** is a privately developed, marina community aimed more at condo owners than at vacationers. **Paamul** and **Xpu-Ha** offer inexpensive seaside inns. If the offbeat beach life is what you're after, grab it now before it disappears. (Other little-known getaways can be found on the **Punta Allen Peninsula** south of Tulum, and the **Majahual Peninsula** south of Felipe Carrillo Puerto; see the next sections for details.) Three water theme parks offer entertaining ways to spend the day immersed in the beauty of this region. One is centered around the crystal-clear cenotes and lagoons at **Xel-Ha.** The other is the immensely popular park development of **Xcaret.** Popular day-trips from Cancún, they are open to anyone traveling along this coast. A more recent development is Xpu-Ha Ecopark.

EN ROUTE SOUTH FROM PLAYA DEL CARMEN   The best way to travel this coast is in a rental car (there are a lot of rental car agencies in Playa). There is a wide, well-paved highway as far as Tulum making for an easy 1-hour drive. Bus transportation from Playa del Carmen south exists but is not great. Buses depart fairly regularly from Playa headed toward Chetumal, stopping several times along the way; however, from the highway it can be a long walk to the coast and to your final destination. There's also bus service to and from Cobá three times a day. Another option is to hire a car and driver; costs run around $10 to $14 per hour, or an all-day rate can be negotiated. Find a driver you like and whose English is good; remember, you'll be with him all day.

XCARET: A DEVELOPED NATURE PARK

Six-and-a-half miles south of Playa del Carmen (and 50 miles south of Cancún) is the turnoff to Xcaret (pronounced ish-car-*et*), a specially built, **ecological and archaeological theme park** that is one of the area's most popular tourist attractions. It's open Monday to Saturday from 8:30am to 8:30pm and Sunday from 8:30am to 5:30pm. Everywhere you look in Cancún are signs advertising Xcaret, or someone is handing you a leaflet about it. They even have their own bus terminal to take tourists from Cancún at regular intervals, and they've added an evening extravaganza. For this reason, we've covered it in the Cancún chapter.

PAAMUL: SEASIDE GETAWAY

About 10 miles beyond Xcaret, 16 miles from Playa del Carmen, and 60 miles from Cancún is Paamul (also written Pamul), which in Maya means "a destroyed ruin." The exit is clearly marked. At Paamul you can enjoy the Caribbean away from the crowds; the water is wonderful, but the beach is rocky. Thirty years ago the Martin family gave up coconut harvesting on this stretch of coast bordering a large, shallow bay, and established this comfortable out-of-the-way respite. Most of the area is dedicated to trailer and RV spaces, but the family also rents nine rooms out.

Scubamex (☎ 9/873-0667; fax 9/874-1729; www.scubamex.com) is a fully equipped, PADI-, NAUI-, and SSI-certified dive shop here, located next to the *cabañas*. Using three 38-foot boats, the staff takes guests on dives 5 miles in either direction. If it's too choppy, the reefs in front of the hotel are also excellent. They also offer a night dive in Paamul, which is considered the best night dive along the Mexican Caribbean. The cost for a two-tank dive is $45, plus $25 if you need to rent gear. The snorkeling is also excellent in this protected bay and the one next to it.

WHERE TO STAY & DINE

✪ **Cabañas Paamul.** Km 85 Carretera Cancún–Tulum (Apdo. Postal 83), 77710 Playa del Carmen, Q. Roo. ☎ **9/876-2691.** (Reservations: Av. Colón 501-C, Depto. D-211 x 6 y 62 97000 Mérida, Yuc.) 9 bungalows; 190 trailer spaces (all with full hookups). July–Aug and Dec–Feb $75 double. March–June and Sept–Nov $50 double. RV space with hookups $7 per day, $95 per month. No credit cards.

The rooms are distributed among four buildings just steps away from the Caribbean. Despite the number of mobile homes (which are occupied more in winter than any other time), there's seldom a soul on the beach. Each bungalow contains two double beds, tile floors, rattan furniture, ceiling fans, hot water, and 24-hour electricity. A large, breezy *palapa* restaurant serves food at reasonable prices. Try the Pescado Paamul or Shrimp Paamul; both are wonderful baked medleys devised by the gracious owner, Eloiza Zapata. For stays longer than a week, ask for a discount. The trailer park isn't what you might expect—some trailers have decks or patios and thatched *palapa* shade covers. Trailer guests have access to 12 showers and separate bathrooms for men and women. Laundry service is available nearby. Turtles nest here June through September. Visitors not staying here are welcome to use the beach, though the owners request that they not bring in drinks or food and use the restaurant instead.

PUERTO AVENTURAS: A RESORT COMMUNITY

Three miles south of Paamul (65 miles from Cancún), you'll come to the large, glitzy development of Puerto Aventuras on Chakalal Bay. What you'll find is a marina community with a nine-hole golf course, and three expensive hotels, one of these being the **OMNI Puerto Aventuras** (☎ **800-the-omni** from the U.S., or 9/873-5101). It has only 30 rooms, which is rather odd—I imagine that it was originally intended to be larger. Although Puerto Aventuras is almost as large as a city, the population of permanent residents is surprisingly low, and you get the feeling that most of these are real estate agents wanting to sell you a condo. You might stop here just to see what the place looks like, to swim with dolphins, to eat at a good restaurant, or to see the museum. But I don't think the resort is as interesting a destination as other places along this coast.

The museum here is the **Museo CEDAM.** CEDAM stands for Center for the Study of Aquatic Sports in Mexico, and the museum houses displays on the history of diving on this coast from pre-Hispanic times to the present. Besides dive-related memorabilia, there are displays of pre-Hispanic pottery, figures, copper bells found in the *cenotes* of Chichén-Itzá, shell fossils, and sunken ship contents. It's open daily from 10am to 1pm and 2 to 6pm. Donations are requested. To make reservations to swim with the dolphins call **Dolphin Discovery** (☎ **9/883-0779**). A 1-hour session costs $119. If you're hungry, Puerto Aventuras has one outstanding restaurant called **Papaya Republic.**

XPU-HA: BEAUTIFUL BEACH HIDEAWAY

Two miles beyond Puerto Aventuras is Xpu-Ha (ish-poo-*hah*), a wide bay lined by a beautiful sandy beach. At one end of the bay is the enclosed **Xpu-Ha Ecopark;** at the other is the enclosed all-inclusive **Robinson Club.** Between these two is a long stretch of uncrowded beach that's open to the public. The beach is dotted with five simple hotels and a few restaurants. Lodging is very simple, almost all of it is in cinder-block rooms with a bed, private bathroom, and lights. Some of it you can rent for as low as $20/night. After you pass the sign for the Xpu-Ha Ecopark you will see a quick succession of turn-offs labeled X-1, X-2, X-3, etc. Ongoing construction keeps affecting the quality of the roads to the beach, but if you turn between X-3 and X-6, you'll have the best bet of finding a decent road. The Xpu-Ha Ecopark is a development along the lines of Xel-Ha or Xcaret, but so far it doesn't offer as many things to do or see. Entrance fees, which include food, drink, and snorkel gear rental, are $40 for adults, $29 for kids over age 5. Activities include snorkeling, kayaks, and sailing. Its 93 acres enclose a small cove and lagoon that are a natural habitat for manatees.

WHERE TO STAY & DINE

Villas del Caribe Xpu-Ha. Carretera Cancún–Tulum Km 88, 77710 Playa del Carmen, Q. Roo. No phone. 9 units. $35 double. No credit cards.

Two stories of rooms face the beach, with communal porches for lounging. Rooms have blue-tile floors and matching blue walls, and each comes with one or two double beds, a tiled bath, and windows facing the beach; one room has a kitchen. There's 24-hour electricity and hot water. The management has radio communication with the Hotel Flores in Cozumel (☎ **9/872-1429**), so if you're there, you can reserve a room ahead (or vice versa).

AKUMAL: BEAUTIFUL BAYS AND CAVERN DIVING

Continuing south on Highway 307 for 1¹/₂ miles, you'll come to the turn-off for Akumal, a small, modern, and ecologically-oriented community built on the shores of two beautiful bays. Signs point the way from the highway, and the white Akumal gateway is less than a half mile down the road. Here you'll find Akumal Bay, largely occupied by the hotel Akumal Caribe, listed below. The road then curves to the left, taking you north along the coast to the shallow and rocky Half Moon Bay, lined with two- and three-story condos, and eventually to Yalku Lagoon. Most of these condos can be rented to vacationers.

You don't have to be a guest to enjoy the beach, swim or snorkel, or eat at one of the restaurants. It's an excellent place to spend the day while on a trip down the coast, but you should consider staying here for a longer time, especially if you are a diver and would like to try **technical diving** and/or **cavern diving.** On Akumal Bay are two dive shops with PADI-certified instructors. The older of these is the **Akumal Dive Shop** (www.akumal.com), one of the oldest and best dive shops on the coast. These people know more about diving in the *cenotes* than just about anyone. Offshore there are almost 30 dive sites to visit (from 30 to 80 feet deep). Both shops offer resort courses as well as complete certification. **Fishing trips** can also be arranged through the dive shops. You're only 15 minutes from good fishing. Two hours (the minimum period) costs $100, and each additional hour is $35 for up to four people with two fishing lines. Windsurfing is also available.

WHERE TO STAY

Club Akumal Caribe/Hotel Villas Maya Club. Km 104 Carretera Cancún–Tulum (Hwy. 307). ☎ **9/875-9012.** (For reservations, P.O. Box 13326, El Paso, TX 79913; ☎ **800/351-1622** in the U.S., 800/343-1440 in Canada, or 915/584-3552.) www.hotelakumalcaribe.com. 70 units. A/C. High season $120 bungalow, $145 hotel room, $160–$420 villa/condo. Low season $95 bungalow, $105 hotel room, $100–$250 villa/condo. Reservations with prepayment by check only. AE, MC, V; cash only at the restaurants. Ask for special packages for low season. Free parking.

The hotel rooms and garden bungalows of this hotel are along Akumal Bay. Both are large and comfortable with tile floors and good size bathrooms. The 40 **Villas Maya Bungalows** are simply and comfortably furnished and come with kitchenettes. The 21 rooms in the three-story **beachfront hotel** are more elaborately furnished and come with refrigerators and either a king-size or two queen-size beds, tile floors, and Mexican accents. There is a large pool on the grounds. Other units belonging to the hotel are condos and the very lovely **Villas Flamingo** on Half Moon Bay. These last ones come with two or three bedrooms and large living, dining, and kitchen areas; and a lovely furnished patio just steps from the beach. The four units share a nice pool. The main part of the hotel has a good restaurant and a beachside bar and snackbar that are very pleasant. If you're traveling with children, ask about the **children's activities program** available during specific times of year (extra charge of $15 per child, per day; with pre-pay discounts available).

Vista del Mar Hotel and Condos. Half Moon Bay, Akumal. ☎ **877/425-8625.** Fax 505/ 988-3882 in the U.S. www.mexico-vacation.com. 27 units. A/C, TV. High season $85 double, $173–$242 condo; low season $45 double, $74–$124 condo. AE, MV, V. Free parking.

All the properties here are beachfront, which makes the rates for these rooms very competitive. The hotel has 15 rooms, which come either with a queen-size bed or a double and a twin. The 12 condos come without A/C (but with ceiling fans) and consist of a kitchen, living area, and either two or three bedrooms and one or two baths. All come with either balconies or terraces facing the sea and are equipped with hammocks. Televisions receive two channels: HBO and Cinemax. There is a pool on the property, and you can rent kayaks, bikes, and snorkeling equipment.

WHERE TO DINE

There are about ten places to eat in Akumal and a good grocery store by the archway called Super Chomak. The **Turtle Bay Café and Bakery** is good for breakfast or lunch. It's by the Akumal Dive Shop. The hotel restaurant **Lol Ha** of the Akumal Caribe serves good Mexican food for breakfast, lunch, and dinner. Another good dining spot is **La Buena Vida**, on Half Moon Bay.

XEL-HA: SNORKELING & SWIMMING

The Caribbean coast is carved by the sea into hundreds of small *caletas* (coves) and lagoons that form the perfect habitat for tropical marine life, both flora and fauna. Xel-Ha (shell-*hah*), 8 miles south of Akumal, is a dramatic example of these and is enjoyed daily by throngs of snorkelers who come to luxuriate in its warm waters and swim among its brilliant fish. Xel-Ha is a swimmer's paradise, with no threat of undertow or pollution. It's a beautiful, completely calm cove that's a perfect place to bring kids for their first snorkeling experience (experienced snorkelers may be disappointed—the crowds here seem to have driven out the living coral and a lot of the fish; you can find more abundant marine life and avoid an admission charge by going to other spots).

The entrance to Xel-Ha is a half mile from the highway. Admission with the base plan is $19 per adult and $12 for children ages 4 to 12; admission with the all-inclusive plan, which includes food and snorkeling gear rental, is $43 for adults and $39 for children. Xel-ha is open daily from 8:30am to 5:30pm, and offers free parking with admission.

Once inside the 10-acre park, you can rent snorkeling equipment and an underwater camera—but you may also bring your own. Food and beverage service, changing rooms, showers, and other facilities are all available. For non-snorkelers, platforms have been constructed that allow decent sealife viewing. When you swim, be careful to observe the SWIM HERE and NO SWIMMING signs. (The greatest variety of fish can be seen right near the ropes marking off the no-swimming areas and near any groups of rocks.) There's also a program for swimming with dolphins. For information and to make reservations the day before, call ☎ **9/871-4120.** The interactive program with the dolphins costs $55.

Just south of the Xel-Ha turnoff on the west side of the highway, don't miss the **Maya ruins** of ancient Xel-Ha. You'll likely be the only one there as you walk over limestone rocks and through the tangle of trees, vines, and palms. There is a huge, deep, dark *cenote* to one side and a temple palace with tumbled-down columns, a jaguar group, and a conserved temple group. A covered *palapa* on one pyramid guards a partially preserved mural. Admission is $2.50.

Xel-Ha is close to Tulum—it's a good place for a dip when you've finished climbing these Maya ruins. A very popular day-trip from Cancún combines the two. You can even make the short 8-mile hop north from Tulum to Xel-Ha by bus. When you get off at the junction for Tulum, ask the restaurant owner when the next buses come by; otherwise you may have to wait as long as 2 hours on the highway.

TANKAH: BEACH AND CENOTE

Four miles beyond Xel-Ha and 5 miles before Tulum, you'll see a sign for Cenote Tankah on your left. Pull in here and you come to a *cenote* by a lovely bay, which (perhaps until now) sees few visitors. Once you get beyond the shallow beach you'll find great snorkeling—in just a short while I managed to see a number of rays and scores of fish. The reefs that protect the bay here are pristine and make for good recreation diving. There's a *palapa* restaurant next to the *cenote* that has good grilled food, and should you elect to stay here, a couple from Texas offer lodging and full dive facilities.

Tankah Inn. Apartado Postal #5, 77780 Tulum, Q. Roo. ☎ **9/874-2188.** Fax 9/871-2092. E-mail: Tankahdiveinn@mailcity.com. 5 units. High season $100 double; low season $80. Rates include continental breakfast. No credit cards.

This place is an uncommon combination of small hotel and full dive shop. The rooms are spacious and attractive. The hotel is right on the shore, and from the second-story dining area you have a great view of the entire bay. This is a great place to hang out after a dive or a snorkeling trip, and the owners are so accomodating that they make you feel very much at home. What's for dinner depends on what the guests are in the mood for; none of the menus are planned far in advance, and the food is good. The hotel offers dive packages and discounts for extended stays or for renting out the entire place.

6 Tulum, Punta Allen & Sian Ka'an

Tulum (80 miles from Cancún) and the Punta Allen Peninsula border on the northern edge of the Sian Ka'an biopreserve. The walled Maya city of Tulum is a large Post-classic Maya site that overlooks the Caribbean in dramatic fashion. Tour companies and public buses make the trip regularly from Cancún and Playa del Carmen. Tulum also has wonderful, sandy beaches and no large resort hotels. It's a perfect spot for those who like to splash around in the water and lie on the beach away from the resort scene. And for those who really want to leave the modern world behind, there's the Punta Allen Peninsula (which can take between 1¹/₂ to 3 hours to reach from Tulum, depending on the current road conditions). It's a place without the crowds, frenetic pace, or creature comforts of the resorts—down here, the generator shuts down at 10pm (if there is one). What you will find is great fishing and snorkeling, the natural and archaeological riches of the Sian Ka'an Biosphere Reserve, and a chance to rest up at what truly feels like the end of the road. A few beach *cabañas* now offer reliable power, telephones, and hot showers.

ORIENTATION   Highway 307 passes the entrance to the ruins (on your left) before cutting through town. A little bit beyond the entrance to the ruins it intersects another highway at the edge of Tulum. To the right is the highway leading to the ruins of Cobá, (see "Cobá," below, for details); to the left is the Tulum hotel zone, which begins about 1¹/₂ miles away. The same road that goes to the hotel zone continues south all the way down the narrow **Punta Allen Peninsula,** entering the **Sian Ka'an Biosphere Reserve,** and eventually arriving at the town of **Punta Allen,** a lobstering/ fishing village at the peninsula's tip. Highway 307, south of this intersection passes through the main part of the village of **Tulum,** and the road continues on towards **Chetumal.** The highway here is lined with businesses, including the bus stations, auto repair shops, markets, restaurants and a dive shop.

EXPLORING THE TULUM ARCHAEOLOGICAL SITE

Located 8 miles south of Xel-Ha, Tulum is a Maya fortress overlooking the Caribbean. By A.D. 900, the end of the Classic period, Maya civilization began to decline and most of the large ceremonial centers were deserted. During the Postclassic period (A.D. 900 to the Spanish Conquest), small rival states developed with a few imported traditions from north-central Mexico. Tulum is one such walled city-state; built in the 10th century, it functioned as a seaport. Aside from the spectacular setting, Tulum is not an impressive city when compared to Chichén-Itzá or Uxmal. There are no magnificent pyramidal structures as are found in the Classic Maya ruins. The primary god here was the diving god, depicted on several buildings as an upside-down figure above doorways. Seen at the Palace at Sayil and Cobá, this curious, almost comical figure is also known as the bee god.

The most imposing building in Tulum is the large stone structure on the cliff called the **Castillo** (castle). Actually a temple as well as a fortress, it was once covered with stucco and painted. In front of the Castillo are several unrestored palace-like buildings partially covered with stucco. And on the **beach** below, where the Maya once came ashore, tourists swim and sun, combining a visit to the ruins with a dip in the Caribbean.

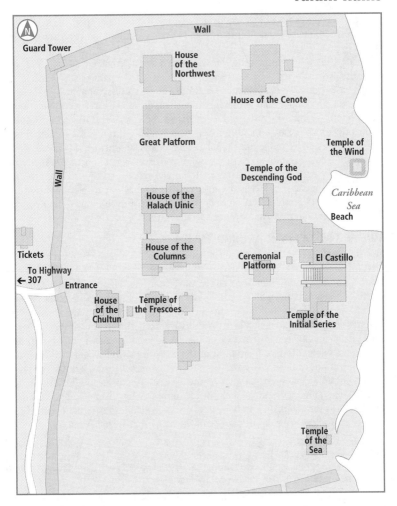

The **Temple of the Frescoes,** directly in front of the Castillo, contains interesting 13th-century wall paintings, but entrance is no longer permitted. Distinctly Maya, they represent the rain god Chaac and Ixchel, the goddess of weaving, women, the moon, and medicine. On the cornice of this temple is a relief of the head of the rain god. If you get a slight distance from the building you'll see the eyes, nose, mouth, and chin. Notice the remains of the red-painted stucco—at one time all the buildings at Tulum were painted a bright red.

Much of what we know of Tulum at the time of the Spanish Conquest comes from the writings of Diego de Landa, third bishop of the Yucatán. He wrote that Tulum was a small city inhabited by about 600 people, who lived in platform dwellings along a street and who supervised the trade traffic from Honduras to the Yucatán. Though it was a walled city, most of the inhabitants probably lived outside the walls, leaving the interior for the residences of governors and priests and ceremonial structures. Tulum survived about 70 years after the Conquest, when it was finally abandoned.

Because of the excess of visitors this site receives, it is no longer possible to climb all of the ruins. In many cases, visitors are asked to remain behind roped-off areas to view them.

In late 1994 a new entrance to the ruins was constructed about a 10-minute walk from the archaeological site. Cars and buses enter a large parking lot; some of the public buses from Playa del Carmen go directly to the visitors' center, where there are artisans' stands, a bookstore, a museum, a restaurant, several large rest rooms, and a ticket booth for Inter-Playa buses, which depart for Playa del Carmen and Cancún frequently between 7:40am and 4:40pm. After walking through the center, visitors pay the admission fee to the ruins ($2; free on Sunday), another fee ($1) if you choose to ride an open-air shuttle to the ruins, and, if you're driving, another fee ($1) to park. You can easily walk, however. There's an additional charge of $4 for a permit to use a video camera at the site. Licensed guides have a stand by the path to the ruins and charge $20 for a 45-minute tour in English, French, or Spanish for up to four persons. They will point out many architectural details you might otherwise miss.

WHERE TO STAY IN & AROUND TULUM

You can stay either on the beach at one of the *cabaña* hotels in the hotel zone or in town. The four hotels in town are generally cheaper than all but the most basic of beach accommodations, but they aren't as much fun. They offer basic lodging for anywhere between $20 and $50 a night. But I really like staying in the *cabaña* hotels. There are more than 20 of these, and they run the gamut from providing only the minimal lodging requirements to refined luxury. To get to the hotels on the beach, turn east at the highway intersection. One-and-a-half miles ahead you have to turn either north or south. North are most of the cheap *cabañas*. I would preach caution in staying at one of these; I've heard from several sources that travelers have had their possesions stolen at one or another of these places. South are the majority of the *cabañas*, including some moderately priced places along the road. The pavement quickly turns into sand, and on both sides of the road you start seeing thatched-roof structures. You can try your luck at one of the many that are located here.

✪ **Restaurant y Cabañas Ana y José.** Punta Allen Peninsula, km 7 Carretera Punta Allen (Apdo. Postal 15), 77780 Tulum, Q. Roo. ☎ **9/887-5470,** in Cancún. Fax 9/887-5469. www.tulumresorts.com. E-mail: anayjose@cancun.rce.com.mx. 15 units. High season $80–$110 double. Low season $70–$100 double. MC, V. Free parking.

This place started as a restaurant and blossomed into a comfortable inn on a great beach for swimming and sunbathing. You can also swim and sunbathe around the hotel's pool. All rooms have tile or wood floors, one or two double beds, and patios or balconies. The rock-walled *cabañas* in front (called "oceanfront") are a little larger than the others, but the second floor "vista del mar" rooms are very attractive and have tall *palapa* roofs. There are also some standard rooms that are much like the others but don't face the sea. Around Christmas and New Year's, the rates are a little higher than normal high season. The hotel also has one suite that costs more. There is 24-hour electricity for lights and ceiling fans. Through the inn, you can rent a car or a bike or hook up with a tour to Sian Ka'an. Excursions organized by the Friends of Sian Ka'an meet at the hotel's restaurant. (See Sian Ka'an box below, for details on making reservations for the Biosphere Reserve trip.) The hotel can have a rental car waiting for you at the Cancún airport. The hotel's restaurant is very pleasant, occupying a screened-in area with sand floors under a large *palapa*. The food is good and moderately priced. The hotel is 4 miles south of the Tulum ruins. Reservations are a must in high season.

Cabañas Tulum. Punta Allen Peninsula, km 7 Carretera Punta Allen. (Apdo. Postal 63), 77780 Tulum, Q. Roo. ☎ **99/25-8295.** 24 units. $40 double. No credit cards.

Next door to Ana y José's is a row of bungalows facing the same beautiful ocean and beach. This place offers the most basic in accommodations. Rooms are simple concrete structures with two double beds, screens on the windows, a table, one electric light (electricity available 6am–11pm), a tiled bathroom, and a veranda facing the beach. Mattresses, which rest on cement platforms, are too thin. There are pool and ping pong tables. A small restaurant serves beer, soft drinks, and all three meals for reasonable prices—just don't expect gourmet fare. In fact, any meal other than breakfast you're better off taking at Ana y José or in town. The *cabañas* are often full between December 15 and Easter and July and August, so arrive early or make reservations. If you're there at any other time, try negotiating a lower rate.

Las Ranitas. Punta Allen Peninsula. Km 9 Carr. Punta Allen 77780 Tulum, Q. Roo. ☎ 9/877-8554. Fax 9/845-0861. www.lasranitas.com. 18 units. High season $150–$170 double; low season $120–$140 double. No credit cards. Rates include continental breakfast.

Almost a mile beyond Cabañas Ana y José, this property offers a little more solitude than the *cabañas* closer to Tulum. The owners built it with ecological principles and privacy in mind. The two-story stucco beach houses are connected by footpaths through dense native vegetation as if they were meant to blend into the landscape as much as possible. Each house holds two units: an upstairs ("premier") with a king-size bed and a downstairs ("conventional") with two doubles. The two different rates for the rooms are shown above. The hotel has four suites, which are quite a bit larger and a little fancier. The rooms in this hotel are probably the nicest on this stretch of coast; they come with large tile bathrooms, chairs, a writing table, and a private patio or balcony. Electricity is provided by solar and wind generators. The beach in front of the hotel is gorgeous, and the hotel has a swimming pool. A beautifully decorated restaurant handles meals.

WHERE TO DINE

There are a few restaurants in the town of Tulum that have reasonable prices and good food. For Mexican food try **Charlie's** or **Don Cafeto's.** For Tex-Mex try **No que No!** (fajitas are the specialty). All of these are located on the main road through town. Also on that road are a couple of roadside places that grill chicken and serve it with rice and beans.

EXPLORING THE PUNTA ALLEN PENINSULA

If you've been captured by an adventurous spirit and have an excessively sanguine opinion of the performance of your rented car, you might want to take a trip down the Punta Allen Peninsula, especially if your interests lie in fly-fishing, bird-watching, or simply exploring new country. The far end of the peninsula is only 30 miles away, but it can be a very slow 30 miles due to the poor condition of the road (1^{1}/$_{2}$–3 hours depending on how much water is in the road). Not far from the last *cabaña* hotel is the entrance to the 1.3-million-acre **Sian Ka'an Biosphere Reserve** (see below). Halfway down the peninsula, at a place called Boca Paila, you come to a bridge that crosses to the lower peninsula (where the Boca Paila Fishing Lodge is). On your right is a large lagoon. Another 15 miles gets you to the village of **Punta Allen,** where you can arrange a bird-watching expedition (available between June and August, with July being best) or boat trips (see Cuzan Guest house, below).

A note about provisions: Since the Punta Allen Peninsula is rather remote and there are no stores, handy provisions to bring along include a flashlight, mosquito repellent, mosquito coils, water, snacks, and bottled water. From October to December winds may make for nippy nights, so come prepared—some hotels don't have blankets.

The Sian Ka'an Biosphere Reserve

Down the peninsula, a few miles south of the Tulum ruins, you'll pass the guard-house of the Sian Ka'an Biosphere Reserve. The reserve is a tract of 1.3-million acres set aside in 1986 to preserve tropical forests, savannas, mangroves, coastal and marine habitats, and 70 miles of coastal reefs. The area is home to jaguars, pumas, ocelots, margays, jaguarundis, spider and howler monkeys, tapirs, white-lipped and collared peccaries, manatees, brocket and white-tailed deer, crocodiles, and green, loggerhead, hawksbill, and leatherback sea turtles. It also protects 366 species of birds—you might catch a glimpse of an ocellated turkey, a great curassow, a brilliantly colored parrot, a toucan or trogon, a white ibis, a roseate spoonbill, a jabiru (or wood stork), a flamingo, or one of 15 species of herons, egrets, and bitterns.

The park is separated into three parts: a "core zone" restricted to research; a "buffer zone," where visitors and families already living there have restricted use; and a "cooperation zone," which is outside the reserve but vital to its preservation. If you drive on Highway 307 from Tulum to an imaginary line just below the Bahía (bay) of Espíritu Santo, all you see on the Caribbean side is the reserve; but except at the ruins of Muyil/Chunyaxche, there's no access. At least 22 archaeo-logical sites have been charted within Sian Ka'an. The best place to sample the reserve is on the Punta Allen Peninsula, part of the "buffer zone." The inns were already in place when the reserve was created. Of these, only the Cuzan Guest House (see "Where to Stay," below) offers trips for birding. But bring your own binoculars and birding books and have at it—the bird life here is rich. At the Boca Paila bridge you can often find fishermen who'll take you into the lagoon on the landward side, where you can fish and see plenty of bird life; but it's unlikely the boatman will know bird names in English or Spanish. Birding is best just after dawn, especially during the April to July nesting season.

Day-trips to the Sian Ka'an are led by the Friends of Sian Ka'an from the Restaurant y Cabañas Ana y José just south of the Tulum ruins. The cost is $50 per person using their vehicle or $40 per person if you drive yourself. Trips start from the Cabañas at 9:30am and return there around 2:30pm. For reservations, contact **Amigos de Sian Ka'an** (☎ **9/884-9583;** fax 9/887-3080) in Cancún. Or you may be able to book the tour once you've arrived at the Restaurant y Cabañas Ana y José (see "Where to Stay in and around Tulum" above) if the tour isn't full.

WHERE TO STAY

There are simple but comfortable lodgings on the peninsula. One or two have elec-tricity for a few hours in the evening, but shut it off around 10pm. The two that I include here are quite different from the standard lodgings in the area and are some-what specialized, but you can easily find cheaper accommodations or stay in one of the places mentioned above for Tulum and go down for just the day.

Boca Paila Fishing Lodge. Km 25 Carreterra Tulum–Punta Allen (Apdo. Postal 59), 77600 Cozumel, Q. Roo. ☎ **9/872-5944** or 9/872-1176. Fax 9/872-0053. (For reservations contact Frontiers, P.O. Box 959, 100 Logan Rd., Wexford, PA 15090; ☎ **800/245-1950** in the U.S., or 412/935-1577; fax 412/935-5388.) 9 *cabañas.* High season (Dec 3–June 2) $2,430 per person double. Low season $1,930 per person double. Rates are for 6 days and

7 nights, including all meals and a private boat and bonefishing guide for each *cabaña,* and round-trip transfer from/to Cancun. Ask about prices for a nonangler sharing a double with an angler. No credit cards are accepted on site;however, if you're prepaying while reserving with Frontiers, MC and V are accepted.

The white stucco *cabañas* offer comfortable but basic lodging. Each individual unit has a mosquito-proof *palapa* roof, large tiled rooms comfortably furnished with two double beds, rattan furniture, hot water in the bathrooms, floor fans, 24-hour electricity, and a comfortable screened porch. This is primarily a fishing lodge; it is not a picturesque hideaway, but it's in a beautiful area. The Boca Paila attracts a clientele that comes for saltwater flyfishing in the flats, mostly for bonefish. Prime fishing months are March to June. But when occupancy is low, nonfishing guests can be accommodated with advance notice. Overnight nonfishing rates are priced high as a discouragement to drop-ins. The lodge is about midway down the Punta Allen Peninsula, just before the Boca Paila bridge.

✪ **Cuzan Guest House.** Punta Allen. For reservations contact Apdo. Postal 24, 77200 Felipe Carrillo Puerto, Q. Roo. ☎ **9/834-0358.** Fax 9/834-0292. members.aol.com/fishcuzan. E-mail: fishcuzan@aol.com. 12 units. $40–$80 double. All-inclusive flyfishing packages offered. No credit cards.

About 30 miles south of the Tulum ruins is the end of the peninsula and Punta Allen, a lobstering and fishing village, planted on a palm-studded beach. Isolated and rustic, it's part Indiana Jones, part Robinson Crusoe, and certainly the most laid-back end of the line you'll find for a long time. The small town has a lobster cooperative, a few streets with modest homes, and a lighthouse at the end of a narrow sand road dense with coconut palms and jungle on both sides. So it's a welcome sight to see the beachside Cuzan Guest House and its sign in English that reads "stop here for tourist information."

Two of the rooms are Maya-style, oval stucco buildings with thatched roofs, concrete floors, hammocks, private bathrooms, and a combination of single and king beds with mosquito netting. The other rooms are comfortable wooden cabins that are loaded with rustic charm—thatched roofs, ocean views, and conveniently placed hammocks. These have two double beds each and come with private bathrooms. A few other rooms or houses elsewhere in the village are sometimes available for rent, but these are more primitive and may suffer from loud village noise at night. There's solar-powered electricity at night and plenty of hot water. The hotel's restaurant, a large *palapa* with a sand floor, serves three meals a day. Breakfast and lunch run about $5 and dinner $12–$15, and could well include lobster if it's in season. The food is good, and, of course, the seafood is fresh. Payment in meals must be in cash or travelers checks. Co-owner Sonja Lilvik, a Californian, makes you feel right at home.

Sonja arranges fly-fishing trips for bone, permit, snook, and tarpon to the nearby saltwater flats and lagoons of Ascension Bay (ask about all-inclusive flyfishing packages). She offers a fascinating 3-hour boat tour of the coastline that includes snorkeling, slipping in and out of mangrove-filled canals for bird-watching, and skirting the edge of an island rookery loaded with frigate birds. November to March is frigate bird mating season, and the male frigate shows off his big billowy red breast pouch to impress potential mates. You can also go kayaking along the coast or simply relax in a hammock on the beach.

7 Cobá Ruins

105 miles (168km) SW of Cancún

The impressive Maya ruins at Cobá, deep in the jungle, are a worthy detour from your route south. You don't need to stay overnight to see the ruins, but there are a few hotels. The village is small and poor, gaining little from the visitors who pass through to see the ruins. Used clothing (especially for children) would be a welcome gift.

From the turnoff at the Tulum junction, travel inland an hour or so to arrive at these mystical ruins jutting up from the forest floor.

ESSENTIALS
GETTING THERE & DEPARTING
BY CAR   The road to Cobá begins in Tulum, across Highway 307 from the turnoff to the Punta Allen Peninsula. Turn right when you see the signs to Cobá and continue on that road for 40 miles. When you reach the village, proceed straight until you see the lake; when the road curves right, turn left. The entrance to the ruins is at the end of that road past some small restaurants. Cobá is also about a 3-hour drive south from Cancún.

BY BUS   Several buses a day leave Cobá for Tulum and Playa del Carmen.

ORIENTATION
The highway into Cobá becomes the one main paved street through town, which passes El Bocadito restaurant and hotel on the right (see "Where to Stay & Dine," below) and goes a block to the lake. If you turn right at the lake you reach the Villas Arqueológicas a block farther. Turning left will lead you past a couple of primitive restaurants on the left facing the lake, and to the ruins, straight ahead.

EXPLORING THE COBÁ RUINS
The Maya built many breathtaking cities in the Yucatán, but few were grander in scope than Cobá. However, much of the 42-square-mile site, on the shores of two lakes, is unexcavated. A 60-mile-long *sacbe* (a pre-Hispanic raised road or causeway) through the jungle linked Cobá to Yaxuná, once a large and important Maya center 30 miles south of Chichén-Itzá. It's the Maya's longest known *sacbe,* and there are at least 50 or more shorter ones from here. An important city-state, Cobá, which means "water stirred by the wind," flourished between A.D. 632 (the oldest carved date found here) until after the founding of Chichén-Itzá, around 800. Then Cobá slowly faded in importance and population until it was finally abandoned. Scholars believe Cobá was an important trade link between the Yucatán Caribbean coast and inland cities.

Once in the site, keep your bearings—it's very easy to get lost on the maze of dirt roads in the jungle. If you're into it, bring your bird and butterfly books; this is one of the best places to see both. Branching off from every labeled path you'll notice unofficial narrow paths into the jungle, used by locals as shortcuts through the ruins. These are good for bird-watching, but be careful to remember the way back.

The **Grupo Cobá** boasts a large, impressive pyramid, the **Temple of the Church** (La Iglesia), which you'll find if you take the path bearing right after the entrance. Walking to it, notice the unexcavated mounds on the left. Though the urge to climb the temple is great, the view is better from El Castillo in the Nohoc Mul group farther back at the site.

From here, return back to the main path and turn right. You'll pass a sign pointing right to the ruined *juego de pelota* (ball court), but the path is obscure.

Continuing straight ahead on this path for 5 to 10 minutes, you'll come to a fork in the road. To the left and right you'll notice jungle-covered, unexcavated pyramids, and at one point, you'll cross a raised portion crossing the pathway—this is the visible remains of the *sacbe* to Yaxuná. Throughout the area, intricately carved stelae stand by pathways or lie forlornly in the jungle underbrush. Although protected by crude thatched roofs, most are so weatherworn as to be indiscernible.

Cobá Ruins

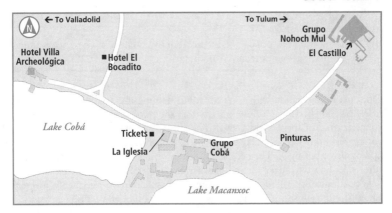

The left fork leads to the **Nohoch Mul Group,** which contains **El Castillo.** With the exception of Structure 2 in Calakmul, this is the tallest pyramid in the Yucatán (rising even higher than the great El Castillo at Chichén-Itzá and the Pyramid of the Magician at Uxmal). So far, visitors are still permitted to climb to the top. From this magnificent lofty perch, you can see unexcavated jungle-covered pyramidal structures poking up through the forest all around.

The right fork (more or less straight on) goes to the **Conjunto Las Pinturas.** Here, the main attraction is the **Pyramid of the Painted Lintel,** a small structure with traces of its original bright colors above the door. You can climb up to get a close look. Though maps of Cobá show ruins around two lakes, there are really only two excavated groups to see once you enter the site.

Admission is $2; children under age 12 enter free daily, and Sunday and holidays it's free to everyone. Camera permits are $4 for each video. The site is open daily from 8am to 5pm.

WHERE TO STAY & DINE

El Bocadito. Calle Principal, Cobá, Q. Roo. No phone. For reservations contact Apdo. Postal 56, 97780 Valladolid, Yuc. 8 units. $16–$21 double. No credit cards. Free unguarded parking.

El Bocadito, on the right as you enter town, could take advantage of being the only game in town besides the much more expensive Villas Arqueológicas, but it doesn't. Next to the hotel's restaurant of the same name, the rooms are arranged in two rows facing an open patio. They're simple, each with tile floors, two double beds, no bed-spreads, a ceiling fan, and a washbasin separate from the toilet and cold-water shower cubicle.

The clean, open-air restaurant offers good meals at reasonable prices, served by a friendly, efficient staff. Busloads of tour groups stop here at lunch.

Villas Arqueológicas Cobá. Cobá, Q. Roo. ☎ **800/258-2633** in the U.S., or 5/203-3086 in Mexico City. 41 units. A/C. $82 double, includes continental breakfast. Half-board (dinner or lunch and breakfast) available for an extra $14 per person; full board (3 meals) available for an extra $29 per person. AE, MC, V. Free guarded parking.

For Your Comfort at Cobá

Because of the heat, visit Cobá in the morning or after the heat of the day has passed. Mosquito repellent, drinking water, and comfortable shoes are imperative.

The mosquito and fly population is fierce, but this is one of the best places along the coast for birding—go early in the morning.

Operated in association with Club Med, but nothing like a Club Med Village, this lovely lakeside hotel is a 5-minute walk from the ruins. It is laid out the same as its counterparts in Chichén and Uxmal. The grounds are beautiful and include a pool and tennis court. The restaurant is top-notch, though expensive. The rooms are stylish and modern, but small. The beds are placed in niches that surround the mattress on three sides and thus make them somewhat uncomfortable for those taller than 6'2". The hotel also has a library on Mesoamerican archaeology (with books in French, English, and Spanish). Make reservations—this hotel fills with touring groups.

To find it, drive through town and turn right at the lake; the hotel is straight ahead on the right.

EN ROUTE TO THE LOWER CARRIBEAN COAST: FELIPE CARRILLO PUERTO

From Tulum you continue along the main Highway 307 past the Cobá turnoff; it heads southwest through Tulum village. Felipe Carrillo Puerto (pop. 47,000) is a busy crossroads in the jungle along the road to Ciudad Chetumal. It has gas stations, a market, a small ice plant, a bus terminal, and a few modest hotels and restaurants. Since the main road intersects the road to Mérida, Carrillo Puerto is the turning point for those making a "short circuit" of the Yucatán Peninsula. Highway 184 heads west from here to Ticul, Uxmal, Campeche, and Mérida.

As you pass through, consider its strange history: This was where the rebels in the War of the Castes took their stand, guided by the "Talking Crosses." Some remnants of that town (named Chan Santa Cruz) still exist. Look for signs in town pointing the way.

8 Majahual, Xcalak & the Chinchorro Reef

If you continue south from Felipe Carrillo Puerto, in 45 minutes you get to the turn-off for Majahual and Xcalak. This area mainly attracts fishermen and divers who come to visit its coastal reefs and the Chinchorro Bank, 30 miles offshore. This is not the place to come if all you're looking for is a stretch of pure sandy beach free of seaweed where you can walk out into the surf and swim without feeling anything under your toes but sand. For this purpose, the beaches around Tulum and Playa del Carmen are better suited. But if you want to snorkel or dive among pristine reefs or kayak in calm turquoise water, or do some flyfishing away from the crowds, you've come to the right place.

There is an old coastal road that passes through Majahual and goes all the way down to Xcalak, and there is a new paved road that runs inland directly to Xcalak. The drive on this latter road was quite pleasant, and I saw an enormous amount of bird life. Once, I even had to brake sharply to avoid hitting a flock of large wild turkeys (known

---

Felipe Carrillo Puerto is the only place to buy **gasoline** between Tulum and Chetumal, although if you're desperate, the tire repairman's family in Limones might sell you a liter or two. Look for the big tire leaning against the fence.

locally as *pavos del monte*), which sauntered off the road more like a herd of goats than a flock of supposedly skittish birds. Taking the new road saves you a lot of time; it's 1¹/₂ hours to get to Xcalak from the turn-off point.

Xcalak is a depopulated, weather-beaten fishing village with a couple of places to stay and to eat. From here you work your way back up the coast to get to the main dive shop for the area and the best lodgings. There are several small inns just beyond the town. The village of Xcalak once had a population as large as 1,200 before the 1958 hurricane; now it has only 200 inhabitants.

ORIENTATION

ARRIVING   By Car   Driving south from Felipe Carrillo Puerto, you'll come to the turnoff (left) onto Highway 10, 1¹/₂ miles after Limones, then it's a 30-mile drive to the coastal settlement of **Majahual** (mah-hah-*wahl*). Before Majahual, there's a military guard station. Tell the guard your destination and turn right to continue to **Xcalak** (eesh-kah-*lahk*) on the new paved highway for 35 more miles. To orient you further, the turnoff from Highway 307 is 163 miles southwest of Cancún and 88 miles southwest of Tulum.

BY PLANE   A new, 4,500-ft. airstrip opened in early 1998, and starting this year **Aero Ferinco** (☎ 9/873-0636 in Cancún for reservations) will have a round-trip flight Cancún-Majahual-Xcalak once a week on Saturday. Check with the **State Tourism Office** in Chetumal (☎ **9/832-0855** or 9/832-5073) for any more developments.

BY BUS   From Chetumal's bus station, two full-size **buses** go to Xcalak daily. There's *combi* (minivan) transportation from behind the Holiday Inn, but they cram in twice as many passengers as will fit comfortably and may carry a pig or goat on top as well. I don't recommend going by bus because it travels the old coastal road and takes forever.

DIVING THE CHINCHORRO REEF

The **Chinchorro Reef Underwater National Park** is a 24-mile-long, 8-mile-wide oval-shaped reef with a depth of 3 feet on the reef's interior and 3,000 feet on the exterior. Locals claim it's the last virgin reef system in the Caribbean. It's invisible from the ocean side; one of its diving attractions is the number of **shipwrecks,** at least 30 of them, along the reef's eastern side. One is on top of the reef. Divers have counted 40 cannons at one wreck site. On the west side are walls and coral gardens.

Aventuras Chinchorro is the fully equipped dive shop for most of the hotels in the Xcalak area. Local diving just offshore costs $45 per diver for a two-tank dive. Chinchorro Banks diving costs between $25 and $65 per person, depending on how long you stay, how far you go, and how many divers are in the group. Fishing and snorkeling excursions and trips into Belize can also be arranged, as well as rental of kayaks and horses. For diving reservations contact **Aventuras Chinchorro,** 812 Garland Ave., Nokomis, FL 34275 (☎ **800/480-4505** or 941/488-4505). Credit cards are only accepted when prepaying reservations from the U.S.

WHERE TO STAY & DINE

Aside from the two places mentioned below, there are several small inns in and about Xcalak and a couple of restaurants. The best thing to do is get information about them in town.

Costa de Cocos Dive Resort. Km 52 Carretera Majahual–Xcalak, Q. Roo. (For reservations contact ☎ **888/968-6181** in the U.S.; www.costadecocos.com; e-mail: ccocos@astro.net.mx.) 12 *cabañas*. High season $120 double with 1 or 2 beds. Low season $100 double. Dive rates and packages available; e-mail your request. Rates include breakfast and dinner. No credit cards.

Important Note about Provisions

Since this is a remote part of the world, travelers should expect inconveniences. When things break down or food items run out, replacements are a long way off. You might arrive to find that the dive boat's broken, that there's no beer, or that the generator powering the water pumps, toilets, and electricity is off for hours or days. Needless to say, a flashlight might come in handy. Bring a large quantity of strong mosquito repellent with DEET as a main ingredient—the mosquitoes are undaunted by anything else. You might want to stow a package or two of mosquito coils to burn at night.

The beautifully constructed thatch-roofed *cabañas* here are fashioned after Maya huts, but have such additions as screened windows with mahogany louvers, wood plank floors, large tile bathrooms, ceiling fans, comfortable furnishings, shelves of paperback books, hot water, and mosquito netting. They have 24-hour wind and solar power, and reverse-osmosis purified tap water. The *cabañas* are located right on the water in a palm grove just north of the fishing village of Xcalak.

All dive equipment is available and included in dive packages or rented separately for day guests. Water-sports equipment for rent includes ocean kayaks, and they now offer day or overnight sea-kayaking trips to Belize, inside the reef. Flyfishing for bonefish, tarpon, and snook inside Chetumal Bay with experienced English-speaking guides is a popular way to spend the day, as is bird-watching at their sanctuary island. NAUI resort or open-water certification can be arranged for an additional fee.

The main building has a bar and restaurant where guests congregate for an afternoon cocktail. The casual restaurant cooks up good home-style cooking, usually with a choice of one or two main courses at dinner, sandwiches at lunch, and full breakfast fare in the morning.

Hotel Tierra Maya. Km. 51 Carr. Majahual-Xcalak, Q. Roo. ☎ **800/480-4505** and 941/488-4505, both in the U.S. www.xcalak.com/aventuras. 6 units. AC. High season $90 double; low season $80 double. Rates include continental breakfast. MC, V.

This is a very comfortable two-story, modern-style hotel. All rooms are spacious and come with two double beds or one king-size. All have private balconies looking out to the sea, cross-ventilation, and ceiling fans, but if this doesn't work for you, there's always air-conditioning. Electricity is provided by solar generators. This hotel is connected to **Aventuras Chinchorro,** which arranges the dive trips to the coastal reefs as well as to the Chinchorro Bank.

9 Lago Bacalar

65 miles (104km) SW of Felipe Carrillo Puerto, 23 miles (37km) NW of Chetumal

Bacalar Lake is an elaborate trick played upon the senses. I remember one time when I visited the place, I couldn't get over the illusion it produced. From a pier in the lake I could gaze down into perfectly clear water, and as I lifted my eyes I could see several hues of blue normally associated with the Caribbean. Beyond the water, the shoreline was clothed in dense tropical vegetation. How could a lake of fresh water surrounded by jungle be anything but murky? A breeze blowing in from the sea smelled of the salt air, and though I knew it to be untrue, I couldn't help but feel that the water I was gazing on was in fact the sea and not freshwater at all, perhaps a well-sheltered lagoon. My senses rebelled against my reason and experience, and the only way to settle the argument was to dive in.

The Yucatán's Lower Caribbean Coast

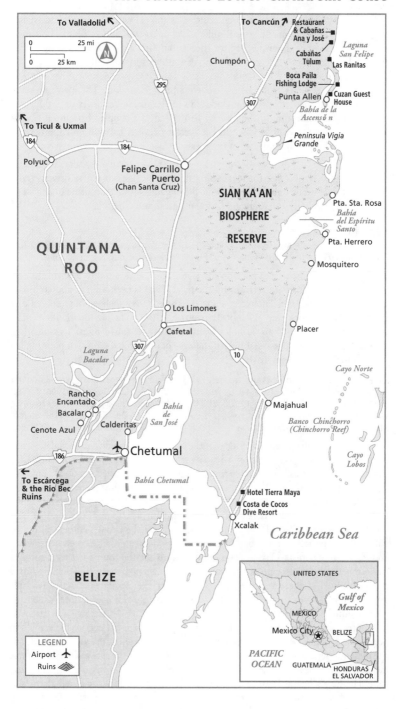

To Valladolid

0   25 mi
0   25 km

Chumpón

To Cancún ↗ Restaurant
& Cabañas
Ana y José

Cabañas
Tulum

*Laguna
San Felipe*

Las Ranitas

Boca Paila
Fishing Lodge

Punta Allen

Cuzan Guest
House

*Bahía de la
Ascensö n*

To Ticul & Uxmal

184

295

307

184

Polyuc

Felipe Carrillo
Puerto
(Chan Santa Cruz)

*Peninsula Vigia
Grande*

SIAN KA'AN

BIOSPHERE

RESERVE

Pta. Sta. Rosa

*Bahía
del Espíritu
Santo*

Pta. Herrero

**QUINTANA
ROO**

Mosquitero

Los Limones

Cafetal

307

10

Placer

*Laguna
Bacalar*

Cayo Norte

Rancho
Encantado

Bacalar

*Bahía
de
San José*

Majahual

*Banco Chinchorro
(Chinchorro Reef)*

Cenote Azul

Calderitas

*Cayo
Lobos*

186

✈ Chetumal

To Escárcega
& the Rio Bec
Ruins

Bahía Chetumal

Hotel Tierra Maya

Costa de Cocos
Dive Resort

Xcalak

Caribbean Sea

BELIZE

LEGEND
Airport ✈
Ruins 📚

UNITED STATES

*Gulf of
Mexico*

MEXICO

Mexico City ✪

BELIZE

*PACIFIC
OCEAN*

GUATEMALA

HONDURAS
EL SALVADOR

Few places I have visited are as enchanting as this. How is it possible that such a large lake, 65 miles long and several miles wide, be so clear and so blue? The answer is that Bacalar is not the watershed for the surrounding area; it is not fed by surface run-off, but only by several *cenotes* that lie beneath its surface. Only in the Yucatán is such a thing possible.

Needless to say, this is the perfect spot for being bone idle. There are, however, plenty of possible activities; these include trips to view the large variety of bird life, the elegant Maya architecture in the near-by Rio Bec area, a couple of beautiful *cenotes*, and a wonderful museum in Chetumal. Given the choice, I would much rather stay in Bacalar and visit Chetumal, than the reverse.

ORIENTATION   If driving south on Highway 307, the town of Bacalar is 1¹/₂ hours beyond Felipe Carrillo Puerto. It is clearly marked by signs. If you're driving north from Chetumal it takes about a half hour. Buses going south from Cancún and Playa del Carmen stop here, and there are frequent buses from Chetumal.

WHERE TO STAY

Hotel Laguna. Costera de Bacalar 479, 77010 Lago Bacalar, Q. Roo. ☎ **9/834-2206.** Fax 9/834-2205. 34 units. $35 double. $60 bungalow for 5 persons. No credit cards.

The Laguna is off the beaten path, so there are almost always rooms available, except in winter, when Canadians seem to fill the place. Rooms overlook the pool and have a lovely view of the lake. The water along the shore is very shallow, but you can dive from the hotel's dock into 30-foot-deep water. The hotel's restaurant offers main courses costing about $5 to $10. It's open daily from 8am to 8pm. To find it, go through town toward Chetumal. Just at the edge of town you'll see a sign pointing left to the hotel and lakeshore drive.

✪ **Rancho Encantado Cottage Resort.** Km 3 Carretera Felipe Carrillo Puerto–Chetumal (Apdo. Postal 233), 77000 Chetumal, Q. Roo. ☎/fax **9/838-0427.** (For reservations contact P.O. Box 1256, Taos, NM 87571; ☎ **800/505-MAYA** in the U.S.; fax 505/776-2102; www.encantado.com; e-mail: mpstarr@laplaza.org.) 12 casitas. Dec–Apr $150–$180 double; May–Nov $140–$160 double; both including continental breakfast and dinner. No credit cards.

This is a beautifully serene lakeside retreat. Rancho Encantado's immaculate white stucco cottages are spread out on a shady manicured lawn beside the smooth Lago Bacalar. Each spacious, comfortable room has mahogany-louvered windows, a red-tile floor, a mahogany dining table and chairs, a living room or sitting area, a porch with chairs, and hammocks strung between trees. All come with small refrigerators and a coffee area; coffeemakers and coffee are provided in each room. Some rooms have cedar ceilings and red-tiled roofs and others have thatched roofs. All are decorated with folk art, murals inspired by Maya ruins, foot-loomed pastel-colored bedspreads, and Zapotec rugs from Oaxaca. The newest rooms are the four waterfront cottages (rooms 9 through 12) with white stucco walls, thatched roofs, and hand-painted murals inspired by those at Bonampak. The owners' villa on the lake is also available several months a year as well as a room apart from the rest of the hotel called the Laguan Suite.

An open-air conference center, with a soaring *palapa* roof, sits next to the water and near the restaurant. Next to this is a large open-air Jacuzzi and a massage area with on-site massage therapists. The large *palapa* restaurant overlooks the lake and serves all three meals. There's no beef on the menu, but plenty of chicken, fish, vegetables, and fresh fruit. The honey here is from Rancho hives. You can swim from the hotel's dock, and kayaks and canoes are available for rent. Orange, lime, mango, sapote, ceiba, banana, palm, and oak trees, wild orchids, and bromeliads on the expansive grounds make great

TIMBUKTU   KALAMAZOO

AT&T Direct® Service

The easy way to call home from anywhere.

Global
connection
with the AT&T
Network

AT&T
direct
service

or the easy way to call home, take the attached wallet guide.

bird shelter, attracting flocks of chattering parrots, turquoise-browed motmots, toucans, and at least 100 more species, many of which are easy to spot outside your room. Luis Téllez, the hotel's guide, keeps an extensive list of birds that have been sighted.

Téllez also keeps abreast of developments at the nearby archaeological sites and is the only source of current information before you reach the ruins. He knows the sites well and leads almost a dozen different excursions from the hotel. Among them are day-trips to the **Río Bec** ruin route, an extended visit to **Calakmul,** outings to the **Majahual Peninsula,** and a riverboat trip to the Maya ruins of **Lamanai** deep in a Belizian forest. Several ruins are easily reachable from the road, while others are so deep in the jungle that a guide is necessary to find them and a four-wheel-drive vehicle is a must. Excursions range in price from $55 to $115 per person, depending on the length and difficulty of the trip, and several have a three-person minimum. Groups interested in birding, yoga, archaeology, and the like are invited to bring a leader and use Rancho Encantado as a base. The Rancho also hosts several workshops on such subjects as writing and speech. Special packages and excursions can be arranged in advance from the hotel's U.S. office. To find the Rancho, look for the hotel's sign on the left about 1 mile before Bacalar.

WHERE TO EAT

Besides the lakeside restaurant of **Rancho Encantado** (see above), you may enjoy the **Restaurant Cenote Azul,** a comfortable open-air thatched-roof restaurant on the edge of the beautiful Cenote Azul. In both places, main courses cost from $5 to $12. To get to Restaurant Cenote Azul, follow the highway to the south edge of town and turn left at the restaurant's sign; follow that road around to the restaurant. At Rancho Encantado you can swim in Lago Bacalar, and at the Restaurant Cenote you can take a dip in placid Cenote Azul, but without skin lotion of any kind, as it poisons the *cenote.*

SIDE TRIPS FROM BACALAR: THE RÍO BEC RUIN ROUTE

A few miles west of Bacalar begins the Yucatán's **southern ruin route,** generally called the Río Bec region. A number of ruins stretch from close to Bacalar and Chetumal westward into the state of Campeche. These ruins are intriguing for their highly stylized architecture and the questions they provoke. They have not been rebuilt to the degree of Uxmal and Chichén Itzá, but in some cases, the archeologists found buildings so well preserved that little rebuilding was needed.

The lands these ruins occupy have not been cleared in the same manner as the marquee ruins mentioned above: trees and jungle foliage have been allowed to remain around the buildings, and this adds greatly to the experience; something suggestive of what John Lloyd Stephens and Catherwood were finding when they traipsed through the Yucatan in the 19th century. Keep an eye peeled for wildlife; I saw several inhabitants of the tropical forest on my last tour through the region. Thanks to the new federal Highway 186, this area is not at all hard to visit. With the exception of the Eco-village in Chicanná and the new Explorean hotel near Kohunlich, accommodations and dining are no-frills, but this is changing. If you decide to visit these ruins, I recommend you take the time to visit the Museo de la Cultura Maya in Chetumal first (see below in the Chetumal section). It will lend a lot of context to what you'll be seeing.

BIRD & ANIMAL LIFE   The fauna along the entire route is especially rich. You might see a toucan, a grand curassow, or a macaw hanging about the ruins; and orioles, egrets, and several birds of prey are extremely common. Gray fox, wild turkey, tesquintle (a bushy-tailed plant-eating rodent), the raccoon relative coati-mundi (with its long tapered snout and tail), and armadillos inhabit the area in abundance. At Calakmul, a family of howler monkeys resides in the trees overlooking the parking area.

THE ROUTE'S STARTING POINT

of Bacalar at the turnoff from Highway 30... ...gins just 9 miles from the edge ...186, which leads to the Río Bec ruin route as well as to Escárcega, Villah... ...alenque. A reminder: Traveling through this region, you will find guard... ...re you will be asked to present your travel papers (birth certificate or ... ...tourist permit). You can divide your sightseeing into several day-trips f... ...r Chetumal, or you can stay the night in Chicanná and continue westward... ...y. If you get an early start, many of the ruins mentioned below can be easil... ...a day from Bacalar.

Evidence shows that these ruins, especia... ...in, were part of the **trade route** linking the Caribbean coast at Cobá to Edzr... ...the Gulf coast and with Lamanai in Belize and beyond. At one time this regio... ...s dense with thriving Maya cities, cultivated fields, lakes, and an elaborate syst... ...f rivers that connected the region with Belize and Central America. Today man... ...hese ancient cities hide under cover of jungle, which has overtaken the land fron... ...zon to horizon.

FACILITIES, OR LACK THEREOF

T... ...e no visitor facilities or refreshments at these sites, so bring your own water and f... The bathrooms at Kohunlich are the only ones at any site on the route. However... ...you cross into the state of Campeche you reach the village of Xpujil (just before... ...uins of Xpujil), and here you can get food and lodging. The **Restaurant Posada** ... ...kmul (☎ **9/832-9162**) is open daily from 6am to midnight. Under the watchful... ...of Doña María Cabrera, it serves good home-style food and caters to ruins enthusi... ...—hung about the room are photos and descriptions of little-known sites by Río Bec... ...cialist Serge Rìou (see below). The new **hotel rooms** behind the restaurant cost $2... ...r a double and are clean and comfortable, with tile floors, private bathrooms wi... ...ot water, good beds, and a small porch.

Just a bit down the road from Xpujil, ...the entrance to the Chicanná ruins, on the north side of the road, is the **Chicann**... **co Village,** km 144 Carretera Escárcega (☎ **9/816-2233** in Campeche for reser... ...ns). This is the best lodging you can get on this road. Here you'll find 28 nicely fu... ...ed rooms distributed among several two-story thatched bungalows. The rooms are... ...nfortable; they come with two doubles or a king-size bed, ceiling fans, a large bath... ...a, and screened windows. The manicured lawns and flower beds are lovely, and p... ...ays link the bungalows to each other and to the restaurant and swimming pool. Double rooms go for $84, which includes breakfast. American Express, MasterCard, and Visa are accepted.

TOURING THE RUINS WITH A GUIDE

At Rancho Encantado in Bacalar (see "Where to Stay," under "Lago Bacalar," above) you can contract the services of a knowledgeable guide who I highly recommend. Either Luis Téllez or Serge Rìou lead tours to some of the local ruins. They both speak English well, are good company, and provide a great deal of background information on what you find at the ruins. There is no comparison between Luis or Serge and regular guides. They have set tours and charge around $75 to $115 per person a day to visit a variety of sites. This includes transportation and food. The higher price is for **Calakmul,** the farthest site from Chetumal. They can also arrange necessary permits to unopened sites.

ADDITIONAL INFORMATION

To make the most of your visit, background reading might include *A Forest of Kings: The Untold Story of the Ancient Maya* by Linda Schele and David Friedel (William Morrow, 1990), *The Blood of Kings: Dynasty and Ritual in Maya Art* by Linda Schele and Mary Ellen Miller (George Braziller, 1968), and *The Maya Cosmos* by David Freidel and Linda Schele (William Morrow, 1993). *Arqueología Mexicana* magazine devoted its July–August 1995 issue to the Quintana Roo portion of the Río Bec ruin route. Last, though it lacks historic and cultural information, and many sites have expanded since it was written, Joyce Kelly's *An Archeological Guide to Mexico's Yucatán Peninsula* (University of Oklahoma, 1993), is the best companion book to have. For a crash course, focus on the meaning of the jaguar, Xibalba (the underworld), and the earth monster.

The following list of sites is in the order in which you would see them, driving from Bacalar or Chetumal. For a map of this area, consult the Yucatán Peninsula map earlier in this book. Entry to each site is $2 to $4, and all are free on Sunday. Informational signs at each building within the sites are in Mayan, Spanish, and English. Keep the mosquito repellent handy.

DZIBANCHÉ

Dzibanché (or Tzibanché) means "place where they write on wood." Exploration began here in 1993, and it opened to the public in late 1994. Scattered over 26 square miles (though only a small portion is excavated), it's both a Classic and a Postclassic site (A.D. 300–900) that was occupied for around 700 years.

TEMPLES & PLAZAS   Two large adjoining plazas have been cleared. The site shows influence from Río Bec, Petén, and Teotihuacán. **The Temple of the Owl,** on the Plaza de Xibalba, has a miniature version of Teotihuacán-style *talud tablero* (slant and straight facade) architecture flanking the sides of the main stairway leading to the top with its lintel and entrance to an underground tomb. (Teotihuacán ruins are near Mexico City, but their influence was strong as far as Guatemala.) Despite centuries of an unforgiving wet climate, a wood lintel, in good condition and with a date carving, still supports a partially preserved corbeled arch on top of this building. Inside the temple, a tomb was discovered, making this the second known temple in Mexico built over an underground tomb (the other is the Temple of Inscriptions at Palenque). A diagram of this temple shows interior steps leading from the top, then down inside the pyramid to ground level, just as at Palenque. The stairway is reached by a deep, well-like drop that held remains of a sacrificial victim and which was sacked during pre-Hispanic times. Uncovered along the stairwell were a number of beautiful, polychromed, lidded vessels, one of which has an owl painted on the top handle, with its wings spreading onto the lid. White owls were messengers of the gods of the underworld in the Maya religion. This interior stairway isn't open to the public, but you can clearly see the lintel just behind the entrance to the tomb. Further exploration of the tomb awaits stabilization of interior walls.

Opposite the Temple of the Owl is the **Temple of the Cormorant,** so named after a polychromed drinking vessel found here depicting a cormorant. Here, too, archaeologists have found evidence of an interior tomb similar to the one in the Temple of the Owl, but excavations of it have not yet begun. Other magnificently preserved pottery pieces found during excavations include an incense burner with an almost three-dimensional figure of the diving god attached to the outside, and another incense burner with an elaborately dressed representation of the god Itzamná attached.

The site also incorporates another section of ruins called **Kinichná** (keen-eech-*nah*), which is about 1½ miles north and is reachable only by a rutted road that's impassable during the rainy season. There, an Olmec-style jade figure was found.

NO ROAD—YET   A formal road to these ruins has not been built, but there's a sign pointing to the right turn to Morocoy approximately 18 miles from the Highway 307 turnoff. You follow that paved road, which turns into an unpaved road, and pass the small settlement (not really a town) of Morocoy to another rough dirt road to the right (there's a sign to the ruins there). Follow it for about a mile to the ruin entrance.

KOHUNLICH

Kohunlich (koh-*hoon*-leek), 26 miles from the intersection of highways 186 and 307, dates from around A.D. 100 to 900. Turn left off the road, and the entrance is 5¹/₂ miles ahead. From the parking area you enter the grand park-like site, crossing a large and shady ceremonial area flanked by four large, conserved pyramidal edifices. Continue walking, and just beyond this grouping you'll come to Kohunlich's famous **Pyramid of the Masks** under a thatched covering. The masks, actually enormous plaster faces, date from around A.D. 500 and are on the facade of the building. Each mask has an elongated face and wears a headdress with a mask on its crest and a mask on the chinpiece, essentially masks within masks. The top one is thought to represent the astral world, while the lower one represents the underworld, suggesting that the wearer of this headdress is among the living and not in either of the other worlds. Note the carving on the pupils, which suggest a solar connection, possibly with the night sun that illuminated the underworld. This may mean that the person had shamanic vision. It's speculated that masks covered much of the facade of this building, which is built in the Río Bec style with rounded corners, a false stairway, and a false temple on the top. At least one theory holds that the masks are a composite of several rulers at Kohunlich. During recent excavations of buildings immediately to the left after you enter, two intact pre-Hispanic skeletons and five decapitated heads were uncovered that were once probably used in a ceremonial ritual. To the right after you enter (follow a shady path through the jungle) is another recently excavated plaza. It's thought to have housed priests or rulers, due to the high quality of pottery found there and the fine architecture of the rooms. Scholars believe that Kohunlich became over-populated, leading to its decline.

CHACÁN BACÁN

Chacán Bacán (chah-*kahn* bah-*kahn*), which dates from around 200 B.C., was first discovered in 1980 with excavation beginning in 1995. It's scheduled to open some-time in 1999, with 30 to 40 buildings uncovered. The discovery of huge **Olmec-style heads** on its facade should make future digs exciting. The heads, showing from the middle of the skull forward, have helmet-like caps similar in style to the full megalithic Olmec heads unearthed in Veracruz and Tabasco on Mexico's Gulf Coast, where the Olmecs originated. These heads are thought to be older than the figures at both Kohunlich and Balamkú. The exact size of the site hasn't been determined, but it's huge. In a densely forested setting, with thousands of tropical hardwood trees, plants, birds, and wild animals, it's been earmarked as an ecological/touristic center. Although not yet open to the public, it's about 50 miles and a 1¹/₂-hour drive from Bacalar. The turnoff (left) to it is at Caoba, where you follow a paved road for about 1¹/₂ miles, then turn left on an unmarked path. From the paved portion you can look left and see the uncovered pyramid protruding over the surrounding jungle. Ask Luis Téllez at Rancho Encantado at Lago Bacalar about the accessibility of this site.

XPUJIL

Xpujil (eesh-poo-*heel*; also spelled Xpuhil), meaning either "cattail" or "forest of kapok trees," flourished between A.D. 400 and 900. This is a small site. Ahead on the left after you enter, you'll see a rectangular ceremonial platform 6¹/₂-feet-high and 173-feet-long supporting an elongated building with three miniature pyramids resembling in shape the conical pyramids of Tikal in Guatemala. In essence, these pyramids have become purely decorative, as the stairways and temples are too small for use. The effect is beautiful. The rest of the building contains the ruins of 12 rooms. To the right after you enter are two newly uncovered structures, one of which is a large acropolis. From the highway, a small sign on the right points to the site that is just a few yards off the highway and 49 miles from Kohunlich.

BECÁN

Becán (bay-*kahn*), about 4¹/₂ miles beyond Xpujil and once surrounded by a moat, means "canyon filled by water" and dates from the early Classic to the late Postclassic (600 B.C. to A.D. 1200) period. This site is extensive. The moat once had seven bridges leading to the seven cities that were pledged to Becán. Following jungle paths beyond the first visible group of ruins, you'll find at least two recently excavated **acropolises.** Although the site was abandoned by A.D. 850, ceramic remains indicate there may have been a population resurgence between A.D. 900 and 1000, and it was still used as a ceremonial site as late as A.D. 1200. Becán was an administrative and ceremonial center with political sway over at least seven other cities in the area, including Chicanná, Hormiguero, and Payan.

To understand this site, you need a good guide. But for starters, the first plaza group you see after you enter was the center for grand ceremonies. From the highway you can see the backside of a pyramid (structure 1) with two temples on top. Beyond and in between the two temples you can see the Temple atop Structure 4, which is opposite Temple 1. When the high priest appeared through the mouth of the earth monster in the center of this Temple (which he reached via a hidden side stairway that's now partly exposed), he was visible from what is now the highway. It's thought that commoners had to watch ceremonies from outside the ceremonial plaza; thus the site's position was for good viewing purposes. The backside of Structure 4 is believed to have been a civic plaza where rulers sat on stone benches while pronouncing judgments. The second plaza group dates from around A.D. 850 and has perfect twin towers on top, where there's a big platform. Under the platform are 10 rooms that are thought to be related to Xibalba (shee-*bahl*-bah), the underworld. Take a flashlight. Earth monster faces probably covered this building (and they appeared on other buildings as well). Remains of at least one ball court have been unearthed. Becán is about 4¹/₂ miles beyond Xpujil and is visible on the right side of the highway, about a half mile down a rutted road.

CHICANNÁ

Slightly over a mile beyond Becán, on the left side of the highway, is Chicanná, which means "house of the mouth of snakes." Trees loaded with bromeliads shade the central square surrounded by five buildings. The most outstanding edifice features a monster-mouth doorway and an ornate stone facade with more superimposed masks. As you enter the mouth of the earth monster, note that you are walking on a platform configured as the open jaw of the monster with stone teeth on both sides. Again you find a lovely example of an elongated building with ornamental miniature pyramids on each end.

CALAKMUL

This area is both a massive Maya archaeological zone, with at least 60 sites, and a 178,699-acre rain forest designated in 1989 as the Calakmul Biosphere Reserve, which includes territory in both Mexico and Guatemala. The best way to see Calakmul is to spend the night at Xpujil or Chicanná and leave early in the morning for Calakmul. If you're the first ones to drive down the narrow access road to the ruins (1¹/₂ hours from the highway) you'll see plenty of wildlife. I saw a constrictor, a flock of wild turkeys, a grand curassow, and several species of birds.

THE ARCHAEOLOGICAL ZONE   Since 1982, archaeologists have been excavating the ruins of Calakmul, which dates from 100 B.C. to A.D. 900. It's the largest of the area's 60 known sites. Nearly 7,000 buildings have been discovered and mapped. At its zenith, at least 60,000 people may have lived around the site, but by the time of the Spanish Conquest in 1519, there were fewer than 1,000 inhabitants. Visitors arrive at a large plaza filled with a forest of trees. You immediately see several stelae; Calakmul contains more of these than any other site, but they are much more weathered and indistinguishable than the stelae of Palenque or Copán in Honduras. On one of them you can clearly see the work of looters who carefully used some sort of stone-cutting saw to slice off the face of the monument. By Structure 13 is a stelae of a woman dating from A.D. 652. She is thought to have been a ruler, which would be exceedingly unusual.

There are several structures here worth checking out; some are built in the Petén style, some in the Rio Bec style. Structure 3 must have been the residence of a noble family. Its design is unique and quite lovely; it managed to retain its original form and was never remodeled the way so many other structures were. Offerings of shells, beads, and polychromed tripod pottery were found inside. Structure 2 is the tallest pyramid in the Yucatán, at 178 feet. From the top of it you can see the outline of the ruins of El Mirador, 30 miles across the forest in Guatemala. Notice the two stairways that ascend along the sides of the principal face of the pyramid in the upper levels. This has no equivalent in Maya architecture; and when appreciated in conjunction with how the masks break up the space of the front face, you can see just how complex the design was. Temple 4 charts the line of the sun from June 21 when it falls on the left (north) corner, to September 21 and March 21, when it lines up in the east behind the middle temple on the top of the building, to December 21 when it falls on the right (south) corner. Numerous jade pieces, including spectacular masks, were uncovered here, most of which are on display in the Museo Regional in Campeche. Temple 7 is largely unexcavated except for the top, where in 1984 the most outstanding jade mask yet to be found at Calakmul was uncovered. In *A Forest of Kings,* Linda Schele and David Freidel tell of wars between the Calakmul, Tikal, and Naranjo (the latter two in Guatemala), and how Ah-Cacaw, king of Tikal (75 miles south of Calakmul), captured King Jaguar-Paw in A.D. 695 and later Lord Ox-Ha-Te Ixil Ahau, both of Calakmul. From January to May the site is open Tuesday to Sunday from 7am to 7pm. The site gets so wet during the rainy season from June to October that it's best not to go.

CALAKMUL BIOSPHERE RESERVE   Set aside in 1989, this is the peninsula's only high-forest *selva,* a rain forest that annually records as much as 16 feet of rain. Notice how the canopy of the trees is higher here then in the forest of Quintana Roo. Here, you are very close to the border with Guatemala, but of course there is no way to get there. Among the plants are cactus, epiphytes, and orchids. Endangered animals include the white-lipped peccary, jaguar, and puma. So far more than 250 species of birds have been recorded. At present, no overnight stay or camping is permitted. If you want a tour of a small part of the forest and you speak Spanish, you can inquire for a guide at one of the two nearby *ejidos.* There are some old *chicleros* living there that have expert knowledge of flora and fauna and can take you on a couple of trails.

The turnoff on the left for Calakmul is located approximately 145 miles from the intersection of highways 186 and 307, just before the village of Conhuas. There's a guard station there where you pay $3 to enter the road/site. From the turnoff it's a 1¹/₂-hour drive on a paved, but very narrow and somewhat rutted, road that may be difficult during the rainy season from May to October.

A Driving Caution

Numerous curves in the road make seeing oncoming traffic (what little there is) difficult, and there have been head-on collisions.

BALAMKÚ

Balamkú (bah-lahm-*koo*) is a sight that should not be missed. There are a couple of buildings in it that were so well preserved that they required almost no reconstruction, just uncovering. Inside one you will find three impressive figures of men sitting in the gaping maws of crocodiles and toads as they descend into the underworld. The whole concept of this building, with its molded stucco facade, is of life and death. On the head of each almost three-dimensional figure are the eyes, nose, and mouth of a jaguar figure; followed by the full face of the human figure; then a neck formed by the eyes and nose of another jaguar; and an Olmec-like face on the stomach, its neck decorated by a necklace. These figures were saved in dramatic fashion from looters who managed to make away with a fourth one. Now they are under the protection of a caretaker, who keeps the room under lock and key, but he can be persuaded to open it for visitors. A tip is appreciated. If you speak Spanish, you can get the caretaker to explain something of the figures and their complex symbolism. There is also a beautiful courtyard and another set of buildings adjacent to the main group. The May 1992 issue of *Mexico Desconocido* features the discovery of Balamkú written by Florentino García Cruz.

10 Chetumal

85 miles (136km) S of Felipe Carrillo Puerto, 23 miles (37km) S of Lago Bacalar

Quintana Roo became a state in 1974, and Chetumal (pop. 170,000) became its capital. While Quintana Roo was still a territory, it was made a free-trade zone to encourage trade and immigration between neighboring Guatemala and Belize. The old part of town, down by the river (Río Hondo), has a Caribbean atmosphere and wooden buildings, but the newer parts are modern Mexican. It is, however, worth a detour to see the wonderful **Museo de la Cultural Maya,** especially if you plan to follow the Río Bec ruin route described above.

ESSENTIALS
GETTING THERE & DEPARTING

BY PLANE   **Aerocaribe** (Mexicana; ☎ 9-832-6336 or 9/832-6675) has daily flights to and from Cancún and flights several times weekly between Chetumal and the ruins of Tikal in Guatemala. **Avio Quintana** (☎ 9/832-9692) flies Monday to Friday to Cancún in a 19-passenger plane for around $85 one-way. Aviacsa has a direct flight to/from Mexico City.

BY CAR   It's a 2¹/₂-hour ride from Felipe Carrillo Puerto along Rte. 307 to Rte. 186. If you're heading to Belize, you'll need a passport and special auto insurance, which you can buy at the border. You can't take a rental car over the border, however.

To get to the ruins of Tikal in Guatemala you must first go through Belize to the border crossing at Ciudad Melchor de Mencos.

BY BUS   The bus station (☎ 9/832-5110) is 20 blocks from the town center on Insurgentes at Niños Héroes. Buses go to Cancún, Tulum, Playa del Carmen, Puerto Morelos, Mérida, Campeche, Villahermosa, and Mexico City. **Omniturs del Caribe** (☎ 9/832-7889 or 9/832-8001) has deluxe buses to Mérida.

To Belize: Two companies make the run from Chetumal (through Corozal and Orange Walk) to Belize City. **Batty's Bus Service** runs 10 buses per day (no AC), and Venus **Bus Lines** (☎ 9/832-2132) has 7 daily buses. Though it's a short distance from Chetumal to Corozal, it may take as much as 1¹/₂ hours, depending on how long it takes the bus to pass through Customs and Immigration. (See "Onward from Chetumal," below, for more Customs information.)

To Limones, Majahual, and Xcalak: Two buses a day run between these destinations.

BY FERRY The docks are ready, but the new ferry was too big and ferry service has been delayed between Chetumal and the Xcalak/Majahual Peninsula. However, check with the **State Tourism Office** in Chetumal (☎ 9/832-6101; fax 9/832-5073) about the status of this service.

VISITOR INFORMATION

The **State Tourism Office** (☎ 9/832-6101 or 9/832-0855; fax 9/832-5073 or 9/832-6097) is located at avenida Hidalgo 22, at the corner of Carmen Ochoa. Office hours are Monday to Friday 8am to 10pm.

ORIENTATION

The telephone **area code** is **983.**

You'll arrive following **Obregón** into town. **Héroes** is the other main cross street. When you reach it, turn left to find the hotels mentioned below.

A MUSEUM NOT TO MISS

Chetumal is really the gateway to Belize or to the Río Bec ruins, and not an interesting city for tourists. But it's worth a detour to Chetumal to see the **Museo de la Cultura Maya.** If you can arrange it, see the museum before you tour the Río Bec ruins, since it will all make more sense after visiting the museum.

Museo de la Cultura Maya. Av. Héroes s/n. ☎ **9/832-6838.** Admission $2.50; children $1. Tues–Thurs 9am–7pm, Fri–Sun 9am–8pm. It's on the left between Colón and Gandhi, 8 blocks from av. Obregón, past the Holiday Inn.

Sophisticated, impressive, and informative, this new museum unlocks the complex world of the Maya. Push a button and an illustrated description appears explaining the medicinal and domestic uses of plants with their Maya and scientific names; another describes the five social classes of the Maya by the way they dress; and yet another shows how the beauty signs of cranial deformation, crossed eyes, and facial scarification were achieved. An enormous screen flashes images taken from an airplane flying over more than a dozen Maya sites from Mexico to Honduras. Another large television shows the architectural variety of Maya pyramids and how they were probably built. Then a walk on a glass floor takes you over representative ruins in the Maya world, clearly depicting the variety of pyramidal shapes at particular sites. And, finally, one of the most impressive sections is the three-story, stylized, sacred ceiba tree, which the Maya believed represented the underworld (Xibalba), earth, and the 13 heavens. From this you'll have a better idea of the symbolism represented by Maya pyramids. Plan no less than 2 hours here.

WHERE TO STAY & DINE

Hotel Holiday Inn Puerta Maya. Av. Héroes 171, 77000 Chetumal, Q. Roo. ☎ **800/ 465-4329** in the U.S., or 9/832-1100. Fax 9/832-1676. 85 units. A/C TV TEL. $105 double. AE, MC, V. Free parking.

This modern hotel (formerly the Hotel Continental) across from the central market was remodeled in 1995 and became a Holiday Inn. The hotel has a good-size pool (a blessing in muggy Chetumal), a good restaurant, and the best air-conditioning in town. The hotel is only 2 blocks from the Museo de la Cultura Maya. To find it as you enter the town on Obregón, turn left on Av. Héroes, go 6 blocks, and look for the hotel on the right, opposite the market.

Hotel Nachancán. Calz. Veracruz 379, 77000 Chetumal, Q. Roo. ☎ **9/832-3232.** 20 units. A/C TV. $30 double, $42 suite. No credit cards.

Opposite the new market, this hotel offers rooms that are plain but clean and comfortable. A restaurant is off the lobby. It's relatively convenient to the bus station, but not close enough to walk if you arrive by bus. It is, however, within walking distance of the Museo de la Cultura Maya. To find it from avenida Obregón, turn left on Calzada Veracruz and follow it for at least 10 blocks; the hotel will be on the right.

ONWARD FROM CHETUMAL

From Chetumal you have several choices. The Maya ruins of Lamanai are an easy day-trip into Belize if you have transportation (not a rental car); or you can explore the Río Bec ruin route directly west of the city heading out on Highway 186. At the Campeche state line there's a military guard post with drug-sniffing dogs; every vehicle is searched. A military guard post at the Reforma intersection just before Bacalar requires motorists to present the identification you used to enter Mexico (birth certificate or passport), plus your tourist permit. Other photo identification may be required, as well as information on where you're staying or where you're headed. The whole procedure should take only minutes.

5

Mérida, Chichén-Itzá & the Mayan Interior

Ask most people about the Yucatán, and they think of Cancún, the Caribbean coast, and Chichén-Itzá. In fact, there's much more to the Yucatán than just those places, and with a little exploring you'll find a great variety of things to do; the kind of variety that can make a trip really fun. One morning you can climb a pyramid and in the afternoon take a dip in the cool, clear water of a *cenote* (deep natural well) or explore a beautiful cave. The next day may find you strolling along a deserted beach or riding in a small boat through mangroves to pay a visit to a colony of pink flamingos, and by nighttime you're dancing in the streets of **Mérida.** This chapter covers the interior of the Yucatán peninsula, including the famous Maya ruins at **Chichén-Itzá** and **Uxmal,** the flamingo sanctuary at **Celestún,** as well as many less well known spots that can be fun to visit.

EXPLORING THE YUCATÁN'S MAYA HEARTLAND

The best way to see the Yucatán is by car. The terrain is flat, the towns are laid out in a simple manner, there is little traffic on the roads, and the main highways are in great shape. But if you do drive around the area, one little Spanish word will be etched in your mind for a long time thereafter: *topes* (*toh* pehs), the ubiquitous speedbumps that come in varying shapes and sizes and with varying degrees of warning. Be on your guard and don't let them catch you by surprise. Off the beaten path, the roads are narrow and rough, but hey—we're talking rental cars. Rentals are in fact a little pricey compared with the U.S. (due perhaps to wear and tear?), but some promotional deals are available. See "By Car," in the Mérida section, below.

There are plenty of buses plying the roads between the main towns and tourist destinations, and there are plenty of tour buses circulating, too—but buses to the smaller towns and ruins and the haciendas are much less frequent than what you would find in the rest of Mexico. One bus company (ADO) controls most of the first-class bus service and does a good job with the destinations it serves. Second-class buses go to some of the out-of-the-way places, but they can be slow, they stop a lot, and they are not air-conditioned, which is the key to comfortable bus travel down here.

The Yucatán is *tierra caliente* (the hotlands). Don't travel in this region without sunblock, mosquito repellent, and water. The coolest weather is from December to February; the hottest is from April to June when the air is still. From July to October, during the rainy season, the air can be a little cooler from winds and thundershowers.

For the tourism industry, the high-season/low-season distinction is less important in the interior than on the Caribbean coast, and most hotels have dropped the two-tiered pricing system. Most high-season travelers are going specifically for the beach and don't move inland, and the low season brings a substantial number of European tours during the hottest months (a fact that astounds most Yucatecans).

From the many possibilities, here's my pick of essential stops in the Yucatán:

MÉRIDA   There's always a lot to do in this vibrant and tropical-style colonial city: Take in the sights and the local culture; enjoy the nightlife; buy some traditional Yucatecan products such as hammocks, *guayaberas* (shirts), Panama hats, and native embroidered dresses or *huipils;* and a whole lot more.

CHICHÉN-ITZÁ & VALLADOLID   These two destinations are 25 miles apart from each other and about midway between Mérida and Cancún. It's 2¹/₂ hours by car from Mérida to Chichén on the new toll road, or *autopista.* You can spend a day at the beautifully restored ruins, then stay at one of the nearby hotels—or drive 25 miles to Valladolid, a quiet and charming colonial town with a pleasant central square. Valladolid features two eerie but accessible *cenotes,* and the spectacular ruins at Ekbalam are only 25 miles to the north. Also nearby is the Río Lagartos nature preserve, teeming with flamingos and other native birds that nest there.

CELESTÚN NATIONAL WILDLIFE REFUGE   This flamingo sanctuary wetlands preserve a large stretch of the Gulf coast with a unique ecosystem. Touring this area by launch is relaxing and rewarding. Only 1¹/₂ hours from Mérida, Celestún makes for an easy day-trip.

DZIBILCHALTÚN   This Maya site, now a national park, is located 9 miles north of Mérida along the Progreso Road. Here you'll find a number of pre-Hispanic ruins, nature trails, a *cenote,* and the new Museum of the Maya. You could make this the first stop in a day-trip to Progreso and other attractions north of Mérida.

PROGRESO   A modern city and Gulf-coast beach escape 21 miles north of Mérida, Progreso has a beautiful oceanfront drive and a wide beach that's popular on the weekends and during the summer. Go on a weekday if you want the beach to yourself. You can also drive down the coast to **Uaymitún** to possibly see some flamingos, and to the recently excavated ruins of **Xcambó.**

UXMAL   Smaller than Chichén, but architecturally more striking and mysterious, it's about 50 miles to the south of Mérida and can be seen in a day, though it's a good idea to extend that somewhat to see the sound-and-light show and spend the night at one of the hotels by the ruins. Several other nearby sites comprise the Puuc route and can be explored on the following day. It's also possible, though a bit rushed, to see Uxmal and the other ruins on a 1-day trip by special excursion bus from Mérida. Sunday is a good day to go, since admission is free to the archaeological sites.

CAMPECHE   This beautiful walled colonial city has been so meticulously restored that it's a delight just to stroll down the streets. Campeche is about 3 hours southwest of Mérida in the direction of Palenque. A full day should give you enough time to see its architectural highlights and museums, but there is something about Campeche that makes you want to linger there.

1 Mérida: Gateway to the Maya Heartland

900 miles (1,440km) E of Mexico City; 200 (320km) miles W of Cancún

Mérida is the capital of the state of Yucatán and has been the dominant city in the region since the Spanish Conquest. The colonial historic center is large but easy to navigate. Mérida is also the only city in the interior that has any nightlife to speak of, and it's more varied and typical of the region than Cancún's. People here know how to have a good time; there's something happening every night, making Mérida the perfect home base for several day trips to nearby attractions.

ESSENTIALS

GETTING THERE & DEPARTING   By Plane   Aeromexico and **Mexicana** have direct nonstop flights to/from Miami. **Continental** has direct nonstop service to/from Houston. Otherwise, you will have to get here through Cancún, Cozumel, or Mexico City. **Mexicana** (☎ 9/924-6633 or 9/924-6910) flies to/from Mexico City. **Aeromexico** (☎ 9/927-9277 or 9/927-9433) flies to/from Cancún and Mexico City. **Aerocaribe** (☎ 9/928-6786), a Mexicana affiliate, provides service to/from Cozumel, Cancún, Veracruz, Villahermosa, and points in Central America. **Aviateca** (☎ 9/946-1312) flies to/from Guatemala City and Flores (Tikal). **Aviacsa** (☎ 9/926-9087) provides service to/from Cancún, Monterrey, Villahermosa, Tuxtla Gutiérrez, Tapachula, Oaxaca, and Mexico City. Taxis from the airport to the city run $8.

BY CAR   Highway 180, coming from Cancún, Valladolid, and Chichén-Itzá, enters Mérida at calle 65, and passes within 1 block of the town square. **Highway 261** from Uxmal (via Muna and Uman) becomes avenida Itzáes; if you arrive by 261, turn right on calle 59 (first street after the zoo). If you arrive from Uxmal via Ticul and the ruins of Mayapán, you can get on Highway 180 into Mérida from the town of Kanasín.

A traffic loop or *periférico* encircles Mérida, making it possible to skirt the city. Directional signs are generally good into the city, but going around the city on the loop requires constant vigilance.

The old federal highway (*carretera federal*) between Mérida and Cancún is labeled 180. The trip takes 6 hours, and the road is in good shape; you will pass through many Maya villages. There is a new four-lane divided **toll road** (known as the *cuota* or *autopista*) that parallels highway 180. It starts at the town of Kantunil, 35 miles east of Mérida. By avoiding the tiny villages and their not-so-tiny speed bumps, the *autopista* cuts 2 hours from the journey between Mérida and Cancún; one-way tolls cost $28. See "En Route to Uxmal," below, at the end of the Mérida section, for suggested routes from Mérida.

BY BUS   There are five bus stations in Mérida, two of which offer first-class buses, the other three provide local service to nearby destinations. The larger of the first-class bus stations, **CAME,** is on calle 70, between calles 69 and 71 (see "City Layout," below). When you get there you'll see the names and logos of a number of different bus lines—ADO, Super Expresso, Maya de Oro, UNO, GL—pay no attention to this, these are all part of the same company. To buy a ticket, just find your destination on the big board above the ticket counter and go to the ticket agent directly below it. The ticket agent might give you a couple of options with different prices for either first class or deluxe. The main difference between the two is that deluxe has more leg room; both are air-conditioned. Unless it's a really long ride, I choose the bus that has the most convenient departure time. Tickets can be purchased in advance.

The other first-class station is the small **Maaya K'iin** used by the bus company **Élite.** It's on calle 65 #548, between calles 68 and 70.

To/from Cancún: You can pick up a bus at the **Came** (50 per day) or with **Élite** (6 per day). Both bus lines also have buses pick up passengers at the Fiesta Americana Hotel, across from the Hyatt (12 per day). Cancún is 4 hours away; a few buses stop in **Valladolid.**

To/from Chichén-Itzá: Three buses per day (2¹/₂ hours) from the **CAME.** Also, check out tours operating from the hotels in Mérida if you want to do it in a day.

To/from Playa del Carmen, Tulum, and Chetumal: From the **CAME** there are 8 departures per day for Playa del Carmen (5 hours); 6 for Tulum (6 hours); 8 for Chetumal (7 hours).

To/from Campeche: From the CAME station there is service to Campeche (2¹/₂ hours) every hour between 6am and 10pm. Élite has 4 per day.

To/from Palenque and San Cristóbal de las Casas: There is first-class service to Palenque twice daily from the Came, once daily from Élite.

The **second-class bus station** is around the corner from the CAME on calle 69, between calles 68 and 70.

To/from Uxmal: Four buses per day. You can hook up with various tour buses through most hotels or any travel agent/tour operator in town. There's also one bus per day that combines Uxmal with the other sites to the south (Kabah, Sayil, Labná, and Xlapak—known as the Puuc route) and does the whole round-trip in a day. It stops for 2 hours at Uxmal and 30 minutes at each of the other sites.

To/from Progreso, Dzibilchaltún: The bus station that serves these destinations is the **Estación Progreso** at calle 62 no. 524, between calles 65 and 67. The trip to Progreso takes an hour by second class.

To/from Celestún: The Celestún station is at calle 71 #585 between calles 64 and 66. The trip takes 1¹/₂ to 2 hours, depending on how often the bus stops. There are 10 buses per day.

ORIENTATION   Arriving by Plane   Mérida's airport is 8 miles from the city center on the southwestern outskirts of town, where Highway 180 enters the city. The airport has desks for renting a car, reserving a hotel room, and getting tourist information. Taxi tickets to town are sold outside the airport doors, under the covered walkway, and cost $9.

VISITOR INFORMATION   There is a city tourism office and a state tourism office. They do not work together, and they have different resources; if you don't get the info you need at one, go to the other. The state operates two downtown tourism offices: one is in the Teatro Peón Contreras, on calle 60 between calles 57 and 59 (☎ 9/924-9290); and the other is on the main plaza, immediately to your left as you enter the Palacio de Gobierno. These are open daily from 8am to 8pm. There are also information booths at the airport and the CAME bus station. The city's **visitor information office** is on calle 59 between calles 60 and 62 (☎ 9/923-0883). Hours are from 9am to 2pm and from 4 to 8pm. In my experience, the city office is more helpful.

Another resource is Canadian Dennis LaFoy, owner of **Yucatán Trails** travel agency, calle 62 no. 482 (☎ 9/928-2582). He is well known and active in the English-speaking community, is a problem-solver and font of information, and he can arrange a variety of individualized tours. He can also hold luggage and facilitate travel in other ways. Also, keep your eye out for a free monthly magazine called *Yucatán Today;* it's a good source of info for Mérida and the rest of the state of Yucatán.

CITY LAYOUT   Mérida has the standard layout for towns in the Yucatán: streets running north-south are even numbers; those running east-west are odd numbers. The numbering begins on the north and the east sides of town so that if you are walking on an odd-numbered street and the even numbers of the cross streets are increasing, then you know that you are heading west; likewise, if you are on an even-numbered street and the odd numbers of the cross streets are increasing, you are going south.

Another useful tip is that address numbers don't tell you anything about what cross-street to look for, so you can't be sure of where your destination is on the city grid. This is why in addition to a street number, you will often see cross-streets listed, usually like this: "calle 60 no. 549 x 71 y 73." The "x" is actually a multiplication sign—shorthand for the word "por" (meaning "by")—and "y" means "and." So the above address is on calle 60 between calles 71 and 73.

The center of town is the bright, busy **Plaza Mayor** (referred to simply as *El Centro*). It's bordered by calles 60, 62, 61, and 63. Calle 60, which runs in front of the cathedral, is an important street to remember; it connects the main square with several smaller plazas, some theaters and lovely churches, and the University of Yucatán just to the north. Here, too, you'll find a concentration of handcraft shops, restaurants, and hotels. Around the Plaza Mayor are the cathedral, the Palacio de Gobierno (state government building), the Ayuntamiento (town hall), and the Palacio Montejo. The Plaza always has a big crowd, but it's full of people on Sundays, when it holds a large street fair. (See the box on "Festivals & Special Events in Mérida," below.) Within a few blocks are several smaller plazas and the bustling market district.

Mérida's most fashionable district is the broad, tree-lined boulevard, **Paseo de Montejo,** and its surrounding neighborhood. The Paseo de Montejo parallels calle 60 and begins 7 blocks north and a little east of the main square. There are a number of trendy restaurants, modern hotels, offices for various banks and airlines, and a few clubs here, but the boulevard is mostly known for its stately mansions built during the boom times of the *henequen* industry. Where the Paseo intersects avenida Colón, you'll find the two fanciest hotels in town: the Hyatt and the Fiesta Americana.

GETTING AROUND **By Car** In general, reserve your car in advance from the U.S. to get the best weekly rates during high season (November to February); in low season I usually do better by renting a car once I get to Mérida. The local rental companies are very competitive and have promotional deals you can get only if you are there on the spot. When comparing, make sure it's apples to apples; ask if the price quote includes the IVA tax and insurance coverage. (Practically everybody offers free mileage.) For tips on saving money on car rentals see "Getting Around," in chapter 2. Rental cars are expensive, averaging $40 to $90 per day after you total all your expenses. By renting for only a day or two, you can avoid the high cost of parking lots in Mérida. These *estacionamentos* charge one price for the night and double that if you leave your car for the following day. Many hotels offer free parking, but make sure they include daytime parking in the price.

By Taxi Taxis are easy to come by and much cheaper than in Cancún.

By Bus City buses are a little tricky to figure out but aren't needed very often since most everything of interest is within walking distance of the main plaza. Still, it's a bit of a walk from the Plaza to the Paseo de Montejo, and you can save yourself some work by taking a bus, minibus, or *pesero* (Volkswagon minivan) that is heading north on calle 60. Most of these will either take you to Paseo Montejo or drop you off at Plaza Santa Ana, right next to the beginning of the Paseo. Most buses on calle 59 go to Mérida's zoological park, or to the Museum of Natural History. "Central" buses stop at the bus station, and any bus marked "Mercado" or "Correo" (post office) will take you to the market district, which is just a couple of blocks southeast of the main square. The *peseros* or *combis* (usually painted white) run out in several directions from the main plaza along simple routes. They're usually lined up along the side streets next to the plaza.

Fast Facts: Mérida

American Express   Paseo de Montejo no. 492 (☎ 9/942-8200). Open 9am to 2pm and 4 to 6pm.

Area Code   The telephone area code is **99.**

Bookstore   The Librería Dante, calle 59 between calles 60 and 62 (☎ 9/928-3674), has a selection of English-language cultural-history books on Mexico. It's open Monday through Saturday from 8am to 9:30pm and Sunday from 10am to 6pm.

Business Hours   Generally, Monday to Saturday 10am to 2pm and 4 to 8pm.

Climate   From November through February, the weather can be pleasantly cool and windy. In other months, it's just hot, especially during the day. Rain can occur anytime of year, especially the July-to-October rainy season, and usually follows the pattern of afternoon tropical showers.

Consulates   The **American Consulate** is located at Paseo de Montejo no. 453 and avenida Colón (☎ 9/925-5409 or 9/925-5011). The **British Vice-Consulate** is located at calle 53 no. 498 at the corner of calle 58 (☎ 9/928-6152). Office hours are 9am to 1pm. The vice-consul fields questions about travel to Belize as well as matters British.

Currency Exchange   Most banks in Mérida are a mess to deal with and do not offer outstanding exchange rates to offset the hassle. Try the **Centro Cambiario del Sureste** (☎ 9/928-2152), open every day from 9am to 9pm. It's in the Pasaje Picheta, a small shopping mall on the north side of the Plaza Mayor.

Hospitals   **Centro Médico de las Américas** at calle 54 no. 365 between 33-A and Av. Pérez Ponce. The main phone number is ☎ **9/926-2619;** for emergencies, 9/927-3199. You can also call the Cruz Roja (Red Cross) at ☎ **9/924-9813.**

Internet   The fastest connections are had at **Mayanet** at calle 60 no. 457A between calles 51 and 53, 2 blocks above Santa Lucía. Hours are Monday to Saturday 9am to midnight.

Police   Mérida has a special body of police to assist tourists. They patrol the downtown area and the Paseo Montejo and are recognizable by their brown-and-white uniforms with the words *Policía Turística.* The phone number for them, as well as the regular police, is ☎ **9/925-2555.**

Post Office   Mérida's main post office (*correo*) is located near the market at the corner of calles 65 and 56. A branch office is located at the airport. Both are open Monday through Friday from 8am to 7pm and Saturday from 9am to 12pm.

Seasons   There are two high seasons, but they aren't as pronounced as on the coast. One is in July and August, when Mexicans most commonly take their vacations, and the other is between November 15 and Easter Sunday, when Canadians and Americans flock to the Yucatán to escape winter weather.

Spanish Classes   Maya scholars, Spanish teachers, and archaeologists from the United States are among the students at the **Centro Idiomas del Sureste,** calle 14 no. 106 at calle 25, Colonia México, 97000 Mérida, Yuc. (☎ **9/926-1155;** fax 9/926-9020). The school has two locations: in the Colonia México, a northern residential district, and on calle 66 at calle 57 in the downtown area. Students live with local families or in hotels; sessions running 2 weeks or longer are available for all levels of proficiency and areas of interest. For brochures and applications, contact Chloe Conaway de Pacheco, Directora.

Festivals & Special Events in Mérida

Many Mexican cities offer weekend concerts in the park, but Mérida surpasses them all with daily public events, most of which are free and fun to watch.

Sunday   Each Sunday from 9am to 9pm, there's a fair called *Mérida en Domingo* (Mérida on Sunday). The main plaza and a section of calle 60 from El Centro to Parque Santa Lucía are blocked off from traffic. Parents come with their children to stroll around and take in the scene. There are booths selling food and drink, along with a lively little flea market and used-book fair. There are children's art classes, educational booths, and concerts of all kinds. At 11am in front of the Palacio del Gobierno, musicians play everything from jazz to classical and folk music. Also at 11am, the police orchestra performs Yucatecan tunes at the Santa Lucía park. At 11:30am, you'll find bawdy comedy acts at the Parque Hidalgo on calle 60 at calle 59. There's a lull in mid-afternoon, and then the plaza fills up again as people walk around and visit with friends. Around 7pm in front of the *Ayuntamiento,* a large band starts playing mambos, rumbas, and cha-cha-chas with great enthusiasm; you may see a thousand people dancing there in the street. Then everyone is invited into the Ayuntamiento to see folk ballet dancers reenact a typical Yucatecan wedding. All events are free.

Monday   Vaquería Regional with the Municipal orchestra perform at 9pm in front of the Palacio Municipal. The music and dancing celebrate the Vaquerías feast, which occurs after the branding of cattle on Yucatecan haciendas. Among the featured performers are dancers with trays of bottles or filled glasses on their heads—a sight to see. Admission is free.

Tuesday   The theme for the Tuesday entertainment, held at 9pm in Parque Santiago, on calle 59 at calle 72, is big-band music from the 1940s, both Latin and American. Admission is free.

Wednesday   At 9pm in the Teatro Peón Contreras on calle 60 at calle 57, the University of Yucatán Folklore Ballet presents "Yucatán and Its Roots." Admission is $5.

Thursday   Yucatecan *trova* music (boleros, baladas) and dance are presented at the Serenata in Parque Santa Lucía at 9pm. Admission is free.

Friday   At 9pm in the patio of the University of Yucatán, calle 60 at calle 57, the University of Yucatán Ballet Folklórico performs typical regional dances from the Yucatán. Admission is free.

Saturday   "*Noche Mexicana*" at the park at the beginning of Paseo de Montejo begins at 9pm. It features several performances of traditional Mexican music and dance. Some of the performers are amateurs who acquit themselves reasonably well; others are professional musicians and dancers who thoroughly know their craft. There are some food stands selling very good *antojitos,* as well as drinks and ice cream.

Also, on the evening of the first Friday of each month, either Canadian Dennis LaFoy of the Yucatán Trails Travel Agency (☎ 9/928-2582) or the Mérida English Library (☎ 9/923-3319) host a get-together for English-speaking residents and visitors. There is a different venue each month, so call either number to get info.

Telephones   There are long-distance phone service centers at the airport, the bus station, at calle 57 corner with calle 60, calle 59, corner with calle 62, and at calle 60 between calles 55 and 53. To use the public phones, you will need to buy a *Ladatel* card from just about any newsstand or store. These cards come in a variety of denominations and work for long distance within Mexico and sometimes even abroad. Also see "Telephone/Fax" in "Fast Facts: Mexico," in chapter 2.

EXPLORING MÉRIDA

Most of Mérida's attractions are within walking distance from the downtown area. But to see a larger area of the city there's a popular **bus tour** that's worth taking. The man who operates these tours has bought a few small buses and given them a fancy paint job, pulled out all the windows, raised the roof several inches, and installed wooden benches so that the buses remind one of the traditional buses of coastal Latin America, known as *chivas* in Colombia and Venezuela or as *guaguas* in other places. You can find these buses on the corner of calles 60 and 55 (next to the church of Santa Lucía) at 10am, 1pm, 4pm, and 7pm. The tour costs $6 per person and lasts 2 hours. Another option for seeing the city is via **horse-drawn carriage.** A 45-minute ride around central Mérida costs $11. You can usually find the carriages beside the cathedral or on calle 60.

EXPLORING THE PLAZA MAYOR   Downtown Mérida is a great example of a lowland colonial city. There is a casual, relaxed feel to the town. Buildings lack the severe baroque features that characterize central Mexico; most are finished in stucco and painted in light colors. Mérida's gardens add to this relaxed, tropical atmosphere. Gardeners here do not strive for the kind of garden where all is exactly in its place, displaying the gardener's control over nature. Here, natural exuberance is the ideal, with plants growing in a wild profusion that disguises human intervention. A perfect example is the patio in the Palacio Montejo, which I will cover shortly. Mérida's plazas are a slightly different version of this aesthetic: Unlike the highland plazas, with their carefully sculpted trees, Mérida's squares are typically built around giant large trees that are left to grow as tall as possible.

The **Plaza Mayor** (often referred to as "el centro") has this sort of informality. Even when there's no orchestrated event in progress, the park is full of people sitting on the benches talking with friends or taking a casual stroll. A plaza like El Centro is a great advantage for a big city such as Mérida, giving it a personal feel and a sense of community that combat the modern bustle of urban life. Notice the beautiful scale and composition of the major buildings surrounding the plaza. The most prominent of these is the cathedral.

The oldest **cathedral** on the continent, it was built between 1561 and 1598, and recently celebrated its 400th anniversary. Much of the stone in the cathedral's walls came from the ruined buildings of Tihó, the former Maya city. Originally, the building was finished with stucco, and you can see some remnants still clinging to the bare rock. People, however, like the way the unfinished walls show the cathedral's age. Notice how the two top levels of the bell towers are built off-center from their bases—an uncommon feature. Inside, decoration is sparse, with altars draped in fabric colorfully embroidered like a Maya woman's shift. The most notable item is a picture of Ah Kukum Tutul Xiú, chief of the Xiu people, visiting the Montejo camp to make peace; it's hanging over the side door on the right.

To the left of the main altar is a small shrine with a curious statue of Jesus that is a replica of one recovered from a burned-out church in the town of Ichmul. The original figure was carved in the 1500s by a local artist from a miraculous tree that was hit by lightning and burst into flames—but did not char. The statue later became blistered in the church fire at Ichmul, but it survived. In 1645 it was moved to the cathedral in Mérida, where the locals attached great powers to the figure, naming it Cristo de las Ampollas (Christ of the Blisters). It did not, however, survive the sacking of the cathedral in 1915 by revolutionary forces, so another figure, modeled after the original, was made. Take a look in the side chapel (open from 8 to 11am and 4:30 to 7pm), containing a life-size diorama of the Last Supper. The Mexican Jesus is covered with prayer crosses brought by supplicants asking for intercession.

Next door to the cathedral is the old bishop's palace, now converted into the city's contemporary art museum, **Museo de Arte Contemporáneo Ateneo de Yucatán (MACAY)** (☎ **9/928-3236**). The palace was confiscated and rebuilt during the Mexican Revolution in 1915. Inside its two stories, 17 exhibition rooms show works by contemporary artists from the Yucatán and around the world. Nine of the rooms hold the museum's permanent collection, the rest hold temporary exhibits. It's open Wednesday through Monday from 10am to 6pm (closed Tuesday). Admission is $2.50; free Sunday.

Across the street, on the south side of the plaza, is the **Palacio Montejo.** Its façade, with heavy decoration around the doorway and windows, is a good example of the Spanish architectural style known as plateresque. But the content of the decoration is very much a New World creation. Conquering the Yucatán was the Montejo family business, begun by the original Francisco Montejo and continued by his son and his nephew (both named Francisco Montejo). Construction of the house started in 1542 under Francisco Montejo El Mozo ("The Younger"; the son). Bordering the entrance are politically incorrect figures of conquistadors standing on the heads of vanquished Indians—borrowed, perhaps, from the pre-Hispanic custom of portraying victorious Maya kings treading on their defeated foes. The posture of the conquistadors and their facial expression of wide-eyed dismay make them less imposing than perhaps the Montejos would have wished. This building is now occupied by a bank, but you can enter the courtyard, view the garden, and see for yourself what a charming residence it must have been for the descendants of the Montejos, who lived here until as recently as the 1970s. (Curiously enough, not only does the society of Mérida keep track of who is descended from the Montejos, it also keeps track of who is descended from the last Maya king Tutul Xiu.)

In stark contrast to the severity of the cathedral and Casa Montejo, is the light and unimposing **Palacio Municipal** (town hall), more commonly known as the *Ayuntamiento*. This is because most of what you see dates from the mid 19th century, when it no longer was necessary to borrow from the architecture of the mother country, and a tropicalist aesthetic began asserting itself across coastal Latin America. Inside on the second floor you can see the meeting hall of the city council, and there's a lovely view of the plaza from the balcony. Sharing the same block with the *ayuntamiento* is a recently completed building called **El Nuevo Olimpo** (The New Olympus). It takes the place of the old Olimpo that was demolished in the 1970s by a misguided town council, to the regret of many older Meridianos. The new building tries to incorporate elements of the original while at the same time presenting something new. It houses a theater, gallery space, and a lovely courtyard.

Cater-corner from the Nuevo Olimpo is the old **Casa del Alguacil** (Magistrate's House). Under its arcades is something of an institution in Mérida: the **Dulcería y Sorbetería Colón,** an ice cream and sweet shop that will appeal to those who prefer less-rich ice creams. Down a little further is a shopping center of boutiques and convenience food vendors. At the end of the arcade is the **Palacio de Gobierno,** dating from 1892. Large murals painted by the Meridiano artist Fernando Castro Pacheco between 1971 and 1973 decorate the walls of the courtyard. Scenes from Maya and Mexican history abound, and the painting over the stairway depicts the Maya spirit with ears of sacred corn, the "sunbeams of the gods." Nearby is a painting of the

Mérida Attractions

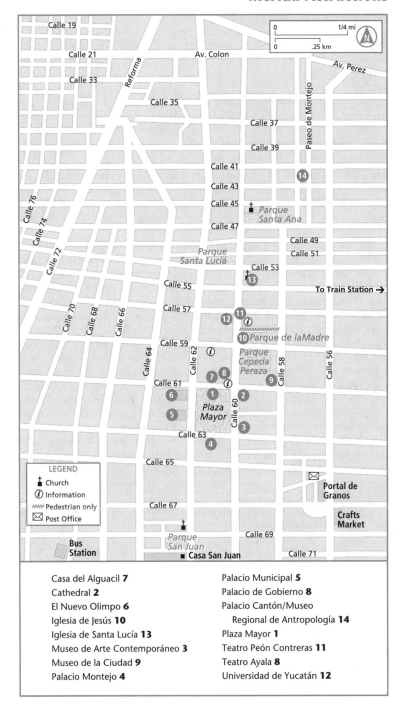

Calle 19
Calle 21
Av. Colon
Av, Perez
Reforma
Calle 33
Calle 35
Paseo de Montejo
Calle 37
Calle 39
Calle 41
Calle 43
14
Calle 45
Calle 76
Parque Santa Ana
Calle 47
Calle 74
Calle 49
Calle 72
Parque Santa Luciá
Calle 51
Calle 53
13
Calle 55
To Train Station →
Calle 57
12 **11** *(i)*
Calle 70
Calle 68
Calle 66
10 Parque de laMadre
Calle 59
(i)
Parque Cepeda Peraza
Calle 64
Calle 62
7 **8**
Calle 58
Calle 56
(i)
Calle 61
6 **1**
9
5
Plaza Mayor
2
Calle 60
Calle 63
3
4
Calle 65

LEGEND
✝ Church
(i) Information
///// Pedestrian only
✉ Post Office

Calle 67
✉ Portal de Granos
Crafts Market
✝
Calle 69
Bus Station
Parque San Juan
■ Casa San Juan
Calle 71

Casa del Alguacil **7**
Cathedral **2**
El Nuevo Olimpo **6**
Iglesia de Jesús **10**
Iglesia de Santa Lucía **13**
Museo de Arte Contemporáneo **3**
Museo de la Ciudad **9**
Palacio Montejo **4**

Palacio Municipal **5**
Palacio de Gobierno **8**
Palacio Cantón/Museo
    Regional de Antropología **14**
Plaza Mayor **1**
Teatro Peón Contreras **11**
Teatro Ayala **8**
Universidad de Yucatán **12**

171

mustachioed Lázaro Cárdenas, who as president in 1938 expropriated 17 foreign oil companies and was hailed as a Mexican liberator. Upstairs is a long and wide gallery with more of his paintings, which achieve their effect by localizing color and imitating the photographic technique of double exposure. The palace is open Monday through Saturday from 8am to 8pm and Sunday from 9am to 5pm. There is a small tourism office to the left as you enter.

Further down calle 61, beside the cathedral, is the **Museo de la Ciudad.** It occupies the former church of San Juan de Dios and holds an exhibit outlining the history of Mérida. It will be of interest to those curious about this city, and there is explanatory text in English. Hours are Tuesday through Friday from 10am to 2pm, 4 to 8pm; Saturday and Sunday 10am to 2pm. Admission is free.

EXPLORING CALLE 60   Heading north from the Plaza Mayor up calle 60, you'll see many of Mérida's old churches and squares. Several stores catering to tourists along calle 60 sell gold-filigree jewelry, pottery, clothing, and folk art. A stroll along this street leads to the Parque Santa Ana and continues to the fashionable boulevard Paseo de Montejo and its Museo Regional de Antropología.

The first place of interest is the Teatro Daniel de Ayala, only because it sometimes has interesting performances. Then on your left you'll come to a small park called **Parque Cepeda Peraza** (or Parque Hidalgo). Named for the 19th-century general Manuel Cepeda Peraza, the *parque* was part of Montejo's original city plan. Small outdoor restaurants front hotels on the *parque,* making it a popular stopping-off place at any time of day. Bordering Parque Cepeda Peraza across calle 59 is the **Iglesia de Jesús,** or El Tercer Orden (the Third Order). Built by the Jesuit order in 1618, it has the richest interior of any church in Mérida, making it a favorite spot for weddings. The entire block on which the church stands belonged to the Jesuits, who are known as great educators. The school they left behind after their expulsion developed into the Universidad de Yucatán.

On the other side of the church is the **Parque de la Madre** (or Parque Morelos). The park contains a modern statue of the Madonna and Child; the statue is a copy of the work by Renoir that stands in the Luxembourg Gardens in Paris. Beyond the Parque de la Madre and across the pedestrian way is the **Teatro Peón Contreras.** This opulent theater was designed by Italian architect Enrico Deserti a century ago. In one corner you'll see a branch of the State Tourist Information Office facing the Parque de la Madre. The theater is noted for its Carrara marble staircase and frescoed dome. Domestic and international performers appear here frequently. Across calle 60 is the main building of the **Universidad de Yucatán.** Inside is a flagstone courtyard where the *ballet folklórico* performs on Friday nights.

A block further north brings you to Parque Santa Lucía. Surrounded by an arcade on the north and west sides, this park once was where visitors first alighted in Mérida when arriving by stagecoach. On Sunday, Parque Santa Lucía holds a used-book sale and small swap meet, and several evenings a week it hosts popular entertainment. On Thursday nights performers present Yucatecan songs and poems. Facing the park is the **Iglesia de Santa Lucía** (1575). From here you are 6 blocks away from the beginning of Paseo de Montejo.

Four blocks farther up calle 60 is Parque Santa Ana; if you turn right, you'll come to the beginning of the paseo in a block-and-a-half.

EXPLORING THE PASEO MONTEJO   The Paseo de Montejo is a tree-lined boulevard, which at one time held many turn-of-the-century mansions belonging to hacienda owners who were enjoying a huge boom in the production of *henequen.* Several have survived, some of which are still in private hands; others have become offices, restaurants, consulates, etc.; many others were demolished. Today, this is thought to be the ritzy part of town, with many fine restaurants, trendy discos, and expensive hotels.

Of the remaining mansions, the most notable is the Palacio Cantón. This mansion, with an entrance on calle 43, houses the ✪ **Museo Regional de Antropología** (Anthropology Museum; ☎ **9/923-0557**). Designed and built by Enrico Deserti, the architect who designed the Teatro Peón Contreras, this is the most impressive mansion on Paseo de Montejo. It was constructed between 1909 and 1911, during the last years of the Porfiriato, as the home of General Francisco Cantón Rosado. The general enjoyed his palace for only 6 years before he died in 1917. The house was converted into a school and later served as the official residence of the governor of Yucatán.

Now the Palacio houses a museum on the pre-Columbian cultures of Mexico, especially the Maya. Its exhibits include cosmology, a pre-Hispanic time computation and comparative timeline, musical instruments, weaving examples and designs, and stone carvings from all over the country. Captions for the permanent displays are mostly in Spanish. Starting with fossil mastodon teeth, the exhibits take you through the Yucatán's history, paying special attention to the daily life of its inhabitants. You'll see how the Maya tied boards to babies' heads in order to create the slanted forehead that was to them a mark of great beauty, and how they filed their teeth or drilled holes in them to inset jewels. There are enlarged photos of the archaeological sites, and drawings illustrate the various styles of Maya dwellings and how they were constructed. Even if you know only a little Spanish, the museum provides a good background for explorations of Maya sites. The museum is open Tuesday through Saturday from 8am to 8pm and Sunday from 8am to 2pm. Admission is $2; free on Sunday.

SHOPPING

Mérida is known for **hammocks, *guayaberas*** (lightweight men's shirts that are worn untucked), and **Panama hats. Baskets** made in the Yucatán and **pottery,** as well as crafts from all over Mexico, are sold cheaply in the **central market.** Mérida is also the place to pick up prepared **achiote,** a paste-like mixture of ground achiote seeds (annatto), oregano, garlic, masa, and other spices used in Yucatecan cuisine. When mixed with sour orange to a soupy consistency, it makes a great marinade, especially on grilled meat and fish. It can be found bottled in this form. It's also the sauce for baked chicken and cochinita pibil.

EXPLORING THE MARKET   Mérida's bustling **market district,** bounded by calles 65 to 69 and calles 58 to 54, is a few blocks southeast of the Plaza Mayor. During the day this part of town is always crowded with hordes of pedestrians. Behind the post office (at calles 65 and 56) and across the way is the oldest part of the market, the **Portal de Granos** (Grains arcade), a dark red building with stone arches. It is called this because years ago this was where the grain merchants sold their wares. Just to the east of it, between calles 56 and 54, is the main market building. Inside, chaos seems to reign, but soon the order becomes apparent. Here you can find anything from fresh fish to flowers to leather goods. In the building directly south of the market, you can find more locally manufactured goods, and on the second floor of the building just to the south of the Portal de Granos is the Municipal Crafts Market, where you can buy just about any handcraft made in the Yucatán.

CRAFTS

Mérida has some interesting shopping outside the market that bears mention.

Casa de las Artesanías. Calle 63 no. 513, between calles 64 and 66. ☎ **9/928-6676.**

This store occupies the front rooms of a restored monastery. Here you can find a wide selection of crafts from throughout Mexico. Stop by here before going to the various crafts markets to see what high-quality work looks like. The monastery's back court-yard is used as a gallery, with rotating exhibits on folk and fine arts. It's open Monday through Saturday from 9am to 8pm, Sunday 9am to 1pm.

Museo Regional de Artes Populares. Calle 59 no. 441, between calles 50 and 48. No phone.

A branch of the Museo Nacional de Artes y Industrias Populares in Mexico City, this museum displays regional costumes and crafts in the front rooms. Upstairs is a large room full of crafts from all over Mexico, including filigree jewelry from Mérida, folk pottery, baskets, and wood carving from the Yucatán. Open Tuesday through Saturday from 9am to 8pm and Sunday from 9am to 2pm. Admission is free.

Miniaturas. Calle 59 no. 507A-4 between calles 60 and 62. ☎ **9/928-6503.**

This fun little store is packed to the rafters in miniatures. Miniatures are a traditional folk art form in Mexico that has been evolving in a number of directions, including social and political commentary, pop art, and bawdy humor. Alicia Rivero, the owner, collects them from several parts of Mexico, so that there's plenty of variety, from traditional miniatures such as furniture for dollhouses, to popular cartoon characters and celebrities. Hours are Monday through Saturday from 10am to 8 pm.

GUAYABERAS

Business suits are hot and uncomfortable in Mérida's soaking humidity, so business-men, politicians, bankers, and bus drivers alike wear the *guayabera,* a loose-fitting shirt that is decorated with narrow tucks, pockets, and sometimes embroidery, and is worn over the pants rather than tucked in. Mérida is famous as the best place to buy *guayaberas,* which can be purchased for under $10 at the market or for over $50 custom-made by a tailor. A *guayabera* made of linen can cost about $65. Most are made of cotton, although other materials are available, and the traditional color is white.

Most shops display ready-to-wear shirts in several price ranges. *Guayabera* makers pride themselves on being innovators. I have yet to enter a shirt-maker's shop in Mérida that did not present its own updated version of the *guayabera.* When looking at *guayaberas,* here are few things to keep in mind: When Yucatecans say *seda,* they do not mean silk but polyester; *lino* is linen or a linen/polyester combination. Take a close look at the stitching and the way the tucks line up over the pockets, etc.; with *guayaberas* the details are everything.

Guayaberas Jack. Calle 59 no. 507A between calles 60 and 62. ☎ **9/928-6002.**

The craftsmanship here is very good, the place has a reputation to maintain, and some of the salespeople can speak English. Prices are as marked. This will give you a good basis of comparison should you want to hunt for a bargain elsewhere. If they do not have the style and color of shirt you want, they will make it for you in about 3 hours. This shop also sells regular shirts and women's blouses. Hours are from Monday through Saturday from 10am to 8pm; Sunday 10am to 2pm.

HAMMOCKS

I am an aficionado of hammocks, having slept in every variety across the length and breadth of Latin America. None is so comfortable as those of the Yucatán, which are woven with local cotton string in a fine mesh. For most of us, of course, the hammock is the equivalent of lawn furniture, something to relax in for an hour or so in the after-noon. But for the vast majority of Yucatecans, hammocks are what they sleep in at night. Many well-to-do Meridianos keep a bed just for show. I know a hotel owner who has 150 beds in his establishment, but won't sleep on a single one of them. He complains that when he does, he wakes up unrested and sore. In hotels that cater to Yucatecans, you will always find hammock hooks in the walls.

My advice to the hammock buyer is this: The woven part should be cotton; it should be made with fine string; and the strings should be so numerous that when you get in it and stretch out diagonally (the way you're supposed to sleep in these hammocks), the gaps between the strings remain small. Don't pay attention to the words used to describe the size of a hammock; they have become practically meaningless. Good hammocks don't cost a lot of money ($15 to $30). If you want a superior hammock, ask for one made with fine crochet thread "*hilo de crochet*" (the word *crochet* is also sometimes bandied about, but you can readily see the difference). This should run about $80.

Nothing beats a tryout when you're shopping for a hammock; the two shops mentioned below will gladly hang one for you to test-drive. When it's up, look to see that there are no untied strings. You can also see what street vendors are offering, but you have to know what to look for—or they are likely to take advantage of you.

Hamacas El Aguacate. Calle 58 no. 604, corner with calle 73. ☎ **9/928-6429.**

El Aguacate sells hammocks wholesale and retail. It has the greatest variety and is the place to go for a really fancy hammock. A good hammock is the size #6 in cotton; it runs $28. The store is open Monday to Friday, 8am to 7pm, Saturday from 8am to 5pm. The store is about 6 blocks south of the main square.

Tejidos y Cordeles Nacionales. Calle 56 no. 516-B, between calles 63 and 65. ☎ **9/928-5561.**

This place near the municipal market sells only cotton hammocks, and they are sold on the basis of weight—a pretty good practice because hammock lengths are standard here. The prices are better than at El Aguacate, but quality control isn't as good. My idea of a good hammock weighs about 1$\frac{1}{2}$ kilos and runs about $18.

PANAMA HATS

Another useful and popular item is this soft, pliable hat made from the fibers of the jipijapa palm in several towns south of Mérida along Highway 180, especially Becal, in the neighboring state of Campeche. The hat makers in these towns work inside caves so that the moist air keeps the palm fibers pliant. They're just the thing to shade you from the fierce Yucatecan sun.

Jipi hats come in various grades determined by the quality (pliability, softness, and fineness) of the fibers and closeness of the weave. The difference in weave is easily seen, as a fine weave improves the shape of a hat. It has more body and regains its shape better. I like two places in particular for Panama hats, and if you speak Spanish, you can hear two different takes on buying a hat. One store is **El Bacaleño** at calle 65 no. 483 across from the post office. The owner can show you differences in qualities, and has some very expensive hats. The other store is a short distance away in one of the market buildings: walk down calle 56 south past the post office and right before the street ends, turn left into a passage way with hardware stores at the entrance. The fourth or fifth shop is the **Casa de los Jipis.** You can always ask people in the area to point it out to you.

WHERE TO STAY

Mérida is easier on the budget than Yucatán resort cities. The stream of visitors is steadier than on the coast so most hotels no longer use a high-/low-season rate structure. This doesn't mean you shouldn't make reservations; Mérida has a new convention center, which attracts large trade shows that can fill a lot of hotels. Most hotels offer at least a few air-conditioned rooms, and some also have pools. In Mérida, free parking is a relative concept—for many hotels free parking means only at night; during the day there is a charge.

VERY EXPENSIVE

✪ **Fiesta Americana Mérida.** Av. Colón 451, Esq. Paseo Montejo, 92127 Mérida, Yuc. ☎ **800/343-7821** in the U.S., 9/942-1111. Fax 9/942-1112. 350 units. A/C MINIBAR TV TEL. $145 double, $184 suite. AE, DC, MC, V. Free guarded parking.

This is a magisterial, five-story hotel on the Paseo Montejo, across from the Hyatt. The exterior architecture does a good job of mirroring the French *fin-de-siecle* style of the old mansions on the Paseo. All rooms have outward-facing windows. They come with spacious, well-equipped bathrooms, tropical-style rattan furniture, and floors of marble and stone. The service is first rate. There is a shopping center on the ground floor, below the lobby.

Dining/Diversions: Two restaurants, one bar. (A disco, not connected with the hotel, is on the ground floor below the lobby.)

Amenities: Swimming pool, tennis courts, gym and spa, business center, shops.

✪ **Hyatt Regency Mérida.** Calle 60 no. 344, 97000 Mérida, Yuc. ☎ **800/223-1234** in the U.S. and Canada, 9/942-0202. Fax 9/942-1284. www.hyatt.com. 300 units. A/C MINI-BAR TV TEL. $160–$180 double. Ask about "supersaver rates." AE, DC, MC, V. Free guarded parking.

This Hyatt is much like Hyatts elsewhere. At 17 stories high, it's not hard to find; the hotel is next to the Paseo de Montejo and across Av. Colón from the Fiesta Americana. The large, modern rooms are carpeted, very quiet, and comfortable. They come with all the amenities and great bathrooms. Regency Club rooms take up the top two floors; guests in these rooms receive complimentary continental breakfast, evening cocktails, and hors d'oeuvres; special concierge service; and access to private lounges and boardrooms. The hotel is at the intersection of calle 60 and avenida Colón.

Dining/Diversions: Several restaurants and bars.

Amenities: Business center, travel agency, and shops. Pool with swim-up bar; fitness center, spa, tennis court.

EXPENSIVE

✪ **Hotel Casa del Balam.** Calle 60 no. 488, 97000 Mérida, Yuc. ☎ **800/624-8451** in the U.S., or 9/924-8844. Fax 9/924-5011. www.yucatanadventure.com.mx. 52 units. A/C MINI-BAR TV TEL. $105 double. AE, DC, MC, V.

The "House of the Jaguar" has the best downtown location of any hotel. Most of the rooms are large and bright, and come with double windows to reduce noise; in most rooms these cannot be opened. The rooms are in two sections: one has three stories, the other six. The quietest rooms are in the three-story section and the top floors of the six-story section. Rooms are decorated with folk art, dark furniture, iron headboards, and tile floors with area rugs. There's a rental-car agency in the lobby and a pool in the rear patio. The hotel has a popular restaurant and bar. The tables scattered around the courtyard have become a favorite spot for evening cocktails.

The owners also operate the hotel **Hacienda Chichén,** at the ruins of Chichén-Itzá; you can make arrangements here to stay there. The hotel is at the corner of 60 and 57.

MODERATE

✪ **Casa Mexilio Guest House.** Calle 68 no. 495, 97000 Mérida, Yuc. ☎ **800/538-6802** in the U.S.; ☎/fax 9/928-2505. www.mexicoholiday.com. 13 units. $52–$67 double, $10 less in summer. Rates include full breakfast. MC, V. Parking on street.

Mérida Accommodations & Dining

LEGEND
- † Church
- ⓘ Information
- ///// Pedestrian only
- ⊠ Post Office

■ **ACCOMMODATIONS**

Casa Mexilio Guest House **18**
Casa San Juan **19**
Fiesta Americana Mérida **3**
Hotel Caribe **14**
Hotel Casa del Balam **8**
Hotel Dolores Alba **13**
Hotel Mucuy **10**
Hotel Trinidad Galería **5**
Hyatt Regency Mérida **2**
Posada Toledo **9**

◆ **DINING**

Alberto's Continental **17**
Café Alameda **11**
Café Amaro **15**
La Casa del Paseo **4**
Pórtico del Peregrino **7**
Restaurant Los Almendros **12**
Restaurant Santa Lucía **6**
Virrey de Mendoza **1**
Vito Corleone **16**

This bed-and-breakfast is unlike any other I know. The owners are geniuses at playing with space in an unexpected and delightful manner. Rooms are at different levels—creating private spaces joined to each other and to roof-top terraces by stairs and cat walks. Rooms are large and comfortable, furnished and decorated in an engaging mix of new and old, polished and primitive. Nine come with air-conditioning. Most of the central patio is taken up by a small pool with whirlpool and exuberant vegetation. There's a new annex across the street that contains two rooms, an apartment with artist studio, and a two-story suite with private pool and terrace ($82–$150/night). Breakfasts are great. The hotel is connected with the Turquoise Reef Group, which runs inns on Mexico's Caribbean coast between Cancún and Chetumal. The hotel is 4 blocks west of the plaza between calles 57 and 59.

Hotel Caribe. Calle 59 no. 500, 97000 Mérida, Yuc. ☎ **888/822-6431** in the U.S. and Canada, or 9/924-9022. Fax 9/924-8733. www.hotelcaribe.com.mx. 53 units. TV TEL. $53–$58 double. AE, MC, V.

I like this three-story hotel (no elevator) for a couple of reasons: Its location at the back of Plaza Hidalgo is both central and quiet. There's a nice little pool and sundeck on the rooftop with a view of the cathedral, and the rooms are comfortable and quiet. Like many hotels in Mexico, rooms are not lit brightly enough for American tastes. Most doubles and all three suites come with air-conditioning. Nearby parking is free at night but costs extra during the day. The restaurant serves good Mexican food. The hotel is on the Parque Cepeda Peraza on calle 60.

INEXPENSIVE

Casa San Juan. Calle 62 no. 545a, 97000 Mérida, Yuc. ☎9/923-6823. Fax 9/986-2937. E-mail: csanjuan@diario1.sureste.com. 6 units, 3 with A/C. $15–$35 double. No credit cards. Rate includes continental breakfast.

Casa San Juan is a small B&B set in a traditional Mérida townhouse. Guest rooms are clean, cheerful, spacious, and comfortable. The lower rate is for rooms that share a bathroom and come without air-conditioning (they come with ceiling and floor fans). Doubles come with either two twin or two double beds. The building and grounds are beautifully kept. There is parking nearby for $2 per day. Breakfasts emphasize tropical fruits and juices and homemade bread. The house is 4 blocks south of the main plaza between calles 69 and 71.

✪ **Hotel Dolores Alba.** Calle 63 no. 464, 97000 Mérida, Yuc. ☎ 9/928-5650. Fax 9/928-3163. www.doloresalba.com. E-mail: asanchez@sureste.com. 90 units. TEL. A/C $27–$33 double. No credit cards. Free guarded parking.

The Dolores Alba has recently been expanded and now offers comfortable rooms at a good price. It's also a good place if you're traveling by car. Three stories of rooms (no elevator) border two courtyards: what was the small courtyard in back is now the large courtyard with a lovely pool. The three stories of rooms that surround it come with air-conditioning, two double beds, and nice bathrooms. They are bright, cheerful, and comfortable. All have windows or balconies that look out over the pool. The front courtyard is dominated by a beautiful mango tree. The older rooms around it are decorated with local crafts. Some of the mattresses in the old section are softer than standard hotel issue, and half of these rooms come with air-conditioning. The bathrooms are clean but small. The hotel is managed by the family that also owns the **Hotel Dolores Alba** outside Chichén-Itzá; you can make reservations at one hotel for the other. This hotel is 3¹/₂ blocks from the Plaza Mayor between calles 52 and 54.

Hotel Mucuy. Calle 57 no. 481, 97000 Mérida, Yuc. ☎ **9/928-5193.** Fax 9/923-7801. 22 units. $20 double. No credit cards.

Guest rooms here are clean and basic, most with two twin beds (and comfortable mattresses) and not a lot in the way of furnishings. But owners Alfredo and Ofelia Comín strive to make guests feel welcome with conveniences such as a communal refrigerator in the lobby and, for a small extra charge, the use of a washer and dryer. The small garden patio is well tended and has comfortable furniture, making it the perfect place for sitting about and reading. The Mucuy is named for a small dove said to bring good luck to places where it alights. This place stays pretty full, and reservations are not accepted. The Mucuy is centrally located on calle 57 between calles 56 and 58.

Hotel Trinidad Galería. Calle 60 no. 456, 97000 Mérida, Yuc. ☎ **9/923-2463.** Fax 9/924-2319. 31 units. $32 double; $48 suite with A/C and TV. AE. Limited free parking.

Walking through this sprawling two-story hotel, one comes across many works of modern art and curios exhibited in the various open spaces created by the hotel's bizarre floor plan. The hotel's owner loves collecting art, and such a sprawling hotel provides him plenty of space to display his collection. Amenities include a small shaded pool, a communal refrigerator, a common dining room, and several sitting areas. Upstairs, a covered porch decorated with antiques and plants runs the length of the hotel, providing yet another place to read or converse. Guest rooms are simply furnished, with comfortable beds, but most don't have windows and can be rather dark. The hotel is at the intersection of calles 60 and 51, 2 blocks north of the Santa Lucía Park.

Posada Toledo. Calle 58 no. 487, 97000 Mérida, Yuc. ☎ **9/923-1690.** Fax 9/923-2256. E-mail: hptoledo@finred.com.mx. 23 units. A/C. $30–$35 double. MC, V. Free parking next door.

This hotel's charm lies in the fact that so much of the original domestic architecture (it was an old mansion) survived the conversion to a hotel. Furniture, decoration, paintings, details of design—from all this one gleans an uncontrived view of the past. As is typical in such old *casonas,* some guest rooms were meant to impress, while others were an unselfconscious expression of simple domesticity; hence there is a great difference—make sure you get one you like. Two of the grandest rooms, with ornate cornices and woodwork, have been converted into a large suite. Those on the third floor (not originally part of the house) are comfortable and have a rooftop terrace. There are a couple of common rooms, a beautiful courtyard lobby, and a restaurant. The hotel's location at the intersection of calles 58 and 57 is very convenient.

WHERE TO DINE

The people of Mérida have definite ideas and traditions about food. Certain dishes are always associated with a particular day of the week. In households across the city, *puchero* (a kind of stew) is served every Sunday. Many Meridianos will tell you that Sundays feel incomplete without this dish. On Mondays, if you go to any restaurant that caters to locals, you are sure to find *frijol con puerco,* another dish that a lot of Meridianos don't miss. Likewise, *potaje* on Thursday; fish, of course, on Friday; and *chocolomo* on Saturday. These dishes are heavy and slow to digest; they are for eating at the midday meal and are not suitable for supper. What's more, Meridianos don't believe that seafood, no matter how it's prepared, is a healthy food to eat at night. All seafood restaurants in Mérida close by 6 pm unless they cater to tourists. The preferred supper food is turkey (which, by the way, is said to be high in tryptophane—a soporific), and it's best served in the traditional *antojitos—salbutes* and *panuchos.* The best of these that I've eaten were at a well-known restaurant in the village of Kanasín, on the outskirts of Mérida, called *La Susana Interncional.* Practically the entire menu is based on turkey. The only way to get there is by taxi, and then you have to come up with a taxi for the return, but if you are a fairly large party, it's worth organizing the expedition.

Another thing you will notice about Mérida is that it has a surprising number of Middle Eastern restaurants. The city received a large influx of Lebanese immigrants around 1900. This population has had a strong influence of local society to the point where *kibbe* is considered to be as Yucatecan as pizza is considered to be American.

EXPENSIVE

Alberto's Continental. Calle 64 no. 482. ☎ **9/928-5367.** Reservations recommended. Main courses $8–$19. AE, MC, V. Daily 1pm–11pm. LEBANESE/YUCATECAN/ITALIAN.

Large and elegantly furnished dining rooms are built around a wonderful old patio framed in Moorish arches. Elegant floors, furniture, decoration, and lighting create a mood best enjoyed at night. There's a sampler plate of four Lebanese favorites, plus traditional Yucatecan specialties, such as *pollo pibil* and fish Celestún (bass stuffed with shrimp). Polish off your selections with Turkish coffee. Alberto's is at the corner of calles 57 and 64.

✪ **La Casa del Paseo.** Paseo de Montejo no. 465. ☎ **9/920-0528.** Main courses $8–$15. AE, MC, V. Daily 1pm–1am. INTERNATIONAL.

Set in one of the lovely mansions on the Paseo de Montejo, this restaurant offers polish and sophistication. The service is excellent, the menu is grand, and the cooking wonderful. Where to begin? Perhaps with a fresh mozarella salad or salmon carpaccio or mushrooms Provençcal. For main dishes, consider the daily specials; if you want something light, the stuffed chicken breast "pechuga suiza" is good; if something more meaty is called for, try the "tres mosquiteros," three grilled beef filets, each with a different sauce. Between calle 35 and Av. Colón, two doors down from the American consulate.

✪ **Virrey de Mendoza.** Calle 60 no. 327. ☎ **9/925-3082.** Main courses $7–$16. AE, MC, V. Daily 12:30–11:30. MEXICAN/YUCATECAN. Parking.

The Virrey de Mendoza offers a peerless dining experience. The food and service are superb, while other essential matters—furniture, lighting, and surroundings—are all handled thoughtfully. The Mexican food is the best in town. Notable house specialties include a poblano chile stuffed with crab and covered in a lobster sauce; filet mignon with cilantro, mushrooms, and olive oil; chicken breast in a sauce of chile *pasilla* and orange; and *huitlacoche* crêpes. My one criticism of the food is that the chef (like most cooks throughout the Yucatán) thinks very highly of Gouda cheese and uses it in dishes for which stronger domestic cheeses are better suited. Across from the Hyatt.

MODERATE

✪ **El Pórtico del Peregrino.** Calle 57 no. 501. ☎ **9/928-6163.** Reservations recommended. Main courses $6–$13. AE, MC, V. Daily noon–11pm. MEXICAN/INTERNATIONAL.

El Pórtico is a favorite among locals and visitors alike. It exudes charm and comfort with a distinctive Mérida flavor. The interior is a lovely garden with three dining areas—two air-conditioned rooms and a patio (one room is nonsmoking, a rarity in Mexico). The menu offers soups (the *sopa de tortilla* is excellent), seafood (a seafood platter or grilled gulf shrimp), and Yucatecan specialties (*pollo pibil*), and other favorites such as baked eggplant with chicken and cheese, and coconut ice cream topped with Kahlúa. The restaurant is 2 blocks north of the main square between calles 60 and 62.

Restaurant Los Almendros. Calle 50A no. 493. ☎ **9/928-5459.** Main courses $4–$9; daily special $5–$9. AE, MC, V. Daily 10am–11pm. YUCATECAN.

If a tourist in Mérida asks where to eat Yucatecan food, locals will inevitably suggest this place because of its reputation. After all, this was the first place to offer tourists such Yucatecan specialties as *cochinita pibil, salbutes, panuchos papadzules,* and *poc chuc.* The menu even comes with color photographs to facilitate acquaintance with these strange-sounding dishes. The food is okay, and not much of a risk, but you can find better food elsewhere. Still, it's a safe place to start getting acquainted with Yucatecan food, and it's such an institution that the idea of a guidebook that doesn't mention this restaurant is unthinkable. It's 5 blocks east of calle 60, facing the Parque de la Mejorada.

Santa Lucía. Calle 60 no. 481. ☎ **9/928-5957.** Main courses $5–$15. MC, V. Reservations recommended. Daily 4pm–2am. YUCATECAN/MEXICAN.

Bistro-like in size and atmosphere, with live music nightly, the restaurant is Mexican in almost every other respect. Judging from the menu, the owners have a sense of humor—the shellfish and ceviche platter is called "Viagra Especial Para Dos." If you want to sample Yucatecan food, you can try the combination platter; the *chiles rellenos* are also good; and the *chuleta yucateca,* too. This place is just before Santa Lucía park.

INEXPENSIVE

Café Alameda. Calle 58 no. 474. ☎ **9/928-3635.** Main courses $2–$4. No credit cards. Daily 7:30am–6pm. MIDDLE EASTERN/MEXICAN/VEGETARIAN.

The trappings are simple and informal (metal tables, plastic chairs) and it's a good place for catching a light meal. The trick here is figuring out the Spanish names for popular Middle Eastern dishes. *Kibbe* is *"quebbe bola,"* not *"quebbe cruda,"* hummus is *"garbanza,"* and shish kebab is *"alambre."* I leave it to you to figure out what a spinach pie is called (and they're excellent). Café Alameda is a treat for vegetarians, and the umbrella-shaded tables in the patio are perfect for morning coffee and pastries. The cafe is located between calles 55 and 57.

✪ **Restaurant Amaro.** Calle 59 no. 507 interior 6. ☎ **9/928-2451.** Main courses $3–$4.50. No credit cards. Mon–Sat 8:30am–11pm. REGIONAL/VEGETARIAN.

This restaurant serves food in a pleasant courtyard beneath the canopy of a large orchid tree. The menu offers many interesting and delicious vegetarian dishes such as the *crema de calabacitas* soup (cream of squash), the apple salad, and the avocado pizza. There is also a limited menu of fish and chicken dishes; try the Yucatecan chicken. Also try the *chaya* water (*chaya* is a leafy vegetable that was a mainstay of the Maya diet before the arrival of the Spanish). All desserts are made in the house. It's a little north of the Plaza Mayor between calles 60 and 62.

Vito Corleone. Calle 59 no. 508 between calles 60 and 62. ☎ **9/928-5777.** Main courses $2–$5. No credit cards. Daily 9:30am–11:30pm. PIZZA.

The reason to come here is the pizza. The tables by the sidewalk are the only bearable places to sit when it's warm, since the oven casts off incredible heat (you can also order a pizza to go). Another section upstairs in the back might be tolerable. The thin-crusted pizzas are smoky and savory. Between calles 60 and 62.

MÉRIDA AFTER DARK

For nighttime entertainment, see "Festivals & Special Events in Mérida," above, or check out the theaters included below.

Teatro Peón Contreras, at calles 60 and 57, and Teatro Ayala, on calle 60 at calle 61, both feature a wide range of performing artists from around the world. Stop in and see what's showing.

Mérida has a club scene that offers everything from ubiquitous rock/disco to some one-of-a-kind spots that are nothing like what you find back home. Most of the discos are in the big hotels or on Paseo de Montejo. For live music and entertainment, try one or more of the places listed below.

El Trovador Bohemio. Calle 55 no. 504. ☎ **9/923-0385.** 9pm to 3am. Cover $1.25.

It's hard to overstate the importance of *música de trio* or *trova* in Mexican popular culture. Boleros may have been at their most popular in the 1940s and 1950s, but every new heartthrob in Mexican pop music feels compelled to release a new version of the classics at some point in his/her career. I like the originals best, and so do most Mexicans. If you know something of this music and are curious about it, El Trovador is your chance to hear how the music should be played. And if you understand collo-quial Spanish, all the better; the language of boleros is vivid, passionate, and quite Mexican—definitely a unique cultural experience. El Trovador is small and dark, and everything is red. The best time to go is Thursday through Saturday. This place faces the Santa Lucía Park.

Pancho's. Calle 59 no. 509. ☎ **9/923-0949.** 6pm to 3am. 2-drink minimum if you do not order food.

If you take this place seriously, you won't like it. Waiters in bandoliers and oversized sombreros, walls adorned with blow-ups of Revolution-era photos, and assorted emblems of Mexican identity—Pancho's, which serves Tex-Mex and international food, is a parody of the tourist attraction, a place for drinking beer and losing the occa-sional *grito.* Live music is performed in the courtyard, beginning at 9pm on most nights, 10:30pm on Saturdays. The five-piece band is quite good, with its large reper-toire of cover tunes; it'll crank out salsa, rock, and jazz.

ECOTOURS & ADVENTURE TRIPS

Recently there's been an explosion of companies that organize nature and adventure tours of the Yucatán Peninsula, but one outfit that's been doing this for a long time and has a great track record is **Ecoturismo Yucatán,** calle 3 no. 235, Col. Pensiones, 97219 Mérida, Yuc. (☎ **9/920-2772;** fax 9/925-9047; www.ecoyuc.com.mx; e-mail: info@ecoyuc.com.mx). It's run by Alfonso and Roberta Escobedo, who create itiner-aries to meet just about any special or general interest you may have for going to the Yucatán or southern Mexico. Alfonso has been creating adventure and nature tours for over a dozen years. Specialties include archeology, bird-watching, natural history, and kayaking. They also are working on tours that explore contemporary Maya culture and life as it is lived today in villages in the Yucatán. Package and customized tours are available.

SIDE TRIPS FROM MÉRIDA
IZAMAL

Izamal is a sleepy town some 50 miles to the east of Mérida. It's an easy day-trip in a car, and you can visit the famous Franciscan convent of San Antonio de Padua, and the ruins of four large pyramids that still overlook the center of town, one of which is partially reconstructed to give the viewer an idea of how they must have appeared before their destruction. Life in Izamal is easy going in the extreme, as evidenced by the *victorias,* the horse-drawn buggies that serve as taxis here. Even if you come by car, you should make a point of touring the town in one of these.

If you're of the slow-boat-to-China school of travel, the best way to visit Izamal is by train on the **Izamal Express,** which leaves every Sunday at 8pm and returns before

5:30pm. "Express" is a misnomer; the train actually moves along at a stately 30 to 40 miles an hour, but the rail car is air-conditioned and comfortable. Your car is met by a local band of musicians who play in the endearing manner of small-town Mexico (with the musicians slipping in and out of the melody). But there's no time for fanfare; you're "whisked" away on one of the *victorias* to tour the town. The tour includes the pyramids, which are explained by a local guide, the convent, and the town center. You'll have some time to visit places on your own, such as the market. Then you sit down to a good meal at the Tumben-Lol restaurant. Here you'll be serenaded by a talented trio, and will see a floor show of traditional dancing that I found most impressive. All of this is included in the price of a ticket. Tickets are limited and should be purchased early (from most travel agencies in town). Cost is $24 per person, $15 for children.

HACIENDA HOPPING

Another kind of relaxing trip would be to one of the former haciendas that dot the countryside around Mérida. In recent years it has become a popular practice to restore these decaying haciendas to their former glory and convert them into attractions, restaurants, and even luxury hotels, usually with an ecological bent. One of the fanciest of these, and the one that gets the most press, is **Hacienda Katanchel** (☎ 9/ 920-0997). It is also one of the most expensive, offering luxury accommodations, Old World service, a pool, 650 acres of forested land, gardens, gourmet food, and excursions. Other haciendas-turned-hotels include **Hacienda Temozón** and **Hacienda Santa Rosa** (☎ 9/944-3637), and **Hacienda Blanca Flor,** in the area of the Puuc route, southeast of Uxmal (☎ 888-BLANCAF in the U.S.). **Hacienda Teya,** just outside Mérida, has a lovely restaurant. **Hacienda Yaxcopoil,** which offers tours of the old buildings and grounds, is covered below, under "en route to Uxmal."

CELESTÚN NATIONAL WILDLIFE REFUGE: FLAMINGOS & OTHER WATERFOWL

On the coast, west of Mérida, in a large area of marshland declared a biopreserve, there is a shallow estuary where fresh water mixes with water from the Gulf, creating a habitat perfect for flamingos and many other species of waterfowl. This estuary (called *ría* in Spanish), unlike other estuaries that are fed by rivers or streams, has fresh water pumped into it through about 80 *cenotes,* most of which lie underwater. It is very shallow (1 to 4 feet deep) and thickly grown with mangrove, but there is an open channel a quarter-of-a-mile wide and 30-miles long, which is sheltered from the open sea by a narrow strip of land. Along this corridor, you can take a launch to see some flamingos as they dredge the bottom of these shallows for a species of small crustacean and a particular insect that make up the bulk of their diet.

You can get here by car or bus; it's an easy 90-minute drive. (For information on buses, see "Getting There: By Bus" above.) To drive, leave from downtown Mérida by calle 57. Shortly after passing Santiago church, 57 ends, and there's a dogleg onto calle 59-A. This crosses Av. Itzáes and changes its name to Jacinto Canek; continue until you see signs for Celestún Hwy. 178. This will take you through Hunucmá where the road joins Hwy. 281, taking you to Celestún. You'll know you have arrived when you get to the bridge.

Immediately to your left after the bridge is where you get a boat for the tour. In the last couple of years, the state agency CULTUR has come into Celestún and established order where once there was chaos. You'll find modern facilities with a snack bar, clean bathrooms, and a ticket window. Prices for tours are fixed. A 75-minute tour costs $33 and can accommodate up to six people. You can join with others or hire a boat by yourself. On the tour you'll definitely see some flamingos; you'll also get to see some mangrove close up and one of the many underwater springs. Please do not urge the boatmen to get any closer to the flamingos than they are allowed to; if pestered too much, the birds will abandon the area for other, less-fitting habitat. The ride itself is quite pleasant—the water is calm, and CULTUR has supplied the boatmen with wide, flat-bottom skiffs that have canopies to shade the passengers from the sun.

In addition to flamingos, you will probably see frigate birds, pelicans, spoonbills, egrets, sandpipers, and other waterfowl feeding on shallow sandbars at any time of year. At least 15 duck species have been counted, and I saw an eagle fishing. Of the 175 bird species that come here, some 99 are permanent residents. The non-breeding flamingos remain here year-round, while the larger group of breeding flamingoes takes off around April to nest on the upper Yucatán Peninsula east of Río Lagartos, returning to Celestún in October.

After the tour, you might want to visit the fishing town of Celestún, which is a little beyond the bridge, on a wide sandy beach facing the Gulf. Here there are several seafood restaurants to choose from (they are all very similar to each other). If you want a quiet night away from Mérida, you can stay at one of the local hotels. My favorite is the **Hotel María del Carmen,** facing the water on calle 12, no. 111. (☎ **9/916-2051**). The accommodations are simple but clean and comfortable, and all come with small balconies facing the water. Rooms cost $22.

Another option would be Eco Paraíso, but that is a whole other kettle of fish.

✪ **Hotel Eco Paraíso.** Km 10 Antigua Carretera a Sisal, 97367 Celestún, Yuc. ☎ **9/ 916-2100.** Fax 9/916-2111. www.mexonline.com/eco-paraiso.htm. E-mail: buger@mail. internet.com.mx. 15 units. $188 for 2 people, double occupancy. AE, MC, V. Rates include breakfast and dinner. Free parking.

Eco Paraíso is meant to be a refuge from the modern world. It sits on a deserted stretch of beach 3-miles long, which was once part of a coconut plantation. It attracts much the same clientele as the former-haciendas-turned-luxury-hotels, but in some ways it has more going for it (like a beach, for instance). Some guests come here for a week of idleness; others use this as a base of operations for visiting the biopreserve and making trips to the Maya ruins in the interior (and the hotel does offer its own tours to various places). Rooms are quite private in that each is an independent bungalow with *palapa* roof. They come with two queen-size beds, sitting area, safety deposit box, ceiling fans, and a private porch with hammocks. The hotel has a swimming pool and a club house with restaurant. The food I had was very good, and service was outstanding. What's more, the concept of the hotel is ecologically friendly in more than name only. Waste is composted, waste water is treated and made use of, and, in fact, the grounds of the hotel are a sort of laboratory for repopulating the area with coconut palms that are resistant to the blight that has laid waste to coconuts across the coast.

DZIBILCHALTÚN: MAYA RUINS AND MUSEUM

This destination makes for a quick morning trip that will get you back to Mérida in time for a siesta, or it could be part of a longer trip to Progreso, Uaymitún, and Xcambó. It's now part of a national park, located 9 miles north of Mérida along the Progreso road and 3 miles east off the highway. To get here from Mérida take calle 60 all the way out and follow signs for Progreso and Hwy. 261. Once you're out of town, look for the sign for Dzibichaltún, which also reads Universidad del Mayab; it will point you right. After a few miles you'll see a sign for the entrance to the ruins and the museum.

Dzibilchaltún was founded about 500 B.C., flourished around A.D. 750, and was in decline long before the coming of the conquistadors, but may have been occupied until A.D. 1600, almost 100 years after the arrival of the Spaniards. Since the ruins were discovered in 1941, more than 8,000 buildings have been mapped. The site covers an area of almost 10-square-miles with a central core of almost 65 acres, but the area of prime interest is limited to the buildings surrounding two large plazas next to the *cenote,* and another building, the Temple of the Seven Dolls, connected to these by a *sacbé.* Dzibilchaltún means "place of the stone writing," and at least 25 stelae have been found, many of them reused in buildings constructed after the original ones were covered or destroyed.

The best thing to do is to start with the **Museo del Pueblo Maya,** which is quite good. It's open from Tuesday to Sunday from 8am to 4pm. Admission is $4. The museum's collection includes artifacts from various sites in the Yucatán. Explanations are printed in bilingual format, and are fairly thorough. Objects include a beautiful example of a plumed serpent from Chichén Itzá and a finely designed incense vessel from Palenque. From this general view of the Maya civilization, the museum moves on to exhibit specific artifacts found at the site of Dzibichaltún, including the rather curious dolls that have given one structure its name. Then there's an exhibit on Maya culture in historical and present times, including a lovely collection of *huipils,* the woven blouses that Indian women wear. From here a door leads out to the site itself.

The first thing you come to is the *sacbé* that connects the two areas of interest. To the left is the **Temple of the Seven Dolls.** The temple's doorways are lined up with the *sacbé* to catch the rising sun on spring and autumnal equinoxes. To the right are the buildings grouped around the Cenote Xlacah, the sacred well, and a complex of buildings around **Structure 38;** the **Central Group** of temples. The Yucatán State Department of Ecology has added nature trails and published a booklet (in Spanish) of birds and plants seen at various points along the mapped trail. The booklet tells where in the park you are likely to see specific plants and birds.

PROGRESO, UAYMITÚN & XCAMBÓ: GULF COAST CITY, FLAMINGO LOOKOUT & MORE MAYA RUINS

For another beach escape, go to the port of Progreso, Mérida's weekend beach resort. This is where Meridianos have their vacation houses and where they come in large numbers for the months of July and August. At other times the crowds and traffic are nowhere to be seen, and you can enjoy the Gulf waters without fuss. Along the Malecón, a wide oceanfront drive that extends the length of a sandy beach, you can pull over and enjoy a swim anywhere that you like. The water here is not as blue as on the Caribbean side, but it is clean. A long pier, or *muelle* (pronounced *mway*-yeh), extends several miles into the bay to service oceangoing ships. Progreso is also the part-time home to some Americans and Canadians escaping northern winters.

Along or near the Malecón are several hotels and restaurants, including **Le Saint Bonnet** (Malecón at calle 78, ☎ **9/935-2299**), where locals dine on fresh seafood. It has a large menu with several good dishes; for something very Mexican, I recommend trying the *pescado al ajillo.*

From Mérida, buses to Progreso leave the special bus station at calle 62 no. 524, between calles 65 and 67, every 15 minutes during the day, starting at 5am. The trip takes almost an hour and costs $2.

If you've got a car, you might want to drive down the coastal road east towards Telchac Puerto. After about 20 minutes you'll see on your right, by the side of the road, a large, solid-looking wooden observation tower for viewing flamingos. There will be a sign reading **Uaymitún.** This was constructed by the state agency CULTUR, who operates it and provides binoculars free of charge for any who want to make the climb to the top. A few years ago, flamingos from Celestún migrated here and established a colony. Your chances of spotting some are good, and this way you don't have to pay for a boat. Twenty minutes farther down this road, there's a turn-off for the road to Dzemul, and a few minutes after that you'll see a sign that reads Xcambó that points to the right, and it's about 100 yards from there. This city is thought to have been a center for maritime trading, and perhaps it made use of some nearby salt flats to produce salt for trade. The central ceremonial center is completely reconstructed, and the archeologists are finding a number of graves. After viewing these ruins, you can continue on the same road through the small towns of Dzemul and Baca. At Baca, take Hwy 176 back to Mérida.

EN ROUTE TO UXMAL

There are two routes to Uxmal, about 50 miles south of Mérida. The most direct is Highway 261 via Uman and Muna. On the way you can stop to see Hacienda Yaxcopoil, which is 20 miles from Mérida. From downtown, take calle 65 or 69 to avenida Itzáes and turn left; this will feed you on to the highway.

If you have the time and would like a more scenic route, try the meandering State Highway 18. This is sometimes known as the Convent Route, but all tourism hype aside, it makes for a good drive. You could make your trip to Uxmal into a loop by going one way and coming back the other, but with so many stops, it would take the better part of 2 days to complete the trip, especially if you want to see the ruins of the Puuc Route. The best way to do this would be to take the long route on Hwy 18, arriving in Uxmal in time to see the sound and light show, then overnight in Uxmal and see the ruins early in the morning before returning to Mérida (the only drawback here is that you might be forced to buy tickets twice to see Uxmal). All the attractions on these routes have the same hours: churches are open from 10am to 2pm and 4 to 6pm; ruins are open from 8am to 5pm.

HIGHWAY 261: YAXCOPOIL & MUNA   Ten miles beyond Uman along Highway 261 is Yaxcopoil (yash-koh-poe-*eel*), a fascinating 19th-century hacienda on the right side of the road between Mérida and Uxmal. It's difficult to reach by bus.

This hacienda, dating from 1864, was originally a cattle ranch comprising over 23,000 acres. Around 1900, it was converted to *henequen* production (for the manufacture of rope). Take half an hour to tour the house (which boasts 18-foot ceilings and original furniture), factory, outbuildings, and museum. You'll see that such haciendas were the administrative, commercial, and social centers of vast private domains; they were almost little principalities carved out of the Yucatecan jungle. It's open Monday through Saturday from 8am to 6pm and Sunday from 9am to 1pm.

HIGHWAY 18: KANASÍN, ACANCEH, MAYAPÁN & TICUL   Take calle 63 east to Circuito Colonias, turn right; then make a left at calle 69, which at that level is a two-way street. This feeds you on to Hwy. 18 to Kanasín (kahn-ah-*seen*) and then Acanceh (ah-kahn-*keh*). In **Kanasín,** watch for signs that say CIRCUKACIÓN or DESVIACIÓN. As in many Yucatán towns, you're being redirected to follow a one-way street through the urban area. Go past the market, church, and the main square on your left and continue straight out of town. (On this route you'll be passing through a lot of small villages without any road signs, so get used to poking your head out the window and *saying "Buenos días, dónde está el camino para . . . ?"* This is what I do, and I ask more than one person.) The next village you come to, at km 10, is **San Antonio Tehuit,** an old *henequen* hacienda. At km 13 is **Tepich,** another hacienda village, with those funny little *henequen*-cart tracks crisscrossing the main road. After Tepich comes **Petectunich** and finally **Acanceh.**

Across the street from and overlooking Acanceh's church is a restored pyramid. On top of this pyramid under a makeshift roof are some recently discovered large stucco figures of Maya deities that are fascinating. The caretaker, Mario Uicab, will find you and guide you up to see them and give you a little explanation if you speak Spanish. Admission is $2. There are some other ruins a couple of blocks away called **El Palacio de los Estucos.** In 1908 a stucco mural was found here in mint condition. Since then it was left exposed and has deteriorated somewhat. Now it is sheltered, and you can still easily distinguish the painted figures in their original colors.

From Acanceh's main square, turn right (around the statue of a smiling deer) and head for **Tecoh** on a good road. Tecoh's parish church sits on a massive pre-Columbian raised platform—the remains of a ceremonial complex that was sacrificed to build the church. With its rough stone and simple twin towers that are crumbling around the edges, the church looks ancient. Inside are three carved *retablos* covered in gold leaf that are unmistakably Indian in style. In 1998 they were cleaned and refurbished and are now quite dazzling.

Continuing on, shortly after the village of Telchaquillo, a sign on the right side of the road will point to the entrance to the ruins of Mayapán.

RUINS OF MAYAPÁN

Founded, according to Maya lore, by the man-god Kukulkán (Quetzalcoatl in central México) in about A.D. 1007, Mayapán ranked in importance with Chichén-Itzá and Uxmal and covered at least $2^1/_2$-square-miles. For more than 2 centuries it was the capital of a Maya confederation of city-states that included Chichén and Uxmal. But before the year 1200, the rulers of Mayapán ended the confederation by attacking and conquering Chichén and by forcing the rulers of Uxmal to live as vassals in Mayapán. Eventually, a successful revolt by the captive Maya rulers brought down Mayapán, which was abandoned during the mid-1400s.

In the last few years, the archeologists and their teams have been very busy excavating and rebuilding the city, and work continues. Several buildings bordering the principal plaza have been reconstructed, including one that is similar to El Castillo in Chichén Itzá. In the process, murals and stucco figures have been discovered that provide more grist for the mill of conjecture: atlantes, skeletal soldiers, macaws, entwined snakes, a stucco jaguar. This place is definitely worth stopping to see.

The site is open daily from 8am to 5pm. Admission is $2; free on Sunday; use of a personal video camera is $4.

FROM MAYAPÁN TO TICUL   The road is a good one, but directional signs through the villages are almost nonexistent; stop and ask directions frequently. The streets in these villages are full of children, bicycles, and livestock, so drive carefully and keep an eye out for the unmarked *topes.* From Mayapán, continue along Highway 18 to **Tekit** (5 miles). The road narrows, then you're on to **Mama,** or Mamita, as it is sometimes called. Stop to see the recently rescued former convent and the church with its lovely façade. Inside are several fascinating *retablos* sculpted in a native form of baroque. In the restoration of these buildings, colonial murals and designs were uncovered and restored. Make sure to get a peek at them in the sacristy. From Mama you head to Ticul, a large (for this area) market town with a couple of simple hotels and the original Los Almendros restaurant.

TICUL

Best known for the cottage industry of *huipil* embroidery (native blouses) and for the manufacture of ladies' dress shoes, Ticul isn't the most exciting stop on the Puuc route—but it's a convenient place to wash up and spend the night. It's also a center for large-size commercially produced pottery; most of the widely sold sienna-colored pottery painted with Maya designs comes from here. If it's a cloudy, humid day, the potters may not be working, since part of the process requires sun drying, but they still welcome visitors to purchase finished pieces.

One place worth a visit is **Arte Maya,** calle 23 no. 301, Carretera Ticul Muna (☎ **9/972-1095;** fax 9/972-0334). It is owned and operated by Luis Echeverría and Lourdes Castillo. This shop and gallery produces museum-quality art in alabaster, stone, jade, and ceramics. Much of the work is done as it was in Maya times; soft stone or ceramic is smoothed with the leaf of the siricote tree, and colors are derived from plant sources. If you buy from them, hang onto the written description of your purchase—their work looks so authentic that U.S. Customs has delayed entry of people carrying their wares, thinking that they're smuggling real Maya artifacts into the U.S.

Ticul is only 12 miles northeast of Uxmal, so thrifty tourists stay here instead of the more expensive hotels at the ruins. I recommend the **Hotel Plaza,** calle 23 no. 202 (on the town square near intersection with calle 26). It's a modest hotel, as you would expect in a town of this sort, but clean and comfortable, and has been recently remodeled. A double room with air-conditioning costs $27, $22 without air-conditioning; in both cases there's a 5% charge if you want to pay with a credit card (MC, V). Get an interior room if you're looking for quiet. Once in Ticul, you can do one of two things: head straight for Uxmal via Santa Elena or loop around the Puuc Route, which gets to Santa Elena the long way. For information on the Puuc route, see below.

FROM TICUL TO UXMAL   Follow the main street (calle 23) west through town. Turn left at the sign to Santa Elena. It's 10 miles to Santa Elena; then, at Highway 261, cut back right for about 2 miles to Uxmal. In Santa Elena, by the side of Highway 261 is a clean restaurant with good food called El Chac Mool.

2 The Ruins of Uxmal

50 miles (80km) SW of Mérida; 12 miles (19km) W of Ticul; 12 miles (19km) S of Muna

One of the highlights of a Yucatán vacation, the ruins of Uxmal—noted for their rich geometric stone façades—are the most beautiful on the peninsula. Remains of an agricultural society indicate that the area was occupied possibly as early as 800 B.C. However, the great building period took place 1,000 years later, between A.D. 700 and 1000, during which time the population probably reached 25,000. After the year 1000, Uxmal fell under the sway of the Xiú princes (who may have come from central Mexico). In the 1440s, the Xiú conquered Mayapán, and not long afterward the glories of the Maya ended when the Spanish conquistadors arrived.

Close to Uxmal, four other sites—**Sayil, Kabah, Xlapak,** and **Labná**—are worth visiting. With Uxmal, these ruins are collectively known as the **Puuc route,** for the Puuc hills of this part of the Yucatán. See the "Puuc Maya Sites" section, below, if you want to explore these sites.

ESSENTIALS

GETTING THERE & DEPARTING   By Car   Two routes to Uxmal from Mérida, via Highway 261 or via State Highway 18, are described in "En Route to Uxmal," at the end of the Mérida section above. *Note:* There's no gasoline at Uxmal.

BY BUS   See "Getting There & Departing" in "Mérida," above, for information about bus service between Mérida and Uxmal. To return, wait for the bus on the highway at the entrance to the ruins. To see the sound-and-light show, don't bother with regular buses, sign up with one of the tour operators in Mérida.

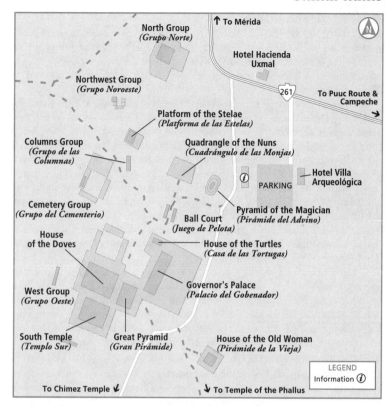

ORIENTATION Uxmal consists of the archaeological site and its visitor center, five hotels, and a highway restaurant. The visitor center, open daily from 8am to 9pm, has a restaurant (with good coffee); toilets; a first-aid station; shops selling soft drinks, ice cream, film, batteries, and books; and a state-run Casa de Artesanía. There are no phones except at the hotels. Most public buses pick up and let off passengers on the highway at the entrance to the ruins. The site itself is open daily from 8am to 5pm. Admission to the archaeological site is $8, which includes admission to the nightly sound-and-light show, but a Sunday visit to Uxmal and other recommended sites nearby will be free. There's a $4 charge for each video camera you bring in. Parking costs $1.

Guides at the entrance of Uxmal give tours in a variety of languages and charge $20 for either a single person or a group. The guides frown on unrelated individuals joining a group. As usual, they'd rather charge you as a solo visitor, but you can ask other English speakers if they'd like to join you in a tour and split the cost. As at other sites, the guides vary in quality, but you will see areas and architectural details you might otherwise miss.

Included in the price of admission is a 45-minute **sound-and light show,** staged each evening at 8pm. It's in Spanish, but headsets are available for rent ($3) for listening to the program in several languages. After the impressive show, the chant *Chaaac, Chaaac* will echo in your mind for weeks.

A TOUR OF THE RUINS

THE PYRAMID OF THE MAGICIAN As you enter the ruins, note the *chultún,* or cistern, where Uxmal stored its water. Unlike most of the major Mayan sites, Uxmal has no river or *cenote* to supply fresh water—perhaps the most mystifying feature of what was once a large and populous city. No wonder they seem so obsessed with Chaac, the rain god.

Just beyond the *chultún,* the remarkable Pyramid of the Magician (also called Pyramid of the Dwarf) looms majestically on the right. The name comes from a legend about a mystical dwarf who reached adulthood in a single day after being hatched from an egg, and who built this pyramid in one night. Beneath it are five earlier structures, which is not an uncommon feature of Maya pyramids since it was the practice of the Maya to build new structures atop old ones at regular intervals. The pyramid is unique because of its rounded sides, height, steepness, and the doorway on the opposite (west) side near the top. The doorway's heavy ornamentation, a characteristic of the Chenes style, features 12 stylized masks of the rain god Chaac.

Next to the Pyramid of the Magician, to the west, is the Nunnery Quadrangle, and left of it is a partially restored ball court, south of which are several large complexes. The biggest building among them is the Governor's Palace, and behind it lies the massive, largely unrestored Great Pyramid. In the distance is the Dovecote (House of the Doves), a small building with a lacy roof comb (false front) that looks like the perfect apartment complex for pigeons. From this vantage point, note how Uxmal is unique among Maya sites for its use of huge terraces constructed to support the buildings; look closely and you'll see that the Governor's Palace is not on a natural hill but rather on a giant platform of packed earth, as is the nearby Nunnery Quadrangle.

THE NUNNERY QUADRANGLE The 16th-century Spanish historian Fray Diego López de Cogullado gave the building its name because it resembled a Spanish monastery. Possibly it was a military academy or a training school for princes, who may have lived in the 70-odd rooms. The buildings were constructed at different times: The northern one was first, then the southern, followed by the eastern, then the western. The western building has the most richly decorated façade, composed of intertwined stone snakes and numerous masks of the hook-nosed rain god Chaac.

The corbeled archway to the south was once the main entrance to the Nunnery complex; as you head toward it out of the quadrangle, look above each doorway in that section for the motif of a Maya cottage, or *nah,* still seen throughout the Yucatán today.

THE BALL COURT A small ball court is conserved to prevent further decay, but compare it later in your trip to the giant, magnificently restored court at Chichén-Itzá.

THE TURTLE HOUSE Up on the terrace south of the ball court is a little temple decorated with colonnade motif on the façade and a border of turtles. Though it's small and simple, its harmony makes it one of the gems of Uxmal.

THE GOVERNOR'S PALACE In its size and intricate stonework, this rivals the Temple of the Magician as Uxmal's masterwork—an imposing three-level edifice with a 320-foot-long mosaic façade done in the Puuc style. Puuc means "hilly country," the name given to the hills nearby and thus to the predominant style of pre-Hispanic architecture found here. Uxmal has many examples of Puuc decoration, characterized by elaborate stonework from door tops to the roofline. Fray Cogullado also gave this building its name. The Governor's Palace may have been just that—the administrative center of the Xiú principality, which included the region around Uxmal. It probably had astrological significance as well. For years, scholars pondered why this building was constructed slightly turned from adjacent buildings. Originally they thought the strange alignment was because of the *sacbé* (ceremonial road) that starts at this building and ends 11 miles away at the ancient city of Kabah. But recently scholars of archaeoastronomy (a relatively new science that studies the placement of archaeological sites in relation to the stars), discovered that the central doorway, which is larger than the others, is in perfect alignment with Venus.

Before you leave the Governor's Palace, note the elaborately stylized headdress patterned in stone over the central doorway. As you stand back from the building on the east side, note how the 103 stone masks of Chaac undulate across the façade like a serpent and end at the corners where there are columns of masks.

THE GREAT PYRAMID   A massive, partially restored nine-level structure, it has interesting motifs of birds, probably macaws, on its façade, as well as a huge mask. The view from the top is wonderful.

THE DOVECOTE   This building is remarkable in that roof combs weren't a common feature of temples in the Puuc hills, although you'll see one (of a very different style) on El Mirador at Sayil.

WHERE TO STAY

There are some lovely hotels in Uxmal. If occupancy is low, you might bargain for a room. If you're on a tight budget, consider this a day-trip or stay in nearby Ticul.

✪ **Hotel Hacienda Uxmal.** Km 80 Carretera Mérida–Uxmal, 97840 Uxmal, Yuc. ☎ **9/976-2011.** (Reservations: Mayaland Resorts, Av. Colón 502, 97000 Mérida, Yuc.; ☎ **800/235-4079** in the U.S., or 9/925-2122; fax 9/925-7022.) 80 units. A/C, TV. High season $160 double. Low season $140 double. AE, MC, V. Free guarded parking.

One of my favorites, this is also the oldest hotel in Uxmal. Located just up the highway from the ruins, it was built as the headquarters for the archaeology staff years ago. Rooms are large and airy, exuding an impression of a well-kept yesteryear, with patterned tile floors, heavy furniture, and well-screened windows. Guest rooms surround a handsome central garden courtyard with towering royal palms, a bar, and a pool. Other facilities include a dining room, gift shop, and a second pool. A guitar trio usually plays on the open patio in the evenings. Checkout time is 1pm, so you can spend the morning at the ruins and take a swim before you hit the road again.

Mayaland Resorts, owner of the hotel, also runs the **Hotel Lodge at Uxmal,** next door. It has a striking appearance and lovely rooms, but the restaurant isn't good, and I like the comforting feel of the older hotel better. Mayaland has a transfer service between the hotel and Mérida for about $30 one-way.

Rancho Uxmal. Km 70 Carretera Mérida–Uxmal, 97840 Uxmal, Yuc. No local phone. (Reservations: Sr. Macario Cach Cabrera, calle 26 no. 156, Ticul, Yuc., 97860; ☎ **9/949-0526** or 9/923-1576.) 18 units. $27–$32 double; $3 per person campsite. No credit cards. Free guarded parking.

This modest hotel is an exception to the high-priced places near Uxmal, and it gets better every year. Air-conditioning has been added to 4 of the rooms, all of which have good screens, hot-water showers, and 24-hour electricity. The restaurant is good; a full meal of *poc chuc,* rice, beans, and tortillas costs about $5, and breakfast is $2.25 to $3. It's a long hike to the ruins from here, but the manager may help you flag down a passing bus or *combi* or even drive you himself if he has time. A primitive campground out back offers electrical hookups and use of a shower. The hotel is 2¼ miles north of the ruins on Highway 261.

Villa Arqueológica. Ruinas Uxmal, 97844 Uxmal, Yuc. ☎ **800/258-2633** in the U.S. 43 units. A/C. $90 double. AE, MC, V. Rates include continental breakfast. Free guarded parking.

This hotel is operated by Club Med, but it is just a hotel and not like one of their self-contained vacation villages. It offers a beautiful two-story layout around a garden patio and a pool. At guests' disposal are a tennis court, a library, and an audiovisual show on the ruins in English, French, and Spanish. Each of the modern, smallish rooms has two oversize single beds that fit into spaces that are walled on three sides. For this reason, I don't recommend this hotel for tall people. You can also ask for rates that include full or half board.

WHERE TO DINE

Besides the hotel restaurants mentioned above and the restaurant at the visitor's center, there are a few other dining choices.

Café-Bar Nicte-Ha. In the Hotel Hacienda Uxmal. ☎ **9/976-2011.** Main courses $5–$8; fixed-price lunch $9. AE, MC, V. Daily 1–8pm. MEXICAN.

This small restaurant attached to the Hotel Hacienda Uxmal is a lovely place to eat. The food is decent, though the prices tend to be high. If you eat here, take full advantage of the experience and spend a few hours by the pool near the cafe: Its use is free to customers. This is a favorite spot for bus tours that fill the place to overcrowding, so come early.

Las Palapas. Hwy. 261. No phone. Breakfast $3; *comida corrida* $3.75. No credit cards. Daily 9am–6pm (comida corrida served 1–4pm). MEXICAN/YUCATECAN.

Three miles north of the ruins on the road to Mérida, you'll find this pleasant open-air restaurant with a large *palapa* roof. The amiable owner, María Cristina Choy, has the lowest prices around. Individual diners can sometimes become lost in the crowd if a busload of tourists arrives, but otherwise the service is fine and the food quite good. There's also a small gift shop with regional crafts and a few books.

THE PUUC MAYA ROUTE & VILLAGE OF OXKUTZCAB

South and east of Uxmal are several other Maya cities worth exploring. Though smaller in scale than either Uxmal or Chichén-Itzá, each contains gems of Maya architecture. The façade of masks on the Palace of Masks at **Kabah,** the enormous palace at **Sayil,** and the fantastic caverns of **Loltún** may be among the high points of your trip. Also along the way are the **Xlapak** and **Labná ruins** and the pretty village of **Oxkutzcab.**

Tips on Seeing Puuc Maya Sites

All these sites are currently undergoing excavation and reconstruction, and some buildings may be roped off when you visit. And photographers, please note: you'll find afternoon light the best. The sites are open daily from 8am to 5pm. Admission is $2 each for Sayil, Kabah, and Labná; $1.25 for Xlapak; and $4 for Loltún. All except the caves of Loltún are free on Sunday. Loltún has specific hours for tours: 9:30am, 11:00am, 12:30, 2, 3, and 4pm, but if the tour guide is there, you might persuade him to do a tour and not wait for a tour bus if you offer him a generous tip. Use of a video camera at any time costs $4, but if you're visiting Uxmal in the same day, you pay only once for video permission and present your receipt as proof at each ruin.

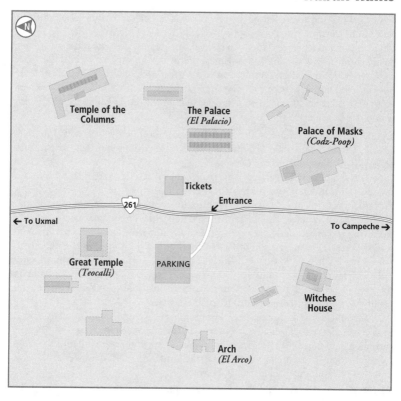

Kabah is 17 miles southeast of Uxmal. From there it's only a few miles to Sayil. Xlapak is almost walking distance (through the jungle) from Sayil, and Labná is just a bit farther east. A short drive beyond Labná brings you to the caves of Loltún. And Oxkutzcab is at the road's intersection with Highway 184, which can be followed west to Ticul or east all the way to Felipe Carrillo Puerto. If you aren't driving, a daily bus from Mérida goes to all these sites, with the exception of Loltún. (See "By Bus" under "Getting There & Departing," in Mérida, above, for more details.)

PUUC MAYA SITES

KABAH   From Uxmal to Kabah, head southwest on Highway 261 to Santa Elena (1/2 miles), then south to Kabah (8 miles). The ancient city of Kabah lies along both sides of the highway. Make a right turn into the parking lot.

The most outstanding building at Kabah is the huge **Palace of Masks,** or *Codz Poop* ("rolled-up mat"), named for its decorative motif. You'll notice it first on the right up on a terrace. Its outstanding feature is the Chenes-style façade, completely covered in a repeated pattern of 250 masks of the rain god Chaac, each one with curling remnants of Chaac's elephant-trunk-like nose. There's nothing like this façade in all of Maya architecture. For years, stone-carved parts of this building lay lined up in the weeds like pieces of a puzzle awaiting the master puzzle-solver to put them into place. Sculptures from this building are in the museums of anthropology in Mérida and Mexico City.

Just behind and to the left of the *Codz Poop* is the **Palace Group** (also called the East Group), with a fine Puuc-style colonnaded façade. Originally it had 32 rooms. On the front you see seven doors, two divided by columns, a common feature of Puuc architecture. Across the highway a large, conical dirt-and-rubble mound (on your right) was once the **Great Temple.** Past it is a **great arch,** which was much wider at one time and may have been a monumental gate into the city. A *sacbé* linked this arch to a point at Uxmal. Compare this corbeled arch to the one at Labná (below), which is in much better shape.

SAYIL   Just about 3 miles south of Kabah is the turnoff (left, which is east) to Sayil, Xlapak, Labná, Loltún, and Oxkutzcab. And 2¹/₂ miles along this road are the ruins of Sayil (which means "place of the ants").

Sayil is famous for **El Palacio.** This tremendous palace of more than 90 rooms is impressive for its size alone, but what makes it a masterpiece of Maya architecture is the building's façade that stretches across three terraced levels. Its rows of columns give it a Minoan appearance. On the second level, notice the upside-down stone figure of the diving god of bees and honey over the doorway; the same motif was used at Tulum several centuries later. The top of El Palacio affords a great view of the Puuc hills. Sometimes it's difficult to tell which are hills and which are unrestored pyramids, since little temples peep out at unlikely places from the jungle. The large circular basin on the ground below the palace is an artificial catch basin for a *chultún* (cistern); this region has no natural *cenotes* (wells) to catch rainwater.

In the jungle past El Palacio is **El Mirador,** a small temple with an oddly slotted roof comb. Beyond El Mirador, a crude stela (tall, carved stone) has a phallic idol carved on it in greatly exaggerated proportions. There is another cluster of buildings called the Southern Group, which are about a quarter-of-a-mile down a trail that branches off from the one heading to El Mirador.

XLAPAK   Xlapak (*shla*-pahk) is a small site with one building; it's 3¹/₂ miles down the road from Sayil. The Palace at Xlapak bears the masks of the rain god Chaac. You wouldn't miss much if you skipped this place.

LABNÁ   Labná, which dates from between A.D. 600 and 900, is 18 miles from Uxmal and only 1³/₄ miles past Xlapak. Descriptive placards fronting the main buildings are in Spanish, English, and German. The first thing you see on the left as you enter is **El Palacio,** a magnificent Puuc-style building much like the one at Sayil but in poorer condition. There is a large, well-conserved mask of Chaac over a doorway with eyes, a huge snout nose, and jagged teeth around a small mouth that seems on the verge of speaking. Jutting out on one corner is a highly stylized serpent's mouth out from which pops a human head with an unexpectedly serene expression. From the front, you can gaze out to the enormous grassy interior grounds flanked by vestiges of unrestored buildings and jungle.

From El Palacio, you can walk across the interior grounds on a reconstructed *sacbé* leading to Labná's **corbeled arch,** famed for its beauty and for its representation of what many such arches must have looked like at other sites. This one has been extensively restored, although only remnants of the roof comb can be seen, and it was once part of a more elaborate structure that is completely gone. Chaac's face is on the corners of one façade, and stylized Maya huts are fashioned in stone above the two small doorways.

You pass through the arch to **El Mirador,** or El Castillo, as the rubble-formed, pyramid-shaped structure is called. Towering on top is a singular room crowned with a roof comb etched against the sky.

There's a snack stand with toilets at the entrance.

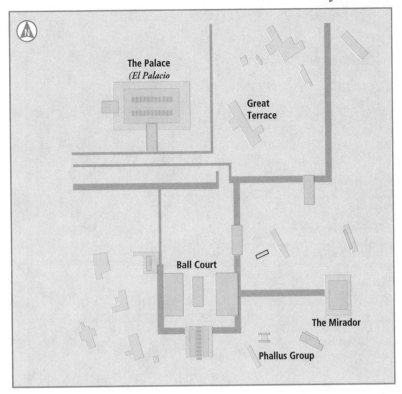

LOLTÚN   The caverns of Loltún are 18½ miles past Labná on the way to Oxkutz-cab, on the left side of the road. These fascinating caves, home of ancient Maya, were also used as a refuge during the War of the Castes (1847–1901). Inside are statuary, wall carvings and paintings, *chultúns* (cisterns), and other signs of Maya habitation. Guides will explain much of what you see. When I was there the guide spoke English, but was still a little difficult to understand.

Tours lasting 1½ hours are given daily at 9:30 and 11am and 12:30, 2, 3 and 4pm and are included in the admission price. The floor of the cavern can be slippery in places, and if you have a flashlight, take it with you. Admission is $4. What you see is quite interesting.

To return to Mérida from Loltún, drive the 4½ miles to Oxkutzcab and from there head northwest on Highway 184. It's 12 miles to Ticul and (turning north onto Highway 261 at Muna) 65 miles to Mérida.

OXKUTZCAB

Oxkutzcab (ohsh-kootz-*kahb*), 7 miles from Loltún, is the heartland of the Yucatán's fruit-growing region. Oranges abound. The tidy village of 21,000 is centered around a beautiful 16th-century church and the market. You can eat at Su Cabaña Suiza, a good restaurant in town. During the last week in October and the first week in November is the **Orange Festival,** when the village turns exuberant with a carnival and orange displays in and around the central plaza.

Labná Ruins

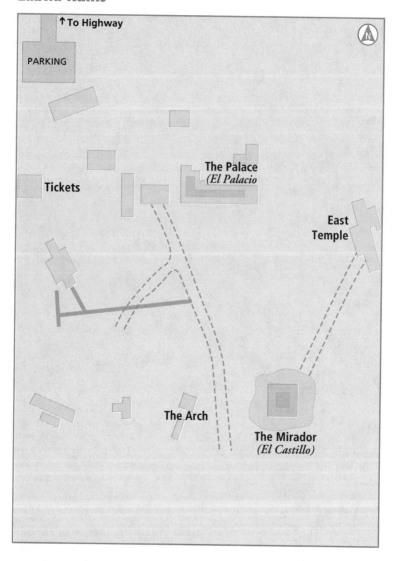

↑ To Highway

PARKING

Tickets

The Palace
(El Palacio)

East Temple

The Arch

The Mirador
(El Castillo)

EN ROUTE TO CAMPECHE

From Oxkutzcab, head back 27 miles to Sayil, and then drive south on Highway 261 to Campeche (78 miles). Along the way are several ruins and caves worth visiting.

XTACUMBILXUNA CAVES Highway 261 heads south for several miles, passing through a lofty arch marking the boundary between the states of Yucatán and Campeche. Continue on through Bolonchén de Rejón (Bolonchén means "nine wells").

About 1³/₄ miles south of Bolonchén, a sign points west to the Grutas de Xtacumbilxuna, though the sign spells it XTACUMBINXUNAN. Another sign reads: IT'S WORTH IT TO MAKE A TRIP FROM NEW YORK TO BOLONCHÉN JUST TO SEE XTACUMBINXUNAN CAVES (JOHN STEPHENS—EXPLORER). The caves are open whenever the guide is around, which is most of the time. Follow him down for the 30- or 45-minute tour in Spanish, after which a $1 to $3 tip is customary.

Legend has it that a Maya girl escaped an arranged marriage by hiding in these vast limestone caverns—which wouldn't be hard to do, as you'll see. Unlike the fascinating caves at Loltún, which are filled with traces of Maya occupation, these offer only the standard gallery of limestone shapes—a dog, an eagle, a penguin, a Madonna and child, a snake—that populate the guide's imagination.

CHENES RUINS   On your route south, you can also take a detour to see several unexcavated, unspoiled ruined cities in the Chenes style. These visits involve a bit of adventure; pack some food and water. When you get to Hopelchén, take the turnoff for Dzibalchén. When you get to Dzibalchén (25½ miles from Hopelchén), ask for directions to Hochob, San Pedro, Dzehkabtún, El Tabasqueño, and Dzibilnocac.

EDZNÁ   From Hopelchén, Highway 261 heads west, and after 26 miles you'll find yourself at the turnoff for the ruins of the city of Edzná, 12 miles farther along to the south.

Founded probably between 600 and 300 B.C. as a small agricultural settlement, it developed into a major ceremonial center over the next 1,500 years. Archaeologists estimate that to build and maintain such a complex center must have required a population in the tens of thousands. Once a network of Maya canals crisscrossed this entire area, making intensive cultivation possible.

The **Great Acropolis** is a unique five-level pyramid with a temple complete with roofcomb on top. Edzná means "house of wry faces," and no doubt there were some of those at one time. Though the buildings at Edzná were mostly in the heavily baroque Chenes, or "well-country" style, no vestige of these distinctive decorative façades remains at Edzná. Several other buildings surround an open central yard. Farther back, new excavations have revealed the **Temple of the Stone Mask,** a structure with several fine stucco masks similar to those of Kohunlich in the Río Bec region near Chetumal. The site takes only 30 minutes or less to see; it may not be worth the price of entry, especially if you've seen many other sites in the Yucatán. (*Note:* The afternoon light is best for photographing the temple.)

It's open daily from 8am to 5pm. Admission costs $3, plus $4 to use your video camera.

Back on Highway 261, it's 12 miles to the intersection with Highway 180, then another 26 miles to the very center of Campeche.

3 Campeche

157 miles (251km) SW of Mérida; 235 miles (376km) NE of Villahermosa

Campeche, capital of the state bearing the same name, is the most thoroughly restored colonial city in Mexico. It's so well restored that, in some places, I can imagine myself having traveled back in time. The façades of all the houses in the old part of town have been repaired and painted, all electrical and telephone cables have been routed underground, and the streets have been paved with stones or bricks. Several Mexican movie companies have taken advantage of this to shoot period pieces here.

Despite all this beauty, not many tourists come to Campeche. Those who do tend to be either people who have stopped on their way to the ruins at Palenque or the Rio Bec region, or the kind of travelers that are more aimless-wanderer types than purposeful sightseers. A couple of things do need to be said: Campeche is not geared to foreign tourism the way Mérida is, so expect less in the way of English translations and such at the museums, etc. And two, Campeche is a sleepy town with little in the way of nightlife.

If you are interested in seeing the ruins and biosphere reserve at Calakmul, and the rest of the ruins along the Río Bec route, see chapter 4, "Side trips from Bacalar." Calakmul is a large and important site, with the tallest pyramid in the Yucatán peninsula, and if you're going as far as Calakmul, you must stop at Balamkú. From the Campeche side you can get information and contract a tour with one of several tour operators. You might talk with a travel agency at the Hotel Delmar and arrange an overnight trip with accommodations at their Ecovillage at Chicanná.

The federal highway that leads to these sights crosses through the Rio Bec region and eventually arrives at Chetumal on Yucatán's southern Caribbean coast. From there you can head up the coast and complete a loop of the peninsula.

Campeche has an interesting history. The first contact between white men and the natives occurred in 1517 when Francisco de Córdoba landed here while exploring the coast. Supposedly, it was the first place on the mainland where a mass was celebrated. Francisco de Montejo the Elder established a settlement here in 1531, but the Spaniards were soon expelled by the Indians. Finally, it was refounded by Montejo the Younger in 1540.

For the next century, the town was plagued by pirates who repeatedly harrassed the city. The list of pirates who have attacked Campeche reads like a *Who's Who of Pirating*. On one occasion, several outfits joined forces under the famous Dutch pirate Peg Leg (who most likely was the inspiration behind the many fictional one-legged sailors) and managed to capture the city. And this wasn't the only time the city was captured. The Campechanos grew tired of playing host to pirate parties and erected walls around the city, showing as much industry then as they now show in renovating their historic district. The walls had a number of bastions at critical locations. For added security, two forts, complete with moats and drawbridges, were built on the hills flanking the city on the north and south sides. There were four entrances to the city, and the two main gates are still intact: the Puerta de Mar (Sea Gate) and the Puerta de Tierra (Land Gate). The pirates never cared to return. Eventually, early in this century, the wall around the city was razed, but the bastions and main gates were left intact, as well as the two hilltop fortresses. Most of the bastions and both of the forts now house museums.

ESSENTIALS

GETTING THERE & DEPARTING   By Plane   Aeromexico (☎ **9/816-6656** at the airport) flies once daily to and from Mexico City.

BY CAR   Highway 180 goes south from Mérida, passing near the basket-making village of Halacho and near Becal, known for its Panama-hat weavers. At Tenabo, take the shortcut (right) to Campeche rather than going farther to the crossroads near Chencoyí. The longer way from Mérida is along Highway 261 past Uxmal. From Uxmal, Highway 261 passes near some interesting ruins and the Xtacumbilxuna caves (see "En Route to Campeche" in the preceding section).

When driving the other direction, toward Celestún and Mérida, use the **Vía Corta** (short route) by going north on avenida Ruíz Cortines, bearing left to follow the water (this becomes avenida Pedro Sainz de Baranda, but there's no sign). Follow the road as it turns inland to Highway 180, where you turn left (there's a gas station at the intersection). The route takes you through Becal and Halacho. Stores in both villages close between 2 and 4pm.

If you're leaving Campeche for Edzná and Uxmal, go north on either Ruíz Cortines or Gobernadores and turn right on Madero, which becomes **Highway 281**. To Villahermosa, take Ruíz Cortines south; it becomes **Highway 180**.

Campeche

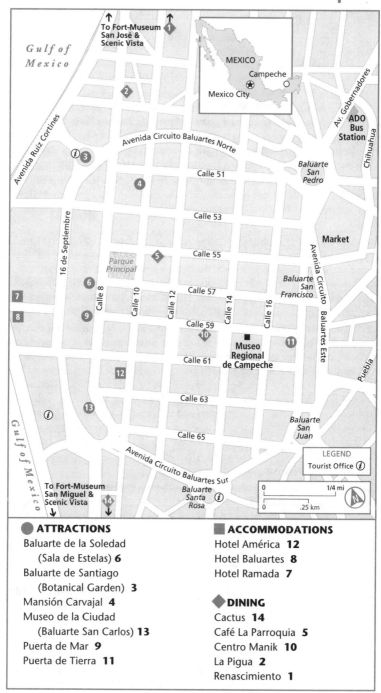

Gulf of Mexico

To Fort-Museum San José & Scenic Vista

MEXICO

Campeche

Mexico City

Av. Gobernadores

ADO Bus Station

Chihuahua

Avenida Circuito Baluartes Norte

Baluarte San Pedro

Calle 51

Calle 53

Market

16 de Septiembre

Parque Principal

Calle 55

Avenida Circuito Baluartes Este

Calle 8

Calle 10

Calle 12

Calle 14

Calle 16

Calle 57

Baluarte San Francisco

Calle 59

Museo Regional de Campeche

Puebla

Calle 61

Calle 63

Baluarte San Juan

Calle 65

Avenida Circuito Baluartes Sur

To Fort-Museum San Miguel & Scenic Vista

Baluarte Santa Rosa

LEGEND

Tourist Office (i)

0   1/4 mi
0   .25 km

● ATTRACTIONS

Baluarte de la Soledad
   (Sala de Estelas) **6**
Baluarte de Santiago
   (Botanical Garden) **3**
Mansión Carvajal **4**
Museo de la Ciudad
   (Baluarte San Carlos) **13**
Puerta de Mar **9**
Puerta de Tierra **11**

■ ACCOMMODATIONS

Hotel América **12**
Hotel Baluartes **8**
Hotel Ramada **7**

◆ DINING

Cactus **14**
Café La Parroquia **5**
Centro Manik **10**
La Pigua **2**
Renascimiento **1**

199

Bus Travel Warning

There have been some bus holdups on highways in the state of Campeche, though none recently. All occurred at night. The U.S. State Department recommends avoiding traveling at night.

BY BUS ADO (☎ **9/816-2802**) offers a first-class *de paso* bus to Palenque (6 hours; $15) five times a day and buses to Mérida (2½ hours; $6) every hour from 5:30am to midnight.

ORIENTATION Arriving   The **airport** is several miles northeast of the town center, and you'll have to take a taxi into town. The **ADO bus station,** on avenida Gobernadores, is 9 long blocks from the Plaza Principal. Turn left out the front door and walk 1 block. Turn right (calle 49) and go straight for 5 blocks to calle 8. Turn left here, and the Plaza Principal is 3 blocks ahead. Taxis are readily available outside the station.

INFORMATION   The **State of Campeche Office of Tourism** (☎/fax **9/816-6767**) is in the Plaza Turística, avenida Ruíz Cortines s/n, 24000 Campeche, Camp. This is in one of the state buildings between the historic center and the shore. There are also information offices in the bastions of Santa Rosa, San Carlos, and Santiago. The tourism offices here are better prepared and more helpful than in most other cities, and they hand out good maps. They keep regular office hours: 9am to 2pm and 4 to 7pm.

CITY LAYOUT   The most interesting part of the city is the restored old part, most of which once lay within the walls. Originally, the seaward wall was at the water's edge, but now land has been gained from the sea between the old walls and the coastline. This is where you'll find the two best hotels in town and most of the state government buildings, which were built in a glaringly modernist style around **Plaza Moch-Couoh.** Here you will find the office tower **Edificio de los Poderes,** or **Palacio de Gobierno**—headquarters for the state of Campeche—and the futuristic **Cámara de Diputados** or **Casa de Congreso** (state legislative chamber), which looks like an enormous square clam.

Campeche's system of street numbering is much like that of Yucatán's cities except that the numbers of the north-south streets increase as you go east instead of the reverse. (See Mérida, "City Layout," above.)

GETTING AROUND   Most of the recommended sights, restaurants, and hotels are within walking distance of the old city, except for the two fort-museums. Campeche isn't easy to negotiate by bus; I recommend taxis for anything beyond walking distance. Taxis are inexpensive.

Fast Facts: Campeche

American Express   Local offices are located at calle 59 no. 4–5 (☎ **9/811-1010**), in the Edificio Belmar, a half block toward town from the Hotel Del Mar. They're open Monday through Friday from 9am to 2pm and 5 to 7pm, and Saturday from 9am to 1:30pm. They do not cash traveler's checks.

Area Code   The telephone **area code** is **9.**

Post Office   The post office (*correo*) is in the Edificio Federal at the corner of avenida 16 de Septiembre and calle 53 (☎ **9/816-2134**), near the Baluarte de Santiago; it's open Monday through Saturday from 7:30am to 8pm. The telegraph office is here as well.

EXPLORING CAMPECHE

With such beautiful surroundings, friendly people, easy pace of living, and orderly traffic, Campeche is a lovely city worthy of at least a day on your itinerary. There are some interesting museums, one outstanding restaurant, and several shops worth investigating.

INSIDE THE CITY WALLS

A good place to begin is the pretty *zócalo,* or **Parque Principal,** bounded by calles 55 and 57 running east and west and calles 8 and 10 running north and south. Construction of the church on the north side of the square began in 1650 and was finally completed 1^1/$_2$ centuries later. A pleasant way to see the city is to take the trolley tour that leaves every hour or so from the main plaza; check with one of the tourist information offices if you don't see it.

For a good introduction to the city, turn south from the park on calle 8 and walk 5 blocks to the **Museo de la Ciudad** (city museum), housed in the Bastion of San Carlos (see below).

Baluarte de la Soledad. Calle 57 and calle 8, opposite the Plaza Principal. No phone. Admission 50¢, Sunday free. Tues–Sat 8am–8pm, Sun 8am–1pm.

This bastion next to the sea gate houses a large number of Maya stelae recovered from around the state. Many are badly worn, but the excellent line drawings beside the stones allow you to admire their former beauty.

Baluarte de San Carlos/Museo de la Ciudad. Circuito Baluartes and av. Justo Sierra. No phone. Voluntary contributions. Tues–Sat 8am–8pm; Sun 8am–1pm.

This museum features a permanent exhibition of photographs and plans about the city and its history. The model of the city shows how it looked in its glory days and provides a good overview for touring within the city walls. There are several excellent ship models as well.

Baluarte de Santiago. Av. 16 de Septiembre and calle 49. No phone. Free admission. Mon–Fri 8am–8pm, Sat–Sun 9am–1pm.

The Jardín Botánico Xmuch'haltun is a jumble of exotic and common plants within the stone walls of this *baluarte.* More than 250 species of plants and trees share what seems like a terribly small courtyard.

Mansión Carvajal. Calle 10 no. 584. No phone. Free admission. Mon–Sat 9am–2pm and 4–8pm.

Restoration was completed in 1992 on this early–20th-century mansion, originally the home of the Carvajal family, owners of a *henequen* plantation. In its latest transformation, the blue-and-white Moorish home contains government agencies. Join the crowd purposefully striding along the gleaming black-and-white tile and up the curving marble staircase. No signs mark the entrance to the building; the entrance is on the west side of calle 10 between calles 53 and 51.

Puerta de Tierra (Land Gate). Calle 59 at Circuito Baluartes/Av. Gobernadores. No phone. Museum free, show $1.50. Daily 8am–9pm.

At the Land Gate there's a small museum displaying portraits of pirates and the city founders. The 1732 French 5-ton cannon in the entryway was found in 1990. On Tuesday, Friday, and Saturday at 8pm there's a light-and-sound show as long as 15 or more people have bought tickets. Some shows are in English, some are in Spanish; it depends on the audience. The show is amusing.

OUTSIDE THE WALLS: SCENIC VISTAS

Fuerte-Museo San Miguel. Ruta Escénica s/n. Admission $1. Tues–Sun 8am–7pm; free admission on Sun.

For a good view of the city and Gulf and a good museum, take a cab ($2–$3) up to Fuerte-Museo San Miguel. San Miguel is a small fort with moat and drawbridge. It houses a wonderful collection of Maya artifacts. Built in 1771, this fort was the most important of the city's defenses. Santa Anna later used it when he attacked the city in 1842. The pride of the collection is the jade masks and jewelry from Maya tombs at Calakmul—a site in southern Campeche. Among the other Calakmul artifacts are human remains that show the burial custom of partially burning the body, then wrapping it in a woven straw mat and cloth. Beans, copal, and feathers—all items deemed necessary to take the person through the underworld after death—were discovered in pottery vessels.

Fuerte-Museo San José el Alto. Av. Morazán s/n. Admission $1. Tues–Sun 8am–8pm.

San José is higher and has a more sweeping view of Campeche and the coast than Fuerte San Miguel but holds only a small exhibit of 16th- and 17th-century weapons and scaled miniatures of sailing vessels. This is a great place for a picnic. Take a cab. On the way, you will pass by an impressive statue of Juárez.

SHOPPING

Casa de Artesanías Tukulna. Calle 10 no. 333 (between calles 59 and 61). ☎ **9/ 816-9088.** Mon–Sat 9am–2pm and 5–8pm.

This store run by DIF (a government family assistance agency) occupies a restored mansion. There is an elaborate display of regional arts and crafts in the back. Everything that is produced in the state is represented in the showrooms. There are quality textiles, clothing, and locally made furniture. It's open Monday through Saturday from 9am to 2pm and 5 to 8pm.

WHERE TO STAY

It's ironic that in this wonderful colonial city there isn't a single good colonial-style hotel or B&B; Campeche is just not that touristy. The most comfortable hotels are outside the historic center; the most economical are inside, though the majority of these don't offer air-conditioning. Those that do are not very attractive or have carpeted rooms, which in Campeche will always smell musty. My favorite of these economical hotels, the Colonial, is simple and pretty. The other two listed, the Baluartes and the Del Mar, are the nicest hotels in the city and come with the most amenities, such as a swimming pool. They are located between the old city walls and the shoreline.

Hotel Baluartes. Av.16 de Septiembre no. 128, 24000 Campeche, Camp. ☎ **9/816-3911.** Fax 9/816-2410. E-mail: baluarte@campeche.sureste.com. 100 units. A/C TV TEL. $45 double. AE, MC, V. Free parking.

Opposite the Gulf of Mexico and next to the Hotel Del Mar, this was the city's original luxury hotel. All the rooms have been completely refurbished with new tile floors, new furniture, and new mattresses. Half of the rooms have a Gulf view, half look toward the city. There's a good restaurant, a coffee shop, a swimming pool, and a bar. You will see the hotel from the sea gate.

Hotel Colonial. Calle 14 no.122, 24000 Campeche, Camp. ☎ **9/816-2222.** 30 units. $18 double. No credit cards.

Despite its name, this hotel doesn't remind one so much of colonial times as it does the 1940s. The furniture, the fancy tiles, the ironwork—the place is loaded with character. It's also very clean, and the hotel's policy is to change sheets daily. Rooms come with basic furniture and small bathrooms. They aren't well lit. Four rooms have air-conditioning, and none have televisions, making this the quietest cheap hotel around. The small lobby and inner courtyard are pleasant places to sit and relax. The hotel is inside the walls between calles 55 and 57.

Hotel Del Mar. Av. Ruíz Cortines 51, 24000 Campeche, Camp. ☎ **9/816-2233** or 9/811-4020. Fax 9/811-1618. E-mail: delmarcp@camp1.telmex.net.mx. 48 units. A/C TV TEL. $90 double. AE, MC, V. Free parking.

Rooms are bright and comfortably furnished and have tile floors. All rooms have balconies facing the Gulf of Mexico. The restaurant, bar, and coffee shop are popular with the locals—always a good recommendation. There's a large swimming pool, a disco, a gym, a children's playscape, and a fenced parking lot behind the hotel. It's on the main oceanfront boulevard, between the coast and the city walls and next to the Hotel Baluartes.

WHERE TO EAT

Campeche is a fishing town, thus its cuisine is seafood. The outstanding restaurant in this place is La Pigua, where I would eat all my afternoon meals. For breakfast, I like one of the traditional eateries such as La Parroquia, and for a light supper, either get some *antojitos* at Renacimiento in the old *barrio* San Francisco, or have one of the vegetarian dishes at Centro Manik. If you want a steak, your best bet is Cactus.

MODERATE

Cactus. Av. Malecón Justo Sierra. ☎ **9/811-1453.** Main courses $5–$9. No credit cards. Daily 7am–2am. STEAKS/MEXICAN.

If seafood isn't to your taste, try this steak house; it's a favorite with the locals. The rib-eyes are good, as is everything but the *arrachera,* which is the same cut of meat as fajitas and very tough.

✪ **La Pigua.** Av. Miguel Alemán no. 179A. ☎ **9/811-3365.** Reservations recommended. Main courses $6–$10. AE, DISC, MC, V. Daily noon–6pm. SEAFOOD/MEXICAN.

La Pigua is the best restaurant in the city. The dining area is an air-conditioned version of the traditional Yucatecan cabin, but with walls of glass looking out on green vegetation. It's lovely. There are not many tables, so by all means, make a reservation. The large menu is peppered with Spanish nautical terms as the headings for different categories. Sure to be on the menu is *pescado relleno de mariscos,* which I whole-heartedly recommend. But, if you're lucky, you might find that they have *pompano* in a green herb sauce with *hierba santa*—unbelievable. Other dishes that are sure to please are the coconut-battered shrimp with applesauce and the *chiles rellenos* with shark. Service is excellent, and the accommodating owner can have your favorite seafood prepared in any style you want. To reach La Pigua from the Plaza Principal, walk north on calle 8 for 3 blocks. Cross the avenida Circuito by the botanical garden where calle 8 becomes Miguel Alemán. The restaurant is 1½ blocks farther up, on the right side of the street.

Renacimiento. Calle 10 no. 90. ☎ **9/811-4257.** Main courses $4–$8, *antojitos* $1–$3. No credit cards. Tues–Sun noon–midnight. REGIONAL/ANTOJITOS.

This is a great place to come for traditional supper fare of tacos, tostadas, and other *antojitos.* It's in the *portales* (arcade) of Plaza de San Francisco, the oldest *barrio* in town. And, if the locals are to be believed, this is where the Spaniards first came ashore in circumstances that allowed the celebration of Mass—the first on the continent.

I recommend the turkey *sincronizadas* and the tacos al pastor. With the *antojitos* come several types of salsas. The cabbage/habañero salsa is for the *sincronizadas,* and the pineapple salsa is for the tacos al pastor (again, according to locals, who I believe are right on target in this matter). The restaurant is a few blocks outside the north wall. Take a cab or just ask anybody for San Francisco (nobody knows this eatery by its official name).

INEXPENSIVE

Centro Manik. Calle 59 no. 22 (between 12 and 14). ☎ **9/816-2448.** Main dishes $2. No credit cards. Mon–Sat 8am–2pm, 6pm–midnight. VEGETARIAN.

This place specializes in vegetarian versions of popular foods—burgers, pizzas, and tamales. It also gets some of its inspiration from local and traditional recipes, such as *pozole* and *brazo de reina.* The restaurant makes its own bread and cakes and can serve them with a cappuccino. The interior is simple and pleasant; most of the tables are in a courtyard or a side room. The restaurant is frequented by all sorts, from college kids to businessmen. There is a small bookstore and a gallery, and some organic local products such as honey are sold.

La Parroquia. Calle 55 no. 9. ☎ **9/816-8086.** Breakfast $1–$3; main courses $3–$6; comida corrida $3.50. No credit cards. Daily 24 hours (comida corrida served 1–4pm). MEXICAN.

This popular local hangout has friendly waiters and offers excellent, inexpensive fare. Here, you can enjoy great breakfasts and *colados,* the delicious regional tamal. Selections on the comida corrida might include pot roast, meatballs, pork, or fish, with rice or squash, beans, tortillas, and fresh-fruit–flavored water.

4 The Ruins of Chichén-Itzá

112 miles (179km) W of Cancún; 75 miles (120km) E of Mérida

The fabled pyramids and temples of Chichén-Itzá (no, it doesn't rhyme with chicken pizza; the accents are on the last syllables chee-*chin* eat-*zah*) are the Yucatán's best-known ancient monuments. The ruins are plenty hyped, but Chichén is truly worth seeing. Walking among these stone platforms, pyramids, and ball courts gives one an appreciation for this ancient civilization that cannot be had from reading books. The city is built on such a scale as to evoke a sense of wonder; to fill the plazas during one of the mass rituals that occurred here a millenium ago would have required an enormous number of celebrants. Even today, with the mass flow of tourists through these plazas, the ruins feel empty.

When visiting this old city, remember that much of what is said about the Maya (especially by tour guides, who speak in tones of utter certainty) is merely educated guessing (or just plain guessing). This Postclassic Maya city was established by Itzáes perhaps sometime during the 9th century A.D. Linda Schele and David Friedel, in *A Forest of Kings* (Morrow, 1990), have cast doubt on the legend that the Toltecs, led by Kukulkán (Quetzalcoatl), came here from the Toltec capital of Tula (in north-central Mexico), and, along with Putún Maya coastal traders, built a magnificent metropolis that combined the Maya Puuc style with Toltec motifs (the feathered serpent, warriors, eagles, and jaguars). Not so, say Schele and Friedel. According to them, readings of Chichén's bas-reliefs and hieroglyphs fail to support that legend and, instead, show that Chichén-Itzá was a continuous Maya site influenced by association with the Toltecs but not by an invasion. Not all scholars, however, embrace this new thinking, so the idea of a Toltec invasion still holds sway.

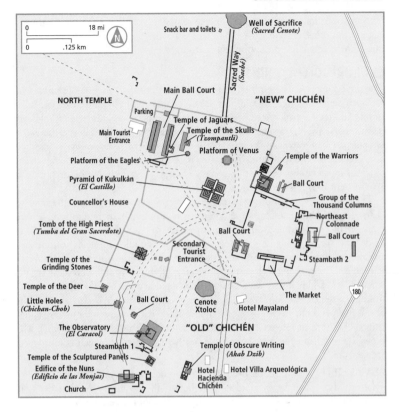

Though it's possible to make a round-trip from Mérida to Chichén-Itzá in 1 day, it will be a long, tiring, and very rushed day. Try to spend at least 1 night at Chichén-Itzá (besides, you've already paid for the sound-and-light ticket), or the nearby town of Valladolid.

ESSENTIALS

GETTING THERE & DEPARTING   By Plane   Day trips from Cancún and Cozumel can be arranged by travel agents in the United States or in Cancún or Cozumel.

BY CAR   Chichén-Itzá is on the main Highway 180 between Mérida (2¹/₂ hrs) and Cancún (1¹/₂ hrs). You can also take the autopista.

BY BUS   From Mérida, there are three first-class **ADO** buses per day, and a couple that go to Valladolid will stop here. Also, there are several second-class buses per day. If you want to make it a day-trip from Mérida, go with a tour company. From Cancún, there are any number of tourist buses, and regular first-class buses leave for Chichén every hour.

ORIENTATION   Arriving   If coming by regular bus, you'll arrive in the village of Pisté, at the station next to the Pirámide Inn.

CITY LAYOUT   The small town of **Pisté,** where most hotels and restaurants are located, is about 1¹/₂ miles from the ruins of Chichén-Itzá. Public buses from Mérida,

Cancún, Valladolid, and elsewhere discharge passengers here. A few hotels are at the edge of the ruins, and one, the Hotel Dolores Alba (see "Where to Stay," below), is out of town about 1¹/₂ miles from the ruins on the road to Valladolid.

EXPLORING THE RUINS

The site occupies 4-square-miles, and it takes most of a day to see all the ruins, which are open daily from 8am to 5pm. Service areas are open from 8am to 10pm. Admission is $8, free for children under age 12, and free for all on Sunday and holidays. A permit to use your own video camera costs an additional $4. Parking is extra. *You can use your ticket to reenter on the same day, but you'll have to pay again for an additional day.* Chichén-Itzá's **sound-and-light** show is worth seeing, and is included in the cost of admission. The show, held at 8pm every night, is in Spanish, but headsets are available for rent ($3) in several languages.

The large, modern visitor center, at the main entrance where you pay the admission charge, is beside the parking lot and consists of a museum, an auditorium, a restaurant, a bookstore, and rest rooms. You can see the site on your own or with a licensed guide who speaks either English or Spanish. These guides are usually waiting at the entrance and charge around $30 for one to six people. Although the guides frown on it, there's nothing wrong with your approaching a group of people who speak the same language and asking if they would like to share a guide with you. The guide, of course, would like to get $30 from you alone. Be wary of the history-spouting guides—some of it is just plain out-of-date—but the architectural details they point out are enlightening. There are actually two parts of Chichén-Itzá: the northern (new) zone, which shows distinct Toltec influence; and the southern (old) zone, which is mostly Puuc architecture.

EL CASTILLO As you enter from the tourist center, the beautiful 75-foot El Castillo pyramid (also called the Pyramid of Kukulkán) will be straight ahead across a large open area. It was built with the Maya calendar in mind. There are 364 stairs plus a platform to equal 365 (days of the year); 52 panels on each side (which represent the 52-year cycle of the Maya calendar); and 9 terraces on each side of the stairways (for a total of 18 terraces, which represents the 18-month Maya solar calendar). If this isn't proof enough of the mathematical precision of this temple, come for the **spring** or **fall equinox** (March 21 or September 21 between 3 and 5pm). On those days, the seven stairs of the northern stairway and the serpent-head carving at the base are touched with sunlight and become a "serpent" formed by the play of light and shadow. It appears to descend into the earth as the sun hits each stair from the top, ending with the serpent head. To the Maya this was a fertility symbol: The golden sun had entered the earth, meaning it was time to plant the corn.

El Castillo was built over an earlier structure. A narrow stairway at the western edge of the north staircase leads into the structure, where there is a sacrificial altar-throne—a red jaguar encrusted with jade. The stairway is open from 11am to 3pm and is claustrophobic, usually crowded, humid, and uncomfortable. A visit early in the day is best. Photos of the figure are not allowed.

MAIN BALL COURT (Juego de Pelota) Northwest of El Castillo is Chichén's main ball court, the largest and best preserved anywhere, and only one of nine ball courts built in this city. Carved on both walls of the ball court are scenes showing Maya figures dressed as ball players decked out in heavy protective padding. The carved scene also shows a headless player kneeling with blood shooting from the neck; the player is looked upon by another player holding the head.

Players on two teams tried to knock a hard rubber ball through one or the other of the two stone rings placed high on either wall, using only their elbows, knees, and hips (no hands). According to legend, the losing players paid for defeat with their lives. However, some experts say the victors were in fact the only appropriate sacrifices for the gods. One can only guess what the incentive for winning might be in such case. Either way, the game must have been riveting, heightened by the perfect acoustics of the ball court.

THE NORTH TEMPLE   Temples are found at both ends of the ball court. The North Temple has sculptured pillars and more sculptures inside, as well as badly ruined murals. The acoustics of the ball court are so good that from the North Temple, a person speaking can be heard clearly at the opposite end, about 450 feet away.

TEMPLE OF JAGUARS   Near the southeastern corner of the main ball court is a small temple with serpent columns and carved panels showing warriors and jaguars. Up the flight of steps and inside the temple, a mural was found that chronicles a battle in a Maya village.

TEMPLE OF THE SKULLS (Tzompantli)   To the right of the ball court is the Temple of the Skulls, with rows of skulls carved into the stone platform. When a sacrificial victim's head was cut off, it was impaled on a pole and displayed in a tidy row with others. Also carved into the stone are pictures of eagles tearing hearts from human victims. The word Tzompantli is not Mayan but came from central Mexico. Reconstruction using scattered fragments may add a level to this platform and change the look of this structure by the time you visit.

PLATFORM OF THE EAGLES   Next to the Tzompantli, this small platform has reliefs showing eagles and jaguars clutching human hearts in their talons and claws, as well as a human head emerging from the mouth of a serpent.

PLATFORM OF VENUS   East of the Tzompantli and north of El Castillo, near the road to the Sacred Cenote, is the Platform of Venus. In Maya–Toltec lore, Venus was represented by a feathered monster or a feathered serpent with a human head in its mouth. It's also called the tomb of Chaac-Mool because a Chaac-Mool figure was discovered "buried" within the structure.

SACRED CENOTE   Follow the dirt road (actually an ancient *sacbé,* or causeway) that heads north from the Platform of Venus; after 5 minutes you'll come to the great natural well that may have given Chichén-Itzá (the Well of the Itzáes) its name. This well was used for ceremonial purposes, not for drinking water, and according to legend, sacrificial victims were drowned in this pool to honor the rain god Chaac. Anatomical research done early this century by Ernest A. Hooten showed that bones of both children and adults were found in the well. Judging from Hooten's evidence, they may have been outcasts, diseased, or feeble-minded.

Edward Thompson, who was the American consul in Mérida and a Harvard professor, purchased the ruins of Chichén early this century and explored the *cenote* with dredges and divers. His explorations exposed a fortune in gold and jade. Most of the riches wound up in Harvard's Peabody Museum of Archaeology and Ethnology—a matter that continues to disconcert Mexican classicists today. Later excavations in the 1960s unearthed more treasure, and studies of the recovered objects detail offerings from throughout the Yucatán and even farther away.

TEMPLE OF THE WARRIORS (Templo de los Guerreros)   Due east of El Castillo is one of the most impressive structures at Chichén: the Temple of the Warriors, named for the carvings of warriors marching along its walls. It's also called the Group of the Thousand Columns for the rows of broken pillars that flank it. During the recent restoration, hundreds more of the columns were rescued from the rubble and put in place, setting off the temple more magnificently than ever. A figure of Chaac-Mool sits at the top of the temple, surrounded by impressive columns carved in relief to look like enormous feathered serpents. South of the temple was a square building that archaeologists called the **Market** (*mercado*); its central court is sur-rounded by a colonnade. Beyond the temple and the market in the jungle are mounds of rubble, parts of which are being reconstructed.

The main Mérida–Cancún highway once ran straight through the ruins of Chichén, and though it has now been diverted, you can still see the great swath it cut. South and west of the old highway's path are more impressive ruined buildings.

TOMB OF THE HIGH PRIEST (Tumba del Gran Sacerdote)   Past the refresh-ment stand to the right of the path is the Tomb of the High Priest, which stood atop a natural limestone cave in which skeletons and offerings were found, giving the temple its name.

The tomb has been reconstructed, and workers are unearthing other smaller temples in the area. As the work progresses, some buildings may be roped off and others will open to the public for the first time. It's fascinating to watch the archaeol-ogists at work, meticulously numbering each stone as they take apart what appears to be a mound of rocks, then reassembling the stones into a recognizable structure.

TEMPLE OF THE GRINDING STONES (Casa de los Metates)   This building, the next one on your right, is named after the concave corn-grinding stones used by the Maya.

TEMPLE OF THE DEER (Templo del Venado)   Past the House of Metates is this fairly tall, though ruined, building. The relief of a stag that gave the temple its name is long gone.

LITTLE HOLES (Chichan-chob)   This next temple has a roof comb with little holes, three masks of the rain god Chaac, three rooms, and a good view of the sur-rounding structures. It's one of the older buildings at Chichén, built in the Puuc style during the Late Classic period.

OBSERVATORY (El Caracol)   Construction of the Observatory, a complex building with a circular tower, was carried out over centuries; the additions and modifications reflected the Maya's careful observation of celestial movements and their need for increasingly exact measurements. Through slits in the tower's walls, Maya astronomers could observe the cardinal directions and the approach of the all-important spring and autumn equinoxes, as well as the summer solstice. The temple's name, which means "snail," comes from a spiral staircase within the structure.

On the east side of El Caracol, a path leads north into the bush to the Cenote Xtoloc, a natural limestone well that provided the city's daily water supply. If you see any lizards sunning there, they may well be xtoloc, the lizard for which the *cenote* is named.

TEMPLE OF PANELS (Templo de los Tableros)   Just to the south of El Caracol are the ruins of a steam bath (*temazcalli*) and the Temple of Panels, named for the carved panels on top. This temple was once covered by a much larger structure, only traces of which remain.

EDIFICE OF THE NUNS (Edificio de las Monjas)   If you've visited the Puuc sites of Kabah, Sayil, Labná, or Xlapak, the enormous nunnery here will remind you at once of the "palaces" at the other sites. Built in the Late Classic period, the new edifice was constructed over an older one. Suspecting that this was so, Le Plongeon, an archaeologist working earlier in this century, put dynamite in between the two and blew away part of the exterior, thereby revealing the older structures within. You can still see the results of Le Plongeon's indelicate exploratory methods.

On the eastern side of the Edifice of the Nuns is an **annex (Anexo Este)** constructed in highly ornate Chenes style with Chaac masks and serpents.

THE CHURCH (La Iglesia)   Next to the annex is one of the oldest buildings at Chichén, absurdly named the Church. Masks of Chaac decorate two upper stories. Look closely and you'll see other pagan symbols among the crowd of Chaacs: an armadillo, a crab, a snail, and a tortoise. These represent the Maya gods, called *bacah,* whose job it was to hold up the sky.

TEMPLE OF OBSCURE WRITING (Akab Dzib)   Beloved of travel writers, this temple lies east of the Edifice of the Nuns. Above a door in one of the rooms are some Maya glyphs, which gave the temple its name, since the writings have yet to be deciphered. In other rooms, traces of red handprints are still visible. Reconstructed and expanded over the centuries, Akab Dzib may well be the oldest building at Chichén.

OLD CHICHéN (Chichén Viejo)   For a look at more of Chichén's oldest buildings, constructed well before the time of Toltec influence, follow signs from the Edifice of the Nuns southwest into the bush to Old Chichén, about half a mile away. Be prepared for this trek with long trousers, insect repellent, and a local guide. The attractions here are the **Temple of the First Inscriptions** (Templo de los Inscripciones Iniciales), with the oldest inscriptions discovered at Chichén, and the restored **Temple of the Lintels** (Templo de los Dinteles), a fine Puuc building.

WHERE TO STAY

The expensive hotels in Chichén are all situated in beautiful grounds, are close to the ruins, and have good food. All have 800 numbers for reservations, which I recommend using. Some of these hotels do a lot of business with tour operators—they can be empty one day and full the next. The inexpensive hotels are in the village of Pisté, $1^1/2$ miles away. There is little to do in Pisté at night; another option would be to go on to the colonial town of Valladolid, 30 minutes away, but you would want reservations because a lot of tour-bus companies use the hotels there (see next section).

EXPENSIVE

✪ **Hacienda Chichén.** Zona Arqueológica, 97751 Chichén-Itzá, Yuc. ☎/fax **9/851-0045** (Reservations: Casa del Balam, calle 60 no. 488, 97000 Mérida, Yuc. ☎ **800/624-8451** in the U.S., or 9/924-2150; fax 9/924-5011. www.yucatanadventure.com.mx). 26 units. A/C, MINIBAR. $115 double. AE, MC, V. Free guarded parking.

This is the smallest and most private of the hotels at the ruins. It is also the quietest and the one least likely to have large tour groups. As a hacienda in 1923, it served as the headquarters for the Carnegie Institute's excavations. Several bungalows were built to house the staff; these have been modernized and are now the guest rooms. Each is simply and comfortably furnished. They are separated from each other by a short distance, and each has a private porch from which you can enjoy the beautiful grounds. The main building belonged to the hacienda. It houses the terrace restaurant, with dining outside by the pool or inside.

Hotel Mayaland. Zona Arqueológica, 97751 Chichén-Itzá, Yuc. ☎ **9/851-0127** (Reservations: Mayaland Resorts, Av. Colón 502, 97000 Mérida, Yuc.; ☎ **800/235-4079** in the U.S., or 9/925-2122; fax 9/925-7022.). 95 units. A/C, Minibar, Tel, TV. High season $140 double, $200 bungalow. Low season 10% off. AE, MC, V. Free guarded parking.

From the lobby doorway you have a great view of El Caracol (the observatory). Rooms in the main building are connected by a wide, tiled veranda, and come with tiled bathrooms (with tubs) and colonial-style furnishings. Maya-inspired bungalows with beautifully carved furniture are tucked into the wooded grounds. The grounds are gorgeous, with huge trees and lush foliage—the hotel has had 75 years to get them in shape. There are three pools, a restaurant, a grill, and a buffet. This is a large hotel, and there are always tour buses parked in front, so get a room on the back side. Mayaland has a shuttle service between the hotel and Mérida for about $35 each way.

Hotel Villa Arqueológica. Zona Arqueológica, 97751 Chichén-Itzá, Yuc. ☎ **800/258-2633** in the U.S., 9/851-0034, or 9/856-2830. 40 units. A/C. High season $105 double. Low season $90. Rates include continental breakfast. AE, MC, V. Free parking.

This is a lovely hotel built around a courtyard and pool partially shaded by two large flamboyant trees; it is one of a chain that has very similar hotels at Cobá and Uxmal. A section of these hotels is leased by Club Med, which operates the 800 number above and includes half-board and full-board rates. Walk-in rates don't include meals and run $20 higher. Bougainvillea drapes down from the walls. The rooms are modern and small but are comfortable, unless you're 6'2" or taller, since each bed is in a niche with walls at the head and foot of the mattress. Most rooms have one double and an oversized single bed. There are tennis courts, and the hotel's restaurant features international and Yucatecan food.

MODERATE

Pirámide Inn. Km 118 Carretera Mérida–Valladolid, 97751 Pisté, Yuc. ☎ **9/851-0115.** Fax 9/8510114. www.piramideinn.com. 44 units. A/C. $47 double. No credit cards.

Less than a mile from the ruins at the edge of Pisté, this hospitable inn has large motel-like rooms equipped with two double beds or one king-size bed. Hot water comes on between 5 and 10am and 5 and 10pm. There is a pool in the midst of landscaped gardens, which include the remains of a Maya wall. Try to get a room in the back. If you're coming from Valladolid, it's on the left, and from Mérida look for it on the right.

INEXPENSIVE

Hotel Dolores Alba. Km 122 Carretera Mérida–Valladolid, Yuc. No phone. (Reservations: Hotel Dolores Alba, calle 63 no. 464, 97000 Mérida, Yuc. ☎ **9/928-5650;** fax 9/928-3163; www.doloresalba.com; e-mail: asanchez@sureste.com). 40 units. A/C. $33 double. No credit cards. Free parking.

This place is of the motel variety, perfect if you come by car. It is a bargain for what you get: two pools (one of them quite nice); *palapas* and hammocks around the place; and large and comfortable rooms. The restaurant serves good meals at moderate prices. Free transportation is provided to the ruins and the Caves of Balankanché during visiting hours, though you will have to take a taxi to get back. The hotel is on the highway 1¹/₂ miles east of the ruins (toward Valladolid).

WHERE TO DINE

Reasonably priced meals are available at the restaurant in the visitors' center at the ruins and at hotels in Pisté. Hotel restaurants near the ruins jump quite a bit in price. In Pisté, however, many places cater to large groups, which descend on them en masse for lunch after 1pm.

Cafetería Ruinas. In the Chichén-Itzá visitors' center. No phone. Breakfast $4; sandwiches $4–$5; main courses $5–$8. No credit cards. Daily 9am–5pm. MEXICAN/ITALIAN.

Though it has the monopoly on food at the ruins, this cafetería actually does a good job with such basic meals as enchiladas, spaghetti, and baked chicken. Eggs and burgers are cooked to order, and the coffee is very good. Sit outside at the tables farthest from the crowd and relax.

La Fiesta. Carretera Mérida–Valladolid, Pisté. No phone. Main courses $4–$6; *comida corrida* $6.50. No credit cards. Daily 7am–9pm (comida corrida served 12:30–5pm). REGIONAL/MEXICAN.

With Maya motifs on the wall and colorful decorations, this is one of Pisté's long-established restaurants catering especially to tour groups. Though relatively expensive, the food is very good. You'll be quite satisfied unless you arrive when a tour group is being served, in which case service to individual diners may suffer. Going toward the ruins, La Fiesta is on the west end of town.

Puebla Maya. Carretera Mérida–Valladolid, Pisté. No phone. Fixed-price lunch buffet $7. No credit cards. Daily 1–5pm. MEXICAN.

Opposite the Pirámide Inn, the Puebla Maya looks just like its name, a Maya town with small white huts flanking a large open-walled *palapa*-topped center. Inside, however, you cross an artificial lagoon, planters drip with greenery, and live musicians play to the hundreds of tourists filling the tables. Service through the huge buffet is quick, so if you've been huffing around the ruins all morning, you have time to eat and relax before boarding the bus to wherever you're going. You can even swim in a lovely landscaped pool.

Restaurant Bar "Poxil." Calle 15 s/n, Carretera Mérida–Valladolid, Pisté. ☎ **9/851-0123.** Main courses $3–$5. No credit cards. Daily 7am–8pm. MEXICAN/REGIONAL.

A *poxil* is a Maya fruit somewhat akin to a *guanábana*. Although this place doesn't serve them, what is on the menu is good, though not gourmet, and the price is right. You will find the Poxil near the west entrance to town on the south side of the street.

A SIDE TRIP TO THE GRUTAS (CAVES) DE BALANKANCHÉ

The Grutas de Balankanché are 3$\frac{1}{2}$ miles from Chichén-Itzá on the road to Valladolid and Cancún. Taxis will make the trip and wait, but they are also usually on hand when the tours let out. The entire excursion takes about half an hour, but the walk inside is hot and humid. The natural caves here became hideaways during the War of the Castes. You can still see traces of carving and incense burning, as well as an underground stream that served as the sanctuary's water supply. Outside, take time to meander through the botanical gardens, where most of the plants and trees are labeled with their common and scientific names.

The caves are open daily. Admission is $3. Use of a video camera costs an additional $4. Children under age 6 are not admitted. Guided tours in English are at 11am and 1 and 3pm, and in Spanish, at 9am, noon, and 2 and 4pm. Tours go only if there is a minimum of 6 people and take up to 30 people at a time. Double-check these hours at the main entrance to the Chichén ruins.

5 Valladolid

25 miles (40km) E of Chichén-Itzá; 100 miles (160km) SW of Cancún

Valladolid (pronounced *bye*-ah-doh-*leed*) is a small, pleasant colonial city halfway between Mérida and Cancún. The people here are friendly and informal, and, except for the heat, life is easy. The city's economy is based on commerce and small-scale manufacture. A large *cenote* is in the center of town, and another one is 3 miles down the road to Chichén. A restoration project has reconstructed several rows of colonial housing in the neighborhood surrounding the convent of San Bernardino de Siena. Side trips to Holbox and Ekbalam (see below) can be mounted from Valladolid.

ESSENTIALS

GETTING THERE & DEPARTING   By Car   From either Mérida or Cancún, you have two choices for getting to Valladolid: the toll road (*cuota*) or Highway 180. The *cuota* passes a few miles north of the city, and the exit is at the crossing of **Highway 295** to Tizimín. **Highway 180** takes significantly longer because it passes through a number of villages with their requisite speed bumps. Both 180 and 295 lead directly to the main square. Leaving is just as easy: from the main square, calle 41 turns into 180 east to Cancún; calle 39 heads to 180 west to Chichén-Itzá and Mérida. To take the *cuota* to either Mérida or Cancún, take calle 40. (See "City Layout," below.)

BY BUS   Expresso de Oriente has eight first-class buses per day to/from Mérida, nine buses to/from Cancún, three to/from Tulum, and three to/from Playa del Carmen. To secure a seat you can buy a ticket a day in advance. In addition, first-class buses make a stop in Valladolid while passing through (*de paso*) on the way to Cancún. To get to Chichén-Itzá you must take a second-class bus, which leaves every hour and sometimes on the half-hour.

ORIENTATION   Visitor Information   There is a small tourism office in the Palacio Municipal where you can get a map but little else. Open daily 10am to 2pm and 4 to 8pm.

CITY LAYOUT   Valladolid has the standard layout for towns in the Yucatán: Streets running north-south are even numbers; those running east-west are odd numbers. The main plaza is bordered by calle 39 on the north, 41 on the south, 40 on the east, and 42 on the west. The plaza is named Parque Francisco Cantón Rosado, but everyone simply calls it **El Centro.** Valladolid has two bus stations at the corners of calles 39 and 46, and 37 and 54. For all practical purposes they are interchangeable; departing buses pass by both stations. Taxis are easy to come by.

EXPLORING VALLADOLID

Before it became Valladolid, the city was a Maya settlement called Zací (zah-*kee*), which means "white hawk." There are two *cenotes* in the area, one of which is called **Cenote Zací**—located at the intersection of calles 39 and 36, in a small park in the middle of town. The walls and part of the roof of the *cenote* have been opened up, and a trail leads down close to the water. Caves, stalactites, and hanging vines contribute to a wild, prehistoric atmosphere. The park features a large *palapa* restaurant that is popular with local residents, plus three traditional Maya dwellings that house a small photograph collection and some historical materials on Valladolid. Admission is 50¢.

To the southwest of El Centro is the Franciscan monastery of **San Bernardino de Siena** (1552). Most of the compound was built in the early 1600s; a large underground river is believed to pass under the convent and surrounding neighborhood, which is called Barrio Sisal. "Sisal" is in this case a corruption of the Mayan phrase *sis-ha,* meaning "cold water." The *barrio* has undergone extensive restoration and is a delight to behold.

Valladolid's main square is the social center of town and a thriving market for the prettiest Yucatecan dresses to be found anywhere. On its south side is the principal church, **La Parroquia de San Servacio.** Vallesoletanos, as the locals call themselves, believe that almost all cathedrals in Mexico point east, and they cherish a local legend to explain why theirs points north—but don't believe a word of it. On the east side of the plaza is the municipal building known modestly as *El Ayuntamiento.* Be sure to appreciate the four dramatic paintings outlining the history of the peninsula. In particular, note the first panel, featuring a horrified Maya priest as he foresees the arrival of Spanish galleons. On Sunday nights, from beneath the stone arches of the *ayuntamiento,* the municipal band plays *jaranas* and other traditional music of the region.

SHOPPING

The **Mercado de Artesanías de Valladolid** at the corner of calles 39 and 44 gives you a good idea of the local merchandise. Perhaps the main handicraft of the town is embroidered Maya dresses, which can be purchased here or from women around the main square. The latter also sell, of all things, Barbie-doll–size Maya dresses! Just ask, "*¿Vestidos para Barbie?*" and out they come. The area around Valladolid is cattle country; the local leather goods are plentiful, and some of the best sandals (*huaraches*) and leather goods are sold over the main plaza, above the municipal bazaar. An Indian named Juan Mac makes *alpargatas,* the traditional everyday footwear of the Maya, in his factory on calle 39, two doors south of the plaza; look for a doorway painted yellow. Most of his output is for locals, but he's happy to knock some out for travelers.

Valladolid also produces a highly prized **honey** made from the tzi-tzi-ché flower. You can find it and other goods at the **town market** on calle 32 between calles 35 and 37. The best time to see the market is Sunday morning.

WHERE TO STAY

Hotels (and restaurants) here are less expensive than the competition in Chichén. Occupancy rates are very high, so you should make reservations. If you arrive without reservations and there is no room in either of the hotels below, then **Hotel San Clemente**, just off the plaza, is your next-best bet.

Hotel El Mesón del Marqués. Calle 39 no. 203, 97780 Valladolid, Yuc. ☎ **9/856-3042** or 9/856-2073. Fax 9/856-2280. 58 units. A/C TV TEL. $48 double. AE. Free secured parking.

The Mesón del Marqués is a very comfortable and gracious hotel. The first courtyard surrounds a fountain and is draped with hanging plants and bougainvillea. This, the original house, holds a good restaurant (see "Where to Dine," below). In back is another courtyard with plenty of greenery and a pool. There is always hot water, and most of the rooms are sheltered from city noise. The rooms are large and quite comfortable. It's on the north side of El Centro, opposite the church.

Hotel María de la Luz. Calle 42 no. 193, 97780 Valladolid, Yuc. ☎/fax **9/856-2071,** or 9/856-2071. www.xaac.com/playacar/maria.htm. E-mail: maria_luz@chichen.com.mx. 67 units. A/C TV. $34 double. MC, V. Rates include breakfast. Free secured parking.

The two-story María de la Luz is built around an inner swimming pool. The guest rooms have been refurbished with new tile floors and bathrooms and new mattresses; three have balconies overlooking the city's main square. The wide interior space holds a restaurant that is quite comfortable and airy for most of the day—a popular place for breakfast. The hotel is on the west side of the main square.

WHERE TO DINE

Valladolid is not a center for haute cuisine, but you should try some of the regional specialties. The lowest restaurant prices are found in the **Bazar Municipal,** a little arcade of shops beside the Hotel El Mesón del Marqués right on the main square.

Hostería del Marqués. Calle 39 no. 203. ☎ **9/856-2073.** Breakfast $3–$5; main courses $3.50–$7. AE. Daily 7am–11:30pm. MEXICAN/YUCATECAN.

This is part of the Hotel El Mesón del Marqués, facing the main square. The patio is calm and cool for most of the day. The menu is extensive and features local specialties.

If you are hungry, try the Yucatecan sampler. Any of the enchiladas are good. The guacamole was a hit on my last visit.

SIDE TRIPS FROM VALLADOLID
CENOTE DZITNUP

The Cenote Dzitnup (also known as Cenote Xkeken), 2¹/₂ miles west of Valladolid off Highway 180, is worth a side trip, especially if you have time for a dip. Descend a short flight of rather perilous stone steps, and at the bottom, inside a beautiful cavern, is a natural pool of water so clear and blue it seems plucked from a dream. If you decide to take a swim, be sure you don't have creams or other chemicals on your skin, as they damage the habitat for the small fish and other organisms living there. Also, no alcohol, food, or smoking is allowed in the cavern.

Admission is $1. The *cenote* is open daily from 8am to 5pm.

EKBALAM: RECENTLY EXCAVATED MAYA RUINS

About 11 miles north of Valladolid, off the highway to Río Lagartos, is the spectacular site at Ekbalam, which means "star jaguar" in Mayan. Recently opened and largely unknown to tourists, the Ekbalam ruins have been undergoing extensive renovation; they are a must-see for travelers who have access to a rental car. Take calle 40 north out of Valladolid, to Highway 295; go 11 miles to the sign marking the Ekbalam turnoff. Follow a narrow, winding road through a small village, and watch the jungle for mounds that indicate the presence of undiscovered ruins leading to the main site. Ekbalam is 8 miles from the highway; the entrance fee is $2, plus $4 for each video camera. The site is open from 8am to 5pm every day; on our last visit, the custodians obligingly admitted us at 6pm to clamber on the main pyramid.

Built between 100 B.C. and A.D. 1200, the smaller buildings are architecturally unique—especially the large and perfectly restored **Caracol.** The principal buildings in the main group have been reconstructed beautifully. Flanked by two smaller pyramids, the imposing central pyramid is 517-feet-long and 200-feet-wide, and at more than 100-feet-high, is easily taller than the highest pyramids in Chichén and Uxmal. You can see the restoration work in progress: stones are carefully separated, numbered, and arranged, then reassembled by archaeologists from INAH, the national institute for anthropology. The caretaker/guide led us up the rocky, forested path to the summit, where we watched a full moon rise to illuminate the jungle for a radius of 35 miles. In the middle distance, unrestored ruins loom to the north and the southwest, and you can spot the tallest structures at **Cobá,** 30 miles to the southeast. Also plainly visible are the **raised causeways** of the Maya—the *sacbé* appear as raised lines in the forest vegetation. More than any of the better-known sites, Ekbalam at dusk excites a sense of mystery and awe at the scale of Maya civilization, and the utter ruin to which it came.

RÍO LAGARTOS NATURE RESERVE: NESTING FLAMINGOS

Some 50 miles north of Valladolid (25 miles north of Tizimín) on Highway 295 is Río Lagartos, a 118,000-acre refuge established in 1979 to protect the largest nesting population of flamingos in North America. Found in the park's dunes, mangrove swamps, and tropical forests are jaguars, ocelots, sea turtles, and at least 212 bird species (141 of which are permanent residents).

To get to Río Lagartos, you pass through Tizimín, which is about 30 minutes away. The best place to stay there is **Hotel 49,** on calle 49 373-A (☎ **9/863-2136**), by the main square. The owner can give you good advice about going to the nature preserve. There is not much to do in Tizimín unless you are there in the first 2 weeks of January, when it holds the largest fair in the Yucatán. The prime fiesta day is January 6: the

Epiphany, known popularly as *Día de los Reyes.* The fiesta is celebrated with lots of music, carnival rides, and more.

SEEING THE RÍO LAGARTOS REFUGE   Río Lagartos is a small fishing village of around 3,000 people who make their living from the sea and from the occasional tourist who shows up to see the flamingos. Colorfully painted homes face the Malecón (the oceanfront street), and brightly painted boats dock along the same half-moon–shaped port. A hotel was going to be opened there, but I can't say if it has been completed yet.

If you arrive by car, you have the option of driving to the salt plant at Los Colorados and out over the flats to the shore of the lagoon, where you can get fairly close to a large colony. Otherwise, go straight to the dock area in Río Lagartos, where you can hire a boat to the large flamingo colony for $75, which can be split among up to 6 people; the trip takes 4 to 6 hours. Or you can get a shorter trip to a closer colony for $20. Ask around for Filiberto Pat Zem, a reliable boatman who takes the time to give a good tour.

Although thousands of flamingos nest near here from April to August, it is prohibited by law to visit their nesting grounds. Flamingos need mud with particular ingredients (including a high salt content) in order to multiply, and this area's mud does the trick. Flamingos use their special bills to suck up the mud, and they have the unique ability to screen the contents they need from it. What you see on the boat trip is a mixture of flamingos, frigates, pelicans, herons in several colors, and ducks. Don't allow the boatman to frighten the birds into flight for your photographs, or the birds will eventually leave the habitat permanently.

ISLA HOLBOX

A remote island off the farthest eastern point of the Yucatán Peninsula, Holbox (pronounced whole-*bosh*) is a half-deserted fishing village, a modest wildlife refuge, and a desert-island getaway for travelers seeking solitude. From Valladolid, take Highway 180 east for 56.2 miles (90km) towards Cancún; turn north after Nuevo Xcan at the tiny crossroads of El Ideal. Drive nearly 62 miles (100km) north (on a poorly maintained state highway) to the tiny port of Chiquilá, where you can leave your car in a secured parking lot; walk 200 yards to the pier and haggle over the $15 boat ride 2 miles to the island. There is a ferry, but it runs only three times per day.

In the late 1840s, Holbox was a refuge for European landowners fleeing Indian mobs during the Caste Wars. Nowadays, the village of Holbox is empty when the fishing fleet is out, and only half-populated in the best of times. Disembark and proceed directly to **Villas Delfines,** a small but elegant *palapa* cluster on the beach, 15 minutes east of the docks by foot, on the Gulf side of the island. Each *palapa* ($80) can accommodate three people and comes with ceiling fans, mosquito netting, and a comfortable porch and hammock. The Villas are exquisitely designed for simple living, and the kitchen is staffed by a very able cook—don't bother with the restaurants in town. Guests do little but eat, drink, and swim off the endless white-sand beach. The Gulf here is clean and shallow; however, it's not the clear turquoise waters of the Caribbean. Take some reading materials, or borrow from the paperback library of German and Spanish best-sellers—there's no TV, no nightlife, and (if you remembered your mosquito repellent) no hassle. Word-of-mouth keeps the *palapas* occupied, so call ahead for reservations at ☎ **9/884-8606** or 9/874-4014, or fax at 9/884-6342.

6 Tabasco & Chiapas

Even though these two states aren't part of the Yucatán, we've included them because it allows us to present Mexico's **Maya region** in its entirety. Many travelers who go to the Yucatán to see Chichén-Itzá and Uxmal also take a side-trip down to Chiapas to see the famous ruins of Palenque, and some go even farther, all the way to San Cristóbal to visit the Highland Maya.

Chiapas and Tabasco differ from the Yucatán in a number of ways. They have higher rainfall levels, and little of the shallow limestone formations that make for underground rivers and *cenotes.* Consequently, you find here two of the largest rivers in Mexico: the Grijalva and the Usumacinta. And you find that the jungle in Tabasco and the eastern lowlands of Chiapas becomes more lush and varied. In the central highlands of Chiapas you find scattered cloud forests wherever the land has been left untouched. Getting there from Palenque is not hard, and it's wonderful to feel the cool mountain air after trekking around in the heat and humidity of the lowlands.

Tabasco is a small state along the Gulf Coast. It is rich in oil, and the capital, **Villahermosa,** has all the marks of a boomtown. It was in this coastal region that the Olmec, the mother culture of Mesoamerica, rose to prominence. In Villahermosa, at the Parque Museo de la Venta, you can see the artifacts that this culture left to posterity, including some of its famous, megalithic heads.

In **Chiapas,** the two areas that hold the most interest are the eastern lowland jungles and the central highlands. In the former lie the famous ruins of **Palenque,** a city of the classic age of Maya civilization. These ruins look unspeakably old, and the surrounding jungle seems poised to reclaim them should their caretakers ever falter in their duties. Deeper into the interior, for those willing to make the trek, are the sites of **Yaxchilán** and **Bonampak.** The central highlands are just as dramatic, but easier to enjoy. Of particular interest is the colonial city of **San Cristóbal de las Casas** and its surrounding Indian villages. The Indians here cling so tenaciously to their beliefs and traditions that this area at one time was more frequented by anthropologists than tourists.

Five years ago, San Cristóbal took center stage when the Zapatista Liberation Army launched an armed rebellion and captured the town. This caught the Mexican government by surprise and forced them to recognize the existence of political and economic problems in Chiapas. After a truce was arranged, negotiations commenced between the two sides, and these have proceeded in fits and starts. Occasionally political violence erupts in the area, as it did in the winter of 1997–98 with a massacre in Acteal, near San Cristóbal, and some killings in the Ocosingo area, which lies between Palenque and San Cristóbal. No foreigners were attacked in these events, and no restrictions were placed on travel to Palenque or the San Cristóbal region. I have toured the area several times since the events took place and have seen little disruption in the day-to-day affairs of the local people. The State Department has not issued a travel advisory for the region, but before you go, get the most current information you can by checking out the State Department Web site: **http://travel.state.gov.**

EXPLORING TABASCO & CHIAPAS

Airline and bus service to this area has improved a lot in the last few years. There is convenient air service from the Yucatán to Villahermosa, Tuxtla Gutiérrez, and Palenque. Coming from the Yucatán by land, you would most likely go through Campeche, which is 5 hours from Palenque and 6 from Villahermosa. From Palenque it is 4 to 5 hours to San Cristóbal depending on road conditions; from Villahermosa it's 5 hours.

Palenque can be seen in a day. A couple of worthwhile side-trips would add a day or two, and if you plan on going to Bonampak and Yaxchilán (Maya ruins bordering Guatemala), add 2 full days. San Cristóbal and the nearby villages have so much to offer that I would consider 4 days to be a minimum. I suggest you do your traveling during the day; not at night.

1 Villahermosa

89 miles (142km) NW of Palenque; 293 miles (469km) SW of Campeche; 100 miles (160km) N of San Cristóbal de las Casas

Villahermosa (pop. 265,000), the capital of the state of Tabasco, is right at the center of Mexico's oil boom—but it's off-center from just about everything else. Nevertheless, oil wealth has transformed this provincial town into a modern city, making it an interesting crossroads for those going overland and a popular port of entry for air travelers.

Prosperity has recently spurred a number of developments, including a beautiful park containing the **Parque Museo de la Venta;** the CICOM center for Olmec and Maya studies containing the **Museo Regional de Antropología Carlos Pellicer Cámara;** and the pedestrian-only area downtown with a few small galleries and museums. These are the three main areas that a visitor would want to see. Of less interest is the modern office building and shopping development called Tabasco 2000.

Two names that you will likely see and hear are Carlos Pellicer Cámara and Tomás Garrido Canabal. The first was a Tabascan poet and intellectual of this century. He is the best known of Mexico's "modernista" poets, and was a fiercely independent thinker. Garrido Canabal was socialist governor of Tabasco in the 1920s and 30s, who tried to turn the conservative, backwater state of Tabasco into a model of socialism. Garrido Canabal supported many socialist causes, but the one that became a highly personal issue with him was anticlericalism. He did such bizarre things as naming his son Lucifer, and his farm animals Jesus and the Virgin Mary. He also destroyed or closed many churches in Tabasco, including the cathedral of Villahermosa. Graham Greene provides a fictional depiction of him in *The Power and the Glory.*

ESSENTIALS
GETTING THERE & DEPARTING
BY PLANE   Getting to Villahermosa on the major Mexican airlines requires going through Mexico City. **Mexicana** (☎ **800/531-7921** or 93/16-3132; 93/56-0101 at

Road Conditions & Warnings

The drive between Villahermosa and Chetumal (about 350 miles) can seem interminable if the road is in poor condition. Vast parts of it are quite lonely; the U.S. State Department includes this road on its warning list due to car and bus hijackings. If you take it, one good stopover between the two would be at Xpujil, 62 miles west of Chetumal. (See "Side Trips from Bacalar: The Río Bec Ruin Route" in chapter 4.) Another potential stopover is Francisco Escárcega, but only in an emergency. Once here, you're not too far from wherever you're going.

the airport) and **Aeromexico** (☎ **800/237-6639** or 93/12-1528) both have three flights a day to/from Mexico City, and all connections go through there. **Aviación de Chiapas (Aviacsa)** (☎ **93/16-5700**, or 93/56-0132 at the airport) flies twice a day to Mexico City, twice a week to Cancún, and every day to Mérida. **AeroLitoral,** another regional airline and a subsidiary of Aeromexico (☎ **800/237-6639** or 93/12-6991), goes through Mexico City with a connection on to Veracruz, Tampico, Monterrey, and Houston. **Aerocaribe** (☎ **800/531-7921** or 93/16-5046), a subsidiary of Mexicana, has flights to several cities of southeast Mexico.

BY CAR   Highway 180 connects Campeche to Villahermosa (7 hours). Highway 186, which passes by the airport, joins highway 199 to Palenque and San Cristóbal de las Casas. The road to Palenque is a good one, and the drive takes 2 hours. Between Palenque and San Cristóbal the road turns mountainous and takes 4 to 5 hours. Because of past problems on this highway, it's a good idea to check at the tourism office to see if it's advisable to drive to San Cristóbal. Another way to get to San Cristóbal is to take highway 195 due south all the way to highway 190, which connects San Cristóbal to Tuxtla Gutiérrez, the capital of the state of Chiapas. This route bypasses Palenque, and isn't much shorter than the other way. On any of the mountainous roads, road conditions are apt to get worse during the rainy season between May and October.

BY BUS   The first-class **bus station** is at Mina and Merino (☎ **93/12-8900**), 3 blocks off Highway 180. Fifteen first-class ADO buses leave for Palenque (2¹/₂ hours) between 6am and 7:45pm. There are 22 first-class buses per day to Mexico City (14 hours) and cities in between. To Campeche there are 12 buses per day (7 hours); some of these go on to Mérida, or you can transfer. Autotransportes Cristóbal Colón has seven daily buses to Palenque, San Cristóbal de las Casas, and Tuxtla Gutiérrez.

ORIENTATION

ARRIVING   Driving in from Villahermosa's **airport,** which is 6¹/₂ miles east of town, you'll cross a bridge over the Río Grijalva, then turn left to reach downtown. Taxis to the downtown area cost $10.

From the **bus station,** local buses marked "Mercado–C. Camionera" or simply "Centro" leave frequently for the center of town. Taxis are readily available in front of the station.

Parking downtown can be difficult; it's best to find a parking lot. Use one that's guarded around the clock.

VISITOR INFORMATION   The **State Tourism Office** is in the Tabasco 2000 complex, Paseo Tabasco 1504, SEFICOT Building, Centro Administrativo del Gobierno (☎ **93/16-2890**). This is an inconvenient location for tourists and, under normal circumstances, not worth a special trip. It is on the second floor of the building

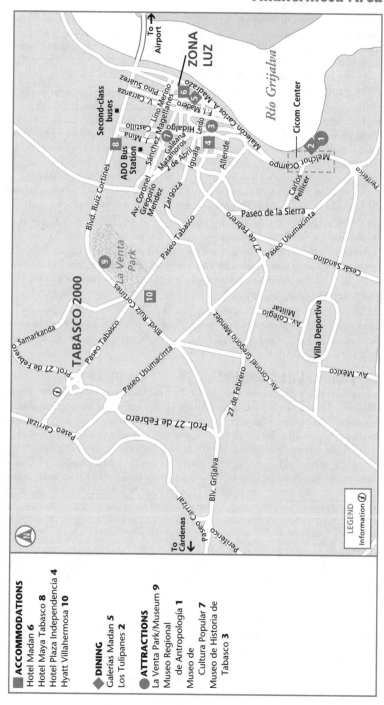

ACCOMMODATIONS
Hotel Madan **6**
Hotel Maya Tabasco **8**
Hotel Plaza Independencia **4**
Hyatt Villahermosa **10**

◆ **DINING**
Galerías Madan **5**
Los Tulipanes **2**

● **ATTRACTIONS**
La Venta Park/Museum **9**
Museo Regional
  de Antropología **1**
Museo de
  Cultura Popular **7**
Museo de Historia de
  Tabasco **3**

facing the Liverpool department store. Office hours are Monday through Friday from 10am to 8pm. There are two other branches—the **airport office** is staffed daily from 10am to 5pm, and **La Venta Park** has an office open Tuesday through Sunday from 10am to 5pm. The staff can supply rates and telephone numbers for the hotels, as well as useful telephone numbers for bus companies and airlines.

CITY LAYOUT   The downtown area, including the **Zona Luz,** is on the west bank of the Grijalva river. A mile upstream (south) is **CICOM,** with the large archaeology museum named for the poet Carlos Pellicer Cámara. On the other side of the river is the **airport.** From the airport, highway 180 crosses the river just to the north of downtown, becoming **bulevar Ruíz Cortines;** turning onto **Madero** or **Pino Suárez** would lead you downtown. Staying on Ruíz Cortines takes you by the Parque Museo de la Venta. It's well marked. Just beyond that is the intersection with **Paseo Tabasco**—then you're right in the heart of the modern hotel and shopping mall district. **Tabasco 2000** would be to the right. This is about 4 miles northwest of downtown.

GETTING AROUND   All the **city buses** converge on avenida Pino Suárez at the market and are clearly labeled for Tabasco 2000, Parque La Venta, and Centro.

Taxis from the center of town to main sites such as the Parque La Venta are inexpensive. If you're getting around **by car,** you'll be glad to know that Villahermosa's streets are well marked, with arrows clearly designating the direction of traffic.

FAST FACTS   **American Express** is represented by Turismo Nieves, bulevar Simón Sarlat 202 (☎ **93/14-1888**); hours are Mon–Fri 10am–2pm and 4–6pm, and Sat 10am–1pm. The telephone **area code** is **93.** There aren't a lot of handy *casas de cambio,* but you can exchange money at the airport, the hotels, and downtown banks on calles Juárez and Madero.

EXPLORING VILLAHERMOSA

Major sights in Villahermosa include the **Parque Museo de la Venta,** the **Museo Regional de Antropología Carlos Pellicer Cámara,** and the **History of Tabasco Museum.** You can hit them all in a day. There is also a new ecological park called **Yumká,** which is 10 miles out of town, in the direction of the airport (see below).

Stroll about the pedestrian-only Zona Luz and you'll see a number of outdoor cafes, ice cream shops, and some modest townhouses with typical features of tropical domestic architecture. Nearby is a small museum on Tabasco's traditional culture and crafts that is rather disappointing. There is also the house of Carlos Pellicer, the Tabascan poet, art collector, and intellectual, who occupied the place in later years with monastic simplicity. You can also walk over to the Plaza de Armas to see the Palacio de Gobierno and look out over the Grijalva river; there's a handsome pedestrian bridge with an observation tower that offers a good view.

✪ **Parque Museo de la Venta.** Blvd. Ruíz Cortines s/n. ☎ **93/14-1652.** Admission $2; Daily 8am–4pm. Take Paseo Tabasco northeast to Highway 180 and turn right; it's less than a mile down on your right.

The museum area occupies a part of a large park named after Tomás Garrido Canabal. The park also includes a lovely lake, a zoo, a natural history museum, and a lot of green space with several walkways frequented by joggers.

La Venta was one of three major Olmec cities during the Preclassic period (2000 B.C.–A.D. 300). Several monolithic heads and altars and other sculptures were discovered there in 1938. These were removed to this park, and now all that remains at La Venta are some grass-covered mounds—once earthen pyramids. At the entrance is an exhibit area that does a good job of displaying how La Venta was laid out, and what archeologists think the Olmec were like. The Olmecs created the first civilization in Mexico and developed several cultural traits that later spread to all subsequent civilizations throughout Mesoamerica. In addition to their monumental works (chiseled without the use of metal), they carved small exquisite figurines in jade and serpentine, which can be seen in the Museo Regional de Antropología (see below).

From the entrance, you follow a trail that leads to the various pieces, one by one. Carved around 1000 B.C., the heads and altars can be as tall as 6½ feet and weigh around 40 tons. The faces seem to be half-adult, half-infantile. They have a highly stylized mouth with thick fleshy lips that turn down. Known as the "jaguar mouth," it is a principal characteristic of Olmec art. The basalt rock used in sculpting these heads and the altars was transported to La Venta from over 70 miles away, which is all the more impressive when you realize the Olmec had no wheels to move it. The rock was thought to have been brought most of the way by raft. At least 17 heads have been found: 4 at La Venta, 10 at San Lorenzo, and 3 at Tres Zapotes—all Olmec cities on Mexico's east coast. As you stroll along, you will see many species of local trees labeled, including a grand Ceiba tree. There are a few varieties of the local critters scurrying about, too, seemingly unconcerned with the humans or with escaping from the park. Allow at least 2 hours to wander through the jungle-like sanctuary and examine the 3,000-year-old sculpture. Mosquito repellent is a must. If you haven't seen enough of the local flora and fauna, try the natural history museum that is right next to where you exit from the *parque museo*, or take a spin around the park's lake.

✪ **Museo Regional de Antropología Carlos Pellicer Cámara.** CICOM Center, av. Carlos Pellicer 511. ☎ **93/12-6344.** Admission $1.50. Daily 9am–7:30pm; gift shop Tues–Sun 10am–4pm.

This museum, on the west bank of the river a mile south of the town center, is well organized, has a great collection, and is architecturally bold and attractive. The pre-Hispanic artifacts on display include not only Tabascan finds (Totonac, Zapotec, and Olmec) but also those of other Mexican and Central American cultures.

The first floor contains the auditorium, bookstore, and gift shop; most interesting are the upper floors, reached by an elevator or the stairs. The second floor is devoted to the Olmec, while the third floor features artifacts relating to central Mexico, including the Tlatilco and Teotihuacán cultures; the Huasteca culture of Veracruz, San Luis Potosí, and Tampico states; and the west-coast cultures of the Nayarit state. Photographs and diagrams provide vivid images, but the explanatory signs are mostly in Spanish. Look especially for the figurines that were found in this area and for the colorful Codex (an early book of pictographs).

Museo de Historia de Tabasco (Casa de los Azulejos). At the corner of 27 de Febrero and Av. Juárez. No phone. Admission 50¢. Daily 10am–4pm, except Sat, 9am–8pm.

I like this place more for the house than for the exhibits. It is an eye-catcher both outside and inside. "Casa de los Azulejos" means house of the tiles, and there are several examples of lovely, intricate tile work here. Other architectural features are fun to look at, too. You can see the place, including the exhibits, in less than an hour. The exhibits mostly include a few antiques and artifacts of Tabasco's history, but it is apparent that not a lot of energy or money went into collecting and displaying them. Most of the descriptive text is in Spanish. The museum is located downtown at one end of the pedestrian-only Zona Luz area.

Yumká. Camino Yumká s/n, 86200 Ejido Dos Montes, Tabasco. ☎ **93/56-0107.** Admission $3. Daily 9am–5pm.

Half safari park, half ecological reserve, Yumká contains native and not-so-native wildlife. There is a guided tour of indigenous tropical forest, a boat tour of the wetlands ($1 extra for the ride), and a small train ride through grasslands populated with various species of African wildlife. This is a large park that takes at least 2 hours to see. There is a restaurant on the premises. Yumká is located 10 miles from downtown in the direction of the airport. There is a minibus that provides transportation (ask at the hotel or at a travel agency), or take a cab ($9).

WHERE TO STAY

Hotels are expensive in this boomtown. If you want to stay downtown, you have your choice of modest hotels; if you would rather stay out by the Parque/Museo La Venta, then the Hyatt has the best location.

EXPENSIVE

Hyatt Villahermosa. Av. Juárez 106, 86000 Villahermosa, Tab. ☎ **800/233-1234** in the U.S., or 93/15-1234. Fax 93/15-5808. 209 units. A/C MINIBAR TV TEL. $175 double; $198 Regency Club room. AE, DC, MC, V. Free guarded parking.

This hotel is not so fancy or as ostentatious as a typical Hyatt, but the rooms are quiet and comfortable and the service is good. The majority of its clients are business travelers. Rooms are ample, with tile floors. The bathrooms are a little smaller than in other hotels in this chain. The fifth floor is nonsmoking; floors 6 through 10 hold the Regency Club, where guests receive special amenities such as separate check-in, daily newspaper, continental breakfast, and evening cocktails. A short walk away is the park, and if you follow the path around the lake, you arrive at the Parque Museo La Venta.

Dining/Diversions: Two restaurants, a bar with live Latin music, and a sports bar. The main restaurant is very good.

Amenities: Laundry and room service, travel agency, car rental, pool, two tennis courts, boutiques, beauty shop, pharmacy, business center, concierge.

Best Western Hotel Maya Tabasco. Blvd. Ruíz Cortines 907, 86000 Villahermosa, Tab. ☎ **800/528-1234** in the U.S. or Canada, or 93/14-4466. Fax 93/12-1097. www. hotelmaya.com.mx. 156 units. A/C TV MINIBAR TEL. $115 double. AE, DC, MC, V. Free parking.

You can't go wrong with this comfortable and busy hotel where the services are that of a more upscale hotel. It's not the Hyatt, however, but it's darn close for comfort and service. The large, carpeted rooms come with a choice of single, double, and king-size beds. Some rooms have individually controlled air-conditioning, while others are centrally controlled. It's located on the main thoroughfare, convenient to the bus station, museums, and downtown. Two restaurants, one formal and one informal, and two bars and a large swimming pool seem to be popular hangouts. Laundry and room service, travel agency, and car rental are available. Free transportation to airport and downtown locations. Business center with e-mail access.

MODERATE

Hotel Plaza Independencia. Independencia 123, 86000 Villahermosa, Tab. ☎ **93/12-1299** or 93/12-7541. Fax 93/14-4724. www.hplaza.indepcia.com.mx. 89 units. A/C TV TEL. $63 double. DC, MC, V. Free parking.

Of the many hotels in this price range, the Plaza Independencia is one of the best. The guest rooms, on six floors served by an elevator, have rattan furnishings, including small desks, carpeted floors, and bathrooms that are larger than most hotels in this price range. Some rooms have balconies, and from the top floor you can see the river. It's the only budget hotel with a pool and enclosed parking, and it has laundry service. There's an off-lobby restaurant and bar. It's 2 blocks south of the Plaza de Armas.

INEXPENSIVE

Hotel Madán. Madero 408, 86000 Villahermosa, Tab. ☎ **93/12-1650.** Fax 93/14-3373. 20 units. A/C TV TEL. $42 double. AE, MC, V. Free secure parking.

The two-story Madán is a convenient downtown hotel within walking distance of the pedestrian-only zone and central-city museums. The rooms are clean and cheerful; they come with two singles, two doubles, or one double. Beds are a little soft. Rooms in the back are the quietest. The hotel's restaurant serves good food. It's between Reforma and Lerdo.

WHERE TO DINE

Like other Mexican cities, Villahermosa is beginning to receive U.S.-franchise restaurants, but if you're going to eat in a franchise-style restaurant, I would try one of the Mexican varieties that do a good job with traditional dishes: Sanborns or VIPS.

Galerías Madán. Madero 408. ☎ **93/12-1650.** Breakfast $3–$4; *comida corrida* (set menu) $4; main courses $3–$6. AE, DC, MC, V. Daily 7am–11pm (*comida corrida* served 1–4pm). MEXICAN.

Situated off the lobby of the hotel Madán, this calm, soft pink, air-conditioned restaurant serves a *comida corrida* of soup, rice, a main course, vegetables, coffee, and dessert. The *empanadas de carne* (meat pies) are worth a try, and the tamales are just plain good. Another popular dish is the *filete a la tampiqueña*. Large windows look onto the street, and the room has the feel of a hotel coffee shop where downtown shoppers and business types gather. It's situated between Lerdo de Tejada and Reforma.

✪ **Los Tulipanes.** CICOM Center, Periférico Carlos Pellicer Cámara 511. ☎ **93/12-9209** or 93/12-9217. Main courses $8–$13. AE, MC, V. Daily 1–9pm. SEAFOOD/STEAKS/ REGIONAL.

Popular with the local upper class, Los Tulipanes offers pricey but good food and excellent service. The staff seems to serve a full house with ease, and on busy days, a guitar trio strolls and serenades. Since the restaurant is located on the Río Grijalva near the Pellicer Museum of Anthropology, you can combine a visit to the museum with lunch here. They may bring you a plate of *tostones de plátano*—a mashed banana chip the size of a tortilla. In addition to seafood and steaks, there are such Mexican specialties as chiles rellenos, tacos, and *rejelagarto empanadas*. They have a wonderful buffet on Sundays for $10.

A SIDE TRIP TO CHOCOLATE PLANTATIONS & THE RUINS OF COMALCALCO

Fifty miles from Villahermosa is Comalcalco, the only pyramid site in Mexico made of kilned brick. Your route will take you through Tabasco's *cacao* (chocolate)-growing country, where you can visit plantations and factories to see the *cacao* from the pod on the tree to the finished chocolate bars.

You'll need a car to enjoy the *cacao* touring, but Comalcalco itself can be reached by bus from Villahermosa. ADO has first-class buses twice daily. From the town of Comalcalco, take a taxi or a VW minivan to the ruins, which are 2 miles farther. Travel agencies in Villahermosa offer a Comalcalco daytrip as well. Generally it leaves at 8am and returns around 5pm.

By car, the fastest route from Villahermosa is on Highway 190 west to Cárdenas, then north on Highway 187. Along the road to Cárdenas are numerous banana plantations and roadside stands, where you can buy direct. As you come into Cárdenas, look for the Alteza chocolate factory of the cooperative **Industriador de Cacao de Tabasco (INCATAB).** There's a sales shop in front where you can buy boxes of chocolate in all its variations. The big boxes are actually filled with small, wrapped, two-bite bars—which make great gifts and snacks.

Cárdenas is the center of *cacao* processing, but the fruit itself is grown on plantations in a wide area west of Villahermosa and as far south as Teapa and north to the coast. After you turn right at Cárdenas onto Highway 187, you'll begin passing trees laden with the heavy *cacao* pod, each full of small beans.

Twelve miles before Comalcalco, in the village of Cunduacán, stop and ask for directions to the **Asociación Agrícola de Productores de Cacao.** It's on the main street, but the sign isn't visible. Mornings are the best time for a tour during November through April when there's an abundance of *cacao.* Here, the *cacao* beans are received from the growers and processing begins. First the beans are fermented in huge tubs for a little over a week, then they are mechanically dried for 16 hours. A fresh white *cacao* bean is slightly larger and fatter than a lima bean, but after roasting it's brown, bitter, and smaller. The roasted beans are sacked and sent to the INCATAB chocolate cooperative in Cárdenas.

Along this route are many mom-and-pop *cacao* plantations, where families grow and process their own *cacao* and sell it at local markets and roadside stands rather than to the cooperative. One of these is **Rancho La Pasadita,** 4¹/₂ miles before Comalcalco on the right. Look carefully for the sign on the pink-and-blue house (it's a bit obscured) that says CHOCOLATE CASERO LA PASADITA. Here Aura Arellano has 19 acres of *cacao* trees that she planted in the 1950s. She will gladly take you out back where the trees grow, and if it's bean season (November through April), you'll more than likely see workers hacking open the football-shaped pods and dumping the contents in big wicker baskets. She ferments her beans the traditional way, in a hollowed-out, canoe-size wooden container. She dries and toasts the beans on a small *comal* (clay pan) over an open fire until they are hard like a nut, after which she grinds them to a powder, mixes it with sugar to cook, and makes it into logs for hot chocolate. These she sells in her living-room storefront. You will see this type of chocolate for sale in shops in Villahermosa.

Comalcalco, 25 miles from Cárdenas, is a busy agricultural center with an interesting market where you can buy wicker baskets, like those used to ferment *cacao,* and *pichanchas* (a gourd with multiple holes in it), used to extract flavor from fresh *cacao* beans for a refreshing drink.

The **ruins of Comalcalco** are about 2 miles on the same highway past the town; watch for signs to the turnoff on the right. Park in the lot and pay admission to the visitors' center by the museum. The museum, with many pre-Hispanic artifacts, is small but interesting and worth the 20 minutes or so it takes to see it. Unfortunately, all the descriptions are in Spanish. There's a history of the people who lived here, the Putún/Chongal Maya, a rough people who were traders, spoke fractured Mayan, and were believed to have founded or greatly influenced Chichén-Itzá.

The neat, grass-covered site spreads out grandly as you enter, with pyramidal mounds left, right, and straight ahead. Comalcalco means "house of the comals" in Nahuatl. A *comal* is a round clay pan used for roasting and making tortillas. All around the grounds you'll see shards of kilned brick that were used to sheath the sides of the pyramidal structures. These bricks were made out of clay mixed with sand and ground oyster shell. Owing to the fragile nature of these ruins, there are many NO SUBIR signs warning visitors not to climb particular structures. Others have paths and arrows pointing to the top. From the **palace** there's a fabulous view of the whole site. On the

Acropolis, under a protective covering, are remains of a few stucco and plaster masks in surprisingly good condition, although there are few of them. Seeing the ruins takes an hour or so. Admission is $2, and the site is open daily from 8am to 5pm. The afternoon light is great for photographs.

2 Palenque

89 miles (142km) SE of Villahermosa; 143 miles (229km) NE of San Cristóbal de las Casas

The ruins of Palenque look out over the jungle from a tall ridge, which projects from the base of steep, thickly forested mountains. It is a dramatic sight colored by the mysterious and ancient feel of the ruins themselves. The temples here are in the classic style with tall, high-pitched roofs crowned with elaborate combs. Inside many are representations in stone and plaster of the rulers and their gods, which give evidence of a cosmology that is and perhaps will remain impenetrable to our understanding. This is one of the grand archaeological sites of Mexico.

Five miles from the ruins is the town of Palenque. There you can find lodging and food, as well as make travel arrangements. Transportation between the town and ruins is cheap and convenient.

ESSENTIALS
GETTING THERE & DEPARTING

BY PLANE The new airport has service to various destinations via **Aerocaribe** (☎ 934/5-0618): Cancún (five flights per week); Mérida (two nonstop flights per week); San Cristóbal (four nonstop flights per week); and Tuxtla (five flights per week—two nonstop). There is one flight per week to Oaxaca with a stop in Tuxtla, and two flights per week requiring a change of planes. Mexico City (five flights per week) requires changing planes. Aerocaribe is a subsidiary of **Mexicana** (☎ 800/531-7921).

BY CAR The 143-mile trip from San Cristóbal to Palenque takes 5 hours and passes through lush jungle and mountain scenery. Take it easy, though, since potholes and other hindrances occur. Highway 186 from Villahermosa is in good condition, and the trip from there should take about 2 hours. There's always the possibility of military roadblocks and a cursory inspection of your travel credentials and perhaps your vehicle.

BY BUS The two first-class bus stations are about a block apart from each other. Both are on Palenque's main street between the main square and the turn-off for the ruins. The smaller company, **Transportes Rodolfo Figueroa,** offers good first-class bus service to/from San Cristóbal and Tuxtla (four per day—5 hours to San Cristóbal, 6½ to Tuxtla). **Cristóbal Colón** offers service to those destinations as well as to Campeche (six per day, 5 hours), Villahermosa (nine per day, 2 hours), and Mérida (two per day, 9 hours).

ORIENTATION

VISITOR INFORMATION The **State Tourism Office** (☎/fax 934/5-0356) is a block before the main square, where avenida Juárez intersects Abasolo. The office is open Monday through Saturday from 9am to 9pm; Sunday from 9am to 1pm.

CITY LAYOUT **Avenida Juárez** is Palenque's main street. At one end of it is the **main plaza,** at the other is the impossible-to-miss **Maya statue.** To the right of the statue is the entrance to the Cañada, to the left is the road to the ruins, straight ahead past the statue is the airport and the highway to Villahermosa. The distance between the main square and the monument is about a mile.

La Cañada, a restaurant and hotel zone, is a small area tucked into the rain forest. Here you'll find shaded, unpaved streets, a few small hotels and restaurants, and stands of artists who carve and paint. Aside from the main plaza area, this is the best location for travelers without cars, since the town is within a few blocks, and the buses that run to the ruins pass right by.

GETTING AROUND   The cheapest way to get back and forth from the ruins is on the white **VW buses,** which run down Juárez every 10 minutes from 6am to 6pm. The buses pass La Cañada and hotels along the road to the ruins and can be flagged down at any point, but they may not stop if they're full.

FAST FACTS   The telephone area code is **934.** As for the **climate,** Palenque's high humidity is downright oppressive in the summer, especially after rain showers. During the winter, the damp air can on occasion be chilly in the evenings. Rain gear is important any time of year.

EXPLORING PALENQUE

The real reason for being here is the ruins; although they can be toured in a morning, many people savor Palenque for days. There are no must-see sights in town. The La Cañada area west of town (see "City Layout," above) is a pleasant spot for a leisurely lunch and for browsing through Maya reproductions made by local artists.

PARQUE NACIONAL PALENQUE

The archaeological site of Palenque underwent several changes in 1994, culminating in the opening of a new **museum/visitor center** not far from the entrance to the ruins. The complex includes a large parking lot, a refreshment stand serving snacks and drinks, and several shops. Though not large, the museum is worth the time it takes to see; it's open Tuesday through Sunday from 10am to 5pm and is included in the price of admission. It contains well-chosen and artistically displayed exhibits, including the jade contents of recently excavated tombs. (The museum was robbed in 1996, but most of the jade pieces have been recovered.) Explanatory texts, in both Spanish and English, explain the life and times of the magnificent city of Palenque. New pieces are always being added as they are uncovered in ongoing excavations.

The **main entrance,** about a half mile beyond the museum, is at the end of the paved highway. There you'll find a large parking lot, a refreshment stand, a ticket booth, and several shops. Among the vendors selling souvenirs by the parking lot are Lacandón Indians wearing white tunics and hawking bows and arrows.

Admission to the ruins is $4; free on Sunday. There's a $4 charge for each video camera used. Parking at the main entrance and at the visitor center is free. The site and visitor center shops are open daily from 8am to 4:45pm; King Pacal's crypt is open daily from 10am to 4pm.

TOURING THE RUINS   Pottery found during the excavations shows that people lived in this area as early as 300 B.C. During the Classic period (A.D. 300–900), the ancient Maya city of Palenque was a ceremonial center for the high priests; the civilization peaked at around A.D. 600 to 700.

When John Stephens visited the site in the 1840s, the cleared ruins you see today were buried under centuries of accumulated earth and a thick canopy of jungle. The dense jungle surrounding the cleared portion still covers yet unexplored temples, which are easily discernible in the forest even to the untrained eye. But be careful not to drift too far from the main paths. In the recent past there have been a few incidents where solitary tourists venturing into the rain forest were assaulted.

Palenque Archaeological Site

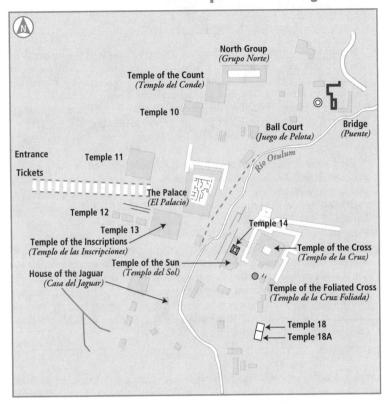

Of all the ruins in Mexico open to the public, this is the most haunting because of its majesty and sense of the past. Scholars have unearthed names of the rulers and their family histories, putting visitors on a first-name basis with these ancient people etched in stone. You can read about it in *A Forest of Kings,* by Linda Schele and David Friedel.

As you enter the ruins from the entrance, the building on your right is the **Temple of the Inscriptions,** named for the great stone hieroglyphic panels found inside. Just to your right as you face the Temple of the Inscriptions is **Temple 13,** which is receiving considerable attention from archaeologists. Recently, the burial of another richly adorned personage was discovered here, accompanied in death by an adult female and an adolescent. These remains are still being studied, but the treasures are on display in the museum.

When you're back on the main pathway, the building directly in front of you will be the **Palace,** with its unique watchtower. The explorer John Stephens camped in the Palace when it was completely tree- and vine-covered, spending sleepless nights fighting off mosquitoes. A pathway between the Palace and the Temple of the Inscriptions leads to the **Temple of the Sun,** the **Temple of the Foliated Cross,** the **Temple of the Cross,** and **Temple 14.** This group of temples, now cleared and in various stages of reconstruction, was built by Pacal's son, Chan-Bahlum, who is usually shown on inscriptions as having six toes. Chan-Bahlum's plaster mask was found in Temple 14 next to the Temple of the Sun. Archaeologists have recently begun probing the depths of the Temple of the Sun in search of Chan-Bahlum's tomb. Little remains of this

King Pacal's Tomb

The great stone hieroglyphic panels found inside the **Temple of the Inscriptions** contain the dynastic family tree of King Pacal. (Most of the panels are in the National Anthropological Museum in Mexico City.) This temple is famous for the tomb, or crypt, of Pacal, that the archaeologist Alberto Ruz Lhuller discovered in its depths in 1952. Ruz's discovery of the tomb is considered by Mayanist scholars to be among a handful of great discoveries in the Maya world. Ruz's own grave site is opposite the Temple of the Inscriptions, on the left as you enter the park.

Pacal began building the temple less than a decade before he died at age 80 in A.D. 683. It took Ruz and his crew four seasons of digging to clear out the rubble designed to conceal the crypt containing the remains of King Pacal. The crypt itself is 80 feet below the floor of the temple and was covered by a monolithic sepulchral slab, 12½-feet-long and 7-feet-wide, engraved with a depiction of Pacal falling backwards from the land of the living into the underworld. Four men and a woman were left at the entrance to the crypt when it was sealed so that they could accompany Pacal on his journey through the underworld. Unless you're claustrophobic, you should visit the tomb to see the burial vault and the sepulchral slab. The way down is lit, but the steps can be slippery. Carved inscriptions on the sides of the crypt (which visitors can't see) show the funerary rites carried out at the time of Pacal's death and portray the lineage of Pacal's ancestors, complete with family portraits.

temple's exterior carving. Inside, however, behind a fence, a carving of Chan-Bahlum shows him ascending the throne in A.D. 690. The panels, which are still in place, depict Chan-Bahlum's version of his historic link to the throne.

To the left of the Palace is the North Group, also undergoing restoration. Included in this area are the **Ball Court** and the **Temple of the Count,** so named because Count Waldeck camped there in the 19th century. At least three tombs, complete with offerings for the underworld journey, have been found here, and the lineage of at least 12 kings has been deciphered from inscriptions left at this site.

Just past the North Group is a small building (once a museum) now used for storing the artifacts found during the restorations. It is closed to the public. To the right of the building, a stone bridge crosses the river, leading to a pathway down the hillside to the new museum. The path, lined with rocks and with steps in the steepest areas, leads past the **Cascada Motiepa,** a beautiful waterfall that creates a series of pools perfect for cooling weary feet. Benches are placed along the way as rest areas, and some small temples have been reconstructed near the base of the trail. In the early morning and evening, you may hear monkeys crashing through the thick foliage by the path; if you keep noise to a minimum, you may spot wild parrots as well. Walking downhill (by far the best way to go), it will take you about 20 minutes to reach the main highway. The path ends at the paved road across from the museum. The *colectivos* going back to the village will stop here if you wave them down.

WHERE TO STAY

The fanciest hotel in town (the Hotel Misión Park Inn Palenque) gets too many complaints for me to recommend it. And with the recent addition of some upscale hotels, it faces stiff competition. English is spoken in most of the good hotels. Transportation

Palenque Accommodations & Dining

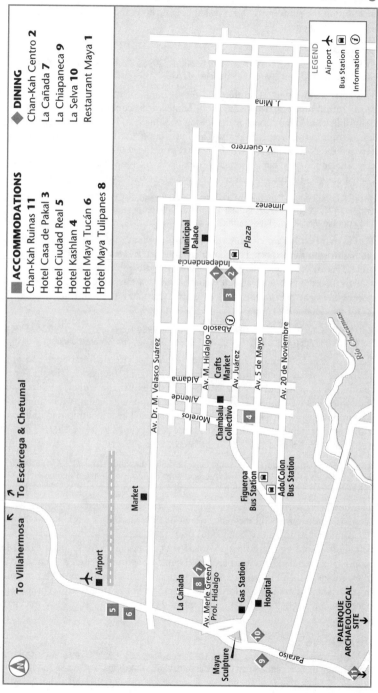

■ ACCOMMODATIONS

Chan-Kah Ruinas **11**
Hotel Casa de Pakal **3**
Hotel Ciudad Real **5**
Hotel Kashlan **4**
Hotel Maya Tucán **6**
Hotel Maya Tulipanes **8**

◆ DINING

Chan-Kah Centro **2**
La Cañada **7**
La Chiapaneca **9**
La Selva **10**
Restaurant Maya **1**

LEGEND
Airport ✈
Bus Station ▣
Information ⓘ

To Villahermosa
To Escárcega & Chetumal

Airport

Market

Av. Dr. M. Velasco Suárez

La Cañada
Av. Merle Green/
Prof. Hidalgo

Gas Station

Hospital

Maya
Sculpture

Paraíso

PALENQUE
ARCHAEOLOGICAL
SITE

Figueroa
Bus Station

Ado/Colon
Bus Station

Chambalu
Collectivo

Morelos
Allende
Aldama
Av. M. Hidalgo
Abasolo
Av. Juárez
Av. 5 de Mayo
Av. 20 de Noviembre

Crafts
Market

Municipal
Palace

Plaza

Independencia
Jimenez
V. Guerrero
J. Mina

Río Chacamax

to and from the ruins is easy from just about any hotel and should not be of concern when choosing one.

MODERATE

✪ **Chan-Kah Ruinas.** Km 30 Carretera Palenque, 29960 Palenque, Chi. ☎ **934/5-1100.** Fax 934/5-0820. 72 units A/C. $85 double. AE, MC, V. Free parking.

This hotel is a grouping of comfortable, roomy bungalows that offer privacy and quiet in the surroundings of a tropical forest. Some are air-conditioned. The grounds are beautifully tended, and there is an inviting pool made to look like a lagoon. A broad stream runs through the property. The hotel is on the road to the ruins midway between the ruins and the town. Christmas prices may be higher than those quoted here, and you may be quoted a higher price if you reserve a room in advance from the United States. The hotel has an outdoor restaurant/bar serving Mexican food.

Hotel Ciudad Real. Carretera a Pakal-Na, 29960 Palenque, Chi. (Reservations made in San Cristóbal.) ☎ **9/678-0187.** E-mail: 103144.2762@compuserve.com. 72 units. A/C TV TEL. $100 double. AE, MC, V. Free secured parking.

This is your best bet for creature comforts and modern convenience. The hotel is on the highway to the airport. The rooms are large, quiet, well lit, and comfortably furnished. Facilities include a large pool, a baby pool, a bar featuring live marimba music at night, a restaurant with an international menu, a travel agency, and a handcrafts store. When making a reservation be sure that the reservation-taker understands that it's for the hotel in Palenque.

Hotel Maya Tucán. Carretera-Palenque Km. 0.5, 29960 Palenque, Chi. ☎ **934/5-0443.** Fax 934/5-0337. 60 units. A/C TV TEL. $75 double. MC, V. Free secured parking.

Get a room in back and you will have a view of the hotel's natural pond. All of the adequately sized and cheerfully decorated rooms come with double beds. The air-conditioner is quiet and gets the job done. Facilities include a pool, restaurant, bar, and sometimes a discotheque—when large tour groups are present (which might bear asking about before checking in). The grounds are well kept in a tropical fashion, and scarlet macaws kept by the hotel fly about the parking lot. The Maya Tucán is a stone's throw from the Ciudad Real on the highway to the airport.

Hotel Maya Tulipanes. Calle Cañada 6, 29960 Palenque, Chi. ☎ **934/5-0201** or 934/5-0258. Fax 934/5-1004. E-mail: mtulipan@mail.ciberpal.com.mx. 50 units. A/C TV TEL. $56 double. AE, MC, V. Free parking.

This hotel tries hard to remind you why you have come to Palenque—Maya statues, carvings, and paintings fill the hallways and public areas in this rambling, overgrown, but comfortable, two-story hotel. And because the hotel is in the Cañada, it has a definite tropical-forest feel; the dark shade is a cool respite from the sun's glare. Most rooms are a little dark and some are small, but it varies from section to section, so ask to see rooms in different parts of the hotel. All in all, this is a fun, very Mexican place to stay, though it's not as comfortable as the others in this category. Recently, a small pool was added. The hotel has a restaurant, and there are a couple of good restaurants nearby.

INEXPENSIVE

✪ **Hotel Casa de Pakal.** Av. Juárez 10, 29960 Palenque, Chi. ☎ **934/5-0443** (at the Maya Tucán; make sure that they understand that you wish to stay at Casa de Pakal). 15 rms. A/C. $33 double. MC, V.

This bright, relatively new, four-story hotel might be the best bargain in town if you don't have a car. The rooms are a little small but far brighter and cleaner than those at nearby choices, and they come with one double and one single bed. The air-conditioning is strong and quiet. A good restaurant is on the premises. The hotel is a half-block west of the main plaza.

Hotel Kashlan. 5 de Mayo 105, 29960 Palenque, Chi. ☎ **934/5-0297.** Fax 934/5-0309. 59 units (27 with A/C). $18–$35 double. MC, V.

This is the closest hotel to the bus station and a dependable choice. The clean rooms have interior windows opening onto the hall, marble-square floors, soft bedspreads, tile bathrooms, small vanities, and luggage racks. Show owner Ada Luz Navarro your *Frommer's* book and you'll receive a discount. Higher prices are for rooms with air-conditioning (there are 27, and some of the new rooms are quite comfortable); ceiling fans (in 30 rooms) are powerful. The hotel restaurant features vegetarian food. Trips around the region, including to Agua Azul and Misol Ha, can also be arranged at the hotel.

WHERE TO DINE

Avenida Juárez is lined with many small restaurants, none of which are noteworthy. There are a couple in the main plaza, some on the road to the ruins, and a couple in the Cañada that I do like.

MODERATE

La Chiapaneca. Carretera Palenque Ruinas. ☎ **934/5-1711.** Main courses $8–$10. AE, MC, V. Daily 8am–12am. MEXICAN.

Considered by many to be Palenque's best restaurant, La Chiapaneca serves top-notch regional cuisine in a pleasant tropical setting. The *pollo Palenque* (chicken with potatoes in a tomato-and-onion sauce) is a soothing choice; save room for the flan. Mexican wines are served by the bottle. La Chiapaneca is about a mile toward the ruins from the Maya statue.

✪ **La Selva.** Km 0.5 Carretera Palenque Ruinas. ☎ **934/5-0363.** Main courses $7–$17. AE, MC, V. Daily 8am–12pm. MEXICAN/INTERNATIONAL.

La Selva (the jungle) offers fine dining in a large, outdoor space under a beautiful thatched roof and beside well-tended gardens. The menu includes seafood, freshwater fish, steaks, and enchiladas. The most expensive thing on the menu is Pigua—a freshwater lobster that is caught in the large rivers of southeast Mexico. These can get quite large—the size of small saltwater lobsters. I especially liked the fish stuffed with shrimp or the mole enchiladas. La Selva is on the highway to the ruins close by the Maya statue.

INEXPENSIVE

Chan-Kah Centro. Juárez 2. ☎ **934/5-0318.** Breakfast $2.25–$3; *comida corrida* $3–$4; main courses $4–$7. AE, MC, V. Daily 7am–11pm. MEXICAN.

This attractive hotel restaurant is the most peaceful place to eat in town. The waiters are extremely attentive, and the food is well prepared (avoid the tough beef, though). The second-story bar overlooks the main plaza—you can have your meal served there. The restaurant is on the west side of the main plaza at the corner of Independencia and Juárez.

La Cañada. Prolongación Av. Hidalgo 12. ☎ **934/5-0102.** Main courses $5–$9. No credit cards. Daily 7am–10pm. MEXICAN.

This *palapa* restaurant tucked into the jungle is one of the best in town and is usually very peaceful. Though the dining room has a dirt floor, the place is spotless, the service attentive, and the food good, if not outstanding. Try one of the local specialties such as *pollo mexicano* or bean soup. This restaurant is in the Hotel La Cañada.

✪ **Restaurant Maya.** Av. Independencia s/n. ☎ **934/5-0042.** Breakfast $3–$5; main courses $4–$5. AE, MC, V. Daily 7am–11pm. MEXICAN/STEAKS.

A popular place in town among tourists and locals, Restaurant Maya faces the main plaza on the northwest corner. The dining area is breezy and open. At breakfast, there are free refills of very good coffee. Try the tamales or any of the other local dishes or traditional Mexican fare. This restaurant was awarded a national prize for quality and service. A new branch has recently opened in the Cañada, called Maya Cañada.

ROAD TRIPS FROM PALENQUE
SPECTACULAR WATERFALLS AT AGUA AZUL & CASCADA DE MISOL HA
The most popular excursion from Palenque is a day-trip to the Misol Ha waterfall and Agua Azul. **Misol Ha** is about 12 miles from Palenque off the road to Ocosingo (sign pointing to the right). Visitors can swim in the waters below the falls and scramble up slippery paths to smaller falls beside the large one, which drops about 90 feet before spraying its mist on the waters below. There's a small restaurant run by the *ejido* cooperative that owns the site. Entrance costs around $1 per person; $2 per car.

Approximately 24 miles beyond Misol Ha on the same road are the **Agua Azul waterfalls,** a truly spectacular series of beautiful cascades tumbling into a wide river. Seeing both is a full day-trip. Visitors can picnic and relax (bring something to sprawl on), swim, or clamber over the slippery cascades and go upstream for a look at the jungle encroaching the water. Agua Azul is prettiest after 3 or 4 consecutive dry days; heavy rains can make the water very murky. Check with guides or other travelers about the water quality before you decide to go. The cost to enter is around $2. Trips can be arranged through **Viajes Shivalva Tours, Viajes Toniná** (see "Bonampak & Yaxchilán: Ruins & Rugged Adventure," below), or the **Hotel Kashlan,** and cost about $10 per person for the day.

BONAMPAK & YAXCHILÁN: RUINS & RUGGED ADVENTURE
Intrepid travelers may wish to consider the 2-day excursion to the Maya ruins of Bonampak and Yaxchilán. The **ruins of Bonampak,** southeast of Palenque on the Guatemalan border, were discovered in 1946. The **mural** discovered on the interior walls of one of the buildings is the greatest battle painting of pre-Hispanic Mexico. Reproductions of the vivid murals found here are on view in the Regional Archaeology Museum in Villahermosa.

You can fly or drive to Bonampak. Several tour companies offer a 2-day (minimum) tour by four-wheel-drive vehicle to within 4 1/2 miles of Bonampak. You must walk the rest of the way to the ruins. After camping overnight, you continue by river to the extensive ruins of the great Maya city, Yaxchilán, famous for its highly ornamented buildings. Bring rain gear, boots, a flashlight, and bug repellent. All tours include meals but vary in price ($80 to $120 per person); some take far too many people for comfort (the 7-hour road trip can be unbearable).

The most reputable tour operators in Palenque are Viajes Shivalva, and Viajes Toniná. **Viajes Shivalva** is located at calle Merle Green 1 (☎ **934/5-0411;** fax 934/5-0392). Office hours are Monday through Friday from 7am to 10pm. A branch office is now open a block from the *zócalo* (main plaza) at the corner of Juárez and Abasolo (across the hall from the State Tourism Office). It's open Monday through Saturday from 9am to 9pm (☎ **934/5-0822). Viajes Toniná** is located at calle Juárez 105 (☎ **934/5-0384).**

3 San Cristóbal de las Casas

143 miles (229km) SW of Palenque; 50 miles (80km) E of Tuxtla Gutiérrez; 46 miles (74km) NW of Comitán; 104 miles (166km) NW of Cuauhtémoc; 282 miles (451km) E of Oaxaca

San Cristóbal (population 90,000) is a colonial town of white stucco walls and red-tile roofs, of cobblestone streets and narrow sidewalks, of graceful arcades and open plazas. It lies in a lush valley nearly 7,000-feet-high. The city owes part of its name to the 16th-century cleric Fray Bartolomé de las Casas, who was the first bishop for the town, and who spent the rest of his life waging a political campaign to protect the indigenous peoples of the Americas.

Surrounding the city are many villages of Mayan-speaking Indians who display great variety in their language, dress, and customs, making this area one of the most fascinating in Mexico. San Cristóbal is for these Indians the principal market town and their point of contact with the outside world. Most of them trek down from the surrounding mountains to sell goods and perform errands; some now even live in San Cristóbal because they have been expelled from their villages for religious reasons.

Probably the most visible among the local indigenous groups are the **Chamula.** The men wear baggy thigh-length trousers and white or black *sarapes,* while the women wear blue *rebozos,* gathered white blouses with embroidered trim, and black wool wraparound skirts.

Another local Indian group is the **Zinacantecan,** whose male population dresses in light-pink overshirts with colorful trim and tassels and sometimes short pants. Hat ribbons (now a rare sight) are tied on married men, while ribbons dangle loosely from the hats of bachelors and community leaders. The Zinacantecan women wear beautiful, brightly colored woven shawls along with black wool skirts. You may also see **Tenejapa** men clad in knee-length black tunics and flat straw hats and Tenejapa women dressed in beautiful reddish and rust-colored *huipils.* Women of all groups are barefooted, while men wear handmade sandals or cowboy boots.

There are several Indian villages within reach of San Cristóbal by road: **Chamula,** with its weavers and highly unorthodox church; **Zinacantán,** whose residents practice their own syncretic religion; **Tenejapa, San Andrés,** and **Magdalena,** known for brocaded textiles; **Amatenango del Valle,** a town of potters; and **Aguacatenango,** known for embroidery. Most of these "villages" consist of little more than a church and the municipal government building, with homes scattered for miles around and a general gathering only for church and market days (usually Sunday).

Evangelical Protestant missionaries recently have converted large numbers of indigenous peoples, and in some villages new converts find themselves expelled from their homelands; in Chamula, for example, as many as 30,000 people have been expelled. Many of these people, called *expulsados* (expelled ones), have taken up residence in new villages on the outskirts of San Cristóbal de las Casas. They still wear their traditional dress. Other villages, such as Tenejapa, allow the Protestant church to exist and villagers to attend it without prejudice.

Although the influx of outsiders is nothing new, and in the last 20 years as been increasing, it doesn't seem to make most Indians want to adopt a more modern style of manners and dress; if anything, it's working in quite the opposite way. It's interesting to note that it is in fact the communities closest to San Cristóbal that are the most resistant to change. The greatest threat to the cultures in this area does not come from tourism, but from the action of large market forces, population pressures, and environmental damage. The Indians aren't really interested in acting or looking like the foreigners they see. They may steal glances at tourists or even stare curiously, but mainly they pay little attention to outsiders, except as potential buyers for handcrafts.

You'll hear the word *ladino* here; it refers to non-Indian Mexicans or people who have taken up modern ways, changed their dress, dropped their Indian traditions and language, and decided to live in town. It may be used derogatorily or descriptively, depending on who is using the term and how.

Other local lingo you should know about includes *Jovel,* San Cristóbal's original name, used often by businesses; and *coleto,* meaning someone or something from San Cristóbal. You'll see signs for *tamales coletos, coleto* bread, and *coleto* breakfast.

ESSENTIALS
GETTING THERE & DEPARTING

BY PLANE   San Cristóbal has a new airport, but regularly scheduled flights are still not available. Most people fly in through Tuxtla Gutiérrez, which is close by. Charter-flight arrangements or flight changes on any airline in another city can be made through **ATC Tours and Travel,** across from El Fogón de Jovel Restaurant in San Cristóbal (☎ **9/678-2550;** fax 9/678-3145).

BY CAR   From Tuxtla, a 1¹⁄₂-hour trip, the road winds through beautiful mountain country. From Palenque, the road is just as beautiful, if somewhat longer (5 hours), and provides jungle scenery, but portions of it may be heavily potholed or obstructed during rainy season. Check with the state tourism office before driving.

BY TAXI   Taxis from Tuxtla Gutiérrez to San Cristóbal cost around $50.

BY BUS   The two bus stations in town are directly across the Pan American Highway from each other. The smaller one belongs to **Transportes Rodolfo Figueroa (TRF),** which provides first-class service to/from Tuxtla (every 40 minutes) and Palenque (four buses per day with a stop in Ocosingo—cheaper than the competition). For other destinations go to the large station run by **ADO** and its affiliates, Cristóbal Colón and Maya de Oro. This company offers service to/from Tuxtla (12 buses per day), Palenque (almost every hour), and several other destinations: Mérida (two buses per day), Villahermosa (two buses per day), Oaxaca (two buses per day), and Puerto Escondido (two buses per day).

ORIENTATION

ARRIVING   To get to the main plaza if you're arriving by car from Oaxaca/Tuxtla, turn left on **avenida Insurgentes** (there's a traffic light); if you're coming from Palenque/Ocosingo, turn right. From the bus station, the main plaza is 9 blocks north up avenida Insurgentes (a 10-minute walk slightly uphill). Cabs are cheap and plentiful.

VISITOR INFORMATION   The **State Tourism Office** is just off the southwest corner of the main plaza, at Av. Hidalgo 1 (☎ 9/678-6570); it's open Monday through Saturday 9am to 9pm, and Sunday 9am to 2pm. The **Municipal Tourism Office** (☎/fax 9/678-0665) is in the town hall, west of the main square. Hours are Monday through Saturday from 9am to 8pm. Check the bulletin board here for apartments, shared rides, cultural events, and local tours. Both offices are helpful, but the state office is open an hour later and usually has more staff to attend the public.

CITY LAYOUT   San Cristóbal is laid out on a grid; the main north-south axis is **Insurgentes/Utrilla** and the east-west axis is **Mazariegos/Madero.** All streets change names when they cross either of these streets. **Real de Guadalupe** seems to have become a principal street for tourism-related businesses. The market is 9 blocks north along Utrilla. From the market, minibuses (*colectivos*) trundle to outlying villages.

Take note that this town has at least three streets named "Domínguez" and two streets named "Flores." There's Hermanos Domínguez, Belisario Domínguez, and Pantaleón Domínguez, and María Adelina Flores and Dr. José Flores.

San Cristóbal de las Casas

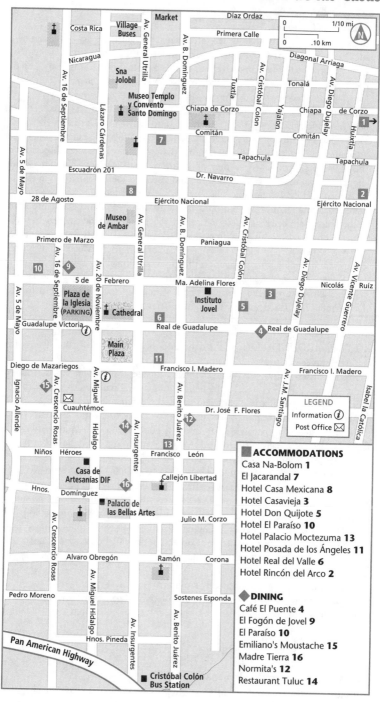

Costa Rica

Nicaragua

Village Buses

Market

Díaz Ordaz

Primera Calle

Diagonal Arriaga

0   1/10 mi
0   .10 km

N

Sna Jolobil

Museo Templo y Convento Santo Domingo

Tonalá

Chiapa de Corzo

Comitán

de Corzo

1

Chíapa

Comitán

Tuxtla

Yajalón

Tapachula

Huixtla

Tapachula

7

Escuadrón 201

Dr. Navarro

28 de Agosto

8

Ejército Nacional

Ejército Nacional

2

Museo de Ambar

Primero de Marzo

Paniagua

10   9

5 de Febrero

Ma. Adelina Flores

Nicolás   Ruíz

Plaza de la Iglesia (PARKING)

Instituto Jovel

3

Cathedral

5

Guadalupe Victoria

6

Real de Guadalupe

Real de Guadalupe

4

Main Plaza

11

Diego de Mazariegos

Francisco I. Madero

Francisco I. Madero

15

Cuauhtémoc

Dr. José F. Flores

12

Niños   Héroes

14

Francisco León

13

Casa de Artesanías DIF

Callejón Libertad

LEGEND
Information (i)
Post Office ✉

16

Hnos.

Domínguez

Palacio de las Bellas Artes

Julio M. Corzo

Alvaro Obregón

Ramón   Corona

Pedro Moreno

Sostenes Esponda

Hnos. Pineda

Pan American Highway

Cristóbal Colón Bus Station

■ ACCOMMODATIONS

Casa Na-Bolom **1**
El Jacarandal **7**
Hotel Casa Mexicana **8**
Hotel Casavieja **3**
Hotel Don Quijote **5**
Hotel El Paraíso **10**
Hotel Palacio Moctezuma **13**
Hotel Posada de los Ángeles **11**
Hotel Real del Valle **6**
Hotel Rincón del Arco **2**

◆ DINING

Café El Puente **4**
El Fogón de Jovel **9**
El Paraíso **10**
Emiliano's Moustache **15**
Madre Tierra **16**
Normita's **12**
Restaurant Tuluc **14**

235

Zapatista Uprising & Lingering Tensions

In January 1994, Indians from this area rebelled against the *ladino*-led towns and Mexican government over health care, education, land distribution, and representative government. Their organization, the **Zapatista Liberation Army (Ejército Zapatista de Liberación Nacional, or EZLN),** and its leader, Subcomandante Marcos, have become world famous. Since the revolt, discussions between government officials and the leadership of the EZLN have stalled. Progress has been made, but the principal issues remain unresolved, and tension still exists in the area. In December 1997 and January 1998 there were more killings, but these have been attributed to local political division rather than the tension between Zapatistas and the national government. We may never know the truth. I was in San Cristóbal shortly afterward, and again a year later, and saw no evidence of tension in the town or the valley. Life was normal. The only visible signs I found of the confrontation were the initials EZLN painted on a few walls and little Subcomandante Marcos dolls, replete with black ski masks, offered for sale by street vendors (a very hot-selling item, by the way). Locals gave no evidence of concern. Tourists were present. Only the newspapers made issue of an impending confrontation. Much to my surprise, there were no military roadblocks on the highway connecting Palenque, Ocosingo, and San Cristóbal, although there are said to be a number of road blocks in the region. Before traveling to Chiapas, check your news sources and see if the State Department has issued any advisories: http://travel.state.gov.

GETTING AROUND   Most of the sights and shopping in San Cristóbal are within walking distance of the plaza.

Urbano buses—minibuses—take residents to and from town and the outlying neighborhoods. All buses pass by the market and central plaza on their way through town. Utrilla and avenida 16 de Septiembre are the two main arteries; all buses use the market area as the last stop. Any bus on Utrilla will take you to the market.

Colectivos to outlying villages depart from the public market at avenida Utrilla. Buses late in the day are usually very crowded. Always check to see when the last or next-to-last bus returns from wherever you're going, then take the one before that—those last buses sometimes don't materialize, and you might be stranded. I speak from experience!

Rental cars come in handy for trips to the outlying villages and may be worth the expense when shared by a group, but keep in mind that insurance is invalid on unpaved roads. There's a **Budget** rental-car office here at Av. Mazariegos 36 (☎ **9/678-3100**). You'll save money by arranging the rental from your home country; otherwise, a day's rental with insurance will cost $62 for a VW Beetle with manual transmission, the cheapest car available. Office hours are Monday through Sunday from 8am to 1pm and 5 to 8pm.

Bikes are another option for getting around the city; a day's rental is about $8, and bike tours to a few out-of-town locations are offered at **Los Pingüinos,** Av. 5 de Mayo 10-B (☎ **9/678-0202**), open daily 10am to 2:30pm and 4 to 7pm.

Fast Facts: San Cristóbal de las Casas

Area Code   The telephone **area code** is **9.**

Books   *Living Maya* by Walter Morris, with photography by Jeffrey Fox, is the best book to read to understand the culture, art, and traditions surrounding

San Cristóbal de las Casas, as well as the unsolved social, economic, and political problems that gave rise to the 1994 Chiapas Indian uprising. *The People of the Bat: Mayan Tales and Dreams from Zinacantán,* by Robert M. Laughlin, is a priceless collection of beliefs from that village near San Cristóbal. Another good book with a completely different view of today's Maya is *The Heart of the Sky* by Peter Canby, who traveled among the Maya to chronicle their struggles (written before the Zapatista uprising).

Bookstore   For the best selection of new and used books and reading material in English, go to **La Pared,** Av. Hidalgo 2 (☎ **9/678-6367**). The owner, Dana Gay Burton, is kind and well informed. She also sells postcards, tee shirts, and amber.

Bulletin Boards   Since San Cristóbal is a cultural crossroads for travelers from all over the world, several places maintain bulletin boards with information on Spanish classes, local specialty tours, rooms or houses to rent, rides needed, etc. These include boards at the **Tourism Office, Café El Puente, Madre Tierra,** and **Casa Na-Bolom.**

Climate   San Cristóbal can be cold day or night year-round, especially during the winter. Most hotels are not heated, although some have fireplaces. There is always a possibility of rain, but I would particularly avoid going to San Cristóbal from late-August to late-October.

Currency Exchange   There are at least five *casas de cambio* on Real de Guadalupe near the main square and a couple under the colonnade facing the square. Most are open until 8pm, and some are open Sunday.

Doctor   The only doctor worth seeing is Dr. Roberto Lobato, calle Guadalupe Victoria 25, ☎ **9/678-1910.**

E-mail   The **Cyberc@fe** is in the little concourse that cuts through the block that is just east of the main square. Look for the entrance on either Real de Guadalupe or Francisco Madero (☎ **9/678-7488**). It is the largest Internet cafe I have seen in Mexico, with several well-connected machines and a few other toys besides.

Parking   If your hotel does not have parking, use the underground public lot (*estacionamiento*) located in front of the cathedral, just off the main square on 16 de Septiembre. Entry is from calle 5 de Febrero.

Post Office   The **post office** (*correo*) is at Crescencio Rosas and Cuauhtémoc, a block south and west of the main square. It's open Monday through Friday from 8am to 7pm and Saturday from 9am to 1pm.

Spanish Classes   The **Instituto Jovel,** María Adelina Flores 21 (Apdo. Postal 62), 29250 San Cristóbal de las Casas, Chi. (☎/fax **9/678-4069**), gets high marks for its Spanish courses. It also offers courses in weaving and cooking. The **Centro Bilingüe,** at the Centro Cultural El Puente, Real de Guadalupe 55, 29250 San Cristóbal de las Casas, Chi. (☎ **800/303-4983** in the U.S., or ☎/fax 9/678-3723), offers classes in Spanish. Both schools can arrange homestays for their students.

Telephone   The best price for long distance telephone calls and faxing is at **La Pared** bookstore at calle Hidalgo #2, across the street from the State Tourism Office.

Photography Warning

Photographers should be very cautious about when, where, and at whom or what they point their cameras. In San Cristóbal, taking a photograph of even a chile pepper can be a risky undertaking; local people just do not like having people take pictures. Especially in the San Cristóbal market, people who think they or their possessions are being photographed may angrily pelt photographers with whatever object is at hand—rocks or rotten fruit. Be respectful and ask first. Young handcraft vendors will sometimes offer to be photographed for money.

In villages outside of San Cristóbal, there are strict rules about photography. Villages around San Cristóbal, especially Chamula and Zinacantán, require visitors to go to the municipal building upon arrival and sign an agreement (written in Spanish) not to take photographs. The penalty for disobeying these regulations is stiff: confiscation of your camera and perhaps even a lengthy stay in jail. And they mean it!

EXPLORING SAN CRISTÓBAL

San Cristóbal, with its beautiful scenery, clean air, and mountain hikes, draws many visitors. However, the town's biggest attraction is its colorful, centuries-old indigenous culture. The Chiapanecan Maya, attired in their beautifully crafted native garb, surround tourists in San Cristóbal, but most travelers take at least one trip to the outlying villages to get a close-up of Maya life. Don't neglect to meander through the San Cristóbal market. It's behind the Santo Domingo church (see attractions below), and it's open almost every day, but never on Sunday. You can witness curious scenes of everyday community life there, plus some that aren't so everyday.

ATTRACTIONS IN TOWN

✪ Casa Na-Bolom. Av. Vicente Guerrero 3, 29200 San Cristóbal de las Casas, Chi. ☎ **9/678-1418.** Fax 9/678-5586. $3 group tour and *La Reina de la Selva,* an excellent 50-minute film on the Bloms, the Lacandóns, and Na-Bolom is available Tues–Sun 11:30am and 4:30pm. The extensive library devoted to Maya studies is open Mon–Fri 10am–2pm. The Artesanía Lacandón gift shop is open Mon–Sun 9am–2pm and 3–7pm. Leave the square on Real de Guadalupe, walk 4 blocks to av. Vicente Guerrero, and turn left; Na-Bolom is 5^1/$_2$ blocks up Guerrero.

If you're interested in the anthropology of this region, you'll want to visit this house-museum. Stay here if you can. The house, built as a seminary in 1891, became the headquarters of anthropologists Frans and Trudy Blom in 1951 and the gathering place of outsiders interested in studying the region. Frans Blom led many early archaeological studies in Mexico, and Trudy was noted for her photographs of the Lacandón Indians and her efforts to save them and their forest homeland. A room at Na-Bolom contains a selection of her Lacandón photographs, and postcards of the photographs are on sale in the gift shop. A tour of the home covers the displays of pre-Hispanic artifacts collected by Frans Blom; the cozy library with its numerous volumes about the region and the Maya; and the gardens Trudy Blom started for the ongoing reforestation of the Lacandón jungle. Trudy Blom died in 1993, but Na-Bolom continues to operate as a nonprofit public trust.

The 12 guest rooms, named for surrounding villages, are decorated with local objects and textiles. All rooms have fireplaces and private bathrooms. Prices for rooms (including breakfast) are $36 single and $43 double.

Even if you're not a guest here you can come for a meal, usually a delicious assortment of vegetarian and other dishes. Just be sure to make a reservation at least 2¹/₂ hours in advance, and be on time. The colorful dining room has one large table, and the eclectic mix of travelers sometimes makes for interesting conversation. Breakfast costs $4, lunch and dinner $7 each. Dinner is served at 7:30. Following breakfast at 8 to 10am, tours to San Juan Chamula and Zinacantán are offered by a guide not affiliated with the house. (See "The Nearby Maya Villages & Countryside," below.)

Catedral. 20 de Noviembre at Guadalupe Victoria. No phone. Free admission. Daily 7am–6pm.

San Cristóbal's main cathedral was built in the 1500s, but has little of interest inside besides a lovely and uncommon beam ceiling and carved wooden pulpit.

Museo de Ambar. Plaza Silvan, Utrilla 10. ☎ **9/678-3507.** Free admission. Daily 9:30am–7pm. From the plaza, walk 2¹/₂ blocks north on Utrilla (going toward the market); the museum will be on your left.

Seen from the street, this place looks like just another store, but pass through the small shop area and you'll find the long, narrow museum a fascinating place to browse. It's the only museum in Mexico devoted to amber, a fossilized resin thousands of years old mined in Chiapas near Simojovel. Owner José Luis Coría Torres has assembled more than 250 sculpted amber pieces as well as a rare collection of amber with insects trapped inside and amber fused with fossils. Amber jewelry and other objects are also for sale.

Museo Templo y Convento Santo Domingo. Av. 20 de Noviembre. ☎ **9/678-1609.** Church free; Museum $2. Museum open Tues–Sun 10am–5pm.

Inside the front door of the carved-stone plateresque façade, there's a beautiful gilded wooden altarpiece built in 1560, walls with saints, and gilt-framed paintings. Attached to the church is the former Convent of Santo Domingo, which houses a small museum about San Cristóbal and Chiapas. Housed on three floors, the museum has changing exhibits and often shows cultural films. It's 5 blocks north of the *zócalo,* in the market area.

Palacio de las Bellas Artes. Av. Hidalgo, 4 blocks south of the plaza. No phone.

Be sure to check out this building if you are interested in the arts. It periodically hosts dance events, art shows, and other performances. The schedule of events is usually posted on the door if the Bellas Artes is not open. There's a public library next door. Around the corner, the Centro Cultural holds a number of concerts and other performances; check the posters on the door to see what's scheduled.

Templo de San Cristóbal. Exit the *zócalo* on Av. Hidalgo and turn right onto the third street (Hermanos Domínguez); at the end of the street are the temple steps.

For the best view of San Cristóbal, climb the seemingly endless steps to this church and *mirador* (lookout point). A visit here requires stamina. By the way, there are 22 more churches in town, some of which also demand strenuous climbs.

HORSEBACK RIDING

The **Casa de Huéspedes Margarita** at Real de Guadalupe no. 34 and **Hotel Real del Valle** (see "Where to Stay," below) can arrange horseback rides for around $15 for a day, including a guide. Reserve your steed at least a day in advance. A horseback-riding excursion might go to San Juan Chamula, to nearby caves, or just up into the hills.

Special Events in & near San Cristóbal

In nearby Chamula, *Carnaval,* the big annual festival that takes place days before Lent, is a fascinating mingling of the Christian pre-Lenten ceremonies and the ancient Maya celebration of the five "lost days" at the end of the 360-day Maya agricultural cycle. Around noon on Shrove Tuesday, groups of village elders run across patches of burning grass as a purification rite. Macho residents then run through the streets with a bull. During *Carnaval,* roads are closed in town, and buses drop visitors at the outskirts.

Nearby villages (except Zinacantán) also have celebrations during this time, although they're perhaps not as dramatic. Visiting these villages, especially on the Sunday before Lent, will round out your impression of *Carnaval* in all its regional varieties. In Tenejapa, the celebration continues during the Thursday market after Ash Wednesday.

During Easter and the week after, when the annual **Feria de Primavera** (Spring Festival) is held, San Cristóbal is ablaze with lights and excitement and gets hordes of visitors. Activities include carnival rides, food stalls, handcraft shops, parades, and band concerts. Hotel rooms are scarce and more expensive.

Another spectacle is staged from July 22 to 25, during the annual **Fiesta de San Cristóbal,** honoring the town's patron saint. The steps up to San Cristóbal church are lit with torches at night. Pilgrimages to the church begin several days earlier, and on the night of the 24th, there's an all-night vigil.

For the **Día de Guadalupe,** on December 12, honoring Mexico's patron saint, the streets are gaily decorated, and food stalls line the streets leading to the church on a hill where she is honored.

THE NEARBY MAYA VILLAGES & COUNTRYSIDE

The Indian communities around San Cristóbal are fascinating worlds unto themselves. If you are unfamiliar with these indigenous cultures, you will understand and appreciate more of what you see by visiting them with a guide, at least for a first foray out into the villages. Guides are acquainted with members of the communities and are viewed with less suspicion than newcomers. These communities have their own laws and customs—and visitors' ignorance is no excuse. Entering these communities is tantamount to leaving Mexico, and should something happen, the state and federal authorities will not intervene except in case of a serious crime.

The best guided trips are the locally grown ones. There are three operators who go to the neighboring villages in small groups. They all charge the same price ($9 per person), use minivans for transportation, and speak English. They do, however, have their own interpretations and focus.

Pepe leaves from **Casa Na-Bolom** (see "Attractions in Town," above) for daily trips to San Juan Chamula and Zinacantán at 10am, returning to San Cristóbal between 2 and 3pm. Pepe looks at cultural continuities, community relationships, and, of course, religion.

Mercedes Hernández Gómez, a very opinionated *mestiza* woman, leads a tour from the main plaza at 9am. She always carries an umbrella so that she can be identified. Mercedes, a largely self-trained ethnographer, is well informed about the history and folkways of the villages and her opinions make for a good tour. She explains (in English) the religious significance of what you see in the churches, where shamans try to cure Indian patients of various maladies. She also facilitates tourists' firsthand contact with Indians.

Alex and Raul can be found in front of the cathedral between 9:15 and 9:30am. They are quite personable and get along well with the Indians in the communities. They focus on cultural values and their expression in social behavior, which provides a glimpse of the details and the texture of life in these communities (and, of course, they talk about religion).

For excursions farther afield, see "Road Trips from San Cristóbal" at the end of this section. Also, the above-mentioned guides (especially Alex and Raul) can be persuaded to go to other communities besides Chamula and Zinacantán; talk to them.

CHAMULA & ZINACANTÁN   A side trip to the village of San Juan Chamula will really get you into the spirit of life around San Cristóbal. Sunday, when the market is in full swing, is the best day to go for shopping; but other days, when you'll be less impeded by anxious children selling their crafts, are better for seeing the village and church.

The village, 5 miles northeast of San Cristóbal, has a large church, a plaza, and a municipal building. Each year, a new group of citizens is chosen to live in the municipal center as caretakers of the saints, settlers of disputes, and enforcers of village rules. As in other nearby villages, on Sunday local leaders wear their leadership costumes with beautifully woven straw hats loaded with colorful ribbons befitting their high position. They solemnly sit together in a long line somewhere around the central square. Chamula is typical of other villages in that men are often away working in the "hot lands" harvesting coffee or *cacao,* while women stay home to tend the sheep, the children, the cornfields, and the fires. It's almost always the women's and children's work to gather firewood, and you see them along roadsides bent under the weight.

Don't leave Chamula without seeing the **church interior.** As you step from bright sunlight into the candlelit interior, you feel like you've been transported to another country. The tile floor is covered with pine needles scattered amid a meandering sea of lighted candles. Saints line the walls, and before them people are often kneeling and praying aloud while passing around bottles of Pepsi Cola. Shamans are often on hand, passing eggs over sick people or using live or dead chickens in a curing ritual. The statues of saints are similar to those you might see in any Mexican Catholic church, but beyond sharing the same name, they mean something completely different to the Chamulas. Visitors can walk carefully through the church to see the saints or stand quietly in the background and observe.

Carnaval, which takes place just before Lent, is the big annual festival. The Chamulas are not a wealthy people, but the women are the region's best wool weavers, producing finished pieces for themselves and for other villages.

In Zinacantán, a wealthier village than Chamula, you must sign a rigid form promising *not to take any photographs* before you are allowed to see the two side-by-side **sanctuaries.** Once permission is granted and you have paid a small fee, an escort will usually show you the church, or you may be allowed to see it on your own. Floors may be covered in pine needles here, too, and the rooms are brightly sunlit. The experience is an altogether different one from that of Chamula.

AMATENANGO DEL VALLE   About an hour's ride south of San Cristóbal is Amatenango, a town known mostly for its **women potters.** You'll see their work in San Cristóbal—small animals, jars, and large water jugs—but in the village, you can visit the potters in their homes. Just walk down the dirt streets. Villagers will lean over the walls of family compounds and invite you in to select from their inventory. You may even see them firing the pieces under piles of wood in the open courtyard or painting them with color derived from rusty iron water. The women wear beautiful red-and-yellow *huipils,* but if you want to take a photograph, you'll have to pay.

To get here, take a *colectivo* from the market in San Cristóbal, but before it lets you off, be sure to ask about the return-trip schedule.

AGUACATENANGO   Located 10 miles south of Amatenango, this village is known for its **embroidery.** If you've visited San Cristóbal shops before arriving here, you'll recognize the white-on-white or black-on-black floral patterns on dresses and blouses for sale. The locals' own regional blouses, however, are quite different.

TENEJAPA   The **weavers** of Tenejapa make some of the most beautiful and expensive work you'll see in the region. The best time to visit is on market day (Sunday and Thursday, though Sunday is best). The weavers of Tenejapa taught the weavers of San Andrés and Magdalena—which accounts for the similarity in their designs and colors. To get to Tenejapa, try either to find a *colectivo* in the very last row by the market or hire a taxi. On Tenejapa's main street, several stores sell locally woven regional clothing, and you can bargain for the price.

THE HUITEPEC CLOUD FOREST   Pronatura, a private, nonprofit, ecological organization, offers environmentally sensitive tours of the cloud forest. The forest is a haven for **migratory birds,** and more than 100 bird species and 600 plant species have been discovered here. Guided tours are Tuesday to Sunday, 9am to 12pm, at a cost of $18 per group (up to eight people). Make reservations a day in advance. Their office is located at av. Benito Juárez 11-B (☎ **9/678-5000**). To reach the reserve on your own, drive on the road to Chamula; the turnoff is at km 3.5. The reserve is open Tuesday through Sunday from 9am to 4pm.

SHOPPING

Many Indian villages near San Cristóbal are noted for their weaving, embroidery, brocade work, leather, and pottery, making the area one of the best in the country for shopping. The craftspeople make and sell beautiful woolen shawls, indigo-dyed skirts, colorful native shirts, and magnificently woven *huipils,* all of which often come in vivid geometric patterns. Working in leather, they are artisans of the highest caliber, making sandals and men's handbags. There's a proliferation of tie-dyed *jaspe* from Guatemala, which comes in bolts and is made into clothing, as well as other textiles from that country. There are numerous shops up and down the streets leading to the market. Calle Real de Guadalupe has more shops than any other street.

CRAFTS

✪ **Casa de Artesanías DIF.** Niños Héroes at Hidalgo. ☎ **9/678-1180.**

Crafts are sold in a fine showroom in one of the city's old houses. Here you'll find such quality products as lined woolen vests and jackets, pillow covers, amber jewelry, and more. In back is a fine little museum showing costumes worn by villagers who live near San Cristóbal. Open Tuesday through Saturday from 9am to 2pm and 5 to 8pm.

Central Market. Av. Utrilla. No phone.

The market buildings and the surrounding streets offer just about anything you need. The market in San Cristóbal is open every morning except Sunday (when each village has its own local market), and you'll probably enjoy observing the sellers as much as the things they sell. See the "Photography Warning" in "Fast Facts," above, regarding photography here. The *mercado* is north of the Santo Domingo church, about 9 blocks from the *zócalo.*

El Encuentro. Calle Real de Guadalupe 63-A. ☎ **9/678-3698.**

You should find some of your best bargains here—at a minimum, you'll think the price is fair. The shop carries many regional ritual items, such as new and used men's ceremonial hats, false saints, and iron rooftop adornments, plus many *huipils* and other textiles. It's open Monday through Saturday from 9am to 8pm and is found between Dujelay and Guerrero.

La Alborada, Centro Desarrollo Comunitario DIF. Barrio María Auxiliadora. No phone.

At this government-sponsored school, young men and women from surrounding villages come to learn how to hook Persian-style rugs, weave fabric on foot looms, sew, make furniture, construct a house, cook, make leather shoes and bags, forge iron, and grow vegetables and trees for reforestation. Probably the most interesting crafts for the general tourist are the rug-making and weaving. Artisans from Temoaya in Mexico State learned rug-making from Persians, who came to teach this skill in the 1970s. The Temoaya artisans in turn traveled to San Cristóbal to teach the craft to area students, who have since taught others. The beautiful rug designs are taken from brocaded and woven designs used to decorate regional costumes. Visitors should stop at the entrance and ask for an escort. You can visit all the various areas and see students at work or simply go straight to the weavers. There's a small sales outlet at the entrance selling newly loomed fabric by the meter, leather bags, rugs, and baskets made at another school in the highlands. La Alborada is in a far southern suburb of the city off the highway to Comitán, to the right. To get there, take a cab. There is a degree of uncertainty about the place being open, but a mid-morning visit is your best chance for success.

La Galería. Hidalgo 3. ☎ **9/678-1547.**

This lovely gallery beneath a cafe has expositions by well-known national and international painters. Also for sale are the paintings and greeting cards by Kiki, the owner, a German artist who has found her niche in San Cristóbal. There are some Oaxacan rugs and pottery, plus unusual silver jewelry. Open daily from 10am to 9pm.

✪ **Taller Leñateros.** Flavio A. Paniagua 54. ☎ **9/678-5174.**

Paper-making isn't all they do here, but it's done with enough creativity and diversity of materials to warrant mention on that alone. This shop/workshop is run as a cooperative effort by six women; five Maya Indians and one American. They also make paper creations, silk screens, wood-cuts, binding, and they've put all those talents together to produce their own magazine, which has garnered quite a bit of attention in Mexico City. Open from 8am to 9pm Mon–Sat; if you want to see paper being made, show up before 4pm.

TEXTILE SHOPS

✪ **Kun Kun SC.** Real de Mexicanos 21. ☎ **9/678-1417.**

The name means "little by little." This cooperative society to aid local native artisans sells mostly ceramic tiles, weavings, and pottery. The weavings are made of locally produced wool that has been spun, dyed, and woven by members. Kun Kun holds workshops for artisans on such things as working with floor looms, which you can watch when visiting the store. The tiles are wonderful. Also, if you're interested, ask about classes in using a backstrap loom. The workshop/store is open 9am–3pm Mon–Sat. They also have a store closer to the Plaza that stays open till 8pm at Real de Guadalupe 55.

Plaza de Santo Domingo. Av. Utrilla.

The plazas around this church and the nearby Templo de Caridad are filled with women in native garb selling their wares. Here you'll find women from Chamula weaving belts or embroidering, surrounded by piles of loomed woolen textiles from their village. More and more Guatemalan shawls, belts, and bags are included in their inventory. There are also some excellent buys in Chiapanecan-made wool vests, jackets, rugs, and shawls, similar to those in Sna Jolobil (see below), if you take the time to look and bargain. Vendors arrive between 9 and 10am and begin to leave around 3pm.

✪ **Sna Jolobil.** Calzada Lázaro Cárdenas 42 (Plaza Santo Domingo). ☎ **9/678-2646.**

Meaning "weaver's house" in the Mayan language, this place is located in the former convent (monastery) of Santo Domingo, next to the Templo de Santo Domingo between Navarro and Nicaragua. This cooperative store is operated by groups of Tzotzil and Tzeltal craftspeople and has about 3,000 members who contribute products, help in running the store, and share in the moderate profits. Their works are simply beautiful; prices are set and high—as is the quality. Be sure to take a look. Open Monday through Saturday from 9am to 2pm and 4 to 6pm; credit cards are accepted.

Unión Regional de Artesanías de los Altos (also known as J'pas Joloviletic). Av. Utrilla 43. ☎ **9/678-2848.**

Another cooperative of weavers, this one is smaller than Sna Jolobil (see above) and not as sophisticated in its approach to potential shoppers. It sells blouses, textiles, pillow covers, vests, sashes, napkins, baskets, and purses. It's near the market and worth looking around. Open Monday through Saturday from 9am to 2pm and 4 to 7pm, and Sunday from 9am to 1pm.

WHERE TO STAY

Keep in mind that among the most interesting places to stay in San Cristóbal is the ex-seminary turned hotel-museum; see **Casa Na-Bolom** in "Attractions in Town," above, for details.

Many hotels will raise their prices by $3 during June and July. For really low-cost accommodations, there are basic but acceptable *hospedajes* and *posadas*, which charge about $8 for a single and $10 to $12 for a double. Usually these places are unadvertised; if you're interested in a very cheap place to stay, ask around in a restaurant or cafe, and you're sure to find one, or go to the tourist office, which often displays notices of new *hospedajes* on the metal flip rack in the office. Some of the best economical offerings are on calle Real de Guadalupe, east of the main square.

VERY EXPENSIVE

✪ **El Jacarandal.** Comitán 7, 29200 San Cristóbal de las Casas, Chi. ☎/fax **9/678-1065.** 4 units. $180 per person for double occupancy includes all meals, drinks, and activities; $60 per person for double occupancy includes breakfast. No credit cards.

El Jacarandal is the home of Nancy and Percy Wood—who choose to entertain guests and, in so doing, elevate the practice to high art. This is not merely a lodging. You can stay here for a week without ever having to look for outside entertainment. The owners keep a stable of horses and like to go for morning rides. They also enjoy showing their guests the Indian villages, the Huitepec cloud forest, and the Maya ruins that are not far from the city. Meals are not to be missed. Fidelia, the cook, is most able, and on many occasions local anthropologists, environmentalists, or prominent citizens drop in for a bite and a chat. The house and grounds themselves are lovely; sometimes it's hard to tear yourself away. From the patio where breakfast is taken, the garden and trees present a lovely foreground against a backdrop of red-tile roofs and church cupolas, and behind everything else, the mountains. The rooms come with one or two beds. Accommodations are gracious and engaging, as is everything in the house.

MODERATE

✪ **Hotel Casa Mexicana.** 28 de Agosto 1, 29200 San Cristóbal de las Casas, Chi. ☎ **9/678-1348.** Fax 9/678-2627. E-mail: hcasamex@mail.internet.com.mx. 51 units. TV TEL. $65 double. AE, MC, V. Free secure parking 1$^1/_2$ blocks away.

Created from a large mansion, this beautiful hotel with a colonial-style courtyard makes for comfortable lodging. Rooms, courtyards, restaurant, and lobby are decorated in modern/traditional Mexican tastes with warm tones of yellow and red. The rooms are carpeted and come with one or two doubles or a king size bed. They are equipped with good lighting, electric heaters, and spacious bathrooms. Guests are welcome to use the sauna, and inexpensive massages can be arranged. The hotel handles a lot of large tour groups; it can be quiet and peaceful one day and full and bustling the next. There is a new addition to the hotel across the street, but I like the doubles in the original section better (the suite there is very comfortable). This hotel is 3 blocks north of the main plaza at the corner of Utrilla.

✪ **Hotel Casavieja.** Ma. Adelina Flores 27, 29200 San Cristóbal de las Casas, Chi. ☎/fax **9/678-6868** or 9/678-0385. www.casavieja.com. 40 units. TV TEL. $55 double. AE, MC, V. Free parking.

The Casavieja is aptly named: It has a charming old feel to it that is San Cristóbal to a "T." Originally built in 1740, restoration and new construction have been faithful to the original design in the essentials such as wood-beam ceilings. One nod toward modernity is carpeted floors, a welcome feature on cold mornings. The rooms also come with electric heaters. Bathrooms vary depending on what section of the hotel you're in, but all are adequate. The hotel's restaurant, Doña Rita, faces the interior courtyard with tables on the patio and inside and offers good food at reasonable prices. I recommend the *molcajete de pollo*. The hotel is 3$^1/_2$ blocks northeast of the plaza between Cristóbal Colón and Diego Dujelay.

Hotel El Paraíso. Av. 5 de Febrero 19, San Cristóbal de las Casas, 29200 Chi. ☎ **9/678-0085.** E-mail: hparaiso@mundomaya.com.mx. 14 units. $49 double. AE, MC, V.

For the independent traveler, this is a safe haven from the busloads of tourists brought in by tour groups, which can upset the tranquillity and service of other hotels. Rooms are small but beautifully decorated, and have comfortable beds with soft patchwork bedspreads and reading lights; some rooms even have a ladder to a loft holding a second bed. The entire hotel is decorated in terracotta and blue with beautiful wooden columns and beams supporting the roof. The hotel's restaurant may be the best in town.

Hotel Rincón del Arco. Ejército Nacional 66, 29200 San Cristóbal de las Casas, Chi. ☎ **9/678-1313.** Fax 9/678-1568. E-mail: htl_rincon_del_arco@sancristobal.com.mx. 50 units. TV TEL. $54 double. MC, V. Free parking.

This well-run hotel has comfortable rooms at a good price. The original section of this former colonial-era home is built around a small interior patio and dates from 1650. Rooms in this part are spacious with tall ceilings and carpet over hardwood floors. The adjacent new section looks out across a grass yard to the mountains and the valley. These rooms are nicely furnished and come with beds covered in thick bedspreads made in the family factory, which you can visit next door. Some rooms have small balconies; all have fireplaces. There's a restaurant just behind the lobby. The only downside is that it's a bit of a walk from the main plaza (8 blocks to the northeast) at the corner of Ejército Nacional and V. Guerrero.

INEXPENSIVE

Hotel Don Quijote. Colón 7, 29200 San Cristóbal de las Casas, Chi. ☎ **9/678-0920.** Fax 9/678-0346. 24 units. TV, TEL. $27 double. MC, V. Free secure parking 1 block away.

Rooms in this three-story hotel (no elevator) are small but quiet, cheerful, carpeted, and well lit. All have two double beds with reading lamps over them, tiled bathrooms, and plenty of hot water. The TVs actually carry English channels (uncommon for hotels in this price range), and there's complimentary coffee in the mornings and Internet access. It's 2¹/₂ blocks east of the plaza, near the corner of Colón.

Hotel Palacio de Moctezuma. Juárez 16, 29200 San Cristóbal de las Casas, Chi. ☎ **9/678-0352** or 9/678-1142. Fax 9/678-1536. 42 units. TV TEL. $25 double. No credit cards. Free limited parking.

This three-story hotel is more open and lush with greenery than other hotels in this price range. Fresh-cut flowers tucked around tile fountains are its hallmark. The rooms have carpeting and modern tiled showers; many are quite large, but, alas, can be cold in winter. The restaurant looks out on the interior courtyard. On the third floor is a solarium with comfortable tables and chairs and great city views. The hotel is 3¹/₂ blocks southeast of the main plaza at the corner of Juárez and León.

Hotel Posada de los Angeles. Calle Francisco Madero 17, 29200 San Cristóbal de las Casas, Chi. ☎ **9/678-1173** or 9/678-4371. Fax 9/678-2581. E-mail: hmansion@mundomaya. com.mx. 20 units. TV TEL. $40 double. AE, MC, V.

This well-managed hotel offers good service and clean rooms and public areas. Guest rooms come with either a single and a double or two double beds, and the well-kept bathrooms are modern; windows open onto a pretty courtyard with a fountain. The rooftop sundeck is a great siesta spot.

Hotel Real del Valle. Real de Guadalupe 14, 29200 San Cristóbal de las Casas, Chi. ☎ **9/678-0680.** Fax 9/678-3955. 36 units. $25 double. No credit cards.

The Real del Valle is just off the main plaza. The 24 new rooms in the back three-story section have new bathrooms, big closets, and tile floors. In addition to a rooftop solarium, you'll find a small cafeteria and an upstairs dining room with a big double fireplace.

WHERE TO DINE

San Cristóbal is not known for its cuisine, but you can eat well at several restaurants. **El Fogón de Jovel,** below, is the place to try typical Chiapanecan fare. Some interesting local dishes include tamales, *butifarra* (a type of sausage), and *pox* (pronounced "posh"; it's a distilled sugar-and-corn drink similar to *aguardiente*). For baked goods, try the **Panadería La Hojaldra** at the corner of Mazariegos and 5 de Mayo (☎ **9/ 678-4286**). It's open daily from 8am to 9:30pm.

MODERATE

El Fogón de Jovel. 16 de Septiembre 11. ☎ **9/678-1153.** Main courses $4–$8. No credit cards. Daily 12:30–10pm. CHIAPANECAN.

The waiters here wear local costumes, and walls are hung with Guatemalan and Chiapanecan prints and folk art. Each dish and regional drink is explained on the menu, which is available in English. A basket of warm handmade tortillas with six filling condiments arrives before the meal. Among the specialties are corn soup, *mole chiapaneco,* pork or chicken *adobado* in a chile sauce, and *pepián,* a dish of savory chile-and-tomato sauce served over chicken. For a unique dessert try the *changleta,* which is half of a sweetened, baked *chayote.* Cooking classes for small groups can be arranged, but make reservations well in advance. The restaurant is a block northwest of the plaza at the corner of Guadalupe Victoria/Real de Guadalupe and 16 de Septiembre.

✪ **El Paraíso.** Av. 5 de Febrero 19 (in the Hotel El Paraíso). ☎ **9/678-0085.** Breakfast $2.25–$3.25; main courses $4–$12. AE, MC, V. INTERNATIONAL.

A small, quiet restaurant where it is obvious that the dishes are prepared by somebody who enjoys the taste of good food; just about anything is good here except for the Swiss rarebit. The cuts of meat are especially tender, the margaritas especially dangerous (one is all it takes). Specialties include the Swiss cheese fondue for two, the Eden salad, and the brochette. This is where locals go for a splurge. It's 2 blocks from the main plaza.

✪ **Madre Tierra.** Insurgentes 19. ☎ **9/678-4297.** Main courses $2–$6; *comida corrida* $6. No credit cards. Restaurant, daily 8am–9:45pm (*comida corrida* served after 12); bakery, Mon–Sat 9am–8pm, Sun 9am–noon. INTERNATIONAL/VEGETARIAN.

For vegetarians and meat-eaters alike, Madre Tierra is a good place for a cappuccino and pastry or an entire meal. The *comida corrida* is very filling, or try the chicken curry, lasagna, and fresh salads. The bakery specializes in whole-wheat breads, pastries, pizza by the slice, quiche, grains, granola, and dried fruit. The restaurant is in an old mansion with wood-plank floors, long windows looking onto the street, and tables covered in colorful Guatemalan jaspe. Madre Tierra is 3½ blocks south of the plaza.

INEXPENSIVE

Café el Puente. Real de Guadalupe 55. No phone. Breakfast $1.75–$2.50; main courses $3–$5. No credit cards. Mon–Sat 7:30am–11pm, Sun 3–11pm. MEXICAN/AMERICAN.

El Puente is more than a cafe, it's a center for cultural activities where tourists and locals can converse, take Spanish classes, arrange a homestay, leave a message on the bulletin board, and send and receive faxes. Movies are presented nightly in a back patio and meeting room. A pleasant cafe occupies the front courtyard; the kind of place where a Brandenburg Concerto accompanies waffles for breakfast, and sub sandwiches or brown rice and vegetables for lunch. There is Mexican fare as well. The long bulletin board is well worth checking out if you're looking for a ride, a place to stay, or information on out-of-the-way destinations. It's 2½ blocks east of the plaza between Dujelay and Cristóbal Colón.

Emiliano's Moustache. Crescencio Rosas 7. ☎ **9/678-7246.** Comida corrida $2.50; main courses $3–$6. No credit cards. Daily 8am–12am. MEXICAN/TACOS.

Like any right-thinking tourist, I initially avoided this place on account of its unpromising name and some cartoon-like *charro* figures by the door. But a conversation with some local folk overcame my prejudice and tickled my sense of irony. Sure enough, when I went in, the place was crowded with *coletos* enjoying the restaurant's highly popular *comida corrida* and delicious tacos, and there wasn't a foreigner in sight. The daily menu is posted by the door for inspection; if it isn't appealing, you can choose from a menu of taco plates (a mixture of fillings cooked together and served with tortillas and a variety of hot sauces). Any Mexican will be quick to confess that Mexico is a nation of *taqueros:* A good taco is much appreciated.

Normita's. Av. Juárez 6 at Dr. Jose Flores. No phone. Breakfast $2–$2.50; *comida corrida* $3.25; *pozole* $2; tacos $1. No credit cards. Daily 7am–11pm (*comida corrida* served 1:30–7pm). MEXICAN.

Normita's is famous for its *pozole*, a hearty chicken and hominy soup to which you add a variety of things. It also offers cheap, dependable, short-order Mexican mainstays. It's an informal "people's" restaurant; the open kitchen takes up one corner of the room, and tables are scattered in front of a large paper mural of a fall forest scene from some faraway place. It's 2 blocks southeast of the plaza.

Restaurant Tuluc. Insurgentes 5. ☎ **9/678-2090.** Breakfast $1.50–$2.50; main courses $3–$4; *comida corrida* $3. No credit cards. Daily 7am–10pm (*comida corrida* served 2–4pm). MEXICAN/INTERNATIONAL.

A real bargain here is the popular *comida corrida*—delicious and filling. Tuluc also has that rarest of rarities in Mexico: a nonsmoking section. Other popular items are the sandwiches and the enchiladas. The house specialty is the filete Tuluc, a beef filet wrapped around spinach and cheese served with fried potatoes and green beans; while not the best cut of meat, it's certainly priced right. The Chiapaneco breakfast is a filling quartet of juice, toast, two Chiapanecan tamales, and your choice of tea, coffee, cappuccino, or hot chocolate. Tuluc is 1 1/2 blocks south of the plaza between Cuauhtémoc and Francisco León.

COFFEEHOUSES

Since Chiapas-grown coffee is highly regarded, it's natural to find a proliferation of coffeehouses here. Most are concealed in the nooks and crannies of San Cristóbal's side streets. Try **Café La Selva,** Crescencio Rosas 9 (☎ **9/678-7244**), for coffee served in all its varieties and brewed from organic beans (and well known for its baked goods), open daily 9am to 11pm. Or for a more traditional-style cafe where locals meet to talk over the day's news, try **Café San Cristóbal,** Cuauhtémoc 1 (☎ **9/678-3861**), open Monday through Saturday from 9am to 10pm and Sunday from 9am to 9pm.

SAN CRISTÓBAL AFTER DARK

San Cristóbal is blessed with a variety of species of nightlife, both resident and migratory. There is a lot of live music, which is surprisingly good and varied. The bars/restaurants are cheap—none charges a cover; only one charges a minimum tab. And they are easy to get to: You can hit all the places mentioned below without setting foot in a cab. Weekends are best, but on any night you'll find something going on.

El Cocodrilo. Plaza 31 de Marzo. ☎ **9/678-0871.** Live music daily 9–11pm.

El Cocodrilo, in the Hotel Santa Clara on the main plaza, is a good place to start the evening off. The band begins to play at 9. The musicians cover a lot of Beatles and Santana tunes, but they put their own stamp on the music, such as playing a rock 'n' roll standard to a reggae beat and mixing in some funk riffs. The live music shuts down at 11.

La Margarita. Real de Guadalupe 34. No phone. Live music daily 9:30pm–12am.

Starting at 9:30 you can catch flamenco/Latin guitar music at this popular restaurant bar a block-and-a-half from the plaza. The band consists of two guitarists, congas, and bass. It plays flamenco-style music with a lot of flair, if not all the passion of real flamenco. As the night progresses, they might get into some Latin jazz. You can't go wrong here unless you are in the mood to dance. The live music ends at around 11:30 to 12.

Las Velas. Madero 14. ☎ **9/678-7584.** $2.50 minimum tab. Live music daily 11pm–1am.

Bands here play with a rougher edge than at El Cocodrilo. Some get into Latin beats and "rock en Español," which is increasingly gaining a foothold all over the world. The crowd is mostly *coletos* in their early 20s. The tight space guarantees that it will be crowded. The cost of admission if you are male is to be frisked for weapons, but this is more for setting the ambiance than actual security. All the locals I spoke with said nothing has ever happened there, or at any other of the bars, that would warrant such a practice.

Latino's. Mazarriegos 19. ☎ **9/678-2083.** Live music Mon–Sat 10pm–2am.

A large dance floor and a really impressive nine-piece house band playing salsa and merengue are all the invitation needed to start dancing. This was the best band I heard in San Cristóbal, and at present it's the most popular. The place fills up on weekends with people of all ages, and everybody dances.

Madre Tierra. Insurgentes 19 (above the restaurant). ☎ **9/678-4297.** Daily 10:30–late.

This would be the place to close out an evening. Here both the crowd and the band are looser than at other places. I come here more for the society and the bohemian setting than the music. The band specializes in blues, reggae, rock—just about anything that has a steady bass line and a solid downbeat. The place is unpretentious, the music is loud, and the mostly young crowd friendly. It closes when the last person leaves—sometimes around 6 in the morning.

ROAD TRIPS FROM SAN CRISTÓBAL

For excursions to nearby villages, see "The Nearby Maya Villages & Countryside," above; and for destinations farther away, there are several local travel agencies. I recommend trying **ATC Travel and Tours,** located across from El Fogón restaurant, calle 5 de Febrero 15 at the corner of 16 de Septiembre (☎ **9/678-2550;** fax 9/678-3145). The agency has bilingual guides and good vehicles. ATC regional tours focus on birds and orchids, textiles, hiking, and camping.

Strangely, the cost of the trip includes a driver but does not necessarily include either a bilingual guide or guided information of any kind. You pay extra for those services, so when checking prices, be sure to flesh out these details.

RUINS OF TONINÁ

Two hours from San Cristóbal is the large and impressive Maya city of Toniná ("house of rocks"), $8^1/_2$ miles east of Ocosingo (midway between San Cristóbal and Palenque). The site dates from the classic period and covers an area of at least 9-square-miles. Excavation and restoration have been relatively recent, otherwise Toniná would be much more famous. If a Maya site can be called a sleeper, Toniná is it. Extensive excavations are under way here during the dry season.

As early as A.D. 350, Toniná emerged as a separate dynastic center of the Maya and has the distinction of having the last recorded date yet found (A.D. 909) on a small stone monument. The date signifies the end of the Classic period. Another stone, dated A.D. 711, depicts the captured King Kan-Xul of Palenque (the younger brother of Chan-Bahlum and the son of King Pacal); the portrait shows him with his arm tied by a rope but still wearing his royal headdress. Recently a huge stucco panel was unearthed picturing the Lord of Death holding Kan-Xul's head, confirming long-held suspicions that the king died at Toniná.

At the moment there are no signs to guide visitors through the site, so you're on your own. The caretaker can also show you around (in Spanish), after which a tip is appreciated. A typical guided tour to Toniná should include the services of a bilingual driver, a tour of the site, lunch, and a swim in the river. From November through February, you'll see thousands of swallows swarming near the ruins.

If you go on your own, the best thing to do is stay overnight at **Rancho Esmeralda** (☎ **9/673-0711;** don't call at night, leave message for owners). For $23–$28, two people can stay in a cabin, just a short walk from the ruins. The owners are American; they offer meals for the guests and horseback riding excursions.

Chiapas Highlands

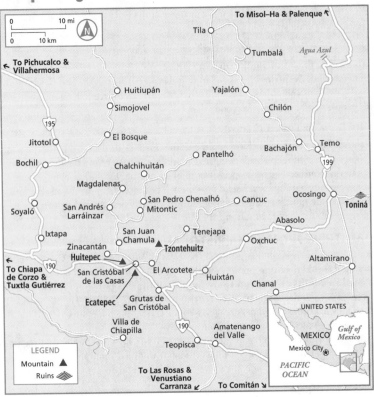

PALENQUE, BONAMPAK & YAXCHILÁN

Many visitors to San Cristóbal want to visit the ruins of Palenque and those of Bonampak and Yaxchilán on Mexico's border with Guatemala. A trip to Palenque can be accomplished in a long day-trip from San Cristóbal, but I don't recommend it because it requires too much traveling.

To get to Bonampak and Yaxchilán you go through Palenque unless you go by small plane. See "Bonampak & Yaxchilán" in the Palenque section under "Road Trips." If you're considering going, talk to the above-mentioned travel agency, ATC Tours. They have a well-organized tour of Yaxchilán and Bonampak, with Tikal thrown in (for a minimum of four people). See also "Active Vacations in the Yucatán" in chapter 2 for U.S. companies offering this trip.

CHINCULTIC RUINS, COMITÁN & MONTEBELLO NATIONAL PARK

Almost 100 miles southeast of San Cristóbal, near the border with Guatemala, is the Chincultic archaeological site and Montebello National Park, with **16 multicolored lakes** and exuberant pine-forest vegetation. Forty-six miles from San Cristóbal is Comitán, a pretty hillside town of 40,000 inhabitants known for its flower cultivation and a sugarcane-based liquor called *comitecho*. It's also the last big town along the Pan–American Highway before the Guatemalan border.

The Chincultic ruins, a late classic site, have barely been excavated, but the main **acropolis,** set high up against a cliff, is magnificent to see from below and worth the walk up for the view. After passing through the gate, you'll see the trail ahead; it passes ruins on both sides. Steep stairs leading up the mountain to the acropolis are flanked by more unexcavated tree-covered ruins. From there, you can gaze upon distant Montebello Lakes and miles of cornfields and forest. The paved road to the lakes passes six lakes, all different colors and sizes, ringed by cool pine forests; most have parking lots and lookouts. The paved road ends at a small restaurant. The lakes are best seen on a sunny day, when their famous brilliant colors are optimal.

Most travel agencies in San Cristóbal offer a daylong trip that includes the lakes, the ruins, lunch in Comitán, and a stop in the pottery-making village of Amatenango del Valle. If you're driving, follow Highway 190 south from San Cristóbal through the pretty village of Teopisca and then through Comitán; turn left at La Trinitaria, where there's a sign to the lakes. After the Trinitaria turnoff and before you reach the lakes, there's a sign pointing left down a narrow dirt road to the Chincultic ruins.

4 Tuxtla Gutiérrez

51 miles (82km) W of San Cristóbal; 173 miles (277km) S of Villahermosa; 151 miles (242km) NW of Ciudad Cuauhtémoc on the Guatemalan border

Tuxtla Gutiérrez (alt. 1,838 ft.; pop. 300,000) is the boomtown capital of Chiapas. Coffee is the basis of the region's economy, along with recent oil discoveries. Tuxtla is a business town; there are some attractive parts, but nothing to keep you here more than a day or two. For tourists, it's mainly a way station en route to San Cristóbal, Oaxaca, or Villahermosa. The main attraction in town is the zoo; the main attraction nearby is the magnificent Sumidero Canyon, which should not be missed (see below).

ESSENTIALS
GETTING THERE & DEPARTING

BY PLANE   **Aviación de Chiapas** (known as **Aviacsa,** ☎ 9/612-6880 or 9/612-8081) can get you to several cities in Mexico, but all flights go through Mexico City—even flights to Cancún, Chetumal, Mérida, Guatemala City, Villahermosa, and Oaxaca. **Aerocaribe,** a subsidiary of Mexicana (☎ 9/612-0020 or 9/612-5402), has five nonstop flights a day to/from Mexico City, with connections to all major cities, and nonstop service to Oaxaca and Villahermosa, Tapachula (on the Guatemalan border), and Veracruz.

Due to its peculiar weather, Tuxtla has two airports: **Terán** and **Llano San Juan.** The airlines use one for 6 months of the year (October to April) and the other for the rest—although there is occasional juggling back and forth. Be sure to double-check which airport you're departing from, and allow enough time to get there. The Terán airport is 5 miles from town; the Llano San Juan airport is 18. There is taxi and mini-van service from both airports.

BY CAR   From Oaxaca you enter Tuxtla by Highway 190. From Villahermosa, or Palenque and San Cristóbal, you'll enter at the opposite end of town on the same highway coming from the east. In both cases, you'll arrive at the large main square at the center of town, La Plaza Cívica. (See "City Layout," below.)

From Tuxtla to Villahermosa, take Highway 190 east past the town of Chiapa de Corzo; soon you'll see a sign for Highway 195 north to Villahermosa. To San Cristóbal and Palenque, take Highway 190 east. The road from Tuxtla to San Cristóbal and Palenque is beautiful but tortuous. It's in good repair to San Cristóbal, but there may be bad spots between San Cristóbal and Palenque. The trip from Tuxtla to Villahermosa takes 8 hours by car; the scenery is beautiful.

BY BUS The first-class bus station (☎ 9/612-2624) is at the corner of streets 2 Norte and 2 Poniente (see "City Layout, below"). All bus lines serving this station and the deluxe section across the street (**Uno, Maya de Oro, Cristóbal Colón, Servicios Altos**) belong to the same parent company, **ADO.** At the main station they sell tickets for all buses. All buses are air-conditioned and have bathrooms. There are two levels of first class; the first-class *económico* has less legroom. Then there's deluxe, which features a few extras: slightly better seats, better movies, and free coffee and soda. There are buses every half hour to San Cristóbal, eight buses a day to Villahermosa, three or four buses a day to Oaxaca, and five to Palenque. There's usually no need to buy a ticket ahead of time, except during holidays.

ORIENTATION

ARRIVING The Llano San Juan airport is off Highway 190 west of town, about 40 minutes away; the Terán airport is off of the same highway going east of town, about 15 minutes away. *Colectivos* are much cheaper if you can find one; they leave as soon as they are full. The **ADO/Cristóbal Colón** bus terminal is downtown.

VISITOR INFORMATION The **Tourist Office** (☎ 800/280-3500 in Mexico or 9/613-4499) is in the Secretaría de Fomento Económico building (previously called the Plaza de las Instituciones) on avenida Central/bulevar Domínguez, near the Hotel Bonampak Tuxtla. It's on the first floor of the plaza and is open Monday through Friday from 8am to 9pm. Most questions can be answered at the information booth in front of the office. There are also information booths at the **international airport** (staffed when flights are due) and at the **zoo** (open Tuesday through Sunday from 9am to 3pm and 6 to 9pm).

CITY LAYOUT Tuxtla is laid out on a grid. The city's main street, **avenida Central,** is the east-west axis and is the artery through town for Highway 190. In the west it becomes **bulevar Belisario Domínguez,** and in the east it becomes **bulevar Angel Albino Corzo. Calle Central** is the north-south axis. The rest of the streets have names that include one number and two directions. This tells you how to get to the street. For example, to find the street 5 Norte Poniente (5 North West) you would walk 5 blocks north from the center of town, and turn west (which is left). To find 3 Oriente Sur, you would walk 3 blocks east from the main square and turn south. When people indicate intersections, they can shorten the names, because it's redundant. The bus station is at the corner of 2 Norte and 2 Poniente.

GETTING AROUND **Buses** to all parts of the city converge upon the Plaza Cívica along calle Central. **Taxi** fares are higher here than in other regions.

FAST FACTS The local **American Express** representative is Viajes Marabasco, Plaza Bonampak, Loc. 4, Col. Moctezuma, near the tourist office (☎ 9/612-6998; fax 9/612-4053). Office hours are Monday through Friday 9am to 1:30pm and 3:30 to 6:30pm. The **telephone area code** is **9.** If you need medical help, the best **clinic** in town is Sanatorio Rojas, calle 2 Sur Poniente 1847 (☎ 9/611-2079 and 9/612-5414).

TUXTLA'S MUSEUM & ZOO

Most travelers simply pass through Tuxtla on their way to San Cristóbal or Oaxaca. The excellent zoo and the Sumidero Canyon are the top sights, though you might also visit the Parque Madero and its anthropology museum.

Calzada de los Hombres Illustres. 11 Nte. Oriente at 5 Oriente Nte. Park and botanical garden free. Museum $2; free on Sunday. Museum Tues–Sun 9am–4pm; botanical garden daily 8:30am–5pm; children's area Tues–Sun 8am–8pm. The park is 15 blocks northwest of the main plaza; catch a *colectivo* along avenida Central or walk about 15 minutes east along 5 Oriente Nte.

Tuxtla's cultural highlights are clustered in this area, once referred to as the Parque Madero. The park also holds the **Regional Museum of Anthropology,** a botanical garden, a children's area, and the city theater. The museum features exhibits on the lifestyles of the people of Chiapas and some artifacts from the state's archaeological sites. In one short stop you can learn about Chiapas's past civilizations, its flora, and its present-day accomplishments. It also has a FONART (government crafts) shop and cafeteria.

Miguel Álvarez del Toro Zoo (ZOOMAT). Bulevar Samuel León Brinois, southeast of downtown. Free admission; donations solicited. Tues–Sun 9am–5:30pm. The zoo is about 5 miles southeast of downtown; buses for the zoo can be found along Av. Central and at the Calzada.

Located in the forest called El Zapotal, ZOOMAT is one of the best zoos in Mexico. The collection of animals and birds indigenous to this area gives the visitor a tangible sense of what the wilds of Chiapas are like. Jaguars, howler monkeys, owls, and many more exotic animals are kept in roomy cages that replicate their home terrain; the whole zoo is so deeply buried in vegetation that you can almost pretend you're in a natural habitat. Unlike at other zoos I've visited, the animals are almost always on view; many will come to the fence if you make a kissing noise.

SHOPPING

The government-operated **Casa de las Artesanías,** Blvd. Domínguez 2035 (☎ 9/612-2275), is both a shop and gallery. The two stories of rooms feature a fine, extensive collection of crafts grouped by region and type from throughout the state of Chiapas. It's open Monday through Saturday from 10am to 8pm.

WHERE TO STAY

As Tuxtla booms, the center of the hotel industry has moved out of town, west to Highway 190. As you come in from the airport, you'll notice the new motel-style hotels, such as the **Hotel Flamboyán, Palace Inn, Hotel Laganja,** and **La Hacienda.** All of these are more expensive than those listed below, which are in the heart of town.

✪ **Hotel Bonampak Tuxtla.** Blv. Domínguez 180, 29030 Tuxtla Gutiérrez, Chi. ☎ **9/ 613-2050.** 70 units. A/C TV TEL. $64 double. AE, MC, V. Free secured parking.

This large, sprawling hotel has a swimming pool, tennis court, travel agency, boutique, coffee shop, and nice restaurant. The rooms facing the street are noisy, even with the air-conditioning on, but the interior rooms are blissfully quiet. The hotel's coffee shop, one of the best in town, is often packed with locals and tourists. The extensive menu includes an economical *comida corrida.* It's on the outskirts of downtown, where avenida 14 de Septiembre becomes bulevar Domínguez.

Hotel Esponda. 1 Poniente Nte. 142, 29030 Tuxtla Gutiérrez, Chi. ☎ **9/612-0080.** Fax 9/612-9771. 50 units. TV TEL. $23 double. AE, MC, V. Free parking.

In a city where inexpensive rooms are hard to come by, the Esponda is a good choice. Its rooms are in a nondescript five-story building with an elevator. The brown, green, and yellow decor is a bit unsettling, but the rooms are perfectly satisfactory—each has one, two, or three double beds; showers (without doors or curtains); big closets; and powerful ceiling fans. The hotel is conveniently located 1 block from the Plaza Cívica, near the Cristóbal Colón bus station.

Gran Hotel Humberto. Av. Central 180, 29030 Tuxtla Gutiérrez, Chi. ☎ **9/612-2080.** Fax 9/612-9771. 112 units. A/C TV TEL. $46 double. AE, MC, V. Free parking.

This older 10-story hotel is your best budget bet in booming Tuxtla. It's clean and comfortable enough, with well-kept furnishings dating from the 1950s. However, it isn't always an oasis of peace and quiet, especially on weekends when church bells compete with the ninth-floor nightclub. The location is ideal—it's in the center of town half a block from Plaza Cívica restaurants and the Mexicana airline office and 1¹/₂ blocks from the Cristóbal Colón bus station.

WHERE TO DINE

Tuxtla's main plaza, the **Plaza Cívica** (avenida Central at 1 Poniente), is actually two plazas separated by avenida Central. Rimming the edges are numerous restaurants, many of which serve customers outdoors under umbrella-shaded tables. The restaurants change names with frequency, so I won't recommend one over another. Just stroll the area and pick one that looks interesting, clean, and reasonably priced.

Las Pichanchas. Av. Central Ote. 837. ☎9/612-5351. Tamales $1–$2 each; main courses $4–$8. AE, DC, MC, V. Daily noon–midnight (live marimba music 2:30–5:30pm and 8:30–11:30pm; patio dinner show Tues–Sun at 9pm). Closed New Year's Day and the 2 days following Easter. MEXICAN.

No trip to Tuxtla Gutiérrez is complete without a meal at this colorfully decorated restaurant devoted to the regional food and drink of Chiapas. Inverted *pichanchas* (pots full of holes used to make *nixtamal masa* dough) are hung on posts as lanterns. For a sampler plate, try the *platón de carnes frías* (cold meat platter that includes different local sausages, ham, cheese, and tortillas) or the *platón de botana regional* (a variety of hot tidbits). The cold meat platter and the especially tasty *butifarra* (sausage) both feed two or three people nicely. Since Chiapan tamales are tastier and larger than those you may have eaten elsewhere, you must try at least one. From the Hotel Humberto in the center of town, walk 6 to 8 blocks south; you'll find the restaurant on the left.

ROAD TRIPS FROM TUXTLA GUTIÉRREZ: CHIAPA DE CORZO & THE SUMIDERO CANYON

The small town of **Chiapa de Corzo** is just off the highway to San Cristóbal, a 30-minute, 8-mile ride by bus from the main square (buses leave every 15 minutes in the morning, every 30 minutes in the afternoon), or a 10- to 15-minute ride by *colectivo*—they leave every 10 minutes from their stand at the corner of 3 Oriente and 3 Sur and cost about $1.

Chiapa de Corzo has a small **museum** on the main square dedicated to the city's lacquer industry; an interesting church; a colonial fountain; and a small **pyramid,** somewhat restored and visible from the road. In the museum, you can often see women learning the regional craft of lacquer painting, and sometimes mask makers give carving demonstrations and lessons.

From this town you can embark on a spectacular trip to the ✪ **Canyon of El Sumidero.** Boat rides through the canyon leave from the docks in Chiapa de Corzo when there are enough people (six to eight). Cost per person is about $7. This is the best way to see the canyon. You can, however, tour the canyon from the top by negotiating a ride along the canyon rim; the cost is around $40 for five people for a 2-hour ride.

Appendix A:
The Yucatán in Depth

I first visited the Yucatán many years ago. At the time, I was attempting to keep my small business afloat, an effort that absorbed every waking minute of my life. It was obvious that I was headed for burnout. My brother suggested we take a vacation to Mexico's oft-visited Yucatán Peninsula. I was reluctant, but my brother was persuasive. And so we flew down for what proved to be the best vacation I could have imagined.

The Yucatán may beckon you with the turquoise-blue waters and perfect temperatures characteristic of the Caribbean, but ultimately it draws you in with an engaging culture and rich history. The people are warm and friendly, and the food is better than you'll find in the Caribbean islands. On subsequent trips I headed inland to check out the famed pyramids. When I came across **Mérida**, I found a vibrant city that manifests a way of being that is perfectly in tune with its tropical surroundings, that is at once relaxed and actively engaged in life. Ever since that first visit (and borne out by the later visits), the Yucatán has in my mind been a place where one goes to escape the excesses of modern society and reclaim some of the simplicity that life used to have.

1 The Land & Its People

SOCIAL MORES It has often been observed by American and English travelers that Mexicans have a different conception of time: life in Mexico obeys slower rhythms. This is true, and yet few of these observers go on to explain what the consequences of this are for the visitor to Mexico. This is a shame, because an imperfect comprehension of this difference causes a good deal of misunderstanding between the tourist and the native Mexican.

Americans, in addition to many Canadians and Northern Europeans, tend to do things at a faster pace and, therefore, skip some of the niceties of social interaction. When walking into a store, many Americans simply smile at a clerk and launch right into a question or request. The smile, in effect, replaces the greeting. In Mexico, it doesn't work that way. One of the most important pieces of advice I can offer travelers is to always give a proper greeting when addressing Mexicans; don't try to abbreviate social intercourse. On several occasions, I have been asked by Mexican acquaintances why Americans grin all the time.

I didn't know what to make of the question at first, and only gradually did I begin to appreciate what was at issue: Mexicans were misinterpreting this American manner of greeting. After all, a smile when there is no context can be ambiguous; it can convey amusement, smugness, superiority, etc.

This goes back to the issue of our different ideas about time. Mexican culture places a higher value on proper social form than on saving time. A Mexican must at least say *"¡Buenos Días!"* or a quick *"¿Qué pasó?"* (or its equivalent), even to total strangers—a show of proper respect. And when an individual meets a group of people he or she will greet each member of the group, which can take quite a while. We might consider such behavior obtrusive and presumptuous; for us the polite thing would be to keep our interruption to a minimum, and give a general greeting to all.

Mexicans, like most people, will consciously or subconsciously make quick judgments about the people they meet. Most divide the world into the well-raised and cultured (*bien educado*), on the one hand, and the poorly raised (*mal educado*) on the other. What's important in Mexico is to be categorized as one of the cultured foreigners and not one of the barbarians. This makes it easier to get the attention of waiters, hotel desk clerks, and people on the street. Unfortunately, many visitors are reluctant to try out their Spanish, preferring to keep exchanges to a minimum. Don't do this. To be categorized as a foreigner isn't a big deal.

TODAY'S MAYA CULTURE & PEOPLES   As with lowlanders elsewhere in Mexico, Yucatecans are exceedingly warm and friendly and show little reserve; entering into conversation with them could not be easier. In the peninsula's interior, you might find people who are unexpectedly reticent, but most likely these are Maya Indians who aren't comfortable speaking Spanish. It may come as a surprise that you don't have to leave Cancún to meet the Maya; thousands come from the interior to work at hotels and restaurants in Cancún, and many can switch easily between Spanish, English, and Yukatek, the local Mayan language. More than 350,000 Maya living in the Yucatán's three states speak Yukatek Mayan, and most, especially men, speak Spanish, too.

Completely different are the estimated 1 million **Tabascan** and **Chiapan Maya,** who speak four different Mayan languages with dozens of dialects. The Maya groups around San Cristóbal de las Casas generally choose not to embrace outside cultures, preferring to live in small mountain hamlets and meeting only for ceremonies and market days. Their forest- and cloud-draped high mountain homeland in Chiapas is cold—in contrast to the heat predominant in the lowland regions of Tabasco and the Yucatán Peninsula. They, too, live much as their ancestors did, but with beliefs distinct from their peninsular relatives.

THE YUCATÁN'S GEOGRAPHY   The Yucatán is edged by the dull aquamarine Gulf of Mexico on the west and north, and the clear cerulean blue Caribbean Sea on the east. The peninsula covers almost 84,000 square miles,

. . . we both learned that the Maya are not just a people of the past. Today, they live in their millions in Mexico, Guatemala, Belize, and western Honduras, still speaking one of the 35 Mayan languages as their native tongue. They continue to cultivate their fields and commune with their living world in spite of the fact that they are encapsulated within a larger modern civilization whose vision of reality is often alien to their own.
                                        —Linda Schele and David Freidel, *A Forest of Kings,* 1990

with nearly 1,000 miles of shoreline. Most terrain is porous limestone, with thin soil supporting a primarily low, scrubby jungle. There are almost no surface rivers; instead, rainwater filters through the limestone into underground rivers. Natural wells called *cenotes,* or collapsed caves, dot the region.

The only sense of height comes from the hills along the western shores of Campeche, rising inland to the border with the Yucatán state. This rise, called the Puuc Hills, is the Maya "Alps," though they are a mere 980 feet high. Locally, the hills are known as the Sierra de Ticul or Sierra Alta. The highways undulate a bit as you go inland, and south of Ticul there's a rise in the highway that provides a marvelous view of the "valley" and the misty Puuc hills lining the horizon.

NATURAL LIFE & PROTECTED AREAS   The Yucatán state's nature preserves include the 118,000-acre **Río Lagartos Wildlife Refuge** north of Valladolid—where North America's largest flock of flamingos nests—and the 14,000-plus acre **Celestún Wildlife Refuge,** which exists for the protection of flamingos and other tropical birds and plant life. The state also has incorporated nature trails into the archaeological site of **Dzibilchaltún,** north of Mérida.

In 1989, Campeche state set aside 178,699 acres in the **Calakmul Biosphere Reserve** that it shares with the country of Guatemala. The area includes the ruins of Calakmul, as well as significant plant and animal life.

Quintana Roo's protected areas are some of the region's most beautiful, wild, and important. In 1986 the state ambitiously set aside the 1.3 million–acre **Sian Ka'an Biosphere Reserve,** conserving a significant part of the coast in the face of development south of Tulum. **Isla Contoy,** also in Quintana Roo, off the coast of Isla Mujeres and Cancún, is a beautiful island refuge for hundreds of birds, turtles, plants, and other wildlife. And in 1990 the 150-acre **Jardín Botánico,** south of Puerto Morelos, was opened to the public. Along with the Botanical Garden at Cozumel's Chancanaab Lagoon, it gives visitors an excellent idea of the biological importance of Yucatán's lengthy shoreline: four of Mexico's eight marine turtle species nest on Quintana Roo's shores—loggerhead, green, hawksbill, and leatherback—and more than 600 species of birds, reptiles, and mammals have been counted.

El Triunfo Biosphere Reserve, near the Lagunas de Montebello in Chiapas, preserves 25,000 acres of the rain-forest habitat of the rare and endangered quetzal bird.

2 A Look at the Past

PRE-HISPANIC CIVILIZATIONS

The earliest "Mexicans" were Stone Age hunter-gatherers coming from the north, descendants of a race that had crossed the Bering Strait and reached North America around 12,000 B.C. They arrived in what is now Mexico by 10,000 B.C. Sometime between 5200 and 1500 B.C., in what is known as the **Archaic period,** they began practicing agriculture and domesticating animals.

THE PRECLASSIC PERIOD (1500 B.C.–A.D. 300)   Eventually, agriculture improved to the point that it could provide enough food to

Dateline

- **10000–1500 B.C.** Archaic period: Hunting and gathering; later, the dawn of agriculture: domestication of chilies, corn, beans, avocado, amaranth, and pumpkin. Mortars and pestles in use. Stone bowls and jars, obsidian knives, and open-weave basketry developed.
- **1500 B.C.–A.D. 300** Preclassic period: Olmec culture

continues

develops large-scale settlements and irrigation methods. Cities develop for the first time. Olmec influence spreads over other cultures in the Gulf Coast, central and southern Mexico, Central America, the lower Mexican Pacific Coast, and the Yucatán. Several cities in central and southern Mexico begin the construction of large ceremonial centers and pyramids. The Maya develop several city states in Chiapas and Central America.

- **1000–900 B.C.** Olmec San Lorenzo center is destroyed; they begin anew at La Venta.
- **600 B.C.** La Venta Olmec cultural zenith. Zapotec culture emerges near Monte Albán Oaxaca.
- **A.D. 300–900** Classic period: Broad influence of Teotihuacán culture and the establishment there of a truly cosmopolitan urbanism. Satellite settlements spring up across central Mexico and as far away as Guatemala. Trade and cultural interchange with the Maya and the Zapotec flourish. The Maya perfect the calendar and improve astronomical calculations. They build grandiose cities at Palenque, Calakmul, Cobá, and in Central America. The Zapotec construct the religious center on Monte Albán.
- **650–800** Teotihuacán suffers a violent attack and is abandoned. Several minor cities in the area reach their zenith as new centers of culture and learning.
- **683** Maya Lord Pacal is buried in an elaborate tomb below the Palace of the Inscriptions at Palenque.
- **800** Bonampak battle/ victory mural painted.
- **900** Postclassic period begins: More emphasis is

continues

support large communities and enough surplus to free some of the population from agricultural work. A civilization emerged that we call the **Olmec**—an enigmatic people who settled the lower Gulf Coast in what is now Tabasco and Veracruz. Anthropologists regard them as the mother culture of Mesoamerica, since they established a pattern for later civilizations in a wide area stretching from northern Mexico into Central America. The Olmec developed the basic calendar used throughout the region, established the predominance of a 52-year cycle—and used it to schedule the construction of pyramids—established principles of urban layout and architecture, and originated the cult of the jaguar and the sacredness of jade. They may also have bequeathed the sacred ritual of "the ball game"—a universal element of Mesoamerican culture.

One intriguing feature of the Olmec was the carving of colossal stone heads. We still don't know what purposes these heads served, but they were immense projects; the basalt stone from which they were sculpted was mined miles inland and transported to the Olmec cities on the coast, probably by river rafts. The heads share a rounded, baby-faced look, marked by a peculiar, high-arched lip—a "jaguar mouth"— that is an identifying mark of Olmec sculpture.

The Maya civilization began developing in the late Preclassic period, around 500 B.C. Our understanding of this period is only sketchy, but Olmec influences are apparent everywhere. The Maya perfected the Olmec calendar and, somewhere along the way, developed their ornate system of hieroglyphic writing and their early architecture. Two other civilizations also began their rise to prominence around this time: the people of Teotihuacán, just north of present-day Mexico City, and the Zapotec of Monte Albán, in the valley of Oaxaca.

THE CLASSIC PERIOD (A.D. 300–900)

The flourishing of these three civilizations marks the boundaries of this period—the heyday of pre-Columbian Mesoamerican artistic and cultural achievements. These include the pyramids and palaces in Teotihuacán; the ceremonial center of Monte Albán; and the stelae and temples of Palenque, Bonampak, and the Tikal site in Guatemala. Beyond their achievements in art and architecture, the Maya made significant discoveries in science, including the use of the zero in mathematics and a complex calendar with which the priests could predict eclipses and the movements of the stars for centuries to come.

The inhabitants of **Teotihuacán** (100 B.C.–A.D. 700—near present-day Mexico City) built a city that, at its zenith, is thought to have had 100,000 or more inhabitants covering 9 square miles. It was a well-organized city, built on a grid with streams channeled to follow the city's plan. Different social classes, such as artisans and merchants, were assigned to specific neighborhoods. At its height, Teotihuacán was the greatest cultural center in Mexico, with tremendous influence as far away as Guatemala and the Yucatán Peninsula. The ceremonial center is so large that it was thought by the Aztecs to have been built by gods. Its feathered serpent god, later known as **Quetzalcoatl,** became part of the pantheon of many succeeding cultures. The ruling classes were industrious, literate, and cosmopolitan. The beautiful sculpture and ceramics of Teotihuacán display a highly stylized and refined aesthetic whose influences can be seen clearly in objects of Maya and Zapotec origin. Around the 7th century, the city was abandoned for unknown reasons. Who these people were and where they went remains a mystery.

Further south, the **Zapotecs,** influenced by the Olmecs, raised an impressive culture in the region of Oaxaca. Their two principal cities were **Monte Albán,** inhabited by an elite of merchants and artisans, and **Mitla,** reserved for the high priests.

THE POSTCLASSIC PERIOD (A.D. 900–1521)

Warfare became a more conspicuous activity of the civilizations that flourished in this period. Social development was impressive, but not as cosmopolitan as the Maya, Teotihuacán, and Zapotec societies. In central Mexico, a people known as the **Toltecs** established their capital at Tula in the 10th century. They were originally one of the barbarous hordes of Indians that periodically migrated from the north. At some stage in their development, the Toltecs were influenced by remnants of Teotihuacán culture and adopted the feathered serpent Quetzalcoatl as their god. They also revered a god known as **Tezcatlipoca** or "smoking mirror," who later became a god of the Aztecs. The Toltecs maintained a large military class divided into orders symbolized by animals. At its height, Tula may have had 40,000 people, and it spread its influence across Mesoamerica. By the 13th century, however, the Toltec had exhausted

placed on warfare in central Mexico. The Toltec culture emerges at Tula and replaces Teotihuacán as the dominant city of central Mexico. Toltec influence spreads to the Yucatán, forming the culture of the Itzaés, who become the rulers of Chichén Itzá.

- **909** A small monument at Toniná (near San Cristóbal de las Casas) has this as the last Long Count date discovered so far, symbolizing the end of the Classic Maya era.
- **1156–1230** Tula, the Toltec capital, is abandoned.
- **1325–1470** Aztec capital Tenochtitlán founded; Aztecs begin military campaigns in the Valley of Mexico, and then thrust farther out, subjugating the civilizations of the Gulf Coast and southern Mexico.
- **1516** Gold found on Cozumel during aborted Spanish expedition of Yucatán Peninsula arouses interest of Spanish governor in Cuba, who sends Juan de Grijalva on an expedition, followed by another, led by Hernán Cortez.
- **1518** Spaniards first visit what is today Campeche.
- **1519** Conquest of Mexico begins: Hernán Cortez and troops make their way along Mexican coast to present-day Veracruz.
- **1521** Conquest is complete after Aztec defeat at Tlatelolco.
- **1521–24** Cortez organizes Spanish empire in Mexico and begins building Mexico City on the ruins of Tenochtitlán.
- **1524–35** Cortez removed from power and New Spain is governed by royal council.
- **1526** Francisco Montejo permitted by King of Spain to colonize the Yucatán.
- **1535–1821** Viceregal period: Mexico governed by

61 viceroys appointed by King of Spain. Control of much of the land ends up in the hands of the church and the politically powerful. Yucatán is led by a governor who reports to the king rather than to viceroys.

- **1542** Mérida established as capital of Yucatán Peninsula.
- **1546** The Maya rebel and take control of the peninsula.
- **1559** French and Spanish pirates attack Campeche.
- **1562** Friar Diego de Landa destroys 5,000 Mayan religious stone figures and burns 27 hieroglyphic painted manuscripts at Maní, Yucatán. Widespread torture and death are meted out to Maya, believed to secretly practice pre-Hispanic beliefs.
- **1767** Jesuits expelled from New Spain.
- **1810–21** War of Independence: Miguel Hidalgo starts movement for Mexico's independence from Spain, but is executed within a year; leadership and goals change during the war years, but a compromise between monarchy and a republic is outlined by Agustín de Iturbide.
- **1822** First Empire: Iturbide ascends throne as Emperor of Mexico, loses power after a year, and loses life in an attempt to reclaim throne.
- **1824–64** Early Republic period characterized by almost perpetual civil war between federalists and centralists, conservatives and liberals, culminating in the victory of the liberals under Juárez.
- **1864–67** Second Empire: The French invade Mexico in the name of Maximilian of Austria, who is appointed Emperor of Mexico. Juárez and liberal government

continues

themselves, probably in civil wars and in battles with the invaders from the north.

Of those northern invaders, the **Aztecs** were the most warlike. At first they served as mercenaries for the established cities in the valley of Mexico—one of which allotted to them an unwanted marshy piece of land in the middle of Lake Texcoco for their settlement. This eventually grew into the island city of Tenochtitlán. Through aggressive diplomacy and military action, the Aztecs soon conquered all of central Mexico and extended their rule east to the Gulf Coast and south to the valley of Oaxaca.

During this period, the Maya built beautiful cities near the Yucatán's Puuc hills. The regional architecture, called **Puuc style,** is characterized by elaborate exterior stonework appearing above door frames and extending to the roofline. Examples of this architecture, such as the Codz Poop at Kabah and the palaces at Uxmal, Sayil and Labná, are beautiful and quite impressive. Associated with the cities of the Puuc region was Chichén Itzá, ruled by the Itzáes. This metropolis evidences strong Toltec influences in its architectural style as well as in its religion, which incorporated a plumed-serpent god called Kukulcán, obviously the god Quetzalcoatl of central Mexico.

The precise nature of this Toltec influence is a subject of debate. But there is an intriguing myth in central Mexico that tells how Quetzalcoatl quarrels with Tezcatlipoca and through trickery is shamed by his rival into leaving Tula, the capital of the Toltec empire. He leaves heading eastwards towards the morning star, vowing someday to return. In the language of myth, this could be a shorthand telling of an actual civil war between two factions in Tula, each led by the priesthood of a particular God. Could the losing faction have migrated to the Yucatán and formed the ruling class of Chichén Itzá? Perhaps, but what we do know for certain is that this myth of the eventual return of Quetazcoatl became, in the hands of the Spanish, a powerful weapon of conquest.

THE CONQUEST

In 1517, the first Spaniards arrived in what is today known as Mexico and skirmished with Maya Indians off the coast of the Yucatán Peninsula. One of these fledgling expeditions ended in shipwreck, leaving several Spaniards stranded as prisoners of the Maya. The Spanish sent out another expedition, under the command of **Hernán Cortez,** which landed on Cozumel in February of 1519. Cortez inquired about the gold and riches of the interior, and the coastal Maya were happy to describe the wealth and splendor of the Aztec empire in central Mexico. Cortez promptly decided to disobey all orders of his superior, the governor of Cuba, and sailed to the mainland.

Cortez arrived when the Aztec empire was at the height of its wealth and power. **Moctezuma II** ruled over the central and southern highlands and extracted tribute from lowland peoples. His greatest temples were literally plated with gold and encrusted with the blood of sacrificial captives. Moctezuma himself was a fool, a mystic, and something of a coward. Despite his wealth and military power, he dithered in his capital at Tenochtitlán, sending messengers with gifts and suggestions that Cortez leave. Meanwhile, Cortez blustered and negotiated his way into the highlands, always cloaking his real intentions. Moctezuma, terrified by the military tactics and technology of the Spaniard, convinced himself that Cortez was in fact the god Quetzalcoatl making his long-awaited return. By the time the Spaniards arrived in the Aztec capital, Cortez had gained some ascendancy over the lesser Indian states that were resentful tributaries to the Aztec. In November of 1519, Cortez confronted Moctezuma and took him hostage in an effort to leverage from him control of the empire.

In the middle of Cortez's dangerous game of manipulation, another Spanish expedition arrived with orders to end Cortez's authority over the mission. Cortez hastened to meet the rival's force and persuade them to join his own. In the meantime, the Aztecs chased the garrison out of Tenochtitlán, and either they or the Spaniards killed Moctezuma. For the next year and a half, Cortez laid siege to Tenochtitlán with the help of rival Indians and a decimating epidemic of smallpox, to which the Indians had no resistance. In the end, the Aztec capital fell, and when it did, all of central Mexico lay at the feet of the *conquistadors*.

The Spanish conquest started out as a pirate expedition by Cortez and his men, unauthorized by the Spanish crown or its governor in Cuba. The Spanish king legitimized Cortez following his victory over the Aztecs and ordered the forcible Christianization of this new

retreat to the north and wage war with the French forces. The French finally abandon Mexico and leave Maximilian to be defeated and executed by the Mexicans.

- **1847–66** War of the Castes in the Yucatán: Poverty and hunger cause the Maya to revolt and gain control of half of the peninsula before being defeated by army. Strife lasts well into the 20th century.

- **1872–76** Juarez dies, and political struggles ensue for the presidency.

- **1877–1911** Porfiriato: Porfirio Díaz is president/dictator of Mexico for 35 years, leads country to modernization by encouraging foreign investment in mines, oil, and railroads. Mexico witnesses the development of a modern economy and a growing disparity between rich and poor. Social conditions, especially in rural areas, become desperate.

- **1911–17** Mexican Revolution: Francisco Madero drafts revolutionary plan. Díaz resigns. Leaders jockey for power during period of great violence, national upheaval, and tremendous loss of life.

- **1917–40** Reconstruction: Present constitution of Mexico signed; land and education reforms are initiated and labor unions strengthened; Mexico expropriates oil companies and railroads. Pancho Villa, Zapata, and presidents Obregón and Carranza are assassinated.

- **1940** Mexico enters period of political stability and makes tremendous economic progress. Quality of life improves, although problems of corruption, inflation,

continues

national health, and unresolved land and agricultural issues continue.

- **1974** Quintana Roo achieves statehood and Cancún opens to tourism.
- **1994–97** Mexico, Canada, and the United States sign the North American Free Trade Agreement (NAFTA). In an unrelated incident, PRI candidate Luis Donaldo Colossio is assassinated 5 months before the election; replacement candidate Ernesto Zedillo becomes Mexico's next president, vowing to be a reformer. Within weeks, the peso is devalued, throwing the nation into turmoil. The middle and lower classes are hurt the most as interest rates soar. An Indian uprising in Chiapas sparks countrywide protests over government policies concerning land distribution, bank loans, health, education, and voting and human rights.
- **1998** Economy improves. Cuauhtémoc Cárdenas becomes the first opposition candidate to become mayor of Mexico City, the second most powerful office in the country.
- **1999** President Zedillo reaffirms his promise not to hand-pick his successor (as has always been the President's prerogative) but to open up the process to all the PRI party faithful.
- **2000** The PRI uses a primary system for the first time to elect its candidate, Francisco Labastida, who faces off against opposition candidates Cuauhtémoc Cárdanas and Vicente Fox.

colony, to be called **New Spain.** Guatemala and Honduras were explored and conquered, and by 1540 the territory of New Spain included possessions from Vancouver to Panama. In the two centuries that followed, Franciscan and Augustinian friars converted millions of Indians to Christianity, and the Spanish lords built up huge feudal estates on which the Indian farmers were little more than serfs. The silver and gold that Cortez looted made Spain the richest country in Europe.

THE COLONIAL PERIOD

Hernán Cortez set about building a new city, the seat of government of New Spain, upon the ruins of the old Aztec capital. For indigenous peoples (besides the Tlaxcaltecans, Cortez's Indian allies), heavy tributes once paid to the Aztecs were now rendered in forced labor to the Spanish. Diseases carried by the Spaniards, against which the Indian populations had no natural immunity, wiped out most of the native population.

Over the three centuries of the colonial period, 61 viceroys appointed by the king of Spain governed Mexico. Spain became rich from New World gold and silver, chiseled out by backbreaking Indian labor. The colonial elite built lavish homes both in Mexico City and in the countryside. They filled their homes with ornate furniture, had many servants, and adorned themselves in velvets, satins, and jewels imported from abroad. A new class system developed. Those born in Spain considered themselves superior to the *criollos* (Spaniards born in Mexico). Those of other races and the *castas* (mixtures of Spanish and Indian, Spanish and Black, or Indian and Black) occupied the bottom rung of society.

It took great cunning to stay a step ahead of the avaricious Crown, which demanded increasingly higher taxes and contributions from its fabled foreign conquests. Still, wealthy colonists prospered grandly enough to develop an extravagant society.

However, discontent with the mother country simmered for years over social and political hot points: taxes, the royal bureaucracy, Spanish-born citizens' advantages over Mexican-born subjects, and restrictions on commerce with Spain and other countries. Dissatisfaction with Spain found an opportune moment in 1808 when Napoleon invaded Spain and crowned his brother Joseph king, in place of Charles IV. To many in Mexico, allegiance to France was out of the question; discontent with the mother country reached the level of revolt.

INDEPENDENCE

The rebellion began in 1810, when a priest, **Father Miguel Hidalgo,** gave the *grito,* a cry for independence, from his church in the town of Dolores, Guanajuato. The uprising soon became a full-fledged revolution, as Hidalgo and Ignacio Allende gathered an "army" of citizens and threatened Mexico City. Although Hidalgo ultimately failed and was executed, he is honored as "the Father of Mexican Independence." Another priest, José María Morelos, kept the revolt alive with several successful campaigns through 1815, when he, too, was captured and executed.

After the death of Morelos, prospects for independence were rather dim until the Spanish king who replaced Joseph Bonaparte decided to make social reforms in the colonies, which convinced the conservative powers in Mexico that they didn't need Spain after all. With their tacit approval, Agustín de Iturbide, then commander of royalist forces, declared Mexico independent and himself emperor. It was not long, however, before internal dissension brought about the fall of the emperor, and Mexico was proclaimed a republic.

The young Mexican republic was inflamed by political instability and ran through a dizzying succession of presidents and dictators as struggles between federalists and centralists, and conservatives and liberals, divided the country and consumed its energy. Moreover, there was a disastrous war with the United States in which Mexico lost half its territory. A central figure was **Antonio López de Santa Anna,** who assumed the leadership of his country no fewer than 11 times and was flexible enough in those volatile times to portray himself variously as a liberal, a conservative, a federalist, and a centralist. He probably holds the record for frequency of exile; by 1855 he was finally left without a political comeback and ended his days in Venezuela.

Political instability persisted, and the conservative forces, with some encouragement from Napoleon III, hit upon the idea of inviting in a Hapsburg to regain control (as if that strategy had ever worked for Spain). They found a willing volunteer in Archduke Maximilian of Austria, who, being at the time unemployed in ruling anyone, accepted the position of Mexican emperor with the support of French troops. The first French force—a modern, well-equipped army—was defeated by the rag-tag Mexican forces in a battle near Puebla (now celebrated annually as **Cinco de Mayo**). The second attempt was more successful, and Ferdinand Maximilian Joseph of Hapsburg became emperor. After 3 years of civil war, the French were finally induced to abandon the emperor's cause; **Maximilian** was captured and executed by a firing squad near Querétaro in 1867. His adversary and successor (as president of Mexico) was **Benito Juárez,** a Zapotec Indian lawyer and one of the great heroes of Mexican history. Juárez did his best to unify and strengthen his country before dying of a heart attack in 1872; his impact on Mexico's future was profound, and his plans and visions bore fruit for decades.

THE PORFIRIATO & THE REVOLUTION

A few years after Juárez's death, one of his generals, **Porfirio Díaz,** assumed power in a coup and ruled Mexico from 1877 to 1911, a period now called the "Porfiriato." He stayed in power through brutal repression of the opposition and by courting the favor of the powerful nations of the time. Generous in his dealings with foreign investors, Díaz became, in the eyes of most Mexicans, the archetypal *entreguista* (one who sells out his country for private gain). With foreign investment came the concentration of great wealth in few hands, and social conditions worsened.

In 1910, Francisco Madero called for an armed rebellion that became the **Mexican Revolution** ("La Revolución" in Mexico; the revolution against Spain is called the "Guerra de Independencia"). Díaz was sent into exile; while in London, he became a celebrity at the age of 81, when he jumped into the Thames to save a drowning boy. Díaz is buried in Paris. Madero became president but was promptly betrayed and executed by a heavy straight out of the Hollywood school of villains—the despicable **Victoriano Huerta.** Those who had answered Madero's call responded again—the great peasant hero **Emiliano Zapata** in the south and the seemingly invincible **Pancho Villa** in the central north with Álvaro Obregón and Venustiano Carranza flanking him. They eventually put Huerta to flight and began hashing out a new constitution.

For the next few years, the revolutionaries Carranza, Obregón, and Villa fought amongst themselves; Zapata did not seek national power, though he fought tenaciously for land for the peasants. He was betrayed and assassinated by Carranza, who was president at that time. Obregón finally consolidated power and probably had Carranza assassinated. He in turn was assassinated when he tried to break one of the tenets of the Revolution—no reelection. His successor, Plutarco El'as Calles, learned this lesson well, installing one puppet president after another until **Lázaro Cárdenas** severed the puppeteer's strings and banished him to exile.

Until Cárdenas's election in 1934, the eventual outcome of the Revolution remained in doubt. There had been some land redistribution, but other measures took a back seat to political expediency. Cárdenas changed all that. He implemented a massive redistribution of land and nationalized the oil industry. He instituted many reforms and gave shape to the ruling political party (now the **Partido Revolucionario Institucional,** or PRI) by bringing under its banner a broad representation of Mexican society and establishing the mechanisms for consensus building. Cárdenas is practically canonized by most Mexicans.

MODERN MEXICO

The presidents who followed were more noted for graft than leadership. The party's base narrowed as many of the reform-minded elements were marginalized. Economic progress, a lot of it in the form of large development projects, became the PRI's main basis for legitimacy. In 1968, the government violently repressed a democratic student movement. Police forces shot and killed an unknown number of civilians in Tlatelolco, a section of Mexico City. Though the PRI maintained its grip on power, it lost all semblance of being a progressive party. In 1985 there was a devastating **earthquake in Mexico City** that brought down many of the government's new, supposedly earthquake-proof buildings, thus exposing shoddy construction and the widespread government corruption that fostered it. There was heavy criticism, too, for how it handled the relief efforts. In 1994, a political/military **uprising in Chiapas** focused world attention on Mexico's great social problems. A new political force, the Zapatista National Liberation Army (EZLN for Ejército Zapatista de Liberación Nacional), has skillfully publicized the plight of the peasant in today's Mexico. The government was forced into negotiations with the EZLN, a position that can bring it little if any political capital. Its tactics have been to make some easy concessions and to stall on other demands.

In recent years, opposition political parties have grown in power and legitimacy. Facing enormous pressure and scrutiny from national and international organizations, and widespread public discontent, the PRI has had to concede electoral defeats for state governors and congresspersons. Elements of the PRI have been trying to reform the party from within, and this has created internal crises as manifested in the several political assassinations that have occurred in the last few years. For the first time ever, the PRI conceded the mayorship of Mexico City in 1998, the second most powerful position in the country, to a leader of the opposition, **Cuauhtémoc Cárdenas**, son of the PRI's brightest star, Lázaro. Now, as the PRI prepares for the upcoming presidential elections, it has for the first time opened up the candidate-selection process by instituting a system of primaries. No longer will the outgoing president be permitted to handpick his successor. The rank and file of the party has responded, and with the recent surge in Mexico's economy and some political mistakes by the opposition, many believe that the PRI will remain the party in power.

3 Art & Architecture 101

Mexico's artistic and architectural legacy reaches back more than 3,000 years. Until the conquest of Mexico in A.D. 1521, art, architecture, politics, and religion were inextricably intertwined. Although the European conquest influenced the style and subject of Mexican art, this continuity remained throughout the colonial period.

PRE-HISPANIC FORMS

Mexico's **pyramids** are truncated platforms, not true pyramids, and come in many different shapes. Many sites have circular buildings, such as El Caracol at Chichén-Itzá, usually called the observatory and dedicated to the god of the wind. El Castillo at Chichén-Itzá has 365 steps—one for every day of the year. The Temple of the Magicians at Uxmal has beautifully rounded and sloping sides. Evidence of building one pyramidal structure on top of another, a widely accepted practice, has been found throughout Mesoamerica.

The Temple of the Inscriptions at Palenque is one of the few pyramids in Mesoamerica specifically built to conceal an underground tomb, although tombs have been found in many other pyramids. Cobá has the longest road (*sacbe*), stretching 62 miles. Numerous sites in Mesoamerica have ballcourts. In Mexico the longest is at Chichén-Itzá—nearly the length of a football field.

Architects of many Toltec, Aztec, and Teotihuacán edifices alternated sloping panels (*talud*) with vertical panels (*tablero*). Elements of this style occasionally show up in the Yucatán. Dzinbanché, a newly excavated site near Lago Bacalar, in southern Quintana Roo state, has at least one temple with this characteristic. The true arch was unknown in Mesoamerica, so the Maya made use of the corbeled arch—a method of stacking stones that allows each successive stone to be cantilevered out a little farther than the one below it, until the two sides meet at the top, forming the shape of an inverted *V*.

The Olmec, considered the parent culture in Mexico, built pyramids of earth. Unfortunately, little remains to tell us what their buildings looked like. The Olmec, however, left an enormous sculptural legacy from small, intricately carved pieces of jade to 40-ton carved basalt rock heads.

Throughout Mexico, carved stone and mural art on pyramids served a religious and historic function rather than an ornamental one. **Hieroglyphs,** picture symbols etched on stone or painted on walls or pottery, functioned as the written language of the ancient peoples, particularly the Maya. By deciphering the glyphs, scholars allow the ancients to speak again, providing us with specific names to attach to rulers and their families, and demystifying the great dynastic histories of the Maya. For more on this, be sure to read *A Forest of Kings* (1990) by Linda Schele and David Freidel and *Blood of Kings* (1986) by Linda Schele and Mary Ellen Miller. Good hieroglyphic examples can be seen in the site museum at Palenque.

Carving important historic figures on freestanding stone slabs, or **stelae,** was a common Maya commemorative device. Several are in place at Cobá; Calakmul has the most, and good examples are displayed in the Museum of Anthropology in Mexico City and the archaeology museum in Villahermosa. **Pottery** played an important role, and different indigenous groups are distinguished by their different use of color and style. The Maya painted pottery with scenes from daily and historic life.

Pre-Hispanic cultures left a number of fantastic painted **murals,** some of which are remarkably preserved, such as those at Bonampak and Cacaxtla. Amazing stone murals or mosaics, using thousands of pieces of fitted stone to form figures of warriors, snakes, or geometric designs, decorate the pyramid facades at Uxmal and Chichén-Itzá.

SPANISH INFLUENCE

With the arrival of the Spaniards, new forms of architecture came to Mexico. Many sites that were occupied by indigenous groups at the time of the conquest were razed, and in their place appeared Catholic churches, public buildings, and palaces for conquerors and the king's bureaucrats. In the Yucatán, existing churches at Izamal, Calkani, Santa Elena, and Muná rest atop former pyramidal structures. Indian artisans, who formerly worked on pyramidal structures, were recruited to build the new buildings, often guided by drawings of European buildings. Frequently left on their own, the indigenous artisans implanted traditional symbolism in the new buildings: a plaster angel swaddled in feathers, reminiscent of the god Quetzalcoatl; the face of an ancient god surrounded by corn leaves. They used pre-Hispanic calendar counts—the 13 steps to heaven or the 9 levels of the underworld—to determine how many florets to carve around the church doorway.

To convert the native populations, New World Spanish priests and architects altered their normal ways of teaching and building. Often before the church was built, an open-air atrium was first constructed so that large numbers of parishioners could be accommodated for services. *Posas* (shelters) at the four corners of churchyards were another architectural technique unique to Mexico, again for the purpose of accommodating crowds during holy sacraments. Because of the language barrier between the Spanish and the natives, church adornment became more explicit. Biblical tales came to life in frescoes splashed across church walls. Christian symbolism in stone supplanted that of pre-Hispanic ideas as the natives tried to make sense of it all. Baroque became even more baroque in Mexico and was dubbed *churrigueresque,* after the Spanish architect José Benito Churriguera (1665–1725). Exuberant and complicated, it combines Gothic, baroque, and plateresque elements.

Almost every village in the Yucatán Peninsula has the remains of **missions, monasteries, convents,** and **parish churches.** Many were built in the 16th century following the early arrival of Franciscan friars (the Franciscans were for a long time the only order allowed to Christianize the Yucatán natives). Examples include the Mission of San Bernardino de Sisal in Valladolid; the fine altarpiece at Teabo; the folk-art *retablo* (altarpiece) at Calkani; the large church and convent at Mani with its *retablos* and limestone crucifix; the façade, altar, and central *retablo* of the church at Oxkutzcab; the 16-bell belfry at Ytholin; the baroque façade and altarpiece at Maxcanu; the cathedral at Mérida; the vast atrium and church at Izamal; and the baroque *retablo* and murals at Tabi.

When Porfirio Díaz became president in the late 19th century, the nation's art and architecture experienced another infusion of European sensibility. Díaz idolized Europe, and during this time he commissioned a number of striking European-style public buildings, including many opera houses still used today. He provided European scholarships to promising young artists who later returned to Mexico to produce Mexican subject paintings using techniques learned abroad.

THE ADVENT OF MEXICAN MURALISM

As the Mexican Revolution ripped the country apart between 1911 and 1917, a new social and cultural Mexico was born. In 1923 Minister of Education José Vasconcelos was charged with educating the illiterate masses. As one means of reaching people, he invited **Diego Rivera** and several other budding artists to paint Mexican history on the walls of the Ministry of Education building and the National Preparatory School in Mexico City. Thus began the tradition of painting murals in public buildings, that you will find in towns and cities throughout the Mexico and the Yucatán.

4 Religion, Myth & Folklore

Mexico is predominantly Roman Catholic, a religion introduced by the Spaniards during the Conquest of Mexico. Despite its preponderance, the Catholic faith in many places in Mexico (Chiapas and Oaxaca, for example) has pre-Hispanic undercurrents. One need only visit the *curandero* section of a Mexican market (where one can purchase copal—an incense agreeable to the gods; rustic beeswax candles, a traditional offering; the native species of tobacco used to ward off evil; etc.), or attend a village festivity featuring pre-Hispanic dancers, to understand that supernatural beliefs often run parallel with Christian ones.

Mexico's complicated mythological heritage from pre-Hispanic religion is full of images derived from nature—the wind, jaguars, eagles, snakes, flowers, and more—all intertwined with elaborate mythological stories to explain the universe, climate, seasons, and geography. Most groups believed in an underworld (not a hell), usually containing 9 levels, and a heaven of 13 levels—which is why the numbers 9 and 13 are so mythologically significant. The solar calendar count of 365 days and the ceremonial calendar of 260 days are numerically significant as well. How one died determined one's resting place after death: in the underworld (*Xibalba* to the Maya), in heaven, or at one of the four cardinal points. For example, men who died in battle or women who died in childbirth went straight to the sun. Everyone else first had to make a journey through the underworld.

One of the richest sources of mythological tales is the *Book of Popol Vuh,* a Maya bible of sorts, recorded after the Conquest. The *Chilam Balam,* another such book, existed in hieroglyphic form at the Conquest and was recorded using the Spanish alphabet to transliterate Maya words that could be understood by the Spaniards. The *Chilam Balam* differs from the *Popol Vuh* in that it is the collected histories of many Maya communities.

Gods & Goddesses

Each of the ancient cultures had its set of gods and goddesses, and while the names might not have crossed cultures, their characteristics or purposes often did. Chaac, the hook-nosed rain god of the Maya, was Tlaloc, the squat rain god of the Aztecs; Quetzalcoatl, the plumed-serpent god/man of the Toltecs, became Kukulkán of the Maya. The tales of the powers and creation of these deities make up Mexico's rich mythology. Sorting out the pre-Hispanic pantheon and mythological beliefs in ancient Mexico can become an all-consuming study (the Maya alone had 166 deities), so below is a list of some of the most important gods:

Chaac: Maya rain god.

Ehécatl: Wind god whose temple is usually round; another aspect of Quetzalcoatl.

Itzamná: Maya god above all, who invented corn, cacao, and writing and reading.

Ixchel: Maya goddess of water, weaving, and childbirth.

Kinich Ahau: Maya sun god.

Kukulkán: Quetzalcoatl's name in the Yucatán.

Ometeotl: God/goddess, all-powerful creator of the universe, ruler of heaven, earth, and the underworld.

Quetzalcoatl: A mortal who took on legendary characteristics as a god (or vice versa). When he left Tula in shame after a night of succumbing to temptations, he promised to return. He reappeared in the Yucatán. He is also symbolized as Venus, the moving star, and Ehécatl, the wind god. Quetzalcoatl is credited with giving the Maya cacao (chocolate) and teaching them how to grow it, harvest it, roast it, and turn it into a drink with ceremonial and magical properties.

Tlaloc: Aztec rain god.

5 Food & Drink

Authentic Mexican food differs quite dramatically from what is frequently served up in the United States under that name. For many travelers, then, Mexico will be new and exciting culinary territory. Even grizzled veterans will be pleasantly surprised by the wide variation in specialties and traditions offered from region to region.

Despite regional differences, some generalizations can be made. Mexican food usually isn't pepper-hot when it arrives at the table (though many dishes must have a certain amount of piquancy, and some home cooking can be very spicy, depending on a family's or chef's tastes). The piquant flavor is added with chiles and sauces after the food is served; you'll never see a table in Mexico without one or both of these condiments. Mexicans don't drown their cooking in cheese and sour cream, à la Tex-Mex, and they use a greater variety of ingredients than most people expect. But the basis of Mexican food is simple—tortillas, beans, chilies, squash, and tomatoes—the same as it was centuries ago, before the arrival of the Europeans.

THE BASICS

TORTILLAS   Traditional tortillas are made from corn that's been soaked and cooked in water and lime, then ground into *masa* (a grainy dough), patted and pressed into thin cakes, and cooked on a hot griddle known as a *comal*. In many households the tortilla takes the place of fork and spoon; Mexicans merely tear them into wedge-shaped pieces, which they use to scoop up their food. Restaurants often serve bread rather than tortillas because it's easier, but you can always ask for tortillas. A more recent invention from northern Mexico is the flour tortilla, which is seen less frequently in the rest of Mexico.

ENCHILADAS   The tortilla is the basis of several Mexican dishes, but the most famous of these is the enchilada. The original name for this dish would have been tortilla enchilada, which simply means a tortilla dipped in a chile sauce. In like manner, there's the *entomatada* (tortilla dipped in a tomato sauce) and the *enfrijolada* (in a bean sauce). The enchilada began as a very simple dish: A tortilla is dipped in chile sauce (usually with ancho chile) and then into very hot oil, then quickly folded or rolled on a plate and sprinkled with chopped onions and a little *queso cotija* (crumbly white cheese) and served with a little fried potatoes and carrots. You can get this basic enchilada in food stands across the country. I love them, and if you come across them in your travels, give them a try. In restaurants you get the more elaborate enchilada, with different fillings of cheese, chicken, pork, or even seafood, and sometimes prepared as a casserole.

TACOS   A taco is anything folded or rolled into a tortilla, and sometimes a double tortilla. The tortilla can be served either soft or fried. *Flautas* and *quesadillas* (except in Mexico City where they are something quite different) are species of tacos. For Mexicans, the taco is the quintessential fast food, and the taco stand (*taquería*)—a ubiquitous sight—is a great place to get a cheap, good, and filling meal. See the section below, "Eating Out: Restaurants, *Taquerías* & Tipping," for information on *taquerías*.

FRIJOLES   An invisible "bean line" divides Mexico: It starts at the Gulf Coast in the southern part of the state of Tamaulipas and moves inland through the eastern quarter of San Luis Potosí and most of the state of Hidalgo, then straight through Mexico City and Morelos and into Guerrero, where it curves slightly westward to the Pacific. To the north and west of this line the pink bean known as the *flor de mayo* is the staple food; to the south and east the standard is the black bean. (Curiously enough, this line also roughly determines whether a taco will come with one or two tortillas; to the north and west you get two tortillas, to the south and east, only one.)

In private households, beans are served at least once a day, and among the working class and peasantry with every meal if the family can afford it. Mexicans almost always prepare beans with a minimum of condiments, usually just a little onion and garlic and perhaps a pinch of herbs. Beans are meant to be a contrast to the other heavily spiced foods in a meal. Sometimes they are served at the end of a meal with a little Mexican-style sour cream.

Mexicans often fry leftover beans and serve them on the side as *frijoles refritos*. "Refritos" is usually translated as refried, but this is a misnomer—the beans are fried only once. The prefix "re" actually means well (as in thoroughly), and what Mexicans actually mean is the beans are well fried.

TAMALES   You make a tamal by mixing corn *masa* with a little lard, adding one of several fillings—meats flavored with chiles (or no filling at all)—then

What's Cooking in the Yucatán

Yucatecan cooking is the most distinct of the many kinds of regional cooking, probably because it was influenced by the Maya and Caribbean cultural traditions. Yucatecans are great fans of *achiote* (or *annatto*, a red seed pod from a tree that grows in the Caribbean area), which is the basic ingredient for perhaps its most famous dish, *cochinita pibil* (pork wrapped in banana leaves, pit-baked, and served with a pibil sauce of *achiote*, sour orange, and spices). And good seafood is readily available. Many of the most common Mexican dishes are given a different name and a different twist here. But waiters are happy to explain what's what, and with a couple of meals under your belt, you'll feel like a native.

wrapping it in a corn husk or in the leaf of a banana or other plant, and steaming it. Every region in Mexico has its own traditional way of making tamales. In some places a single tamal can be big enough to feed a family, while in others they are barely three inches long and only about an inch thick.

CHILES   There are many kinds of chile peppers, and Mexicans call each of them by one name when they're fresh and another when they're dried. Some are blazing hot with only a mild flavor; some are mild but have a rich, complex flavor. They can be pickled, smoked, stuffed, stewed, chopped, and used in an endless variety of dishes.

MEALTIME

MORNING   The morning meal, known as *el desayuno*, can be something very light, such as coffee and sweet bread, or something more substantial: eggs, beans, tortillas, bread, fruit, and juice. It can be eaten early or late and is always a sure bet in Mexico. The variety and sweetness of the fruits is remarkable, and you can't go wrong with Mexican egg dishes.

MIDAFTERNOON   The main meal of the day, known as *la comida*, is eaten between 2 and 4pm. Stores and businesses close, and most people will go home to eat and perhaps take a short afternoon siesta before going about their business. The first course is the *sopa*, which can be either soup (*caldo*) or rice (*sopa de arroz*) or both; then comes the main course, which ideally would be a meat or fish dish prepared in some kind of sauce and probably served with beans, followed by dessert.

EVENING   Between 8 and 10pm, most Mexicans will have a light meal called *la cena*. If eaten at home, it will be something like a sandwich, bread and jam, or perhaps a couple of tacos made from some of the day's leftovers. At restaurants, the most common thing to eat is *antojitos* (literally, "little cravings"), a general label for light fare. *Antojitos* include tostadas, tamales, tacos, and simple enchiladas, and are big hits with travelers. Large restaurants will offer complete meals as well. In the Yucatán, *antojitos* include *papadzules* (a species of enchilada filled with hard-boiled egg), *sincronizadas* (small tostadas), and *panuchos* (fried tortillas filled with bean paste and topped with *cochinita* pibil and marinated onions).

EATING OUT: RESTAURANTS, *TAQUERÍAS* & TIPPING

First of all, I feel compelled to debunk the prevailing myth that the cheapest place to eat in Mexico is in the market. Actually, this is almost never the case.

You can usually find better food at a better price without going more than 2 blocks out of your way. Why? Food stalls in the marketplace pay high rents, they have a near-captive clientele of market vendors and truckers, and they get a lot of business from many Mexicans for whom eating in the market is a traditional way of confirming their culture.

On the other side of the spectrum, avoid eating at those inviting sidewalk restaurants that you see beneath the stone archways that border the main plazas. These places usually cater to tourists and don't need to count on getting any return business. But they are great for getting a coffee or beer and watching the world turn.

In most nonresort towns, there are always one or two restaurants (sometimes it's a coffee shop) that are social centers for a large group of established patrons. These establishments over time become virtual institutions, and change comes very slowly to them. The food is usually good standard fare, cooked as it was 20 years ago; the decor is simple. The patrons have known each other and the staff for years, and the *charla* (banter), gestures, and greetings are friendly, open, and unaffected. If you're curious about Mexican culture, these places are fun to eat in and observe the goings-on.

During your trip you're going to see many *taquerías* (**taco joints**). These are generally small places with a counter or a few tables set around the cooking area; you get to see exactly how they make their tacos before deciding whether to order. Most tacos come with a little chopped onion and cilantro, but not with tomato and lettuce. Find one that seems popular with the locals and where the cook performs with brio (a good sign of pride in the product). Sometimes there will be a woman making the tortillas right there (or working the *masa* into *gorditas, sopes,* or *panuchos* if these are also served). You will never see men doing this—this is perhaps the strictest gender division in Mexican society. Men do all other cooking and kitchen tasks, and work with already-made tortillas, but will never be found working *masa*.

For the main meal of the day, many restaurants offer a multicourse blue-plate special called ***comida corrida*** or ***menú del día.*** This is the most inexpensive way to get a full dinner. In Mexico, you need to ask for your check; it is generally considered inhospitable to present a check to someone who hasn't requested it. If you're in a hurry to get somewhere, ask for the check when your food arrives.

Tips are about the same as in the United States. You'll sometimes find a 15% **value-added tax** on restaurant meals, which shows up on the bill as "IVA." This is a boon to arithmetically challenged tippers, saving them from undue exertion.

To summon the waiter, wave or raise your hand, but don't motion with your index finger, which is a demeaning gesture that may even cause the waiter to ignore you. Or if it's the check you want, you can motion to the waiter from across the room using the universal pretend-like-you're-writing gesture.

Most restaurants do not have **nonsmoking sections;** when they do, we mention it in the reviews. But Mexico's wonderful climate allows for many open-air restaurants, usually set inside a courtyard of a colonial house, or in rooms with tall ceilings and plenty of open windows.

DRINKS

All over Mexico you'll find shops selling **juices** and **smoothies** made from several kinds of tropical fruit. They're excellent and refreshing; while traveling I take full advantage of them. You'll also come across *aguas frescas*—water flavored with hibiscus, melon, tamarind, or lime. Soft drinks come in more flavors than in any other country I know. Pepsi and Coca-Cola taste the way they did in the United States years ago, before the makers started adding corn syrup. The coffee is generally good, and **hot chocolate** is a traditional drink, as is *atole*—a hot, corn-based beverage that can be sweet or bitter.

Of course, Mexico has a proud and lucrative **beer**-brewing tradition. A lesser-known brewed beverage is *pulque*, a pre-Hispanic drink: the fermented juice of a few species of maguey or agave. Mostly you find it for sale in *pulquerías* in central Mexico. It is an acquired taste, and not every *gringo* acquires it. **Mezcal** and **tequila** also come from the agave. Tequila is a variety of mezcal produced from the *a. tequilana* species of agave in and around the area of Tequila, in the state of Jalisco. Mezcal comes from various parts of Mexico and from different varieties of agave. The distilling process is usually much less sophisticated than that of tequila, and, with its stronger smell and taste, mezcal is much more easily detected on the drinker's breath. In some places like Oaxaca it comes with a worm in the bottle; you are supposed to eat the worm after polishing off the mezcal. But for those teetotalers out there who are interested in just the worm, I have good news—you can find these worms for sale in Mexican markets when in season. *¡Salud!*

6 Recommended Books

BOOKS

HISTORY By the time Cortez arrived in Mexico, the indigenous people were already masters of literature, recording their poems and histories by painting in fanfold books (*códices*) made of deerskin and bark paper or by carving on stone. To record history, gifted students were taught the art of bookmaking, drawing, painting, reading, and writing—abilities the general public didn't possess. A contemporary book that tells the story of the natives' "painted books" is *The Mexican Codices and Their Extraordinary History* (Ediciones Lara, 1985), by María Sten.

The ancient Maya produced two important epic works, the *Book of Popol Vuh* and the *Chilam Balam*. Dennis Tedlock produced the most authoritative translation of the *Popul Vuh* (Simon & Schuster, 1985). Anthropologist Michael D. Coe said, "The *Popul Vuh* is generally considered to be the greatest single work of Native American literature." Unfortunately, other than the *Popul Vuh* and the *Chilam Balam*, there are only four surviving *códices* (or portions of them) because, after the Conquest, the Spaniards deliberately destroyed native books. However, several Catholic priests, among them Bernardo de Sahagun and Diego de Landa (who was one of the book destroyers), encouraged the Indians to record their customs and history. These records are among the best documentation of life before the Conquest.

During the Conquest, Cortez wrote his now-famous five letters to King Charles V, the first printed Conquest literature, but the most important record is that of Bernal Díaz de Castillo. Enraged by an inaccurate account of the Conquest written by a flattering friend of Cortez, 40 years after the conquest, Bernal Díaz de Castillo, himself a *conquistador,* wrote his lively and very readable version of the event, *True History of the Conquest of Mexico;* it's regarded as the most accurate.

In an attempt to defend himself for burning 27 Maya hieroglyphic rolls in 1562, Diego de Landa collected contemporary Maya customs, beliefs, and history in his *Relación de las Cosas de Yucatán* (today entitled *Yucatán Before and After the Conquest*, Dover Press, 1978). It was first published in 1566 and remains the most significant record of its kind.

Ancient Mexico: An Overview (University of New Mexico Press, 1985), by Jaime Litvak, is a short, very readable history of pre-Hispanic Mexico. *The Hummingbird and the Hawk* (Columbus, 1967), by R. C. Padden, is an excellent account of the Conquest of Mexico. *The Wind That Swept Mexico* (University of Texas Press, 1971), by Anita Brenner, is an illustrated account of the Mexican Revolution. *Barbarous Mexico* (University of Texas Press, 1984), by John Kenneth Turner, was written in the early 1900s as a shocking exposé of the atrocities during the Porfiriato.

CULTURE *Mexican and Central American Mythology* (Peter Bedrick Books, 1983), by Irene Nicholson, is a concise illustrated book that simplifies the subject.

Though not focused on life in the Yucatán or Chiapas and Tabasco—where thinking, culture, and customs developed apart from the rest of Mexico— several books, nevertheless, are good background reading on Mexico in general. A good, but controversial, all-around introduction to contemporary Mexico and its people is *Distant Neighbors: A Portrait of the Mexicans* (Random House, 1984), by Alan Riding. In a more personal vein is Patrick Oster's *The Mexicans: A Personal Portrait of the Mexican People* (Harper & Row, 1989), a reporter's insightful account of ordinary Mexican people. A novel with valuable insights into the Mexican character is *The Labyrinth of Solitude* (Grove Press, 1985), by Octavio Paz. *The Lost World of Quintana Roo* (E. P. Dutton, 1963), by Michel Peissel, is the thrilling account of a young man's journey on foot in search of undiscovered ruins along the Yucatán's almost uninhabited Caribbean coast in the late 1950s.

Passionate Pilgrim (Paragon House, 1993), by Antoinette May, is the fascinating biography of Alma Reed, an American journalist and amateur archaeologist whose life spanned the 1920s to 1960s. Her journalistic assignments included early archaeological digs at Chichén-Itzá, Uxmal, and Palenque; breaking the story to the *New York Times* of archaeologist Edward Thompson's role in removing the contents of the sacred *cenote* at Chichén-Itzá to the Peabody Museum at Harvard; and serving as a columnist for the *Mexico City News*. She also had a love affair with Felipe Carrillo Puerto, the governor of Yucatán, who commissioned the famous Mexican song, "La Peregrina," in her honor. She later championed the career of Mexican muralist José Clemente Orozco at her art gallery in New York.

Anyone going to San Cristóbal de las Casas should first read *Living Maya* (Harry N. Abrams, 1987), by Walter F. Morris, with excellent photographs by Jeffrey J. Foxx. The book is all about the Maya living today in the state of Chiapas. Peter Canby's *Heart of the Sky: Travels Among the Maya* (Kodansha International, 1994) takes readers on a rare and rugged journey as he seeks to understand the real issues facing the Maya of Mexico and Guatemala today.

The best single source of information on Mexican music, dance, and mythology is Frances Toor's *A Treasury of Mexican Folkways* (Crown, 1967).

ART, ARCHAEOLOGY & ARCHITECTURE Travelers heading for the Yucatán should consider reading amateur archaeologist John L. Stephens's wonderfully entertaining accounts of travel in that region in the 19th century. His book, *Incidents of Travel in Central America, Chiapas ,and Yucatán,* and also his account of his second trip, *Incidents of Travel in Yucatán,* have been reprinted by Dover Publications. The series also includes Friar Diego de Landa's *Yucatán Before and After the Conquest.*

The Maya (Thames and Hudson, 1993), by Michael D. Coe, is extremely helpful in grasping the different Maya periods. *A Forest of Kings: The Untold*

Story of the Ancient Maya (William Morrow, 1990), by Linda Schele and David Freidel, uses the written history of Maya hieroglyphs to tell the incredible dynastic history of selected Maya sites. You'll never view the sky the same way after reading *Maya Cosmos: Three Thousand Years on the Shaman's Path* (William Morrow, 1993), by David Freidel, Linda Schele, and Joy Parker. This scholarly work filled with personal insights takes us along a very readable path into the amazing sky-centered world of the Maya. *The Blood of Kings: Dynasty and Ritual in Maya Art* (George Braziller, Inc., 1986), by Linda Schele and Mary Ellen Miller, is a pioneer work that unlocks the bloody history of the Maya.

In *Breaking the Maya Code* (Thames & Hudson, 1992), readers follow Michael D. Coe on the fascinating 100-year journey of reading the mysterious written texts left by the Maya in partially remaining books, pottery, murals, and carved in stone. Another must-read, and a real page-turner, it's a modern-day mystery complete with a cast of real-life characters. *Maya History* (University of Texas Press, 1993), by Tatiana Proskouriakoff, is the last work of one of the most revered Maya scholars. Linda Schele, a contemporary Maya scholar, calls Proskouriakoff "the person who was to our field as Darwin was to biology." Her contributions included numerous drawings of now-ruined Maya temples and glyphs, of which there are over 300 in this book.

Try a used bookstore for *Digging in Mexico* (Doubleday, Doran, 1931), by Ann Axtell Morris. The book is as interesting for its photographs of Chichén-Itzá, before and during the excavations, as it is for the author's lively and revealing anecdotes. Morris was a young writer and the wife of Earl Morris, director of excavations at Chichén-Itzá during the Carnegie Institution's work there in the 1920s.

In *Maya Missions* (Espadana Press, 1988), authors Richard and Rosalind Perry reveal the mysteries of the Yucatán Peninsula's many centuries-old colonial-era missions with inviting detail. *An Archaeological Guide to Mexico's Yucatán Peninsula* (University of Oklahoma, 1993), by Joyce Kelly, is a companion to *Maya Missions* that covers the other side of the peninsula's architecture; it is the most comprehensive guide to Maya ruins. Carrying these two books with you will enrich your visit many times over.

Mexico: Splendors of Thirty Centuries (Metropolitan Museum of Art, 1990), the catalog of the 1991 traveling exhibition, is a wonderful resource on Mexico's art from 1500 B.C. through the 1950s. Another superb catalog, *Images of Mexico: The Contribution of Mexico to 20th Century Art* (Dallas Museum of Art, 1987), is a fabulously illustrated and detailed account of Mexican art gathered from collections around the world. *Art and Time in Mexico: From the Conquest to the Revolution* (Harper & Row, 1985), by Elizabeth Wilder Weismann, illustrated with 351 photographs, covers Mexican religious, public, and private architecture with excellent photos and text. *Casa Mexicana* (Stewart, Tabori & Chang, 1989), by Tim Street-Porter, takes readers through the interiors of some of Mexico's finest homes-turned-museums, public buildings, and private homes. *Mexican Interiors* (Architectural Book Publishing Co., 1962), by Verna Cook Shipway and Warren Shipway, uses black-and-white photographs to highlight architectural details from homes all over Mexico.

FOLK ART   Chloë Sayer's *Costumes of Mexico* (University of Texas Press, 1985) is a beautifully illustrated and written work. *Mexican Masks* (University of Texas Press, 1980), by Donald Cordry, based on the author's collection and travels, remains the definitive work on the subject. *Cordry's Mexican Indian Costumes* (University of Texas Press, 1968) is another classic. Carlos Espejel wrote both *Mexican Folk Ceramics* and *Mexican Folk Crafts* (Editorial Blume, 1975 and 1978), two comprehensive books that explore crafts state by state. *Folk Treasures of Mexico* (Harry N. Abrams, 1990), by Marion Oettinger, curator of folk art and Latin American art at the San Antonio Museum of Art, is the fascinating illustrated story behind the 3,000-piece Mexican folk-art collection amassed by Nelson Rockefeller over a 50-year period. This book also provides much information about individual folk artists.

NATURE *A Naturalist's Mexico* (Texas A&M University Press, 1992), by Roland H. Wauer, is a fabulous guide to birding in Mexico. *A Hiker's Guide to Mexico's Natural History* (Mountaineers, 1995), by Jim Conrad, covers Mexican flora and fauna and tells how to find the easy-to-reach, as well as out-of-the-way spots he describes. *Peterson Field Guides: Mexican Birds* (Houghton-Mifflin, 1973), by Roger Tory Peterson and Edward L. Chalif, is an excellent guide to the country's birds. *A Guide to Mexican Mammals and Reptiles* (Minutiae Mexicana), by Normal Pelham Wright and Dr. Bernardo Villa Ramírez, is a small but useful guide to some of the country's wildlife.

Appendix B:
Useful Terms & Phrases

1 Telephones & Mail

USING THE TELEPHONES

In 1999, an important change in local telephone service took place. Where previously you would dial a five- or six-digit number within a city for local calls, these now all conform to international standards of seven-digit numbers. In order to access any local number in this book, dial the last seven digits listed (most numbers listed in this book are a total of eight digits—the number plus the area code within Mexico). For local numbers within Mexico City only, eight digits are required: dial 5, and the remaining seven digits of the number.

To call long distance within Mexico, you'll need to dial the national long distance code **01** prior to dialing the two- or three-digit area code, and then the number. In total, Mexico's telephone numbers are eight digits in length. Mexico's area codes (*claves*) are usually listed in the front of telephone directories. Area codes are listed before all phone numbers in this book. For long-distance dialing you will often see the term "LADA," which is the automatic long distance service offered by Telmex, Mexico's former telephone monopoly and the largest phone service company in Mexico. To make a person-to-person or collect call inside Mexico, dial ☎ **020.**

International long distance calls to the United States or Canada are accessed by dialing ☎ **001,** then the area code and seven-digit number. To make a person-to-person or collect call to outside of Mexico, dial ☎ **090.** For other international dialing codes, dial the operator at ☎ **040.**

While in Cancún and the Yucatán, you might find that when you request a phone number, you'll get only five or six digits. Don't panic—that's how local numbers are given. Just ask for the local area code as well, and add it to the beginning of the number you were given. When you dial the number, use the *last seven digits* of the area code plus phone number.

For additional details on making calls in Mexico and to Mexico, see chapter 3.

POSTAL GLOSSARY

Airmail   **Correo Aéreo**
Customs   **Aduana**
General Delivery   **Lista de Correos**

Insurance (insured mail) **Seguro (correo asegurado)**
Mailbox **Buzón**
Money Order **Giro Postal**
Parcel **Paquete**
Post Office **Oficina de Correos**
Post Office Box (abbreviation) **Apartado Postal**
Postal Service **Correos**
Registered Mail **Registrado**
Rubber Stamp **Sello**
Special Delivery, Express **Entrega Inmediata**
Stamp **Estampilla or Timbre**

2 Basic Vocabulary

Most Mexicans are very patient with foreigners who try to speak their language;
it helps a lot to know a few basic phrases.

I've included a list of certain simple phrases for expressing basic needs,
followed by some common menu items.

ENGLISH-SPANISH PHRASES

English	Spanish	Pronunciation
Good day	**Buenos días**	*bway*-nohss *dee*-ahss
How are you?	**¿Cómo está?**	*koh*-moh ess-*tah*?
Very well	**Muy bien**	mwee byen
Thank you	**Gracias**	*grah*-see-ahss
You're welcome	**De nada**	day *nah*-dah
Good-bye	**Adiós**	ah-*dyohss*
Please	**Por favor**	pohr fah-*vohr*
Yes	**Sí**	see
No	**No**	noh
Excuse me	**Perdóneme**	pehr-*doh*-ney-may
Give me	**Déme**	*day*-may
Where is . . . ?	**¿Dónde está . . . ?**	*dohn*-day ess-*tah*?
the station	**la estación**	lah ess-tah-*seown*
a hotel	**un hotel**	oon oh-*tel*
a gas station	**una gasolinera**	*oon*-uh gah-so-lee-*nay*-rah
a restaurant	**un restaurante**	oon res-tow-*rahn*-tay
the toilet	**el ban–o**	el *bahn*-yoh
a good doctor	**un buen médico**	oon bwayn *may*-thee-co
the road to . . .	**el camino a/hacia**	el cah-*mee*-noh ah/*ah*-see-ah
To the right	**A la derecha**	ah lah day-*reh*-chuh
To the left	**A la izquierda**	ah lah ees-ky-*ehr*-thah
Straight ahead	**Derecho**	day-*reh*-cho
I would like	**Quisiera**	key-see-*ehr*-ah
I want	**Quiero**	*kyehr*-oh
to eat	**comer**	ko-*mayr*
a room	**una habitación**	*oon*-nuh ha-bee-tah-*seown*
Do you have . . . ?	**¿Tiene usted?**	tyah-nay oos-*ted*?
a book	**un libro**	oon *lee*-bro
a dictionary	**un diccionario**	oon deek-seown-*ar*-eo
How much is it?	**¿Cuánto cuesta?**	*kwahn*-to *kwess*-tah?
When?	**¿Cuándo?**	*kwahn*-doh?
What?	**¿Qué?**	kay?

Useful Terms & Phrases

English	Spanish	Pronunciation
There is (Is there . . . ?)	(¿)Hay (. . . ?)	eye?
What is there?	¿Qué hay?	kay eye?
Yesterday	Ayer	ah-*yer*
Today	Hoy	oy
Tomorrow	Mañana	mahn-*yahn*-ah
Good	Bueno	*bway*-no
Bad	Malo	*mah*-lo
Better (best)	(Lo) Mejor	(loh) meh-*hor*
More	Más	mahs
Less	Menos	*may*-noss
No smoking	Se prohíbe fumar	say pro-*hee*-bay foo-*mahr*
Postcard	Tarjeta postal	tar-*hay*-ta pohs-*tahl*
Insect repellent	Rapelente contra insectos	rah-pey-*yahn*-te *cohn*-trah een-*sehk*-tos

MORE USEFUL PHRASES:

Do you speak English?	¿Habla usted inglés?	ah-blah oo-*sted* een-*glays*?
Is there anyone here?	¿Hay alguien aquí?	eye *ahl*-ghee-en kay
Who speaks English?	¿qué hable inglés?	*ah*-blay een-*glays*?
I speak a little Spanish.	Hablo un poco de español.	*ah*-blow oon *poh*-koh ess-pah-*nyol*
I don't understand Spanish very well.	No (lo) entiendo muy bien el español.	noh (loh) ehn-tee-*ehn*-do moo-ee bee-aynl el ess-pah-*nyol*
The meal is good.	Me gusta la comida.	may *goo*-sta lah koh-*mee*-dah
What time is it?	¿Qué hora es?	kay *oar*-ah ess?
May I see your menu?	¿Puedo ver el menú (la carta)?	*puay*-tho veyr el may-*noo* (lah *car*-tah)?
The check please.	La cuenta por favor.	lah *quayn*-tah pohr fa-*vorh*
What do I owe you?	¿Cuánto lo debo?	*Kwahn*-toh loh *day*-boh?
What did you say?	¿Mande? (colloquial expression for American "Eh?")	*Mahn*-day?
More formal:	¿Cómo?	*Koh*-moh?
I want (to see)	Quiero (ver)	Key-*yehr*-oh vehr
a room	un cuarto or una habitacióno	on *kwar*-toh, *oon*-nuh ha-bee-tah-*seown*
for two persons	para dos personas	*pahr*-ah doss pehr-*sohn*-as
with (without) bathroom	con (sin) baño.	kohn (seen) *bah*-nyoh
We are staying here only one night one week	Nos quedamos aquí solamente una noche una semana	nohs kay-*dahm*-ohss ah-*key* sohl-ah-*mayn*-tay oon-ah *noh*-chay oon-ah say-*mahn*-ah
We are leaving tomorrow	Partimos (Salimos) man–ana	Pahr-*tee*-mohss; sah-*lee*-mohss mahn-*nyan*-ah
Do you accept? traveler's checks?	¿Acepta usted? cheques de viajero?	Ah-*sayp*-tah oo-*sted* *chay* kays day bee-ah-*hehr*-oh

English	Spanish	Pronunciation
Is there a Laundromat? near here?	¿Hay una lavandería? cerca de aquí?	Eye *oon*-ah lah-*vahn*-day-ree-ah sehr-ka day ah-*key*
Please send these clothes to the laundry	Hágame el favor de mandar esta ropa a la lavandería.	*Ah*-ga-may el fah-*vhor* day mahn-*dahr ays*- tah *rho*-pah a lah lah- *vahn*-day-*ree*-ah

NUMBERS

1	**uno** (*ooh*-noh)		17	**diecisiete** (de-*ess*-ee-*syeh*-tay)
2	**dos** (dohs)		18	**dieciocho** (dee-*ess*-ee-*oh*-choh)
3	**tres** (trayss)		19	**diecinueve** (dee-*ess*-ee-*nway*-bay)
4	**cuatro** (*kwah*-troh)		20	**veinte** (*bayn*-tay)
5	**cinco** (*seen*-koh)		30	**treinta** (*trayn*-tah)
6	**seis** (sayss)		40	**cuarenta** (kwah-*ren*-tah)
7	**siete** (*syeh*-tay)		50	**cincuenta** (seen-*kwen*-tah)
8	**ocho** (*oh*-choh)		60	**sesenta** (say-*sen*-tah)
9	**nueve** (*nway*-bay)		70	**setenta** (say-*ten*-tah)
10	**diez** (dee-ess)		80	**ochenta** (oh-*chen*-tah)
11	**once** (*ohn*-say)		90	**noventa** (noh-*ben*-tah)
12	**doce** (*doh*-say)		100	**cien** (see-*en*)
13	**trece** (*tray*-say)		200	**doscientos** (*dos*-se-en-tos)
14	**catorce** (kah-*tor*-say)		500	**quinientos** (keen-ee-*ehn*-tos)
15	**quince** (*keen*-say)		1,000	**mil** (meal)
16	**dieciseis** (de-*ess*-ee-sayss)			

TRANSPORTATION TERMS

English	Spanish	Pronunciation
Airport	**Aeropuerto**	Ah-ay-row-*por*-tow
Flight	**Vuelo**	Boo-*ay*-low
Rental car	**Arrendadora de Autos**	Ah-rain-da-dow-rah day autos
Bus	**Autobús**	ow-toh-*boos*
Bus or truck	**Camión**	ka-mee-*ohn*
Lane	**Carril**	kah-*rreal*
Nonstop	**Directo**	dee-*reck*-toh
Baggage (claim area)	**Equipajes**	eh-key-*pah*-hays
Intercity	**Foraneo**	fohr-ah-*nay*-oh
Luggage storage area	**Guarda equipaje**	gwar-daheh-key-*pah*-hay
Arrival gates	**Llegadas**	yay-*gah*-dahs
Originates at this station	**Local**	loh-*kahl*
Originates elsewhere	**De Paso**	day *pah*-soh
stops if seats available	**Para si hay lugares**	*pah*-rah-see-aye-loo-gahr-ays
First class	**Primera**	pree-*mehr*-oh
Second class	**Segunda**	say-*goon*-dah
Nonstop	**Sin Escala**	seen ess-*kah*-lah
Baggage claim area	**Recibo de Equipajes**	ray-see-boh day eh-key-*pah*-hay
Waiting room	**Sala de Espera**	*Saw*-lah day ess-*pehr*-ah
Toilets	**Sanitarios**	Sahn-ee-tahr-*ee*-oss
Ticket window	**Taquilla**	tah-*key*-lah

3 Menu Glossary

Achiote   Small red seed of the *annatto* tree.

Achiote preparado   A prepared paste found in Yucatán markets made of ground *achiote,* wheat and corn flour, cumin, cinnamon, salt, onion, garlic, and oregano. Mixed with juice of a sour orange or vinegar and put on broiled or charcoaled fish (tikik chick) and chicken.

Agua fresca   Fruit-flavored water, usually watermelon, canteloupe, chia seed with lemon, hibiscus flour, rice, or ground melon-seed mixture.

Antojito   A Mexican snack, usually *masa*-based with a variety of toppings such as sausage, cheese, beans, and onions; also refers to *tostadas, sopes,* and *garnachas.*

Atole   A thick, lightly sweet, warm drink made with finely-ground rice or corn and usually flavored with vanilla, pecan, or chocolate.

Botana   A light snack—an *antojito.*

Buñuelos   Round, thin, deep-fried crispy fritters dipped in sugar.

Carnitas   Pork that's been deep-cooked (not fried) in lard, then steamed and served with corn tortillas for tacos.

Ceviche   Fresh raw seafood marinated in fresh lime juice and garnished with chopped tomatoes, onions, chiles, and sometimes cilantro and served with crispy, fried, whole corn tortillas or crackers.

Chayote   Vegetable pear or merleton, a type of spiny squash boiled and served as an accompaniment to meat dishes.

Chile en nogada   Poblano peppers stuffed with a mixture of ground pork and chicken, spices, fruits, raisins, and almonds, fried in a light batter and covered in a walnut-and-cream sauce.

Chiles rellenos   Poblano peppers usually stuffed with cheese, rolled in a batter, and fried; other stuffings include ground beef spiced with raisins.

Churro   Tube-shaped, bread-like fritter, dipped in sugar and sometimes filled with *cajeta* or chocolate.

Cochinita pibil   Pork wrapped in banana leaves, pit-baked in a *pibil* sauce of *achiote,* sour orange, and spices; common in Yucatán.

Enchilada   Tortilla dipped in a sauce and usually filled with chicken or white cheese and sometimes topped with tomato sauce and sour cream (enchiladas Suizas—Swiss enchiladas), or covered in a green sauce (enchiladas verdes), or topped with onions, sour cream, and guacamole (enchiladas Potosinas).

Escabeche   A lightly pickled sauce used in Yucatecan chicken stew.

Frijoles charros   Beans flavored with beer; a northern Mexican specialty.

Frijoles refritos   Pinto beans mashed and cooked with lard.

Garnachas   A thickish small circle of fried *masa* with pinched sides, topped with pork or chicken, onions, and avocado, or sometimes chopped potatoes and tomatoes, typical as a *botana* in Veracruz and Yucatán.

Gorditas   Thickish fried-corn tortillas, slit and stuffed with choice of cheese, beans, beef, chicken, with or without lettuce, tomato, and onion garnish.

Gusanos de maguey   Maguey worms, considered a delicacy, and delicious when deep-fried to a crisp and served with corn tortillas for tacos.

Horchata   Refreshing drink made of ground rice or melon seeds, ground almonds, and lightly sweetened.

Huevos Mexicanos   Scrambled eggs with chopped onions, hot peppers, and tomatoes.

Huevos Motuleños   Fried eggs atop a tortilla, garnished with beans, peas, ham, sausage, plantain, and grated cheese; a Yucatecan specialty.

Huevos rancheros   Fried eggs on top of a fried corn tortilla covered in a spicy or mild tomato sauce.

Huitlacoche   Sometimes spelled "cuitlacoche," mushroom-flavored black fungus that appears on corn in the rainy season; considered a delicacy.

Machaca   Shredded dried beef scrambled with eggs or as salad topping; a specialty of northern Mexico.

Manchamantel   Translated means "tablecloth stainer," a stew of chicken or pork with chiles, tomatoes, pineapple, bananas, and jícama. Sometimes listed as "mancha manteles."

Masa   Ground corn soaked in lime used as the basis for tamales, corn tortillas, and soups.

Mixiote   Rabbit, lamb, or chicken cooked in a mild chile sauce (usually chile *ancho* or *pasilla*), then wrapped like a tamal and steamed. It is generally served with tortillas for tacos, with traditional garnishes of pickled onions, hot sauce, and lime wedges.

Pan de Muerto   Sweet bread made around the Days of the Dead (Nov 1 to 2), in the form of mummies, dolls, or round with bone designs.

Pan dulce   Lightly sweetened bread in many configurations, usually served at breakfast or bought at any bakery.

Papadzules   Tortillas stuffed with hard-boiled eggs and seeds (pumpkin or sunflower) in a tomato sauce.

Pavo relleno negro   Stuffed turkey Yucatán-style, filled with chopped pork and beef, cooked in a rich, dark sauce.

Pibil   Pit-baked pork or chicken in a sauce of tomato, onion, mild red pepper, cilantro, and vinegar.

Pipián   Sauce made with ground pumpkin seeds, nuts, and mild peppers.

Poc chuc   Slices of pork with onion marinated in a tangy sour orange sauce and charcoal broiled; a Yucatecan specialty.

Pulque   Drink made of fermented sap of the maguey plant; best in state of Hidalgo and around Mexico City.

Quesadilla   Corn or flour tortillas stuffed with melted white cheese and lightly fried.

Queso relleno   "Stuffed cheese" is a mild yellow cheese stuffed with minced meat and spices; a Yucatecan specialty.

Rompope   Delicious Mexican eggnog, invented in Puebla, made with eggs, vanilla, sugar, and rum.

Salsa verde   A cooked sauce using the green tomatillo and puréed with spicy or mild hot peppers, onions, garlic, and cilantro; on tables countrywide. As a rule, green sauce is hotter than red sauce.

Sopa de calabaza   Soup made of chopped squash or pumpkin blossoms.

Sopa de lima   A tangy soup made with chicken broth and accented with fresh lime; popular in Yucatán.

Sopa seca   Translated means "dry soup." Any pasta or rice served as a first or second course.

Sopa Tlalpeña   A hearty soup made with chunks of chicken, chopped carrots, zucchini, corn, onions, garlic, and cilantro.

Sopa Tlaxcalteca   A hearty tomato-based soup filled with cooked nopal cactus, cheese, cream, and avocado, with crispy tortilla strips floating on top.

Sopa de Tortilla   A traditional chicken broth–based soup, seasoned with chiles, tomatoes, onion, and garlic, bobbing with crisp fried strips of corn tortillas.

Sope   Pronounced "*soh*-pay," a *botana* similar to a *garnacha,* except spread with refried beans and topped with crumbled cheese and onions.

Tacos al pastor   Thin slices of flavored pork roasted on a revolving cylinder dripping with onion slices and juice of fresh pineapple slices. Served in small corn tortillas, topped with chopped onion and cilantro.

Tamal   Incorrectly called tamale (tamal singular, tamales plural); meat or sweet filling rolled with fresh *masa,* then wrapped in a corn husk or banana leaf and steamed; many varieties and sizes throughout the country.

Tepache   Drink made of fermented pineapple peelings and brown sugar.

Tikin xic   Also seen on menus as "tikik chick," charbroiled fish brushed with *achiote* sauce.

Tinga   A stew made with pork tenderloin or chicken, sausage, onions, garlic, tomatoes, chiles, and potatoes; popular on menus in Puebla and Hidalgo states.

Torta   A sandwich, usually on *bolillo* bread, usually with sliced avocado, onions, tomatoes, with a choice of meat and often cheese.

Tostadas   Crispy fried corn tortillas topped with meat, onions, lettuce, tomatoes, cheese, avocados, and sometimes sour cream.

Venado   Venison (deer) served perhaps as *pipian de venado,* steamed in banana leaves and served with a sauce of ground squash seeds.

Xtabentun (shtah-ben-*toon*)   A Yucatán liquor made of fermented honey and flavored with anise. It comes *seco* (dry) or *crema* (sweet).

Zacahuil   Pork leg tamal, packed in thick *masa,* wrapped in banana leaves, and pit-baked, sometimes pot-made with tomato and *masa;* specialty of mid- to upper Veracruz.

Index

Index

FROMMER'S® COMPLETE TRAVEL GUIDES

Alaska
Amsterdam
Arizona
Atlanta
Australia
Austria
Bahamas
Barcelona, Madrid & Seville
Beijing
Belgium, Holland & Luxembourg
Bermuda
Boston
British Columbia & the Canadian Rockies
Budapest & the Best of Hungary
California
Canada
Cancún, Cozumel & the Yucatán
Cape Cod, Nantucket & Martha's Vineyard
Caribbean
Caribbean Cruises & Ports of Call
Caribbean Ports of Call
Carolinas & Georgia
Chicago
China
Colorado
Costa Rica
Denmark
Denver, Boulder & Colorado Springs
England
Europe
European Cruises & Ports of Call
Florida
France
Germany
Greece
Greek Islands
Hawaii
Hong Kong
Honolulu, Waikiki & Oahu
Ireland
Israel
Italy
Jamaica
Japan
Las Vegas
London
Los Angeles
Maryland & Delaware
Maui
Mexico
Miami & the Keys
Montana & Wyoming
Montréal & Québec City
Munich & the Bavarian Alps
Nashville & Memphis
Nepal
New England
New Mexico
New Orleans
New York City
New Zealand
Nova Scotia, New Brunswick & Prince Edward Island
Oregon
Paris
Philadelphia & the Amish Country
Portugal
Prague & the Best of the Czech Republic
Provence & the Riviera
Puerto Rico
Rome
San Antonio & Austin
San Diego
San Francisco
Santa Fe, Taos & Albuquerque
Scandinavia
Scotland
Seattle & Portland
Singapore & Malaysia
South Africa
Southeast Asia
South Pacific
Spain
Sweden
Switzerland
Thailand
Tokyo
Toronto
Tuscany & Umbria
USA
Utah
Vancouver & Victoria
Vermont, New Hampshire & Maine
Vienna & the Danube Valley
Virgin Islands
Virginia
Walt Disney World & Orlando
Washington, D.C.
Washington State

FROMMER'S® DOLLAR-A-DAY GUIDES

Australia from $50 a Day
California from $60 a Day
Caribbean from $70 a Day
England from $70 a Day
Europe from $60 a Day
Florida from $60 a Day
Hawaii from $70 a Day
Ireland from $60 a Day
Italy from $70 a Day
London from $85 a Day
New York from $80 a Day
Paris from $85 a Day
San Francisco from $60 a Day
Washington, D.C., from $60 a Day

FROMMER'S® PORTABLE GUIDES

Acapulco, Ixtapa & Zihuatanejo
Alaska Cruises & Ports of Call
Bahamas
Baja & Los Cabos
Berlin
California Wine Country
Charleston & Savannah
Chicago
Dublin
Hawaii: The Big Island
Las Vegas
London
Maine Coast
Maui
New Orleans
New York City
Paris
Puerto Vallarta, Manzanillo & Guadalajara
San Diego
San Francisco
Sydney
Tampa & St. Petersburg
Venice
Washington, D.C.

FROMMER'S® NATIONAL PARK GUIDES

Family Vacations in the
  National Parks
Grand Canyon

National Parks of the
  American West
Rocky Mountain

Yellowstone & Grand Teton
Yosemite & Sequoia/
  Kings Canyon
Zion & Bryce Canyon

FROMMER'S® MEMORABLE WALKS

Chicago
London

New York
Paris

San Francisco
Washington D.C.

FROMMER'S® GREAT OUTDOOR GUIDES

New England
Northern California

Southern California & Baja
Southern New England

Washington & Oregon

FROMMER'S® BORN TO SHOP GUIDES

Born to Shop: China
Born to Shop: France

Born to Shop: Italy
Born to Shop: London

Born to Shop: New York
Born to Shop: Paris

FROMMER'S® IRREVERENT GUIDES

Amsterdam
Boston
Chicago
Las Vegas

London
Los Angeles
Manhattan
New Orleans

Paris
San Francisco
Seattle & Portland
Vancouver

Walt Disney World
Washington, D.C.

FROMMER'S® BEST-LOVED DRIVING TOURS

America
Britain
California

Florida
France
Germany

Ireland
Italy
New England

Scotland
Spain
Western Europe

THE UNOFFICIAL GUIDES®

Bed & Breakfasts in
  California
Bed & Breakfasts in
  New England
Bed & Breakfasts in
  the Northwest
Beyond Disney
Branson, Missouri
California with Kids
Chicago

Cruises
Disneyland
Florida with Kids
Golf Vacations in the
  Eastern U.S.
The Great Smoky &
  Blue Ridge
  Mountains
Inside Disney

Hawaii
Las Vegas
London
Miami & the Keys
Mini Las Vegas
Mini-Mickey
New Orleans
New York City
Paris

Safaris
San Francisco
Skiing in the West
Walt Disney World
Walt Disney World
  for Grown-ups
Walt Disney World
  for Kids
Washington, D.C.

SPECIAL-INTEREST TITLES

Frommer's Britain's Best Bed & Breakfasts and
  Country Inns
Frommer's Britain's Best Bike Rides
The Civil War Trust's Official Guide
  to the Civil War Discovery Trail
Frommer's Caribbean Hideaways
Frommer's Food Lover's Companion to France
Frommer's Food Lover's Companion to Italy
Frommer's Gay & Lesbian Europe
Frommer's Exploring America by RV
Hanging Out in Europe
Israel Past & Present

Mad Monks' Guide to California
Mad Monks' Guide to New York City
Frommer's The Moon
Frommer's New York City with Kids
The New York Times' Unforgettable
  Weekends
Places Rated Almanac
Retirement Places Rated
Frommer's Road Atlas Britain
Frommer's Road Atlas Europe
Frommer's Washington, D.C., with Kids
Frommer's What the Airlines Never Tell You